Creative Dissent

For Ann Lakhdhir
with Best Wishes

Douglas Roche
October 7/08

Creative Dissent

A Politician's Struggle for Peace

Douglas Roche

NOVALIS

© 2008 Novalis, Saint Paul University, Ottawa, Canada

Cover design: Audrey Wells
Layout: Audrey Wells and Dominique Pelland

Cover photograph: Con Boland
Interior photographs: courtesy of the author, except for the following: Artona Studio, Pembroke, Ontario (p. 3 bottom); Murray Mosher Photography, Ottawa (p. 8); Merle Prosofsky Photography Ltd., Edmonton (p. 9); The Canadian Press (Peter Bregg) (p. 11); © www.fotografiafelici.com (p. 13, p. 21); UN Photo 168763 / Yutaka Nagata (p. 15 top); UN Photo 173425 / Y. Nagata (p. 15 bottom); Toronto Star photo 92-01-23-20-6A (p. 18, top); Michael Bedford Photography, Ottawa (p. 20 top); Photo Service of *L'Osservatore Romano*, Vatican City (p. 32). Every effort was made to contact copyright holders. Any omissions will be corrected in the next edition of the book.
Family tree on page 29: by Michael McBane

Business Offices:
Novalis Publishing Inc.
10 Lower Spadina Avenue, Suite 400
Toronto, Ontario, Canada
M5V 2Z2

Novalis Publishing Inc.
4475 Frontenac Street
Montréal, Québec, Canada
H2H 2S2

Phone: 1-800-387-7164
Fax: 1-800-204-4140
E-mail: books@novalis.ca
www.novalis.ca

Library and Archives Canada Cataloguing in Publication
Roche, Douglas, 1929–
       Creative dissent : a politician's struggle for peace / Douglas Roche.
Includes index.
ISBN 978-2-89646-029-8
       1. Roche, Douglas, 1929–. 2. Legislators–Canada–Biography.
3. Ambassadors–Canada–Biography. 4. Politicians–Canada–Biography.
5. Pacifists–Canada–Biography. I. Title.
FC601.R64A4 2008   971.064'4092   C2008-903550-X

Printed in Canada.

We acknowledge the financial support of the Government of Canada through the Book Publishing Industry Development Program (BPIDP) for our publishing activities.

5 4 3 2 1   12 11 10 09 08

For my grandchildren, Isabelle and Nicholas

and all the grandchildren in the world

Contents

Acknowledgments

I f fully done, the acknowledgements in my memoirs would be very long, indeed. Countless individuals on my journey of nearly 80 years have shaped me, inspired me, guided me and, in short, contributed to the richness of my life. Many of these people are mentioned in the book in the appropriate places; many others are not. These memoirs are not a catalogue of everyone I have known or of all my relatives and friends. They are essentially an account of my public life, interconnected with memorable personal moments.

I want the reader to know who I am, where I came from and how my ideas for peace developed. Thus, a description of my formative years is important. My children are introduced, one by one, as they come on the scene, and there are glimpses—happy and sad—of family life. But the purpose of the book is not to tell my personal life story, as such; rather, it is to examine my struggle as a political figure in Canada to give the values of peace and human security a higher priority in public policy. My children, of course, are intertwined with the public Doug Roche, but, as adults, they have the right to privacy in their own lives.

It would be hard to deny that writing one's memoirs requires a certain amount of ego, a quality not usually in short supply in politicians. But I have never considered myself as the be-all and end-all to whom people should give their votes, let alone their affection. Life is not all about me. Instead, I have tried always to see myself as an instrument for conveying, with increasing sharpness as the years have gone by, a message of peace and social justice.

I see myself as part of God's plan for the continued development of the planet. I have been blessed enormously with experiences that have enabled me to understand what globalization is all about, and how dangerous it is to all of humanity for a growing list of countries to maintain nuclear arsenals. Along with curbing global warming, abolishing nuclear weapons is the supreme challenge of the 21st century. I want people to wake up and demand that politicians take effective steps to avert the catastrophe that every expert says is coming unless the nuclear powers take seriously their moral and legal obligation to eliminate nuclear weapons.

This is the continued purpose of my life. Parliamentarians are usually afraid of being labelled as one-issue politicians. This does not bother me. I have paid my dues to politics. Now I want politics to pay attention to the essential requirement for true human security.

Although this book recounts a number of my political battles, I have not set out, by any means, to settle any scores. In my heart, I am truly reconciled with those whose political philosophy is, to put it mildly, not the same as mine. More important, I want students to be uplifted as they see in my life the struggle that the world faces to build the conditions for peace, and why that struggle is so worthwhile. This is the point that the Rt. Hon. Joe Clark has focused on in his introduction. I am very grateful to the former prime minister for his sensitivity to it. His conduct in public life is a model of the type of political reconciliation that I cherish. The views expressed in his hitherto unpublished report on Canada's role in arms control and disarmament (see chapter 9) are Joe Clark at his best.

Firdaus Kharas, an outstanding television and animation producer who understands what I am about, has embarked on a documentary on my life based on these memoirs.

The team around me at the Middle Powers Initiative (MPI) has given me the confidence to speak out. I want to acknowledge the deep involvement of the MPI executive in my work: Jonathan Granoff, president of the Global Security Institute, which provides the structure for MPI's work; Alyn Ware from New Zealand; Michael Christ, David Krieger and Alice Slater from the U.S.; Karel Koster from the Netherlands; Xanthe Hall from Germany; Ron McCoy from Malaysia; Hiromichi Umebayahsi from Japan; Rebecca Johnson from the U.K.; and Jayantha Dhanapala from Sri Lanka.

In Canada, my work has been greatly aided by Ernie Regehr, Bev Delong, Debbie Grisdale, Murray Thomson, Steve Staples, Erika Simpson, Adele Buckley, Walter Dorn, Michael Byers, Ann Gertler, Judy Berlyn, Metta Spencer, Janis Alton and Phyllis Creighton—valiant figures all. Tariq Rauf has been a special friend and guide for nearly three decades.

I would not have been able to write this book without the records kept through the years by Pam Miles-Séguin. These records of what I was doing on virtually every day of my political career triggered my long-term memory, no small blessing when one is recounting a whole life.

Personal records and memory would still not have been enough for me to develop my themes fully. The staff at the Library of Parliament, as they have for so many of my books, came to my assistance. I am deeply grateful to Hugh Finsten, former associate librarian, and Danielle Séguin, who invariably found the documents I needed. At Foreign Affairs and International Trade Canada, historian Mary Halloran provided valuable help and eased the way for documents originating in my time as Canada's ambassador for disarmament to be declassified. Ryan Touhey at Library and Archives Canada located key files for me. I received help from the Dag Hammarskjöld Library at the United Nations, New York. Loree Semeluk, my former student, also helped with the research.

Two of my long-time friends, Duncan Edmonds and Ruth Bertelsen, critiqued the first draft of the book. Their suggestions for improvement were trenchant and insightful.

My sister Marion Kerans proved very helpful in providing material on my early years. I have quoted a scene from her own memoirs, which she wrote for her grandchildren. Frank Dolphin, my colleague at the *Western Catholic Reporter*, reviewed Chapter 5, on my years as the paper's editor.

Bonnie Payne, who has been my assistant since I left the ambassador for disarmament job in 1989, once again prepared the manuscript for publication. I deeply appreciate her devoted and constantly cheerful assistance.

Khalid Yaqub, who maintains my website (www.douglasroche. ca) and created PowerPoint presentations of my last three books, *The Human Right to Peace, Beyond Hiroshima* and *Global Conscience*, helped me again during computer challenges.

The team at Novalis has become part of my professional family. Michael O'Hearn, publisher, has given me constant support. Kevin Burns, editorial director, keeps raising my confidence level with his perceptive comments that reveal that he understands the interplay between the public and the private Doug Roche. Anne Louise Mahoney, managing editor (whose father, Ed Mahoney, appears in the book), takes care of the details of turning a manuscript into a book. And Amy Heron, copy editor, saves me constantly from linguistic gaffes.

My own family—Evita, Francis, Mary Anne and Tricia—has given me an enduring love that has sustained me through the years. My wife, Patricia McGoey, contributed enormously to this book, first of all through her love and also through her support of the lonely hours of writing in my study.

Douglas Roche
Edmonton
May 16, 2008

Introduction

The Rt. Hon. Joe Clark, PC

When Doug Roche and I came to the House of Commons together in 1972—same election, same party, same province—he was already an established figure on Canada's international stage. Over time, he introduced me to many of the individuals, and some of the issues, that constituted my own steep learning curve on international affairs. His reach ranged from the Secretary General of the United Nations, especially Javier Perez de Cuellar, through to most of the effective Canadian NGOs operating overseas, and he conscientiously connected us.

At one critical period, when the Progressive Conservative Party was preparing to win the 1979 general election, and wanted to be as ready as possible to govern, he played a seminal role in bringing together leaders of the foreign policy community and our party caucus. Many members of our caucus were suspicious of what Mr. Diefenbaker had called the "Pearsonalities" at External Affairs, and there was reciprocal skepticism in parts of the foreign policy and NGO communities. We needed to bring down those mutual suspicions. Doug made the case to diplomats and NGOs that the two groups needed one another, and helped establish a working relationship that, with some notable bumps, served the country very well.

It is worth recalling how national political parties saw their role in Canada at that time. They sought to be inclusive, not ideologic. Robert Stanfield said, famously, "There are enough natural divisions in a country like Canada without political parties creating new ones." His purpose was to reflect the whole broad country and, as much as possible, to attract candidates who were forward-looking. That certainly guided his approach to Quebec, but also to Alberta. Doug Roche was of natural interest to Bob Stanfield.

As a prospective federal candidate myself in Alberta, I wanted company in our parliamentary caucus—people like Doug Roche in Edmonton and Harvie André in Calgary who, while we might disagree on critical issues, came to office looking forward, looking like the future. That 1972 election transformed the Progressive Conservative Party, bringing to Parliament people such as Flora MacDonald, Allan McKinnon, John Fraser, Jake Epp, Ron Atkey, Perrin Beatty—and Doug and Harvie and me. Mr. Stanfield had constructed a party able to govern the modern country and, because it was designed to be a broad tent, representative of the diverse country, Doug Roche was free and encouraged to espouse the causes that were central to his life.

Doug and I were not particularly close as parliamentary colleagues. I had become party leader, he continued to build his international networks, and we both worked conscientiously in our neighbouring, but quite different, constituencies. We came to disagree sharply on some basic domestic issues—the Charter, the Clarity Act, Doug's decision to accept an Alberta Senate appointment. But we came to office with a similar and guiding commitment to the public interest and worked together effectively.

There are two stories in this autobiography. One recounts an unconventional, accomplished life, dealing with crucial issues, in important settings and at historic times, and having an influence upon both opinion and events. The parallel story traces the uncomfortable tension between the serious "arms control" community and any Canadian government and, on a very personal basis, the struggle between effective action and deeply held belief.

Doug Roche is both an idealist, whose hopes are as high as his standards, and a believer, driven by some bedrock certainties. Moreover, he is fluent, forceful, informed. Those would be powerful attributes for a commentator, a teacher, or an adviser. But commentary was not enough for Doug and, time and again, he thrust himself into the arena directly, taking the lead, and taking the heat.

His titles have included editor, Member of Parliament, ambassador, senator. But his real calling is as an advocate and an activist.

His *Western Catholic Reporter* was an outspoken instrument of Vatican II, to an audience that was frequently skeptical of that vision. As a Member of Parliament and senator, his interest was not really in the "art" of the possible, but in the boundaries of the possible, and how far they could be pushed. His Roman Catholicism was often questioning and, at times, courageous. His diplomatic career was successful and effective, but it was also characterized by tensions—between his instructions and his beliefs, himself and his colleagues, his "constituency" in the peace movement and his office as Ambassador.

The personal story is marked by ambition, audacity at critical times, some great strokes of luck, particularly in marrying his wife Eva and raising their family, and a sense of humour that softens the intensity that Doug often carries like a cloak through his public ventures.

But most interesting is his handling of the inherent tensions in being simultaneously activist/advocate/official/actor.

As ambassador, he wanted to act to the limits of his mandate, and then push beyond those limits. That's natural for someone who takes his work seriously; it is valuable in any serious discussion or decision, and it sometimes worked. But it is not a comfortable role and, as this book makes clear, Doug was keenly aware of the conflict zones within which he lived.

A diplomat usually performs in two rings. One is public discussion, in which he engages and informs interested Canadians and others. The second is private persuasion, where he works with his colleagues, sometimes including his minister and prime minister, in developing a Canadian position, and then with other countries in trying to find a broader agreement. Doug Roche also operated actively in a third ring, which was private advocacy, both with his diplomatic colleagues and minister, and his large network of friends.

In one sense, all ambassadors for disarmament forcefully argue internally for arms control—that is part of their mandate and responsibility. Canada's peace movements and practising diplomats don't come from different planets. They are both rooted in the same country, the same democratic and internationalist tradition, the same culture of respect for human rights and difference. But the Roche case was different. He came with a public reputation and record on the issues, and a predilection for digging in. In his case, arms control was clearly a cause, as well as a belief.

The prime minister and I knew that—it was a calculated risk as, in a similar circumstance, was Brian Mulroney's decision to name Stephen Lewis, with his passionate commitment to the developing world, as Canadian Ambassador to the United Nations. They both performed invaluable service for Canada, but it was not a comfortable role.

A country is more than what it earns or produces. It is also what it argues about, what it objects to, what it stands up for. Canada's international reputation is high because that reputation is seen to be authentic. While Canadians are skilled and gallant, when engaged in conflict, our distinguishing strength is in mediating conflict: we are a peaceable community—not passive, but moderate, respectful, constructive and conciliatory.

In many ways, our most consistent contribution to international affairs has been in the active encouragement of multilateral diplomacy and co-operation. We believe that arms control, like trade rules, like agreed environmental standards, allows the moderate majority of nations to constrain the powerful minority, in what can genuinely be called a common interest.

Yet, the community interested in arms control and international development is usually underrepresented in Parliament, and in the decision-making levels of government. For all its passion and intelligence, that community often lacks the financial resources and access of the corporate and other interests that may be their adversaries in critical discussions. They merit a strong voice in any political system presumed to rely on democratic debate and genuine dialogue. So they need a voice in the system, and enough institutional strength to ensure their case is considered. Doug Roche set a high standard.

He has been a relentless and skillful advocate of international peace and development. His highest profile is on issues of arms control, both as Canada's respected and effective Ambassador for Disarmament, and as a citizen-catalyst for initiatives that sought to frame public debate and force governments to face the nuclear weapons threat. More than a strong voice, he has become a creative force in the arms control debate.

Clearly, his proudest moments were those when he and others had pushed an idea forward to a point where actual, enduring change seemed to have been secured. Too often, those changes came undone, or otherwise proved illusory, but, remarkably, those reverses didn't dampen his ardour.

But his commitments—and his influence—are broader than the critical issues of arms control. They are rooted in his direct encounters with what he describes as "the stark contrast between rich and poor in the modern world." As a young journalist from cloistered North America, he describes his first days in Bombay as "one shock after another." He found his vocation, and then mobilized his considerable talents and determination to engage others of us in confronting those brutal, dangerous and growing gaps between rich and poor.

Doug Roche's career helps us reflect on when, and how, a country like Canada—highly respected, but not a superpower—can exert leadership in international affairs. One clear reality is that we cannot have that influence on every issue, nor even on critical issues simply at a time of our choosing. We need a confluence of initiative and circumstance—as occurred in the campaign against apartheid, or our contribution to the Contadora peace process in Central America, or the partnership with civil society on the land mines treaty.

Timing always matters. Prime Minister Trudeau developed an intense interest in arms control at the end of his second regime, but there was no international current running in that direction, and the Canadian prime minister had no capacity to create one. Mr. Trudeau became another voice in that debate rather than a factor in real change.

We are not the principal architects of international change, but have an unusual ability to shape that change when opportunities arise. We need to nourish our capacity and our reputation to be able to act when circumstances create the opportunity. So, if timing always matters, so does preparation.

We need to keep our credentials fresh and current on the issues where we hope to make a difference. That is how Doug Roche played a major role in sustaining Canada's capacity to play "above our weight" on arms control. He did that day by day, argument by heated argument, at the United Nations and elsewhere. As important was his forceful, often lonely, role within the government and Parliament of Canada, always putting the arms control case vigorously. He has been a constant, conscious source of the internal tension that sustained Canada's crucial credentials on arms control, and on the broader issues of international development.

The Rt. Hon. Joe Clark
was the sixteenth Prime Minister of Canada.

Prologue

A Landmark Achieved

During the night of January 25, 2000, a raging snowstorm pounded the Atlantic seaboard, sweeping as far south as Atlanta. For several hours the next morning, the Atlanta airport was closed. Fortunately, I had flown south from Edmonton a day earlier to do the final preparations for a consultation on nuclear weapons that the Middle Powers Initiative was holding at the Carter Center. Jimmy Carter, the former president of the United States for whom the centre was named, was scheduled to speak.

By nine o'clock, only a few of the 40 expected participants were on hand. One of them was actor Michael Douglas, who had been invited in his capacity as United Nations Messenger of Peace. Michael was sitting alone near the back of the room. I had hosted him at a meeting in Ottawa in 1998, and went over to greet him. I sat beside him, expressing my chagrin that he had made a great effort to arrive on time at a meeting that might not happen. Michael tried to console me. "In show business, the show always goes on," he said. Not feeling very consoled, I said to Senator Alan Cranston of California, "Let's start the show and we'll see what happens." Over the next hour, several participants trickled in and by noon most had arrived. Disaster had been averted.

The Carter Center is a complex of buildings located on 37 acres and with a view of the Atlanta skyline two miles away. When Jimmy Carter lost the presidency to Ronald Reagan in 1980, he founded the centre in partnership with Emory University as a place to advance human rights and alleviate unnecessary human suffering. The centre has become famous for strengthening democracies by monitoring elections in Asia, Africa and Latin America, and for mediating civil conflicts around the globe. In 2002, Carter won the Nobel Peace Prize for his work.

It was a great honour that the former president had invited the Middle Powers Initiative (MPI), still young and untested, to hold our consultation in this prestigious setting, and with the centre as a co-sponsor. MPI, a non-governmental organization, was founded in 1998 to stimulate middle-power governments to use their access to the nuclear weapons states to urge them to fulfill their legal responsibilities to nuclear disarmament. As chairman, I had led MPI delegations to several European countries, but we were still in the early stages of figuring out how we could most effectively build multilateral co-operation to eliminate nuclear weapons.

With the Nuclear Non-Proliferation Treaty (NPT) scheduled to be reviewed at a major conference in May 2000, MPI decided to work to influence the major states to fulfill their promises to take steps towards nuclear disarmament. We invited representatives of the New Agenda Coalition, a group of states (Brazil, Egypt, Ireland, Mexico, New Zealand, South Africa and Sweden) also founded in 1998 to work on nuclear weapons issues. Representatives of some NATO countries, such as Germany and Canada, attended. The biggest surprise was the presence of six senior officials from the U.S. government, including John Holum, then senior adviser to the secretary of state for arms control and international security, and Ambassador Norman A. Wulf, special representative for nuclear non-proliferation to then President Clinton.

I seized the opportunity to push the U.S. As a politician, I am always wary of being labelled as "anti-American" in my criticism of the U.S. So I noted at the outset of my remarks to launch the consultation that I had had the good fortune to live in the U.S. for eight years, and that three of my children were born in that country. "I know, from first-hand experience, the greatness of the U.S. The human energy and creativity, so abundant here, have animated me." Because the nuclear weapons issue sweeps across borders in the most dramatic way, I said, what the U.S. does affects the life of every person on the planet. Because the U.S. was not only maintaining nuclear weapons but also seeking to modernize them, the window of opportunity for nuclear disarmament that had opened at the end of the Cold War was now closing. As the leader of the Western nations, the linchpin of NATO and the strongest military power in world by far, the U.S. must provide the leadership needed to encourage all states to foster dialogue and openness and to take other trust- and confidence-building measures with their neighbours. A credible American commitment to a world free of nuclear weapons would spur other states to strengthen collective and co-operative means of addressing their security concerns. The U.S., I said, should send a powerful signal to the Non-Proliferation Treaty Review Conference: "First, it is in its own direct security interest to head off the complete breakdown of the non-proliferation regime; second, it is the right thing to do in the interest of humanity."

President Carter was at the table while I spoke. When I finished, he took the microphone and said, "I wish every member of the U.S. Administration and Congress had just heard Senator Roche." My confidence took a big leap forward.

President Carter went on to criticize the major nuclear powers for not honouring the agreements they had made. He also pointed to the lack of political discourse on the topic among politicians in his own country. "If you look at the political debates going on between the Republicans and Democrats, not one word is mentioned of non-proliferation or nuclear agreements or some of the policies our own country has adopted or failed to adopt. My own belief is that this group [at the Atlanta consultation] ... is the only one I know that collectively can bring this issue forward. I think it has a fairly good chance of making the NPT debate successful."

The consultation delved into the need for the nuclear weapons states to unequivocally undertake the negotiations required under NPT to completely eliminate their nuclear arsenals. Chris Westdal, who was then Canada's ambassador for disarmament, remembers the Atlanta consultation as a high point in nuclear disarmament discussions, with MPI playing an important role in bringing key players together. "It was important to get other American opinions than the government line," he said. The informal gatherings were perhaps just as important as the working sessions in breaking down barriers and developing trust, that most elusive of diplomatic requirements.

Along with Michael Douglas, Jane Fonda, known as much for her peace activism as for her movies, brought some glamour to the gala dinner. Aside from their celebrity, Douglas and Fonda belonged in the gathering. Two decades earlier, they had made *The China Syndrome*, a film that had alerted the world to the risks posed by nuclear energy. Many in the press said at the time that the film was unrealistic and alarmist, yet the nuclear disaster at Three Mile Island occurred less than three weeks after the movie was released, and the Chernobyl explosion happened several years later. "Pride and the refusal to recognize the likelihood of technical or human error made these disasters inevitable," Douglas told the dinner audience. "Today we face an even greater risk. Before nuclear weapons go off from accident or design ... let us find a way to negotiate their elimination. I ask this not as an expert, but as a citizen concerned that public focus and pressure on this most serious of issues are not adequate." Jonathan Granoff (a protegé of Senator Cranston), who chaired the dinner, said in his concluding remarks, "In these past two days, we have seen that with dialogue bridges can be built ... This kind of gathering has value and we want the process to continue."

There was considerable follow-up to the Atlanta consultation. President Carter wrote an article, "A Nuclear Crisis," for the *Washington Post*. Senator Cranston prepared a statement calling for U.S. action for 100 top U.S. leaders to sign. David Krieger, an MPI executive member and head of the Nuclear Age Peace Foundation in Santa Barbara, California, sponsored an appeal, "End the Nuclear Weapons Threat to Humanity!" It ran in the *New York Times* on the opening day of the NPT review conference and was signed by fourteen Nobel Peace Prize laureates. Michael Douglas went to Britain to speak to an all-party parliamentary group in the House of Commons. Carter Center and MPI representatives convened several meetings with U.S. policy-makers.

★ ★ ★

On April 24, the month-long 2000 NPT review conference opened in the General Assembly Hall of the United Nations in New York, with 155 of the 187 parties to the Treaty attending.

Fifteen years earlier, as Canada's ambassador for disarmament, I had led the Canadian delegation to the 1985 NPT review conference. After I left the post in 1989, the Holy See's permanent representative at the United Nations, Archbishop Renato Martino, invited me to become an adviser on disarmament to the Holy See's UN mission.

Martino wanted me to help strengthen the Holy See's opposition to nuclear weapons. With my Holy See credentials, I subsequently had access to the floor at all the international meetings, so had a ringside seat when UN Secretary-General Kofi Annan opened the 2000 meeting with a stern warning: "Nuclear conflict remains a very real and terrifying possibility at the beginning of the 21st century."

Tensions surfaced immediately between the nuclear weapons states, which wanted to postpone nuclear disarmament commitments as long as possible, and the Non-Aligned Movement (mostly the developing states), which wanted a phased program of nuclear disarmament according to a specified timetable.

The New Agenda Coalition immediately seized the initiative by issuing a working paper setting out the "unequivocal undertaking" for total nuclear disarmament that became the leitmotif of the conference. The nuclear weapons states responded with a joint statement that they were committed to the "ultimate" goal of complete elimination. By using the word *ultimate*, and maintaining their decades-long stand that nuclear disarmament was linked to general and complete disarmament, the nuclear weapons states revealed that they saw the NPT review conference as business as usual. The New Agenda Coalition leaders responded directly: "Total elimination of nuclear weapons is an obligation and a priority and not an ultimate goal, and even less a goal that is linked, subject or conditioned to general and complete disarmament."

The nuclear weapons states asked to meet with the New Agenda Coalition leaders. Thus started a set of negotiations involving key players who had been at the Atlanta consultation: John Holum, leader of the U.S. delegation; and, on behalf of the New Agenda Coalition, Darach MacFhionnbhairr of Ireland and Peter Goosen of South Africa. For several days, they wrestled with a text centering on Article VI of the NPT, which obliges states to "pursue" negotiations on nuclear disarmament. Though the New Agenda Coalition had to give up on securing a time frame for nuclear negotiations, it did obtain a clear commitment from the nuclear weapons states that "systematic and progressive efforts to implement Article VI" would include an "unequivocal undertaking by the nuclear weapons states to accomplish the total elimination of their nuclear arsenals leading to nuclear disarmament to which all states parties are committed under Article VI."

Conference participants then agreed on thirteen practical steps to implement this commitment. Holum told me that the Atlanta consultation "helped advance the U.S. position." Goosen said that the level of personal trust generated by the MPI meeting "played an important role in this success."

At the end of the conference, Ambassador Antonio de Icaza of Mexico, speaking on behalf of the New Agenda Coalition, said that the conference's final report "signified an important landmark on which to build a nuclear weapons–free world." Despite the absence of a time-bound program for nuclear disarmament, the document gave the nuclear weapons abolition movement the strongest political basis it has ever had. The door to the long-standing doctrine of nuclear deterrence had cracked open. The nuclear weapons states now accepted the total elimination, not merely reductions, of nuclear weapons.

For good reason had the nuclear weapons states hitherto resisted committing to total elimination; they correctly saw it as challenging the underlying doctrine of nuclear deterrence. But the New Agenda Coalition, as well as the Middle Powers Initiative, had always realized that if the nuclear deterrence doctrine could be exposed as the immoral, illegal and militarily unsustainable policy it is, then the whole framework supporting nuclear weapons could crumble.

Given the tenacity of the nuclear weapons states to hold onto their nuclear arsenals, I knew it would be unrealistic to think they would immediately implement the agreement they had just signed. Nonetheless, a gain of historic proportions had been made. Victory always has a hundred fathers, as the saying goes. One of those fathers was the Middle Powers Initiative, which had brought together key diplomats in a stimulating and creative environment.

I felt justified in telling my colleagues that MPI could now do even more important work in implementing the "unequivocal undertaking ... to total elimination." The future looked bright. But, eight months later, George W. Bush took office and ripped apart the 2000 agreement. New tensions and frustrations were around the corner as the nuclear weapons crisis deepened.

I

The Formative Years:
1929–1971

1

English and French: A Contest

A major decision point in my life came when I was six. Of course, I didn't make the decision, my father did. He wanted me to attend Garneau School in Ottawa to learn French, but he acquiesced to the entreaties of my three aunts and sent me to the English-speaking school, St. Joseph's. My father understood the deepening bilingual nature of Canada, but for the sake of good relations in the family he gave in. My life had hardly begun and already I was at a turning point.

I was born June 14, 1929, in Catherine Booth Mothers' Hospital in Montréal. That was the year of the stock market crash and the onset of the Great Depression. Also that year, the British Privy Council reversed the Supreme Court of Canada's decision of the previous year and legally declared women as "persons under the law." This cleared the way for women to be appointed to the Senate of Canada. Seventy-five years later, in 2004, I devoted my last major speech in the Senate to the role women senators have played in bringing human security values to the Senate, and I challenged them to do much more in the fields of peace and development. I'm sure the thought of my becoming a senator or an ambassador or a Member of Parliament never occurred to the various members of my family. They were preoccupied with surviving the tough economic times.

My great-grandfather, Michael Roche, had had his own struggles with poverty. He grew up in County Mayo, Ireland, the son of Thomas Roche, a sharecropper. In the last years of the eighteenth century, Thomas farmed a small plot of land, which he rented for twelve shillings and sixpence a year. County Mayo was known as one of the poorest and most isolated counties in Ireland. The Celtic language and Irish culture and folk beliefs remained strong until the early 20th century. The Roches had emigrated from France at the time of the Norman invasion in the eleventh century, with one branch going to England and the other to Ireland. Roche is a French name that means "rock." The family motto, handed down through the ages, is "Mon Dieu est Ma Roche," God is my rock.

In the years leading up to the Irish potato famine, the desperate economic conditions forced hundreds of thousands of young Irish men to choose between breaking stones in workhouses or emigrating. Michael saw his chance for a future in the far-off land of British North America. On May 13, 1842, at the age of 31, he married Ann Keenan, who had been a governess for English families and was well educated. One week after the wedding, they sailed from Westport on the barque *Britannia*, a 556-ton vessel. At that time, it normally took six weeks to cross the Atlantic, usually in wretched conditions. Disease and death were constant companions of the Irish emigrants. Some vessels lost a third of their passengers when "the plague" struck, and burials at sea were a daily occurrence. In *The Ocean Plague,* published in 1847, Robert Whyte described the worst of the suffering:

> "Ah! Sir," said a fellow-passenger to me, after bewailing the folly that tempted him to plunge his family into aggravated misfortune, — "we thought we couldn't be worse off than we war; but now to our sorrow we know the differ; for sure supposing we were dyin of starvation, or if the sickness overtuk us. We had a chance of a doctor, and if he could do no good for our bodies, sure the priest could for our souls; and then we'd be buried along wid our own people, in the ould church-yard, with the green sod over us; instead of dying like rotten sheep thrown into a pit, and the minit the breath is out of our bodies, flung into the sea to be eaten up by them horrid sharks."

I think with profound gratitude of my great-grandparents and the other Irish immigrants every time I fly to and from Europe, enjoying a glass of wine, a good book and a movie.

The Law of Killaloe

Michael and Ann appear to have dodged the worst of the travel misery and they landed at Quebec in early July. They made their way by wagon to McNab Township, in Renfrew County in the Ottawa Valley, where Michael began to clear and cultivate 10 acres of land. Less than a year after their migration from the Irish seaside to the backwoods of Upper Canada, their first child, Thomas Joseph Roche, was born. Three other children, Mary Ann, Catherine and Michael Jr., followed.

In the winter of 1856, Michael and Ann moved their family up the Opeongo Line to Hagarty Township, where the government granted land to settlers who would keep the road between the Ottawa River and Georgian Bay in repair. For the second time, Michael and Ann took on the heavy work of clearing land and constructed, out of the maple bush, an 18- by 20-foot log house in a place that became known as Rochefort. Michael and Ann both lived into their late 80s and are buried in the cemetery of St. Mary's Church in Brudenell.

Thomas, my grandfather, married Bridget Devine, the daughter of Irish settlers, and became the first postmaster of Rochefort. He took his politics seriously and was a lifelong conservative as well as a staunch and loyal Catholic. Thomas moved a few miles away to Killaloe, where, as justice of the peace and licence commissioner, he became known as the Patriarch of Killaloe. His wit was endearing. When he died, the *Eganville Leader* wrote, "He was a brilliant conversationalist, and his sense of humor and his sparkling sayings will be remembered as long as there is a drop of Irish blood remaining in this vicinity."

Apparently, one of those he charmed was Leslie Frost, who became premier of Ontario in 1949. A favourite Frost story was how "Judge Roche" of Killaloe would handle the objections of big-city lawyers appearing before him: "What you say may be in all them books, all right, but it ain't the law of Killaloe." (This story made its way into *Colombo's Canadian Quotations,* John Robert Colombo, ed., Hurtig Publishers, 1974.)

As a reporter for the *Toronto Telegram*, I covered Premier Frost and travelled Ontario widely with him in election campaigns. One day, Frost said to me, "Douglas, I want you to run for me in a seat where your grandfather lived."

"Mr. Frost," I replied, "I'll never become a politician."

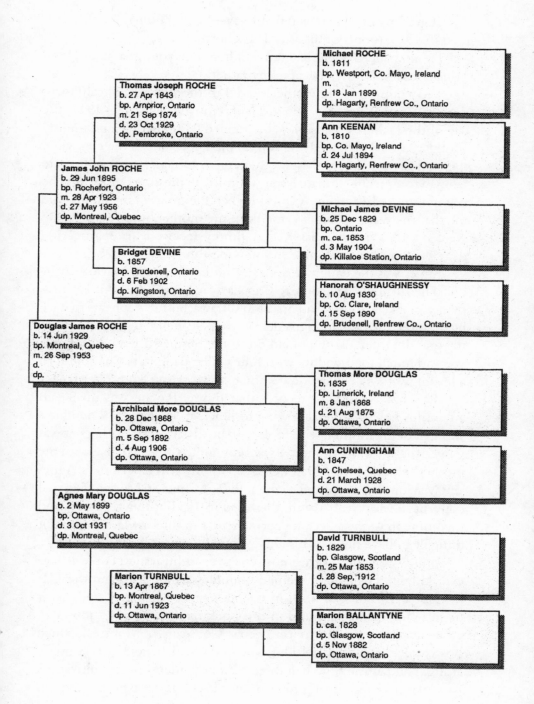

Michael ROCHE
b. 1811
bp. Westport, Co. Mayo, Ireland
m.
d. 18 Jan 1899
dp. Hagarty, Renfrew Co., Ontario

Thomas Joseph ROCHE
b. 27 Apr 1843
bp. Arnprior, Ontario
m. 21 Sep 1874
d. 23 Oct 1929
dp. Pembroke, Ontario

Ann KEENAN
b. 1810
bp. Co. Mayo, Ireland
d. 24 Jul 1894
dp. Hagarty, Renfrew Co., Ontario

James John ROCHE
b. 29 Jun 1895
bp. Rochefort, Ontario
m. 28 Apr 1923
d. 27 May 1956
dp. Montreal, Quebec

Michael James DEVINE
b. 25 Dec 1829
bp. Ontario
m. ca. 1853
d. 3 May 1904
dp. Killaloe Station, Ontario

Bridget DEVINE
b. 1857
bp. Brudenell, Ontario
d. 6 Feb 1902
dp. Kingston, Ontario

Hanorah O'SHAUGHNESSY
b. 10 Aug 1830
bp. Co. Clare, Ireland
d. 15 Sep 1890
dp. Brudenell, Renfrew Co., Ontario

Douglas James ROCHE
b. 14 Jun 1929
bp. Montreal, Quebec
m. 26 Sep 1953
d.
dp.

Thomas More DOUGLAS
b. 1835
bp. Limerick, Ireland
m. 8 Jan 1868
d. 21 Aug 1875
dp. Ottawa, Ontario

Archibald More DOUGLAS
b. 28 Dec 1868
bp. Ottawa, Ontario
m. 5 Sep 1892
d. 4 Aug 1906
dp. Ottawa, Ontario

Ann CUNNINGHAM
b. 1847
bp. Chelsea, Quebec
d. 21 March 1928
dp. Ottawa, Ontario

Agnes Mary DOUGLAS
b. 2 May 1899
bp. Ottawa, Ontario
d. 3 Oct 1931
dp. Montreal, Quebec

David TURNBULL
b. 1829
bp. Glasgow, Scotland
m. 25 Mar 1853
d. 28 Sep, 1912
dp. Ottawa, Ontario

Marion TURNBULL
b. 13 Apr 1867
bp. Montreal, Quebec
d. 11 Jun 1923
dp. Ottawa, Ontario

Marion BALLANTYNE
b. ca. 1828
bp. Glasgow, Scotland
d. 5 Nov 1882
dp. Ottawa, Ontario

One of my great regrets is that I never knew Thomas Roche, who died in 1929, four months after I was born.

Thomas and Bridget had ten children. The youngest, James John (usually called Jimmy), became my father.

As a young man, my father served in the Navy Medical Corps during World War I. He was in Halifax on December 6, 1917, the day of the Halifax explosion, which killed 2,000 people and injured another 9,000. Fortunately, he was on the upper side of the city when the explosion occurred. My mother, Agnes Douglas, then in her late teens, wrote an affectionate letter to Jimmy, expressing her joy that he was not injured. I was always proud when members of my family told me that my writing ability came from my mother. Jimmy and Agnes were married six years later, after Jimmy received his engineering degree from Queen's University in Kingston.

Agnes was the daughter of Archibald Douglas and Marion Turnbull. The Turnbulls had come to Canada from Scotland. Archie Douglas owned a bakery on Rideau Street in Ottawa; business appears to have been good, for he had eight delivery rigs. When Archie died at 38, my grandmother Turnbull held on to the business for a while, but it was too much for a widow with four young daughters. She sold it to a leading Ottawa bakery, now known as Morrison-Lamothe.

The *Eganville Leader* records that Jimmy Roche was unable to attend his father's funeral "owing to illness in his family." The illness was that of my mother, who took sick shortly after my birth. That was why, at the age of six months, I was brought to Ottawa to live with my mother's sister, Marion Daley. The care of my two elder sisters, Agnes and Marion, was entrusted to the nuns at Mount St. Mary, a bilingual convent in Montréal. My mother died in 1931 at the age of 32, and my home in Ottawa became permanent. I'm sure my father found it difficult to have none of his children living under his roof.

Jimmy was one of the most creative, enthusiastic people I have ever known. His energy seemed boundless. After a stint in the U.S. (my sister Marion was born in Grand Rapids, Michigan) and a year or so living off his earnings in the stock market, he got a job as an efficiency expert at Northern Electric Company, in Montréal, which was a forerunner of Nortel. During World War II, he sold victory bonds at night and at the time had three victory gardens under cultivation. At Christmas and during the summer holidays, he would scoop up

Agnes and Marion from their convent and take them by train to Ottawa to visit all the relatives.

Chief among them, of course, was our aunt, Marion Daley, who was raising me. She was married to James J. Daley, a pharmacist; they had one son, Archie, who was six years older than me. Archie and I were raised as brothers. He went into the novitiate of the Missionary Oblates of Mary Immaculate at eighteen, so I had the run of the house at 45 Hastey Avenue in Sandy Hill, small as it was. I attended Archie's ordination to the priesthood in Roviano, Italy, and have grown closer to him as the passing years erased the difference in our ages. He is now in retirement at the Oblate residence in Ottawa, and I treasure the moments I spend with him.

When Jimmy Relented

Marion Daley, whom I called "Mom," was my surrogate mother, Jim Daley a second father, and Maude Daley, Jim's sister, who was a public health nurse, a live-in aunt. Maude busied herself in church affairs and was forever collecting clothing for the families of poor children she encountered. Mom's two sisters, Nell and Bess, were lovingly referred to as the "maiden aunts." They, like Maude, belonged to the generation of Canadian women who were without male partners because of the First World War. I have vivid memories of Jimmy's and my sisters' visits to Ottawa. The Depression notwithstanding, the Christmas dinner table was piled high with food and there were plenty of presents under the tree. My sister Marion, in a lovely memoir she wrote for her grandchildren, describes the concerts we kids put on for the grown-ups. "Our stage was the entrance hallway which ran between the vestibule and the stairway to the second floor. Red velvet curtains on brass rings hung from the archway into the living room. After supper, with the adults seated in the tiny living room, we would close the curtains and gather in the hallway. Then, when we were ready, Archie would introduce the acts and we would sing, tap dance, recite, play the piano or perform a play we had made up. The audience was duly appreciative."

Mom would throw her head back and laugh at our antics. She always welcomed my two sisters with the same warmth she showed me, and treated them with a butterscotch pie, with a golden meringue that was at least three inches thick. I was always a bit in awe of my sister Agnes, four years older than me, who insisted that things be done properly. Marion, closer to me in age, was more my pal in whom I could confide. Archie, of course, was a role model for us all.

For treats, Archie, Agnes, Marion and I were given money for the matinee at the Capitol Theatre, with its impressive marble staircase and huge crystal chandeliers. I loved the Laurel and Hardy movies. Every July, Jimmy would take the girls to Pembroke to stay at his sister Lottie Shea's house. When I was older, I went along for a week or two and developed a close bond with my Shea cousins. Jimmy revelled in cycling, picking raspberries and teaching any child he could find, including his own, to swim by holding a branch with a long cord attached at one end to the branch and at the other end to the child's waist.

Because he depended on his wife's family for so much emotional support for my sisters and me, Jimmy was reluctant to oppose them when the time came for me to begin school. Jimmy wanted to enroll me at Garneau, a French school that was a block away, but my Ottawa family wouldn't hear of it. The idea of French immersion was foreign to them. Hardly anyone they knew spoke French and they could see no need of it. A few years earlier, the University of Ottawa, located at the end of our street, had officially become a bilingual university. This divisive experience left scars on the English-speaking community in Ottawa. Two blocks from our house stood St. Joseph's Church, for English-speaking Catholics; across the street was Sacré-Cœur, for French-speaking Catholics. Though the Oblate Fathers staffed them both, they could have been on different planets. There was absolutely no interaction between the two.

Jimmy relented and off to St. Joseph's I went. As a compromise, I would take French lessons on Saturday mornings from the Holy Cross Sisters, who had a small convent at the corner of Chapel and Daly streets, close to Laurier House, where Prime Minister Mackenzie King lived. It was at the Saturday French lessons that I met John Turner, who would be King's successor seven times removed. Turner did much better than I did learning French and started his political career as a Member of Parliament from Montréal.

When it came time to educate my children, they went into French immersion and all became bilingual. But for me, French was always a struggle. I never did acquire the proficiency of my sisters who, when they were bickering, were told by our father to argue in French so he wouldn't have to listen to them. Without proficiency, I lost confidence and thus, stupidly, resisted practising. It was a vicious circle I couldn't escape. I learned enough French to pass high school and college exams, but because I couldn't become "perfect" (how many anglophones are "perfect" in the second language?), my interest waned. When I became a Member of Parliament, second-language instruction was highly recommended, so I went on courses to St. Jean, Québec. One summer, when I was an ambassador, I even studied for a month in France. My proficiency improved, but I could never rate myself as fully bilingual and I know my political career suffered as a result.

All this was undoubtedly more than Jimmy had in mind when I was six years old, but he was certainly prescient. However, I ask myself: if I had gone to Garneau School for my elementary education, would I have received the excellent grounding in English that St. Joseph's gave me, a grounding that definitely led to my journalism career? I have learned in my life that it's better not to dwell on the "what ifs."

Security in Religion

My boyhood was a happy one. I used to lie in bed listening to the sturdy peal of the bell in the Peace Tower, about a mile away on Parliament Hill. Sandy Hill was a pleasant neighbourhood to grow up in. I remember bread, milk and ice being delivered by horse-drawn carts. We never seemed to mind the mess the horses made on the street. St. Joseph's Church, where I became head altar boy, was like a second home to me. (It wasn't that I prayed that much; there were tennis courts beside the church and socials in the parish hall.) Priests were frequent visitors to our home and the religious atmosphere provided its own kind of security. The parish mission, Forty Hours Devotions, Sunday night benediction (I would listen to Jack Benny on the radio and then dash to church at the last minute) and dramatic candlelight processions on Christmas Eve were all staples. Catholic faith and Catholic culture: the two were so intertwined, they were as one.

I don't know how many schoolboys can say this, but I looked forward every day to going to school. The St. Joseph's teachers were wonderful: I have particularly fond memories of Florence Mulvihill in Grade 1, Genevieve Quinn in Grade 2, Bill O'Meara in Grade 7 and Gabrielle Bourke, the principal, in Grade 8. Bill O'Meara taught me English and instilled in me a respect for books; he drilled us on punctuation and spelling, and to this day I rail against anyone who doesn't put the second "m" in accommodation. I don't think there was a time in those seven years (like everyone at that time, I did grades 3 and 4 in one year) that I wasn't first or second in the class. Sports was another story. Although I did manage to make the St. Joseph's hockey team, I was so weak a player that the coach would not put me in to play in important games.

It was a shock to me when I started high school. This time, Jimmy had his way. He had just married Florence McCarney and set up house on Melrose Avenue in the Notre-Dame-de-Grâce section of Montréal. My sisters were thrilled to get out of the convent at last. Jimmy asked me whether I would like to move to Montréal, so the family would be together. I was so taken with my life in Ottawa, and I felt so close to Mom, that I said no. That must have hurt him, but he was gracious and always welcoming when I would, increasingly, take the train to Montréal to visit him and Florence and my sisters. However, he did insist that I go to high school at the University of Ottawa.

In those days, the U of O had an English and a French high school. I went into the English, but the atmosphere of the school was mostly French. I found the teachers, both lay and clerical, to be narrow-minded and, it seemed to me, resentful of the English. It was as if a quiet war was going on between the two cultures. I didn't like the place, and my grades began to slip. I was barely passing some subjects. I hated when Monday morning came around. One day in my second year, the football team was playing a big game against its rivals at St. Patrick's College High School in Ottawa East. Why the authorities would not let us go to the game remains a mystery to me. With a couple of pals, I skipped school to attend, whereupon my next report card showed the dreaded 69 in conduct. Anything below 70 was considered grounds for dismissal. When I brought the report card home, my uncle Jim Daley took at look at it and said with a grunt and the slightest of smiles on his face, "Well, I don't suppose there's any hurry for your father to see this. Let's wait till the next time he's in town."

When the summer rolled around, my misconduct long forgotten, I went to my father. "Dad, I can't go back there. Please let me switch to St. Pat's. All my friends are there and I know I'll do better in that school." Jimmy, who had likely been prepped by Mom beforehand, agreed. I was so excited, I jumped on my bicycle and pedalled to St. Pat's to register—two weeks early.

My attitude to life changed the minute school began. Like the U of O, St. Pat's was also run by the Oblate Fathers, but this English-speaking group was definitely different from their French-speaking counterparts. Father "Hank" Conway, Father "Spike" Hennessy, Father "Zack" Zachary, approachable and keenly interested in student activities, were role models. Brother Pollack taught ancient history with a verve that made me think he had actually been there.

Editor of the *Patrician*

I joined the staff of the *Patrician*, the school paper, whose editor that year was John Turner. I covered sports and was thrilled to see my words in print. I even went out for football and made the junior team, though I wasn't very good. The best thing about it was my new friendship with fellow linebacker Pat Murphy, who would later be an usher at my wedding. Murphy and I became stalwart figures of the Sodality, a spiritual group, which we thought was a pretty neat organization because it brought us into contact with the girls at Immaculata High School on Bronson Avenue. I took up downhill skiing, and was fairly good, though I didn't win any races. I did excel in the Camera Club, and the *Patrician* noted that I won the junior trophy with a photo entitled "So comfortable" of my sister Marion stretched out beneath a tree. My grades quickly rose again. The next year I found myself promoted to associate editor of the *Patrician*. The editor was John Grace, who later earned a Ph.D. at the University of Michigan and became editor of the *Ottawa Journal*. Grace and I began a lifelong friendship that we still celebrate with an annual Christmas luncheon.

In my third year, I was editor-in-chief. For a series on the benefits of university education, I interviewed Grattan O'Leary, editor of the *Ottawa Journal*. Nervous, I went to his home for our talk. He received me graciously and patiently answered my questions. O'Leary's advice was for students to follow any natural tendencies to a profession. "Therein lies the key to happiness in the world," he said, "by working at what you like." O'Leary himself went on to the Senate. Many times through the years, students have interviewed me. Using

The next summer, I worked as a labourer during the building of the Stewartville Dam, which was located at the west end of Lake Madawaska near Arnprior. We worked a ten-hour day and slept in bunks in dormitories. For a while, I spent days in the blistering sun hauling rocks. Then I was sent into the railway cars to shovel out cement powder. We had to wear masks to save our noses and throats from the sting of the dust, which permeated my clothing and got into my boots and underneath my socks. The result was big blisters on my feet, which Jim Daley treated when I would go home on weekends. When the foreman finally took pity on me and reassigned me to be a carpenter's helper—and all I had to do was store lumber—I thought I was in heaven.

I spent part of another summer cutting grass in a cemetery in Ottawa. I didn't put this experience in my resumé because I was fired. I never fully understood why. Maybe it was because another fellow and I used to take naps in the shade of the gravestones. Losing this job didn't bother me too much, though, because I went right over to the construction site for an apartment building near our house and signed on as a labourer. Actually, I had a fairly strong work ethic, which intensified over the years, as babies arrived and bills piled up. In fact, my working life began when I was eleven. One day, my Aunt Bess, who was a secretary in a law firm uptown, called to say that the office boy had broken his leg and that I should get on my bike and come right up to help them. Years later, I realized I was getting old when I met Ian Scott, then the attorney-general of Ontario, and remembered that his grandfather, W. L. Scott, was the senior partner in Aunt Bess's law firm when I worked there.

The Best Trip to Europe

In 1949, I had the student-in-Europe-trip-of-a-lifetime. I had just turned 20 and Archie was about to be ordained in Italy. His father, Jim Daley, had died the year before, and such a journey was out of the question for Mom, who hated even short trips. Designated the family representative, I sailed from Halifax to Southampton on the SS *Aquitania*. On the five-day trip across the Atlantic, I fell into a spontaneous friendship with a group of young Americans off to tour Europe. One of them was a good-looking girl on whom I developed a boyish crush. When the ship docked, we went our separate ways and I never saw her again.

I took the boat train to London and found a small hotel, then set off by foot to explore London, which still showed the ravages of the war. I went to Paris and soaked in the atmosphere of the Left Bank and Montmartre, then made a pilgrimage to Lourdes. There I first encountered the commercialization of religion; it seemed to me the shops selling religious trinkets overpowered the sanctity of the grotto. I travelled along the Mediterranean coast of France, stopping in Marseilles and Nice, and spent a couple of days in Lausanne, Switzerland.

Finally, I reached Rome. Archie took me to the Oblate summer residence in the hills of Roviano, where he was to be ordained. I took copious notes and photos to share with the family back home. There was a great feast after the ordination, then a two-week holiday for Archie. We took the train back to Rome and the Oblates gave me a room at the Scholasticate at 5 Via Vittorino da Feltre. Every day, Archie led the way, on foot, of course, to a church or other great monument. We went to the four major basilicas by day and to the Baths of Caracella for concerts by night. I fell in love with the city; over the years, I have found Rome to be the perfect combination of antiquity and levity. The Italians are probably the most interesting people on earth, with their insouciance being not the least of their charms.

Archie managed to get two tickets to a "private" audience with Pope Pius XII. The Pope went around the room of about 50 people greeting everyone. When he reached me, I blurted out, "I'm going to be a priest." The Pope seemed to look through me and said nothing. Archie had to stay on in Rome for a further year's study, so I made my way back to Southampton and the return voyage on the *Aquitania*. I suppose, since that long-ago summer, I have been to Europe at least a hundred times by air. The journey by ship in the summer of 1949 was the only time I travelled by boat, and that experience definitely outshone them all.

Through my late teens, the mixture of happy education experiences, association with priests, the mix of jobs and probably my desire to follow in Archie's footsteps had led me to think that I had a vocation to the priesthood. Without a great deal of intellectual and spiritual probing (I am sure the standards for seminary entrance are much higher today), I applied to the Oblate novitiate in Arnprior. After spending three months there in the fall of 1949, the novice master and I came to the mutual conclusion that I was not cut out to be a priest.

The day I left the novitiate, I went straight to the *Ottawa Journal* and was hired as a reporter at $25 per week. It may sound glamorous, but the job entailed writing obituaries all day long. In those days, the *Ottawa Journal*, sadly now defunct, carried a short article on nearly everyone in the city who had died. My job was to call up the undertaker and the family and get the pertinent details on the deceased. Woe to you if you got any fact wrong, because the family would always complain. The city editor was Dick Jackson, a gruff and cynical newspaperman whose peremptory style, just as in the movies, covered a soft heart. Jackson was demanding. Under his tutelage, I learned to "get it right the first time" and write fast. I took to the life.

Jackson liked me (I could tell by the way he yelled at me) and started giving me interesting assignments. One summer day, beseeched by bird lovers who apparently felt the *Journal* wasn't expressing enough appreciation for Ottawa's avian culture, he sent me out on birdwatching with members of the Ottawa Field-Naturalists' Club. I trekked along for a few hours and learned to tell the difference between an American robin and a northern cardinal. We also spotted blue jays, grey partridges and mallards, giving me the basis for a lively piece. Jackson put it on page one, with a byline.

The newspaper business was exciting, but I knew I had to get back to college after the novitiate interruption. Following high school, I had stayed on at St. Pat's to start university work. In my sophomore year, I started a school yearbook. I held a contest for the best name and then awarded the prize to myself for coming up with "The Best Years." St. Pat's was a small college, with no more than a couple of hundred students, so the sense of community was strong. On registration day, I spotted a girl with long black hair, wearing a white and black diamond sweater. The first moment I saw her, I said to myself, "I'm going to marry that girl." (In fact, I did marry her, but she professed not to believe the story.)

Eva Nolan was the eldest child of Gertrude Smythe and Michael Nolan, who farmed in Bowesville (now part of the expanded Ottawa airport). She loved the theatre, music, dancing, bridge and debating. It seemed to me that half the men in the college were in love with her. But I persisted, and our friendship turned into a romance. A gang of friends developed, and every so often we would troop out to Eva's farmhouse in Bernie Benoit's car (Bernie was best man at our wedding) for parties, the highlight of which was always Eva's father's playing jazz on the piano.

Eva had a bit of an Irish temper and occasionally she would direct it at me. During these crises, I would seek solace from her mother, who would take my side of the argument and fix things up with Eva. When our children were small, "Nanny," as we called her, was always on hand. She loved to tell the story that one day Eva and I, children in tow, were getting off a train in Grand Central Station in New York. Nanny was with us, and one of the children cried out, "Come on, Nanny!" Two porters were standing by and Nanny heard one of them say, "I'll take this family. They must be rich; they've got a nanny." At Nanny's funeral, I recounted that story and added, "Yes, in having Gertrude Nolan as a mother-in-law, Doug Roche was the richest man in the world." I meant it.

Social Justice and the Catholic Press

One of the requirements for an honours degree at St. Patrick's College was completing a thesis on an original subject. I was becoming interested in Catholic newspapers and had begun to submit articles to the *Canadian Register* in Kingston, so I chose "The Apostolate of Canada's Catholic Press" as my topic. Under the supervision of my English professor, Father Leo Cormican, I set out to judge the effectiveness of Canada's English Catholic press in promoting a spirit of Catholic action. With this project, two tendencies within me were converging. I had discovered Catholic social teaching in two papal encyclicals: *Rerum Novarum* by Leo XIII, and *Quadragesimo Anno* by Pope Pius XI. Pope Leo's 1891 encyclical, subtitled "Rights and Duties of Capital and Labour," set out the Catholic Church's response to the social instability and labour conflict that had arisen in the wake of industrialization. The Pope defended the rights of workers and condemned unrestricted capitalism. Forty years later, Pope Pius expanded on these themes in his encyclical, subtitled "On Reconstruction of the Social Order," contending that blind economic forces cannot create a just society on their own. The most powerful social teaching of the Church was yet to come, but my own desire for social justice was awakening.

The other tendency was, of course, journalism. The processes that produce the news of the day fascinated me. I thought the press and social justice should go together. My thesis critiqued three Catholic publications: the *Ensign*, the *Canadian Register* and the *Canadian Messenger*. I found the *Ensign* the most interesting, probably because it was owned and operated by Catholic laymen, not the hierarchy. Because it was outwardly focused—it did not dwell incessantly on the internal matters of the Church—I found it more effective than the papers the dioceses put out. Its one big drawback, I found, was its excessive anti-communism, which stemmed from its editor, Robert W. Keyserlingk, a brilliant White Russian who had escaped from the Soviet Union and was determined to crusade against communism. The Cold War was then just getting started. Some Canadian Catholics undoubtedly were fearful of "the Reds," but a weekly diatribe against communism distorted what the Catholic Church in Canada was all about.

I thought my 94-page tome would win the prize for best thesis, but it didn't. Instead, I won the philosophy medal. And who should show up as the main speaker at our college convocation but Keyserlingk? I managed to get a few words with him and told him about my thesis, which he asked me to send to him. I resumed my job at the *Ottawa Journal*; a few weeks later, John Thompson, managing editor of the *Ensign,* called me to say he liked the thesis and that I should consider whether I had a vocation to work in the Catholic press. Would I like to work at the *Ensign*? I was excited at the idea of laymen in the Church standing up for social values, so I jumped at the chance and set out for Montréal, the *Ensign's* home base.

Eva, meanwhile, went on to do a second degree in social work and was assigned to do her fieldwork in Brooklyn. I started making regular trips to New York to visit her. With three other budding social workers, she had an apartment in Flatbush at the very end of the subway line. It took an hour to reach Times Square and the theatre district, where we spent every hour we could spare. One night, after dancing into the wee hours, Eva and I took a subway train to her apartment. She made me tiptoe in so as not to wake her roommates. She mussed up her bed to make it appear slept in, changed her clothes, and then we took off again to spend the day in Manhattan. I didn't have a care in the world.

At the *Ensign*, John Thompson became a mentor and a hero for me. A captain in the Canadian army, he had fought at Dieppe, lost an eye and spent time as a prisoner of war. He smoothed out my writing style and taught me how to edit. He had a concept of the Church— involved with the world rather than standing apart from it—that I admired. He was determined to get more Canadian stories with Catholic content into the paper rather than run just purely Catholic stories. This took us out of the pews and into the public arena. He sent me across Canada to dig up stories. My first time in western Canada, I travelled across the Prairies and into Alberta by train. When the train stopped in Banff, I left my papers and portable typewriter in the club car and went for a walk around town. I was enthralled with the beauty of the mountains; the landscape was luminescent and I kept walking. Suddenly I heard a train whistle and realized that my train was departing from the station. I couldn't believe I had been so oblivious. All I could do was send a wire to the next station, get my belongings taken off the train and wait twelve hours in Banff for the next train. It made for a great story about Banff life, and Thompson loved it.

The *Ensign* had a rocky financial life due to what can best be described as a feud between Keyserlingk and Cardinal James McGuigan, who was archbishop of Toronto. The original idea had been for the new *Ensign* to take over the *Register* chain of diocesan papers, but McGuigan developed second thoughts. Keyserlingk went ahead anyway, though his financial base was shaky. Fortunately, these problems were far over my head, and I was having a great time being news editor. My duties included "putting the paper to bed," which meant journeying every Thursday night to Ottawa to work Friday at *Le Droit*, where the paper was printed. Often, I would push the composing room staff to close the paper in time for me to catch the afternoon train to Toronto and then on to Sarnia, where Eva was by this time working as a social worker. I would arrive in Sarnia at 2 a.m. and Eva would be standing at the station. Time meant nothing. We were in love. Saturday night we would frequently drive over the U.S. border to Port Huron for dinner. The Sunday night train arrived back in Montréal at 7:30 a.m. on Monday, just in time for work.

During those bachelor days, I shared a small apartment downtown with Marceil Saddy, who also worked at the *Ensign*, and Don Hunt, another newspaperman. One night we got the urge to bake a cake. We put the batter in the oven to bake and decided to go to the Press Club for a quick drink. Either the drink wasn't so quick or the cake cooked faster than it should have, because when we got back to the apartment, the firemen were just arriving to deal with the smoke pouring out of the oven. The neighbours were not amused.

Typing as Fast as I Could

On Christmas Day, 1952, I took Eva to the chapel at St. Pat's College, a site filled with so many happy memories for us both, and asked her to marry me. She did not jump at the prospect. Far from it. She wanted to go back to university to get her master's degree. I said I didn't want to wait. We argued all the way back to her parents' home. It wasn't very romantic! We stood on the porch. I decided to stop arguing and let her think quietly. After a few minutes, she looked at me. There were tears in both our eyes, and we hugged each other. We set the date for September 26, 1953.

Since it seemed like a good idea to start married life with both of us living in the same city, Eva found a job as a caseworker at Catholic Children's Services in Toronto. Don Hunt gave me a lead that the *Toronto Telegram* had an opening for a reporter. I went to see Laurie McKechnie, the city editor. He was only mildly impressed by my *Ottawa Journal* background and not at all with my work at the *Ensign*. "Sit down at that typewriter over there," he said. "You've got ten minutes to write why I should hire you." Without a second's hesitation, I started pounding out a news story about the arrival in Toronto of a great reporter, Doug Roche, and what an asset he would be to the *Toronto Telegram* if McKechnie were to hire him before anybody else got him. It was pure stream-of-consciousness and I kept it going as fast as I could type. In ten minutes, I had written close to a column. McKechnie looked at it. "Seventy-five dollars a week," he said.

The pressures at the *Ottawa Journal* were nothing compared to those I found waiting for me at the *Tely*. It vigorously competed with the *Toronto Star*, each paper putting out six editions a day. When the movies show the harried reporter yelling into the phone, "Get me rewrite!" they must have had the *Tely* in mind. That's the way it was.

I was assigned to the rewrite desk. With headphones clamped on and a copy boy ready to yank short pieces of paper out of the typewriter and run them to the copy desk, I would try to make sense out of a reporter shouting in my ear about something—a robbery, a chase, an accident—and write it coherently—and fast. Bedlam became normal.

When an RCAF trainer collided with a Trans-Canada Airlines North Star over Moose Jaw, Saskatchewan, killing 36 passengers and one woman on the ground, the *Tely* sent me and a photographer to the scene. We raced to the Toronto airport just in time for a flight to Winnipeg. The *Tely* had chartered a plane to take us directly from Winnipeg to Moose Jaw. But the *Toronto Star* had done the same for its news crew. On the tarmac, I raced to the pilot of the *Tely*'s plane. "I'll give you a bonus of $100 if you take off before the *Star*'s plane," I shouted. (I knew the *Tely* would cover it.) We got in the air first and landed a few minutes ahead of the *Star* plane. We had a taxi waiting. We raced to the home of the dead woman to scoop up all the family pictures, so the *Star* wouldn't have any. I covered the story for three days, constantly searching for exclusive quotes and theories about how the accident happened. When I returned to Toronto, a bonus was waiting for me.

I was assigned one day to help fellow reporter Ed Mahoney cover Marilyn Bell's swim across Lake Ontario. Mahoney, who also went to St. Pat's College, and I were roommates in a house we rented on Centre Island. Ed was determined to get an exclusive interview with Bell when she finished the swim. He rented an ambulance to try to sneak Bell away after her swim and get exclusive quotes—even though the *Star* had her under contract. The *Star* discovered the plot and guarded Bell on the way to their ambulance. But Ed was able to talk to her on the run and phoned the quotes back to rewrite. The *Star* reporters thought they had lots of time to get Bell's own story about the swim and were not concerned when she went promptly to sleep. Meanwhile, the *Tely* hit the streets with "exclusive" Bell quotes. I was somewhere in the melee of reporters dashing to and fro on the waterfront. All this was "fire engine" journalism with a vengeance.

Time to Grow Up

Archie married Eva and me on a glorious autumn Saturday. My father, Jimmy, toasted Eva and made a great hit with her folks. The *Tely* gave me two weeks' vacation for my honeymoon. Eva and I flew to Boston right after the reception to start a week's holiday at a resort in the Berkshires; we spent the second week in New York. Julie Andrews was starring in *The Boy Friend*. We drank champagne in the Roosevelt Hotel to the strains of Guy Lombardo. Life couldn't have been sweeter.

The next June, Eva was standing at the kitchen sink after dinner in our one-bedroom apartment in Etobicoke. She was seven-and-a-half months pregnant and preparing to go on maternity leave. "I don't feel well," she said. I got her into the car and drove downtown to St. Michael's Hospital. The nurses took her immediately into the labour room. I paced the floor all night. There was no news. At 6 a.m., a nurse came to me and told me to sit down. "You have two babies," she said, "a boy and a girl." I was stunned. Neither Eva nor I had had any idea twins were on the way. When I recovered my composure, the nurse said that the little boy's lungs were not sufficiently developed and that he might not make it. He had already been baptized. I went to see Eva. We named the boy Francis and the girl Evita. Eva went to sleep and I returned home. I sat on the edge of the bed with one shoe off and the other still on. I felt a weight I had never felt before. "Doug Roche," I said out loud, "you're 25 years old. You've got a wife and two children. It's time to grow up."

3

A Welcome to the U.S.

Francis lived 36 hours. I was the one to tell Eva that he had died. We took comfort that we still had Evita. The next day, I rode in the back seat of the undertaker's car, the little white casket on the front seat, to Mount Pleasant cemetery. Ed Mahoney and my brother-in-law Bill Kellerman, Marion's husband, who happened to be in Toronto at the time, were the only people with me. Though, at four pounds, eight ounces, Evita was actually two ounces lighter than Francis had been, her lungs were better developed. The doctors kept her in an incubator for six weeks. After Eva returned home, I took a jar of mother's milk to the hospital every day for the tiny baby. The day the nurses let me hold her in my arms I knew she was going to thrive.

My journalism career started to flourish when the *Tely* assigned me to cover Queen's Park, the seat of the Ontario government. There I came into contact with Premier Leslie Frost, a shrewd politician from Lindsay, who charmed everyone with his avuncular style. He was nicknamed "Mr. Ontario." One day in Kenora during an election campaign, Frost was holding forth with a roomful of admirers. I could see him winding up for one of his Ontario-is-the-greatest-place-in-the-world speeches.

"We have beautiful human relationships in Ontario," he beamed. "I look around me and I see three distinguished journalists covering my campaign. There's Ben Rose of the *Toronto Star*, a proud member of the Jewish community, there's Bill Kinmond of the *Globe and Mail*, an outstanding Protestant, and there's Doug Roche of the *Telegram*, a devout Roman Catholic. Friends, inter-religious harmony is what makes Ontario great." After the event, I cornered Frost in the hallway.

"Mr. Premier," I said, "my paper sent me here to cover your campaign, not to be a prop in one of your speeches. My religion has nothing to do with your campaign. If you do that again, I'm going to report that you are trading on religion."

"Douglas, my boy," Frost said, with a pat on my back, "you should be proud to live in such a great province." You couldn't help but like Frost, which is why he stayed in office for twelve years. When our next child, Michaelene, was born in 1955, he sent Eva and me a gift of a sweater and booties.

Frost campaigned relentlessly, even chartering small planes to reach remote towns. At the end of one campaign, I went back to Lindsay with him to be on hand for yet another victory celebration. The election was the next day and we were all exhausted from non-stop travel. I rested in the hotel for an hour, then decided I had better get down to Frost's headquarters in case anything was happening. There he was, coat off and shirt sleeves rolled up, poring over voters' lists.

"Mr. Premier," I said, "you've just campaigned all over the province. Why don't you get someone else to do the detail work in your own riding?"

"Douglas," he said, "in politics, you've got to know where the votes are."

A Dream Denied

The *Tely* was exciting and fun and, while many of the stories I wrote had substance, I knew I would not be satisfied with mere sizzle; I wanted some steak. That meant journalism with a purpose. The *Ensign* had just been put under the ownership of Christ the King Cultural Foundation Inc., whose president was Bishop John C. Cody of London, Ontario. Robert Keyserlingk was still the publisher and editor, but now he had a new board of prominent bishops and laymen to report to, and brighter prospects for more stable financing. I wrote to Bishop Cody, expressing renewed interest in "some aspect of the field of Catholic communications."

A few weeks later, Keyserlingk met with me in Toronto to offer me the job of associate editor of the *Ensign* and assistant to the publisher. Hope for a truly national Catholic paper, outwardly focused and supported by at least a good number of important bishops, was rekindled. But by this time, the *Ensign* had acquired a bad reputation as a place to work because of Keyserlingk's imperious demands. John Thompson had stuck it out for four years, but even he was gone. Keyserlingk needed to prove to his board that he was not impossible to work for. His goal, I think, was to secure a former employee who wanted to redirect his life to a greater good. Me.

He was willing to pay me what I was then earning at the *Tely*, $7,000 a year. I asked for and received a contract, co-signed by Bishop Cody, stating that I was to be trained as Keyserlingk's successor and that, if anything precipitated termination, the company would pay me six months' salary. I thought this provided me with opportunity and protection at the same time.

Eva and I prepared to move to Montréal to a rented three-bedroom flat in the west end. Before leaving Toronto, I wrote to John Bassett, publisher of the *Tely*, to tell him that I was leaving not out of any unhappiness but because I felt an attraction and suitability to work in the Catholic press. "We all seek professional happiness," I wrote, "and at this stage of my life, having tasted both fields, I think I know where mine lies." Then I paid him a deserved compliment. When I joined the *Telegram*, some of my friends and family looked askance at a Catholic working for the paper because of its past strong ties with the Protestant Orange Order. But in my time, I never observed one anti-Catholic or anti-any-other-minority act, neither at the office nor on the printed pages. Moreover, the paper's promotion of inter-religious harmony was an important contribution to the unity of Canada.

It's a good thing that my contract with the *Ensign* specified that the "company," not the "paper," was liable for my severance pay, since eleven months after I took up my duties, it folded. Keyserlingk had scoured financial circles for new capital, but his lingering problems with Cardinal McGuigan and the Toronto Archdiocese made investors uneasy. I toured Canada and wrote stories from all the provinces to boost Canadian content and shift the focus away from Keyserlingk's incessant anti-communist articles. The paper even evolved into an attractive magazine format, copied off *Time* magazine. But it was too late. The *Ensign* died, and with it the hope of a national Catholic newspaper. Bishop Cody asked me to write my analysis of what went wrong; it turned out to be almost as long as my college thesis on the Catholic press.

This analysis stood me in good stead when, a decade later, I took on the editorship of the *Western Catholic Reporter*. A future *Ensign*, I had written to Cody, must have the initial and continuing support of the hierarchy, without which it is almost impossible to operate. A broad program of financing has to be arranged from the start to avoid the pitfalls of a second-class publication. The board of directors would require active financial and editorial committees to surround the publisher with expert advice. The paper should not equate vigorous Catholicism with anti-communism. "It should show all readers that a press that seeks to enlighten against a background of eternal truth can be as well written, researched and edited as the slick presentations of those whose only God is money." Of course, that last sentence makes me squirm today. I can only say that a certain broadening of my views has taken place since my sweet-bitter experience at the *Ensign*. In any event, the Christ the King Cultural Foundation, the "company" owning the *Ensign*, continued to pay my salary, so I had some time to think about the future.

How to Make Important Decisions

It was a year of blows for me. My father, Jimmy, died that May. He was only 60 years old. Not long after Eva and I were married, he had been diagnosed with colorectal cancer. He suffered a great deal. One good thing about having moved to Montréal for the *Ensign* was that I could be with him a lot in that final year, along with his wife, Florence, and my sister Agnes. The summer before, Jimmy had brought my sister Marion, who was then living in Vancouver, and her two babies to Lake Clear, near Killaloe, for a family reunion. We all knew it would be his last.

When he was being anointed by Father Alex Carter, later a leading Canadian bishop at the Second Vatican Council, Jimmy motioned for me to get his wallet. I knew what was coming. Jimmy took out a $20 bill and handed it to Father Carter. The priest was chagrined and tried to refuse. I piped up, "Better take it, Father, that's the way they do it in Kilalloe." When Jimmy died, we took him back to Killaloe, as he had requested, and buried him beside his father, the Patriarch of Killaloe.

Forty years later, on what would have been my father's 100th birthday, Marion gathered up the family and we went to St. Andrew's Church, beside the cemetery, for a memorial mass for Jimmy. Archie was the celebrant. We shared some memories, Marion laughing as she told of Jimmy taking his kids to a burlesque show in Montréal. I made the speech about the Patriarch that I said Jimmy would have given had he been able to attend his own father's funeral. Afterwards, the grandchildren laid flowers on the graves, and Marion gathered us in a circle to sing what she claimed was our father's favourite song: "O, What a Beautiful Morning!"

Jimmy once gave me some good advice. When you have to make an important decision, never make it when you are tired, hungry or in a bad mood. Go out and have a good dinner with a rich dessert, he said. Then go for a long walk and weigh the pros and cons of the choices before you. Eva and I talked about our future over several dinners. I felt the *Toronto Telegram* would take me back—but did I really want to go? I believed in Catholic journalism, but it was clear that if I were to stay in the field, I would have to leave Canada for the United States. Did I want to leave Canada? Feeling a bit sorry for myself, I wrote to a friend, "In my reluctance to deprive my native land of my unwanted talents, I am slowly arriving at the conviction that I am a study in stupidity." Eva, adventure in her soul as always, encouraged me to at least not be afraid of going to the U.S. One night, as I sat on the steps to the basement, my mind cleared. I immediately wrote to half a dozen leading Catholic papers in the U.S. Within a week, I heard back from the *Catholic Universe Bulletin*, the diocesan paper of Cleveland, Ohio.

At Home in the United States

I took a reporter's job and flew to Cleveland, where I came under the influence of Joe Breig, a prolific columnist with an overflowing appreciation of the great Catholic writer G. K. Chesterton. Breig, who had a gift for making the mundane seem important, was a man of boundless faith and a very large heart. He and his wife, Mary, took me into their home in Cleveland Heights, while I searched for a house for my family. I was proud that I could make a down payment on a house I found around the corner from Joe's. Eva flew to Cleveland with our two little girls. It was late at night when she arrived at our first house with two overtired children. There on the porch was a huge vase of flowers with a note signed by the neighbours: "Welcome, Eva!"

The next day, a smartly dressed woman from the New Neighbors League came to the door to tell us about various local organizations and activities. The welcome book she left contained coupons for a pound of coffee, car lubrication, a box of candy, ice cream and cleaning. We had hardly recovered from this burst of generosity when the Welcome Wagon representative appeared with still more gifts, including cocktails for two and a beauty parlour treatment. But the nicest part of the welcome brigade was our new neighbours. When the lady next door brings a cake and refreshes the movers with a bottle of beer, and the lady next to her sends in a basket of groceries and lunch besides, and then they and a couple of other neighbours spend an afternoon helping you unpack and set up the family operation, you know you're welcome. I felt very much at home in the United States. My struggles with the U.S. government were to come, but in those Eisenhower years, I was struck by the zest and energy of Americans, who didn't seem anything like the loud-mouthed show-offs who too frequently personified the U.S. abroad.

The *Universe Bulletin* was run by Joe Gelin, a no-nonsense newspaperman, assisted by Breig. These were the years immediately preceding the Second Vatican Council, which emphasized the role of the layman in projecting the Church into the wider community. Gelin and Breig were already well advanced in doing just that, and I learned from them how to write about Catholic values in an interesting way. Breig wrote articles and books on the side, and I wondered whether I could ever turn out the same quantity of work and maintain the family values he reflected in his paean to his wife, *Life with My Mary*, which he wrote in 1955. I used to say that Joe could not endure the sight of a piece of paper not covered with words. Mary had a more practical theory: the family budget would collapse without the extra income from Joe's writing. I started freelancing myself; for many years, I wrote article after article for Catholic magazines in the dead of night to keep up with increasing family expenses. One major article I wrote while in Cleveland was a long profile of Cardinal Paul-Émile Léger of Montréal, known as the Crusading Cardinal of Charity. The *Sign*, a leading Catholic monthly magazine, published it.

Interviewing John F. Kennedy

Early in my tenure at the *Universe Bulletin*, Gelin assigned me to write a ten-part series, "A Canadian Looks at Us." In it, I pointed out how the Church in the United States had made a big leap forward by using modern communications. "Only in America could a soft-spoken Irish priest [Patrick Peyton] use movie stars to bring the message of the rosary to millions. Only in America could a bishop [Fulton J. Sheen] become a television star by bringing the message of love to the people." The Church, I wrote, has reached an influential position largely because it has recognized the tremendous value of modern communication—a centrepiece of Western progress.

Gelin suggested I write my own column, called "Eyewitness," in which I could explore the lives of everyday people in the Church. I interviewed teenagers, grandmothers and nuns (the latter because I felt they didn't get enough publicity). One person I interviewed who was not at all ordinary was Senator John F. Kennedy, then beginning his campaign for the presidency. Kennedy had come to Cleveland to speak at a book launch. I waited all afternoon in a hotel lobby for him to finish a meeting with Ohio Democratic leaders. He had promised me an interview and invited me to ride with him to the airport.

Kennedy sat in the front passenger seat; I sat in the back, with a Cleveland detective beside me. I asked the Senator straightaway about the issue of a Catholic running for the White House. Kennedy said he had stopped talking about it because he didn't want to be put on the defensive about his religion. Ever since Al Smith's defeat for the presidency in 1928 was blamed on his Catholic faith, it was assumed that no Catholic would reach the White House. Even the *Christian Century*, a liberal Protestant publication, said that it could not "look with unconcern upon the seating of a representative of an alien culture, of a medieval, Latin mentality, of an undemocratic hierarchy and of a foreign potentate in the great office of the President of the United States." Kennedy said he would repeat to me what he was then telling journalists across the country. "The people are running ahead of politicians who say a Catholic would have no chance for the presidency. The people today are more interested in a man's talent and ability than in his religious convictions."

He went on to talk about his wife, Jacqueline, his two-month-old daughter, Caroline, and his daily task as a senator. He said he kept up on Catholic events by reading *America*, the Jesuit publication. Why, he wondered, does a religious wall exist only around the White House? If there was such a wall, he thought it would crumble when the time came to test its strength.

Obviously, Kennedy decided later to do some destruction himself. In 1960, having won the Democratic nomination, he faced the issue head-on in a speech before the Greater Houston Ministerial Association. "I do not speak for my Church on public matters—and the Church does not speak for me," he said. His biographers agree that, with the Houston speech, Kennedy knocked religion out of the campaign as an intellectually respectable issue. With his election to the presidency, barriers to Catholics in American politics melted away.

A Jolting Discovery

I discovered another kind of barrier I would have to deal with. At the age of two, Michaelene (we called her Mickey, after Eva's father), began to show delayed development. She had sat up and walked more or less on time, but we gradually noticed that we couldn't get any response from her. She could walk about 80 per cent normally, but wasn't improving. She ceased doing little things that she had previously done, such as holding a ball or spoon. Our pediatrician suggested a hearing clinic, which, in turn, recommended a clinic for retarded children.

A battery of physical, psychological and neurological examinations followed. The doctors who had participated in the tests, reviewing their findings, concluded that Mickey was severely retarded due to extensive damage on the right side of her brain. The damage was irreparable, they said; surgery was not an option. They unanimously recommended that Mickey be placed in an institution.

Their last comment was the most difficult to accept. Eva and I decided that we would not place Mickey in an institution unless we were convinced that she would be better off there than at home. That time might arrive, but not yet. We were in a sort of denial; it would take time for the full significance of Mickey's condition to sink in. Facing the prospect of giving up our child was so frightening that we just kept hoping the problem would go away. As time went on, Mickey required a lot of parental energy—especially Eva's. But we were sure we had made the right decision to keep her with us.

One evening, the phone rang. Out of the blue, Father Ralph Gorman, CP, editor of the *Sign*, offered me a job as associate editor. He had been following my work, he said, and he liked what I did. The *Sign* would give me responsibility for a part of the magazine and a boost in salary. He asked me to come to the office for an interview. When I hung up, I told Eva.

"Where's the *Sign* located?" she asked.

"In Union City, New Jersey," I said. "Just beside New York City."

"New York!" Eva exclaimed, dancing around the room—slowly, because Douglas Francis was about to be born.

4

Journeys Through
the Global Village

In July 1958, with six-week-old Doug in tow (when he turned 21, he opted to be called Francis, on the grounds, I think, that one Doug Roche in the world is enough), Eva and I put Evita and Mickey in the back seat of the family car and drove to New Jersey. For the first two months, we lived in a hotel on Journal Square in Jersey City that had a view of the Statue of Liberty from the bathroom window. Our two-bedroom apartment had maid service, which definitely appealed to Eva.

Most evenings, we would put the children in the car and drive through the towns that are practically contiguous in the eastern side of the state, looking for a house to buy. In Rutherford, we found an old Queen Anne house sided with English fieldstone, and with four bedrooms, three bathrooms and a finished basement. One block away, an express bus took 25 minutes to reach the Port Authority, which stands beside Times Square in Manhattan. I could drive to work in 15 minutes. Eva pronounced it perfect, and we scrambled to put every dollar we could find into the down payment towards the price tag of $21,000.

The *Sign*, a monthly magazine with a circulation of 350,000, was considered in the top rank of Catholic publications in the U.S. With its blend of text and photos, it had the appearance of *Life* and *Look*. It did not profess to serve intellectual Catholics, as *America* and *Commonweal* did, but was edited to have the widest appeal to a mass audience. The Passionist Fathers owned it, and the editor was Father Ralph Gorman, a Scripture scholar with a common touch. Though a soft-mannered man in conversation, he fired out his editorials in fusillades. He was one of the first Catholic editors to attack the ultra-conservative thinking of Catholics who would sooner fight communism by looking under beds than correct the social disorders that communists feed on. He made the *Sign* stand for international-minded Catholicism and social justice. It was liberal in applying the social teaching of the Church and conservative in the arts, and tried to pull readers along a progressive path.

After my experience with Bob Keyserlingk at the *Ensign*, I found Father Ralph very appealing. He taught me to stand up against right-wing ideology that cares little about human suffering. When the *Sign* explored and explained the fallacies in Senator Barry Goldwater's principles (long before he ran for the presidency), the response from readers was as angry as if the publication had insulted the Pope. A series of editorials on the theme of government and welfare provoked thousands of indignant and abusive letters. Father Ralph was undeterred. "It strikes us as strange," he wrote, "that these people never give any indication of having read authoritative sources of Catholic teaching on social problems, such as [in the papal encyclicals] *Rerum Novarum, Quadragesimo Anno, Mater et Magistra* or *Pacem in Terris*, nor do they show that they are aware of the existence of standard Catholic works by specialists in this field."

I was put in charge of the People section, which featured pieces about interesting Catholics, and photo stories, which were a staple of the magazine. At the start of each monthly cycle, a magazine is just an idea. I learned how to develop ideas from their genesis to the finished editorial product. We were trying constantly to project a Christian vision of life in terms that the "average family" could understand and respect. I not only produced but also wrote profiles on Clare Boothe Luce, the playwright, congresswoman and ambassador; Norman St. John-Stevas, a bit of a Catholic rebel, who became a leading Member of Parliament in the United Kingdom; and Ellen Sullivan, a member of the Catholic Evidence Guild in New York, who preached from a small platform in Times Square. I mixed stories called "What Is a Bishop?" with an in-depth report from Connecticut titled "What Suburbia Does to a Diocese." I went to Atlanta to do a story on educated blacks in the South and to Reno to depict what the gambling culture was doing to Nevada.

It was a learning experience to see America from the suburban congestion of Long Island to the peaceful panorama of San Francisco Bay, from stylish Michigan Avenue in Chicago to cluttered Bourbon Street in New Orleans. During a swing through several states, I interviewed bishops and historians, judges and journalists, politicians and housewives. The people I talked to surveyed the American scene from such diverse points as a carpeted office in a Chicago skyscraper overlooking Lake Michigan and a tax assessor's office in a small town in Nevada. I encountered progress everywhere: urban renewal in Pittsburgh, interracial improvement in Illinois, scores of new churches and schools in California. Every day brought thrilling sights: the city of Denver and the snow-capped Rockies from the steps of Colorado's state capitol, the endless expanse of yellow-and-green checkerboard fields of the Plains states, the Spanish villas of Santa Barbara from Mount Calvary high overhead. I met good people, greedy people, brilliant people and malicious people. All of this left me with an image of America in wild array.

America in Shame and Glory

One morning in Oklahoma City I had breakfast with an interesting woman named Mrs. Clara Luper. Her grandmother was a slave; her mother finished sixth grade. She herself had a master's degree, and her teenage daughter, who accompanied us, wanted to be a psychiatrist. Mrs. Luper, a black woman, was the leader of Oklahoma City's sit-in demonstrators, whose passive protests over the previous three years had resulted in about 140 restaurants "opening up" to blacks. But 200 were still closed to black people. Mrs. Luper asked me if I wanted to feel what it is like to be refused service in a restaurant. So the three of us went into a drugstore and sat down at the counter in the small dining room. Everyone's eyes turned on us. I felt the tension in the air, as if someone had suddenly shouted an obscene word. The Lupers and I talked quietly among ourselves as if nothing special were going on. Then a waitress came over and told us we would not be served. We said nothing and just remained in our seats for half an hour. Hateful glances were thrust at us. Finally, we left.

We approached five or six other restaurants in the downtown area. Each place was guarded by a stalwart white citizen, who denied us admission. Since the sit-ins had begun, I learned, most of the restaurants that would not serve blacks put guards on the door so their white customers would not be disturbed by demonstrations. I remember one place in particular: two gum-chewing, slovenly dressed waitresses in a department store basement barred our way into the lunchroom with a filthy rope; they stared at us and grinned at each other. Hardened as she was by years of interracial work, Mrs. Luper could not disguise the hurt in her heart. For the first time in my life, I was ashamed of my white skin.

I marvelled at the ability many black people had to laugh at their troubles. When I was in Oklahoma, people were still chortling over a choice incident: a white mother with a three-year-old child at her side and carrying a baby wrapped in a blanket entered a segregated restaurant. She placed an order, including custard for the baby, and asked that a bottle of milk be heated. When the waitress returned with the order, the mother had unwrapped the baby. There in all his dark splendour was a black child.

One day, I stood in a Kansas field, hip-deep in a sea of wheat gracefully swaying in the breeze. A solitary farmer in a distant field was methodically ploughing for a late crop. The stutter of his tractor was the only sound. Off to the left, beside a clump of tall trees, was the farmer's white stucco house with its red roof and a television antenna. For a long time I absorbed this pastoral scene of man, labour and the bounty of grain that resulted from his efforts. A sense of confidence replaced the confusion in my mind about the strength and ambitions of Americans. Once or twice, the farmer ploughing his field passed by me; I could see his weather-beaten, sweat-stained face. He looked up at the sky, determining whether he would finish his work before rain came. Suddenly, with a fierce emotion, I wanted all America to see this scene—the people in the slums, the people on the subways, the people in the towering apartment buildings, the people in split levels. I wanted them to see America in its pristine glory.

Expanding Horizons

Back at the *Sign*, I hired writers and photographers, and the magazine paid them well (at least by religious publication standards) in an effort to compete not only with secular publications but also with television and its growing influence. Our star photographer was Jacques Lowe, who went on to fame as the private photographer for President Kennedy. Lowe's photographs of the Kennedys have become the iconic imagery of a time and remain vividly etched in the minds of people everywhere. A naturalized American citizen who emigrated from Germany, Lowe was hired by Kennedy's father to take a family portrait, and they loved his work. He started going everywhere with JFK on his campaign for the presidency and, in the end, had taken 40,000 Kennedy photographs. He gave me some original prints, which I still have. Naturally, we published some of his best in the *Sign*.

When the *Sign* published a memorial to Kennedy after his assassination, I wrote the text for Jacques's tribute, using his spoken words: "He was a young President, and he believed in youth and the value of young ideas. He believed in the value of creative man and the future of creative mankind." When Robert Kennedy was killed five years later, a despondent Lowe, unable to take the violence in America any longer, returned to Europe. He stayed there for 18 years before coming back to the U.S. All his priceless Kennedy negatives were carefully stored in a vault in the World Trade Center. They were incinerated in the collapse of the Twin Towers in the terrorist attack of 9/11.

Lowe had died a few months before. His daughter Thomasina persevered with existing files and produced a stunning book, *Remembering Jack*, with a foreword by Robert F. Kennedy Jr. and an afterword by the novelist Tom Wolfe, one of Jacques's close friends. Jacques taught me what constituted great photography and considered me one of the unwashed when I argued with him that some of his photos were too dark. We became good friends. In fact, he was probably my first non-Catholic friend. (Jacques was Jewish.) He lived on Perry Street in Greenwich Village, and Eva and I thought it was very bohemian to tour the Village galleries and cafés with him.

My working life at the *Sign* expanded my horizons. Father Ralph assigned me to go to Nigeria to do articles on how "the Black Colossus" was throwing off its colonialism and preparing to celebrate independence. Fortunately, Nanny was on hand to help Eva, and I got back before the birth of Mary Anne. Blonde, shy and almost always happy, Mary Anne was a joy from the moment of her birth.

Nigeria was a showplace of how a country could achieve independence without violence. It was destined to be a leader of Black Africa. But the packed slums of the capital city of Lagos, situated on a lagoon on Nigeria's swampy south Atlantic coastline, were a shock to me. A principal reason why there never was a white settlement of any size in Nigeria, as occurred in eastern and southern Africa, is that the country became known as the "White Man's Grave." Besides an enervating tropical climate, the early explorers, administrators and missionaries had to combat yellow fever and malaria. Many of the groundbreaking Irish missionaries died within three months of their arrival. The story is told of a British consular officer, who, finding himself posted to Nigeria, asked about his pension. "Pension?" his Chief in the Colonial Office replied. "My dear fellow, nobody who goes to Nigeria ever lives long enough to be retired."

Nigeria was also of growing importance from a religious viewpoint. The Muslims, who dominated the northern half of the country, were starting to fan down through the western section. How would this affect the Christian areas? The prayer of the Catholic hierarchy was for ten years of peace in order to sink the roots of the Church even deeper in the soil. I started learning about the Muslim faith, a subject on which I had been blithely ignorant. I watched as, five times a day, turbaned Muslims turned to Mecca and prayed with their faces to the ground.

Life of an Ibo Family

I travelled to the eastern section of Nigeria, where the Ibos, who are mostly Christian, are strong. I had an introduction to an Ibo tribesman, James Ibole, from his clansman, Mark Mere, whom I had met in New York. A master's student in education at Fordham, Mere brought his young family to our house a few times, but generally he felt lonely in the crowded but impersonal milieu of New York. When I reached his relatives at their compound in Owerri, Ibole, a 44-year-old teacher, ceremoniously presented a *kola* nut to me, a symbol of acceptance and friendship.

I could see why Mark was lonesome in the U.S. Ibole and his wife, Theresa, had nine children, aged 23 to four. One of the daughters was married; the other eight children lived with their parents in a compound. Although their mud and clay house was small, it didn't hinder family activities, which were carried on for the most part out of doors. Behind the main house, containing a living room surrounded by four bedrooms, was a cookhouse where the family's staple diet of beans, yams and ground corn was cooked over a fire of twigs and sticks. Ibole's teaching salary was $200 a year. Theresa augmented the family income by selling vegetables every day in a nearby market.

By Owerri standards, the family was reasonably prosperous. By the standards of the West they had few possessions indeed. Water had to be hauled half a mile. There was no electricity. Ironing was done with a coal iron. Yet a pristine joy shone through Ibole's family life.

Seven years later, the area erupted in the Biafran war, when the Ibos, then sitting on valuable oil reserves in the southern Niger Delta, tried to secede and set up their own nation state. The Yoruba in the West and the Hausa and Fulani tribes in the north wanted to maintain their access to the oil. A terrible civil war was fought; images of starving Biafran children appeared around the world. The war petered out in 1970, and a military bloc governed the whole country for many years. It was estimated that up to three million people died due to the conflict, most from hunger and disease. When the Biafran war exploded, I looked back on the peaceful scenes I had observed in Owerri and realized, probably for the first time, how vulnerable innocent people are to corrupt politics and the ravages of war.

A Venezuelan Communist and the Church

Two years after the Africa trip, I went to Central America and saw in Honduras and Nicaragua the same kind of dehumanizing slums I had witnessed in Lagos. These were Catholic countries, without any interfaith conflicts to impair economic development. Yet there was massive poverty. In Honduras, I called on the Papal Nuncio. The opulence of his house took me aback.

Thanks to President Kennedy's Alliance for Progress and Pope John XXIII's crash program to save the faith on a continent containing one third the numerical strength of the Catholic Church, Latin America was in the news. The spotlight was on the "oligarchy," who controlled vast amounts of land and wealth. Fidel Castro had recently taken over Cuba, and other communist leaders were making inroads in the media, universities and unions through the continent. The press in North America usually portrays communists, wherever they are, as ogres, but this does little to tell us why a man turns to communism as a way of life. I wanted to know who the Latin America communist was. What did he want? Why had the Church lost him?

When I went to Venezuela, I looked around for one person who would personify this story. A trustworthy contact introduced me to Aristides Bastidas, a science reporter for the daily *El Nacional*, who was also secretary-general of the National Union of Press Workers and a card-carrying communist. The previous year, he had received a national newspaper award for his science reporting. He was intrigued that a Catholic journalist—and from an American publication no less—was genuinely interested in him.

We met in a café in downtown Caracas on a Sunday afternoon. Outside, the traffic was light, unusual in the bustling capital. There was no sign of the police roundup, going on at that very moment, of communist demonstrators who a few days earlier had bombed the American embassy and rioted against the government. "I'm sorry I couldn't take part in those riots," Bastidas said, "but I was in Cuba at the time." For the next several hours, he maintained this matter-of-fact tone, though his brown, steely eyes gave away his emotion about events that had seared his innermost feelings.

Bastidas was born of farming parents in the village of San Pablo, which is 180 miles west of Caracas in barren country rising gently to the mountains. His father was one of two thousand *campesinos* who rented a patch of land from a wealthy landowner. Half of each man's crop of corn and black beans had to be returned to the owner. His family lived in a three-room hut made of wood and baked mud. The floor was cement; cardboard walls separated the rooms. Water was obtained at a public well where pigs and burros, as well as humans, came to drink. Aristides was the eldest of three children.

"The landowners never got to know the poor people," Bastidas told me. "They would go to Caracas and then to Europe and then come back to their homes. They lived in another world. They wouldn't even go to mass in the church with us, but would go to a private chapel on some landowner's estate. My family was literally starving on sterile land. I had to get out and help them and the only place that looked promising for us was Caracas. When I told the priest that we were leaving, he indicated that, well, he would have one less problem. I guess when you have a thousand flies buzzing around you and one leaves you don't really notice that it's gone."

The shack on the edge of the cemetery that became the family's home in Caracas was worse by far than the one they had left. His father found work as a labourer in the sewage system, while the mother contributed to the family income by making *arepas*, a type of cornbread, and selling them in neighbourhood *bodegas*.

Bastidas had a variety of jobs during his first year of high school, but when he was fifteen his father, who was 41, died of overwork and poor nutrition. Even though Aristides went to work full time, the family's survival became an almost insuperable problem. Looking back, he commented, "There was an erosion in the belief as well as the practice of my faith. There was just enough time to stay alive."

He got a job as a guard in a psychiatric hospital (he still carried the scar of a 17-inch wound suffered when an inmate threw a pot at him), where he took his first step into union activities. He organized the nurses and guards, who were badly treated by the management, into a union. At the age of sixteen, Bastidas was its president. The government outlawed the union and Bastidas was sent to jail, the first of several sentences.

This was the turning point in his life: "In jail I met communists who were political prisoners. They were great fighters for agrarian reform. I began to see communism as a solution to the misery of the people I knew. I was young and scared, but the communists befriended me. The next year I joined the Party. I didn't know much about it, but I began to read and study."

A few nights after my meeting with Bastidas, I called on him and his family in their two-bedroom apartment in *Bloque 9*, a housing development in Casalta, where the communists numerically were quite strong. I met his wife, Aura, and their two children who, though they would soon be joining communist youth groups, had been baptized in the Catholic Church. Aura insisted that her husband had not pressured her to stop practising her religion. "I just lost confidence in the Church," she told me. Later in the evening, when the children had gone to bed, Bastidas returned to the subject of violence. He had learned, he said, that violence leads to power.

I entitled the article "Christ to Marx—Step by Step." It won the Catholic Press Association 1962 Journalism Award for Best Non-Fiction Article.

The Medicine of Broadway

In March of that year, our youngest child, Patricia Theresa (in later years, she preferred to be called Tricia) arrived. We had acquired a home-movie camera and filmed all the great family moments. Tricia was photographed in a pink snowsuit, and we began to call her "the little girl in the pink suit." Evita was eight years old. Eva and I were not yet ten years married and we had had five children. I did not forget Francis I, to whom I fervently prayed to look after his sisters and brother. I thanked God that Nanny was on hand much of the time; the sheer daily routine would have been crushing without her.

Mickey was then seven and required increasing care. We had found an osteopathic physician who had helped to bring improvement in cases like hers by moving, through deft massage, certain bones blocking the passages to the brain. So far, we could see a little improvement in Mickey's condition, enough to prompt us to continue the treatments, even though the doctor lived in Philadelphia, almost 200 kilometres away. Every Saturday morning for months, I would drive Mickey to her treatment, until the doctor advised us to stop.

Through my work, I had met John Hodgson, director of the Catholic Travel Bureau, who organized pilgrimages to religious shrines in Europe. He took an interest in Mickey and invited Eva to take her on a pilgrimage to Lourdes. What a gift! Eva was thrilled at the prospect of such a wonderful journey. I can't say we prayed for a miracle, but we did pray that we would be able to accept God's will for our daughter. Eva said that when she arrived at Lourdes and saw the terrible state so many people were in, she didn't dare ask God for a special favour for us. She told me that when she wheeled Mickey through the candlelight processions each evening to the grotto, the huge crowd singing "*Ave, Ave, Ave Maria ...*" brought her an indescribable peace.

For the second week of the pilgrimage, Hodgson had arranged for Eva's group to go to Rome to see all the religious sites in the Eternal City. Thus, on October 11, 1962, Eva, with Mickey at her side, found herself in the traffic jam crossing the Tiber onto the Via della Conciliazione, the broad avenue that leads straight to St. Peter's Basilica. In the car immediately ahead of her was Cardinal Paul-Émile Léger of Montréal, on his way to participate in the opening ceremonies of the Second Vatican Council. The Council, with its immense repercussions, would alter my life, and here were my wife and daughter right in its midst.

Eva and Mickey returned home. A social worker warned us that the continuing drain on parental strength and emotions could short-change the other children. We tried not to let that happen. We did not stop having family parties or going places, but the timing and duration of the events coincided with Mickey's schedule. We made sure that the other children got their little treats and attention, and both Eva and I kept up outside interests. One day, some children came to play at our house for the first time. They were hardly in the door when Evita marched over to the biggest lad in the group and announced, pointing to Mickey, "That's my sister, and she can't talk, so you be nice to her." A little short on tact, but heartwarming. I'm not saying that life in our household ran like clockwork or that there never was an emotional crisis. But each member of the family seemed to know instinctively that there had to be a little more "give" than normal.

One way Eva found to restore her energies was to spend a full day in New York every second Wednesday. In the periods when Nanny was not staying with us, we hired a housekeeper to come in at 9 a.m. Eva would take the bus to New York and spend the morning in an actor's class; at one point she studied under the famous actress Uta Hagen. Then she had a quick lunch and went to see a Broadway matinee; in those days, tickets cost about three dollars. After the show, Eva would go to her tap-dancing class. I would come straight home from work, feed the kids and put them to bed. Eva would return home around nine or ten o'clock with a bounce in her step. There never was a minute in New York she didn't love.

In 1964, when Evita was 10, Francis, 6, and Mary Anne, 4, Eva and I took them for a three-day adventure at the New York World's Fair. Nanny minded Mickey, 9, and Tricia, 2, at home. The kids loved this fantastic fiesta. We stared at fighting dinosaurs, drove through the city of tomorrow, romped on the moon, rode the People Wall, shot rapids in a hollow log, and gasped at what they had done to ordinary movies. Every moment was exciting. The kids loved it. I kept track of the expenses—$186.80 for the three days—and made more than this by selling an article entitled "Family at the Fair" to a magazine.

As you can see, living with a child who, in the language of the time, was called "retarded," was not the depressing existence that some might think. The problem, of course, wasn't thrown at us. We eased ourselves into it with the gradual discovery of Mickey's condition. At first, in the days of uncertainty, everything Mickey did wrong upset us. After we knew what to expect, everything she did right, even little things like winking, greatly pleased us. There were other compensations. Mickey did not aggravate us the way healthy children sometimes can. And she made the hopes and dreams we had for Evita, Francis, Mary Anne and Tricia seem even more precious.

Christians Comporting Badly

Since I had already done special reports from Africa and Latin America, the *Sign* sent me to India in 1963. No other country has had such a profound effect on the development of my thinking about the stark contrasts between rich and poor in the modern world. My journey took me first to the Vatican Council and then to the Holy Land. These stops proved to be a valuable preparation for what I would see in India. Each taught me to be more generous than I might have been in my judgments of the Church's performance there.

I had stopped in Rome to interview the tall and imposing Cardinal Valerian Gracias, India's first cardinal. Rome was filled with the politics of the Church in change. At the press briefings, the cocktail parties, the sidewalk conversations, I felt the tug-of-war between the progressives and the conservatives. I sensed the anachronisms of the Church slowly giving way to the intensive desire of the Council Fathers, or at least most of them, to rediscover the Church that Christ gave to Peter and the other apostles. But why, I kept asking myself, had it taken this long—1900 years—to find out what we are?

In the Holy Land I had hoped to be inspired, as I walked the paths of the Lord, to perceive the Church that all people could recognize as one, holy, catholic and apostolic. But I was chagrined. I searched for the simplicity of Christ's love and found human strife. The lack of concern of the non-Christian world for the Christian and the fractures of Christianity itself are flung in the face of the visitor. On my trip, the hatred between Arabs and Jews seemed no more scandalous to me than the sharp divisions within the Christian body. The supreme example of this conflict is the Church of the Holy Sepulchre, built on Calvary, the place where Jesus died. The church is partitioned among Roman Catholics, Greek Orthodox, Armenian Catholics and

Coptic Christians: each conducts services, oblivious of the others. It is a monument to the pride of distrustful Christians everywhere and a disgrace to the memory of Christ, who died that all might be one in him. Is it any wonder, I wrote at the time, that the Muslims in Jerusalem stand in bemused disdain of Christianity?

Of course, I felt privileged to pray at the manger in Bethlehem and to kneel on the Lithostrotos, the flagstones upon which Pilate judged Jesus. And the morning I spent in silence in the Garden of Gethsemane will always live with me. The effect, though, was not the triumph of Christianity that I had been taught in school but humiliation that we Christians depict ourselves so badly. If the pure message of Christ's love failed to sway the people living in the very area he sanctified, I thought, how much can we expect in distant lands?

My first days in Bombay, or Mumbai as it is now called, brought one shock after another. To read or see pictures of inhuman crowding and destitution is one thing; to walk among such poverty, to smell it, to face myriad pathetic, staring eyes is another. Mumbai, the New York of India, then had a population of four million jammed on a peninsula big enough for a third that many. Today, at thirteen million, it is one of the largest cities in the world. The surrounding suburbs swell the population to twenty million. Waves of people continually surged through the streets, just like Times Square when a parade had passed. The shacks at Worli, on the way into the city from the airport, were unsurpassed in filth.

Every night I saw thousands upon thousands of men, women and children sleeping in the streets. I was told many times that people preferred this indignity to stifling tenements jammed fifteen and 20 people to a room, but it didn't make me feel any better. Each morning, near the Taj Mahal Hotel, I noticed a particular little boy, about eight years old, getting up, folding a thin, straw mat, and shaking the dust off himself as he began another day of foraging. Outside the cathedral, the distorted hands of beggars were thrust out at me; I thought, with shame, of the bacon-and-egg breakfast that would be impeccably served to me by white-gloved waiters back at the hotel. One night, I came away from a dinner party, at which I had been treated to Indian delicacies, and stumbled over human bodies lining the steps of the dwelling and the sidewalk. I said a hasty farewell to my host, who was as embarrassed as I, and climbed into a taxi in frustrated rage.

The very next morning, the lead editorial in the *Times of India* discussed the "grim and bitter taste" left in the mouths of foreigners encountering India's poverty. "The struggle for survival, the fierce fight for existence, is an astonishing thing to see," the editorial said, "and an observer is left wondering how it is that humans so ill-equipped to fight continue to show so much grit and cling on to life."

My Love Affair with India

I set out to see as much of the religious, political, cultural and family life as I could on a trip lasting nearly three weeks through central and south India and then up to New Delhi in the north. Elephants and caves bore me, so I skipped the game sanctuaries and archeological sites. I spent my time with Christian missionaries and dedicated Hindus—merchants and farmers, politicians and students. I was invited into homes of people of almost every economic class, and once in a while got a chance to eat with my fingers in the Indian manner.

I remember the towering Hindu temples, adorned with the carvings of hundreds of human figures, that I saw in Madras (now called Chennai), and the serenity of a shrine to Gandhi that features Jesus' Sermon on the Mount among his favourite quotations chiselled in stone. I still see the millions of candles outlining the homes of New Delhi on the night of Diwali, the Hindus' joyous festival of lights. Castes, languages and wildly coloured clothing were mingled everywhere. Men in their long wraparounds called *dhotis*, women in their saris alive with violet, green and fuchsia, the bazaars rich with the odour of spices and the chatter of trade, the bent bodies plucking at the fields, barefoot children in a new school, the philosophers and illiterates, the spinning wheels and steel mills—everything the eye can see weaves a pattern in the Indian fabric. India absorbs everything. One day in a train compartment, I watched, fascinated, as a Sikh did up his hair in long plaits, which he carefully wrapped in a turban six feet long. He powdered his beard, shed his *dhoti* and donned the smart, white uniform of the Indian navy.

Many Westerners think of the East as a "mass of people," forgetting that this "mass" is made up of individuals, each with his or her own hopes and fears, fun and frustrations. One night a man I was visiting offered me a drink. Since he was living in an area of prohibition, he peered up and down the hallway to make sure no one was spying, bolted the door and produced a bottle that he gleefully announced was "homemade." My stomach was shuddering even before the vile liquid hit it, but I managed to down the glass. Another time, I needed a taxi, but the only one available was a rickshaw. The driver urged me in, but my spirit rebelled at the idea of another human being pulling me along the street; I rented a bicycle instead and pedalled off, to the bewilderment of the rickshaw driver.

One time I was driving with a friend through the countryside in the south of India at night. Suddenly, the car's headlights picked out men milling around a truck on the road. A man had been hit in an accident. I gave up my place in the car, and my companion sped off with him to a hospital a few miles away. This simple act seemed to amaze the village men, who clustered about me with great excitement. One of them brought a bench for me to sit on. Clad in their loincloths, they came up, one by one, to peer at me in the darkness. Finally, an old man shook his head and said, "Only a foreigner would stop and help one of us!"

It was at this moment that my love affair with India began. As I sat in that remote village, the turbulence inside me subsided. For the first time in many days, I felt at peace with a nation and a mentality that had both angered and enraptured me. After that, I became more relaxed, and the Indians responded with a friendship that lowered the barriers between us.

I was never able to get out of my mind that about 90 per cent of the people in India have virtually nothing of a material nature. But despite this immense sadness, I began to feel the dignity and promise of India. Through the bedlam of a nation in motion, I saw a yearning for greatness that might be achieved by the coupling of a 5,000-year history to Western technology.

Meeting a Kerala Farmer

As I had done in Africa and Latin America, I wanted to see India through the eyes of one person. So I went to the village of Trichur in Kerala, one of the most beautiful places in India. Its magnificent green rice paddies were surrounded by orchards bearing coconuts, mangoes, papaya, bananas and pineapples. A Westerner can hardly walk unobtrusively into a village in India, but even so I wasn't prepared for the sensation I caused when I sought out a farmer named

Krishnankutty. A hundred farmers gathered around me as I set out across a field of sugar cane, which glowed with the mauve reflection of the setting sun.

Krishnankutty showed me his clay hut with a straw roof, which he had built himself. He was glad, he said, that it didn't leak very much during the monsoons. The only furniture in the three small, dark rooms were a few benches and some straw mats spread on the floor for sleeping.

His six children, ages seventeen to two, joined the cluster around us. I could see their scabies and eczema and the strange shape of the bodies of the little ones caused by a diet severely low in nutrients. Krishnankutty's wife, Karthiayini, who looked much older than her 35 years, told me the children get tapioca with a little rice twice a day. "Sometimes when we have the money, we give them a little breakfast of coffee or tea," she said. The children never got milk.

By his own standards, Krishnankutty was a simple man who wanted a better home and education for his children and a regular income. These simple desires had been a powder keg in Kerala. It was a stronghold of Christianity in India, but it was also the first place in the world ever to adopt a communist government in a free election. The travel books describe Kerala as a palm-fringed paradise. But a missionary uttered a more realistic view of the lives of Krishnankutty and his fellow villagers: "They work, they starve, they love."

The world for Krishnankutty was some far-off place. He only hoped that in his next incarnation he would be born into a higher caste and have a better share of life's goods. Once in a while, he walked a mile to the house of his friend, a doctor, and listened to the news on the radio, but he found everything far beyond him. Every two or three months, he found a little release from his cares by scraping together a few pennies and buying a bottle of cheap liquor. Otherwise the family's annual diversion was limited to *Onam*, the four-day harvest festival, during which all the villagers wear new clothes and sing and dance day and night in what one of them called a glorious celebration.

Shortly after his marriage, Krishnankutty got a job as a coolie building a highway on the India-China border for the Indian government. The job lasted for only a year and Krishnankutty returned home to work in the fields for 30 cents a day. "Why are you starving down there?" his older brother asked him one day. "Come up and cultivate the land near me." The brother had been given five acres of government forest land as a gratuity for military service. The land had not been properly surveyed, so the brothers extended the plot by half an acre and Krishnankutty moved his growing family to their new home. He cleared the land and planted tapioca. Since he couldn't exist on half an acre, he went into the forest, marked off an additional acre and began to cultivate it.

On my final day in India, I went to the Lok Sabha, the Indian Parliament in Delhi, to observe the new democracy in action. It was raucous, with dissident members switching back and forth between English and Hindi. On a plane that night back to Mumbai, where I would catch my flight home, I happened to sit beside an Indian Member of Parliament. He had taught school while studying law so he could embark on a political career. Now he represented one million people, and he talked happily about how the gigantic power dams the government was building would better their lives by making it possible to irrigate millions of hectares. He spoke gratefully of the $5 billion that India had received from the United States in aid, and predicted that President Kennedy, in his forthcoming visit to India, would receive a welcome surpassing any he had received anywhere in the world. A day after I landed back in New York, the shots rang out in Dallas and Kennedy was dead.

Non-white, Non-Western, Non-Christian

It seems now that I must have been in a trance for four days while the final observances for Kennedy took place. My personal innocence was over. I now knew how brutal the world is. But I could not deny its beauty, which I had see up close in my travels through Africa, Latin America and Asia, not to mention Europe, the U.S. and, of course, Canada. But the vastness of the poverty I had seen and the disdain of the rich gnawed at me. I remembered the culture shock I had experienced after many of my trips—not from the first exposures to poverty abroad but from the return to a North America teeming in riches. I had seen the diversity of the world, and the local parish seemed a very parochial place to me. I found white superiority repugnant and just plain dumb considering the total picture of the people of the world—a world beginning to shrink technologically and wanting the same decencies of life that seemed to be reserved for rich, white Westerners. It was about then that I woke up one morning and declared to myself: "Doug Roche, you have made a great discovery. You have discovered that most of the world is non-white, non-Western and non-Christian. And it's about time that we started to get along with one another."

I thank James Ibole, the Ibo teacher, Aristides Bastidas, the Venezuelan communist, and Krishnankutty, the Kerala farmer for opening my eyes to the human condition today. Our lives touched only briefly, but that was enough to enlighten me. These three men, from very different backgrounds, helped me to understand the meaning of the term *global village*.

5

The Catholic Revolution

Six months after I had joined the *Sign*, Pope John XXIII surprised the Catholic Church with the announcement on January 25, 1959, of his plan to convoke the 21st ecumenical council, and the first since Vatican I of 1869–1870. The portly and smiling father figure was supposed to be a stop-gap pope after the long reign of Pius XII. Instead, after only 90 days in office, his vision of Vatican II unleashed changes that reshaped the face of Catholicism and opened the Church to the world.

It was only after 2,500 bishops from around the globe had gathered at St. Peter's Basilica in Rome for the formal opening of the Council in the fall of 1962 that I began to pay attention. I found that I had a lot to learn. An ecumenical, or general, council is a solemn assembly of the world's bishops, called by the Pope to decide, under his presidency, matters concerning the life of the Church. The idea had come to him, Pope John said, "like a flash of heavenly light." He immediately set the tone of the gathering: "We feel we must disagree with those prophets of gloom, who are always forecasting disaster, as though the end of the world was at hand. In the present order of things, Divine Providence is leading us to a new order of human relations ...." He spoke of "opening the windows" to let fresh air sweep through the Church.

That something momentous was about to happen became clear by the attention the Council paid to Vatican II's central document, *Lumen Gentium*, the "Dogmatic Constitution on the Church." The first draft, done by the Curia (which, together with the Pope, comprises the central governing authority of the Catholic Church), placed heavy emphasis on the hierarchical and juridical aspects of the Church, including the supremacy of the Pope. But when the Council Fathers came together, they immediately saw the need to set out a radically different vision of the Church, one that was more biblical, vital and dynamic. They insisted that the Church is foremost a people to whom God communicates himself in love. A fierce drama unfolded, pitting progressives against traditionalists.

The following June, only one year into the Council, John XXIII died of cancer. The cardinals elected a new pope: Giovanni Battista Montini, Pope Paul VI. Many expected him to rein in the Council, but when it assembled for its second session in the fall of 1963, the Council continued the movement towards a pastoral rather than an institutional Church. In Rome to do some stories on the human dimension of the struggle, I focused on Bishop Ernest Primeau of Manchester, New Hampshire, following him around for several days to write "Life of a Council Father." The debate over the nature of the Church was in full flight.

"It's surprising that after more than 1900 years, we're asking these questions; but they've never been settled," Bishop Primeau told me. It was only after the Council decided what the real image of the Church should be that it could then look outward at the great problems of the world.

The new draft of the Constitution on the Church sought to get rid of the idea, once and for all, that bishops, priests and religious alone make up the Church. It emphasized that all the faithful, through baptism and confirmation, are incorporated into the holy community of the people of God and are dedicated to the task of the salvation and sanctification of the world. The lay person, in this sense, ceased to be something negative or, as some had put it, at the bottom of the ecclesiastical pyramid that thrust upward to the Pope.

When it was approved the following year by a vote of 2,151 bishops for and only 5 opposed, the Constitution on the Church amounted to, in my view, a revolution. By devoting a whole chapter to a description of the Church as the "new people of God," the Council put great emphasis on the human and communal side of the Church. This was encapsulated in one beautiful sentence: "The heritage of this people are the dignity and freedom of the [people] of God, in whose hearts the Holy Spirit dwells as in His temple."

The document emphasized that the laity are called in a special way to make the Church "present and operative" in the world. Thus, while laypeople would continue to assist the hierarchy, the term *lay apostolate* should refer primarily to apostolic tasks particular to the laity. This new understanding of the integrity of the laity, especially as it applied to communications, profoundly affected my thinking of the role of the Catholic press, a role I had first begun to explore in my college thesis.

The other great document of Vatican II was *Gaudium et Spes*, the "Pastoral Constitution on the Church in the Modern World." While it arose from a challenging intervention from the floor by Cardinal Léon-Joseph Suenens of Belgium at the first session, the document was heavily influenced by Pope John XXIII's encyclical *Pacem in Terris* ("On Establishing Universal Peace in Truth, Justice, Charity, and Liberty"), one of the great encyclicals of all time. Only two months before his death, John XXIII sent this message of peace to the whole world. Addressing all humanity, he affirmed that people have "the right to live." They have "the right to bodily integrity ... to food, clothing, shelter, medical care, rest and social services." People are living in the grip of constant fear of war and violence. "Nuclear weapons must be banned ... True and lasting peace among nations cannot consist in the possession of an equal supply of armaments but only in mutual trust ... In this age which boasts of its atomic power, it no longer makes sense to maintain that war is a fit instrument with which to repair the violation of justice ... The attainment of the common good is the sole reason for the existence of civil authorities." And then: "No state can fittingly pursue its own interests in isolation from the rest." With his powerful message, Pope John gave the world a roadmap for peace.

The Council picked up on this intimate bond between the Church and humanity by declaring in the opening sentence of the Constitution on the Church in the Modern World: "The joys and the hopes, the griefs and the anxieties of the [people] of this age, especially those who are poor or in any way afflicted, these too are the joys and hopes, the griefs and anxieties of the followers of Christ."

I was deeply affected by the passages calling for the complete outlawing of war by international consent, based on the logical proposition that, in the new age, the use of weapons of mass destruction imperilled the continuation of life on the planet: "Any act of war aimed indiscriminately at the destruction of entire cities or of extensive areas along with their population is a crime against God and man himself. It merits unequivocal and unhesitating condemnation."

By the time it concluded in December 1965, Vatican II had produced sixteen documents on a range of subjects, including religious liberty, ecumenism, the liturgy and strengthening internal processes. I found the central message of Vatican II to be a powerful one: the Church is a dynamic body of pilgrims, always developing, and we preach the love of Christ best by serving humanity. Not the least of the remarkable changes in the new outwardness of the Church was this sentence from *Nostra Aetate*, the "Declaration on the Relationship of the Church to Non-Christian Religions": "Upon the Muslims too, the Church looks with esteem." The full import of this shift from the ideological wars of the past would be seen only following the terrorist attacks of 9/11.

Invitation to Edmonton

In November 1964, I received a phone call from Archbishop Anthony Jordan of Edmonton. He told me that he wanted to make the present archdiocesan newspaper a better reflection of what was happening at Vatican II. Would I come up to Edmonton, look over the present operation, and make a recommendation to him? His call caught me in a reflective moment, with two factors intersecting in my mind.

First, Eva and I had been living in the U.S. for more than seven years. Our family, we were fairly sure, was complete. Did we want to stay permanently in the U.S? I had gone so far as to obtain the papers setting in motion American naturalization. Eva and I sat down at the kitchen table to examine them. I said to Eva, "I don't think I can sign this." She said she was also hesitant. Much as we enjoyed the country, and certainly the New York area, we both felt a pull back to Canada.

The other factor was my job. I liked the *Sign*, and Father Ralph Gorman had given me marvellous opportunities, but I could never be editor of the magazine, no matter how good my work was. That was never stated explicitly to me; there was simply an assumption that the editor of the *Sign* would always be a priest. There was every possibility that Father Ralph's successor would be a man who knew considerably less about the publishing business than I did, but would nonetheless hold the job because he was a priest. I was not prepared to sublimate my own professional career in this way.

There was no crisis on either the U.S. citizenship front or the *Sign* editorship; both of these problems could drift. It was Archbishop Jordan's phone call that made me start thinking seriously about the future. I flew to Edmonton for a long weekend. I found the *Western Catholic*, founded in 1919, to have a weak editorial structure; it was valiantly held together by a priest. As I told Archbishop Jordan in a memo, if he wanted a paper to reflect fully the values of Vatican II and to be respected in the community for its professionalism, he would have to revamp the entire operation and put a decent amount of capital into it.

I recommended that the new paper be called the *Western Catholic Reporter* and be classed as an independent Catholic paper, even though owned by the archdiocese, to give it wider latitude for dialogue among Catholics themselves and between the Catholic Church and the general community. I pointed out that the dynamic concept of the people of God had a great potential for teaching Catholics what it means for the Church to be a community rather than only an institution. I thought it would be good to have a Catholic newspaper that would firmly have the stamp of the people of God on it, rather than the Chancery Office stamp. In order to get this idea across, I proposed a board of advisers made up of priests, nuns, laymen and at least two married women. The final legal and moral responsibility for the paper would remain with the archbishop as publisher, but the editor would edit the paper as he saw fit. He would report to the board of advisers as well as the archbishop. If two thirds of the board voted non-confidence in the editor, he would be required to resign.

Archbishop Jordan must have liked the memo because he called again in February and offered me the job of editor. I wasn't happy about the $10,000 annual salary, a drop from what the *Sign* was paying me, but I figured I would make it up in other ways. The challenge was irresistible. I was 35 and could be my own editor. I would prove myself at last.

Although she agreed with my analysis, Eva was sad at the prospect of leaving New York, which she loved. She went on a final binge of Broadway shows. One of my Canadian friends predicted that, having lived the glamorous life in New York, we would never last in the "boonies" of Alberta. But he was wrong. We took to the "big sky country" and the easy livability of a medium-sized city after the frenetic crowding of the greater New York area.

For one last and great look at the United States before departing, Eva and I, with Nanny along to look after Mickey, piled the children into the back of the station wagon and set out on an unforgettable trip that the family talks about to this day. We headed for an Amish farmhouse in Pennsylvania, then to the monuments of Washington, D.C., across to Oklahoma and north to St. Louis and Springfield, Illinois, to see the birthplace of Abe Lincoln. We drove through the northern states to Montana for a Wild West rodeo and spent some time at Waterton Park, Alberta.

Every day began about 5 a.m., with the kids getting into the car still in their pajamas. We would drive for about three hours, with them asleep, until breakfast. Then they could run for an hour or so and we would drive for another four hours. At 2 p.m. the kids knew they would be in the next motel's swimming pool. About every fourth day, we didn't drive at all and they could frolic in the pool. The home movies caught us all having the time of our lives.

A Time Not to Haggle

In Edmonton, we stayed temporarily in a house owned by the Archdiocese, but we couldn't settle in because the house stood in the way of the University of Alberta's forthcoming expansion. We were having trouble finding an affordable house with enough space. Eva spent evenings driving around looking for a place to live. One night she returned with a possibility. She had found an empty lot on a lovely street on the edge of a park overlooking the city's downtown. I located the owner, Ambrose Holowach, a minister in the Alberta government, and went to see him.

"Mr. Holowach," I said, "my name is Doug Roche. I've got a wife and five children, and I've just moved to Edmonton to be the editor of a new Catholic paper. I need a home. I see that you have an empty lot on Strathearn Drive. Would you like to sell it?"

"Well, I was keeping it to build a house for my mother," he said.

"I understand," I said. "Sorry to have bothered you."

He replied, "I think she's getting too old. Maybe I won't be able to build for her."

"Does that mean you might sell it?" I asked.

"I might," he said.

"I'll offer you $7,000,"

"No," he answered. "I'd have to get $10,000."

Without a second's hesitation, I said, "I'll offer you $10,000," and held out my hand. Holowach seemed a bit surprised, but he shook my hand.

The deal went through and a month later, Holowach was sitting in the steam room of the YMCA with my lawyer, Allan Wachowich, a member of the paper's board of advisers (now the chief justice of Alberta).

"Allan," Holowach said, "will you tell me why I sold that lot to Doug Roche for $10,000? Why, I could get twelve-five for it today."

Wachowich said he could hardly keep from laughing. I told my children in later life, "There's a time to haggle and a time not to haggle. When you see a good deal, don't quibble. Do it." The property today, with its view of the striking Edmonton skyline, is worth many times what I paid for it.

We hired an architect and Eva did a rough design of what she wanted, which included giving the kitchen a view of the park and placing the living room on the second floor. Construction started in October. Eva told the builder she wanted to move into the new house for Christmas. He rolled his eyes and said he'd try. Two days before Christmas, the workers were falling over one another to get the house livable. On Christmas Eve, the movers brought in the furniture while I went to the airport to pick up Eva's family. The house was in chaos. The Christmas tree went up at the last minute. We couldn't find the roasting pan for the turkey, so the children were dispatched on a great treasure hunt. It was, without a doubt, the best Christmas I have ever had. God was blessing us. I knew we had made the right move.

The house, or rather the backyard, was the scene of a party for my 40th birthday, which has gone down in family annals. Eva decided it would be an intergenerational party, for young people as well as adults, so she hired a rock band made up of local teenagers. Our children were recruited to string up lights in the backyard. It was a warm June night; in Edmonton, the sun doesn't set at that time of the year until 10:30 p.m. The crowd was happy, the music was blaring and everyone was having a good time, when suddenly a police officer appeared. Too much noise, he said. He hardly made a dent in our enthusiasm. Half an hour later, he was back. "The neighbours are complaining," he said, "so this time I have to give you a summons." Eva went to court to deal with the charge. "How do you plead?" asked the judge. "Well, guilty, Your Honour," Eva said, "but I would like to make a statement. You see, Your Honour, it was my husband's 40th birthday and I thought it would be good for the kids to see our whole society, old and young, just having a good time together. It would be very good for unity and a little music would help." The judge could barely keep a straight face as he slid lower in his chair. "Five dollars," he said. Eva said it was the best five dollars she ever spent.

Modern Canada: Reach for Greatness

Even before moving the family to Edmonton, I had travelled across Canada from the East Coast to the West to rediscover my own country. I found a new self-respect in Canada: the St. Lawrence Seaway, Saskatchewan potash, Alberta oil and enough untapped minerals under the tundra to make Canadians dizzy. More than the flow of wealth, the new-found appreciation of ourselves was becoming a characteristic, soon to burst open in the Centennial celebration of 1967 and Expo 67. The new civic pride, the frenzy of culture, the awakened interest in religion, the facing up to the demands of biculturalism, the spirit of get-up-and-go all excited me. Among those I interviewed were two people who would later have a deep influence on me: Robert Stanfield, then the premier of Nova Scotia, and Claude Ryan, editor of *Le Devoir*, the leading French-language newspaper in Canada.

With the outbreak of self-determination in Quebec, the "two solitudes" era of Canada was over. A national unity crisis was building. I looked for religious leadership and went to see Bishop Alex Carter of Sault Ste. Marie, who as a young priest had anointed my father and who was now one of the Canadian leaders at Vatican II. "At a time when our country is going through a dangerous crisis, it seems to me that spiritual leaders do not have the right to remain silent," he told me. The rise and fall of Prime Minister John Diefenbaker had occurred during my time in the U.S., so I went to the gallery in the House of

Commons to study the new Canadian political leaders. Prime Minister Lester Pearson, who had just given Canada its new flag, was locked in combat with Opposition leader Diefenbaker, whose cutting speeches seemed to make most of the Commons quake.

One of the most stirring sights I came across in Ottawa was in the National Gallery. A teacher was explaining to her class the paintings of the Group of Seven, the Canadian artists who had finally won the acclaim at home they deserved. There, better than anything else in the gallery, were some Canadian masterpieces: Tom Thomson's *The Jack Pine*, Frederick Varley's *Georgian Bay* and A.Y. Jackson's *The Red Maple*. These artists long ago discovered the sturdy splendour of Canada. For many years, Canadians, with our inferiority complex, had ignored them. Now the prophets were honoured in their homeland.

I finished my cross-country tour by interviewing Bruce Hutchison, a journalistic sage whose books *The Unknown Country* and *Canada: Tomorrow's Giant* had years before awakened me to Canada's potential. We met at his summer camp at Shawnigan Lake on Vancouver Island.

"Doesn't it seem strange that, after nearly a century of existence, we're still worrying whether this nation can endure?" I asked him. "Our future seems to lie in one of two directions: as an appendage, even if basically unwanted by both sides, to the United States, or full national partnership with the French-Canadians. Is that basically the problem of Canada today?"

"Yes," he replied. "Essentially, it has always been the problem since the American revolution. It's more strident and difficult now. The self-realization of Quebecers presents the same old problem in a new and different guise. Also, the influence of the Americans in our culture is more intense than ever before in this age of mass communication. Not to mention our dependence on the Americans for defence."

I titled the first article in my "Coming Home" series "Modern Canada: The Reach for Greatness," and published it in the inaugural edition of the *Western Catholic Reporter*.

A Paper for the People of God

Pope John XXIII declared in *Pacem in Terris* that the right to information is among the "universal, inviolable, unalterable" rights of the human person. Moreover, every person has "the right to freedom in searching for truth and in expressing and communicating his opinions." I made this view the hallmark of the paper. The first issue, published September 9, 1965, contained a policy statement by Archbishop Jordan, who wrote, "The paper will be an independent Catholic paper fully encouraged by myself as Archbishop." The *Reporter* would not be independent in reflecting the defined teaching of the Catholic Church in the area of faith and morals, but would be independent in providing reports and a forum for discussion of the issues of the day from a Catholic viewpoint. "I do not believe that those in authority in the Catholic Church should control the flow of information," Jordan added. "Consequently, I have entrusted to the editor responsibility for the editorial content and operation of the paper."

I felt confident in the staff I had hired, including Frank Dolphin, an experienced CBC journalist and excellent writer as associate editor, and Stuart Lindop, with whom I had worked on the *Ensign* in Montréal, as business manager. I switched from the old linotype operation to offset printing and gave the paper a modern look.

The first edition contained a twelve-page supplement on Vatican II with lots of photos and background articles. My editorial contained these words:

> The Catholic Church is firmly committed to Pope John's "aggiornamento," the bringing up to date that was symbolized in the Pope's "open window." For many years to come, we will be a Church in transition. And an age of transition, historians tell us, is always an age of confusion. But out of the confusion and the questioning that characterize the monumental undertaking of the Second Vatican Council will emerge a religious vibrancy that will be, with God's grace, capable of reshaping the face of the earth. The creative force unleashed after the Council closes will be just as important as the actual Council sessions. A new energy must be stirred up at home.

I put the "people of God" quotation from Vatican II on the masthead and wrote in my opening editorial that the paper was aimed at the people of God, meaning all Christians of whatever denomination. "The cause of Christian unity and the heartening pace of the ecumenical movement are uppermost in our mind as we begin publishing," I said. In the first edition, I published a column by a local Baptist minister, the Rev. Ed Checkland, who observed that the old days of

Protestants and Catholics fighting had given way to a new awareness "of the common foundation of their faith in Jesus Christ as Lord and Saviour." Today, I find the identification of the people of God with only Christianity far too limiting. I believe in a God who embraces not only Christians but Muslims, Jews, Hindus and other people of faith. But in 1965, despite the fact that the *Reporter*'s philosophy was rooted in the Second Vatican Council, the people of God concept was too much for many to bear.

While many members of the Catholic audience may have been ready to move slightly forward from the notion of a religious paper being a "house organ," they were not prepared to wrestle with the great themes and changes in the life of the Church brought on by Vatican II. A lot of Catholics were bewildered at seeing the delicate subjects of birth control, mandatory celibacy, and the question of women priests debated in the pages of their "Catholic" newspaper. The pastors were also split, but it was the older ones, dubious about where all this was heading, who continued to support the paper (when they did not actually frown on it).

Only rarely did I seek controversy. One instance when I did provoke reaction was in challenging the Catholic Women's League to spend less time "taking a whack at the CBC or dirty books" and more time working to alleviate alcoholism, drug addiction, child neglect, juvenile delinquency and inferior education. Though I was duly castigated by a number of the leading ladies in the community, some officers of the League told me they agreed with me.

The reality was that much of the material flowing across my desk was by nature controversial: the changes in the liturgy, the role of pastoral councils, the desire of women to play a more active and decisive role in the Church. It wasn't the paper as such that upset a lot of pastors, it was the outcome of Vatican II itself. Unlike the bishops, who had experienced the crucible of debate in Rome, the pastors had only heard of the Council from afar and, in most cases, had no deep knowledge of it.

Although the paper carried many news items each week that were benign, if not outright "feel-good," the controversies in the Church multiplied and clamoured for coverage. When priests started leaving the ministry, my editorial problem was compounded. If a priest was well known, how could I ignore the newsworthy nature of his move?

When Charles Davis, one of the theological luminaries of Vatican II, left the priesthood and moved from Britain to teach at the University of Alberta, how could I ignore a world figure in our midst? But many pastors certainly didn't want to read about the views of an "ex-priest" in the paper they were asked to support. Archbishop Jordan had a particular aversion to seeing photos in the paper of priests without their Roman collar. It was the only time he ever made a direct request of me not to publish something. I figured this was a small concession for me to make.

While I tried to "accentuate the positive" (in the words of the wonderful song Bing Crosby used to sing), I could not "eliminate the negative." One way I tried to build a positive spirit was co-sponsoring, along with the Catholic Information Centre, a thirteen-week series of lectures, "Vatican II and You," in Edmonton and Calgary. Close to 3,000 people attended the sessions, which featured experts, movies, panel discussions and audience participation. Closed-circuit television was necessary to accommodate the crowds. The first speaker was Bishop Remi De Roo, the young Bishop of Victoria, British Columbia, who was then coming to prominence as a staunch advocate of the Vatican II reforms. He described the four goals of the Council: knowledge of self by the people of God, increased awareness of God's plan for renewal of the Church, co-operation with other churches towards Christian unity, and dialogue with the entire world to promote harmony. Asked about birth control, he said that the Council proclaimed the principle of responsible parenthood. "It [the Council] states that in this matter the parents themselves and no one else should ultimately bear judgment in the sight of God."

Exhilaration—and Cold Cash

The crisis in the Church was now becoming identifiable. For some it was a crisis of faith, for others a crisis of hope. It was, at the very least, a crisis of understanding, resulting from a general misunderstanding of Vatican II teaching. The bishops, who had appeared brave in Rome, softened their message once they faced a traditionalist backlash at home. By their silence, the bishops dampened the enthusiasm of progressives for reform. The people of God needed to hear the voices of the bishops alerting and encouraging them to assume new responsibilities in building the Church after the Council, I wrote in an editorial.

> Rather than the bishops' voices, we are hearing the voices of dissent. They are telling us that the institutional Church is so enmeshed in medieval anachronisms that it cannot be reformed quickly enough to make any impact on a world that is racing ahead technologically. Moreover, we are told that the institution is so bound in legalisms that it chokes off the love of Christ from the millions who are waiting to embrace Him. We are persuaded that the bishops are more worried about the priests and nuns who are rebelling against authoritarianism than they are about the millions of laity who are gradually drifting farther and farther away from any meaningful relationship with the Church.

Because of my openness, I was increasingly asked to speak in Protestant churches and other non-Catholic places of worship. There was a genuine desire in the larger community to learn what Vatican II was all about and how this would affect relationships between the churches. I gave a Lenten series of talks in Edmonton's Anglican Cathedral and spent two days covering the Synod of the Anglican Diocese of Edmonton. The *WCR* sponsored an ecumenical pilgrimage to the Holy Land; I invited a Catholic pastor, Father W. A. Reynolds, and the dean of All Saints Anglican Cathedral, R. F. Shepherd, to go along as spiritual directors. I published Dean Shepherd's account of their poignant journey.

The paper was catching on, at least in important circles. The religious editor of the *Toronto Star* called it "genuinely outstanding." The apostolic delegate to Canada, Archbishop Sergio Pignedoli, wrote to commend the mature and responsible tone, "in keeping with the entire orientation of Catholicism today as crystallized in Vatican II." Basil Dean, publisher of the *Edmonton Journal*, the city's main newspaper, said, "It will not be long before the intelligent public in Alberta, inside and outside the Church, will be paying careful attention to what you have to say." *Time* magazine took notice: "Improbably in Alberta, a province slowly thawing from its ice-age conservatism, Pope John's historic call for an *aggiornamento* has inspired a powerful echo, in the form of the liveliest and most liberal Catholic newspaper in the country." In its first two years, the *Western Catholic Reporter* won the Catholic Press Association's Journalism Award for General Excellence in its circulation category. The judges praised the paper's ability to "grab" readers with dramatic presentations of copy and art.

All this was exhilarating, but I was brought back to cold reality every time I looked at the circulation figures. We needed 25,000 subscribers at $5 a subscription and about $75,000 in advertising to bring annual revenues to $200,000, which is what the paper cost to produce. The circulation stalled at 18,000, despite intensive efforts by Sandy Williams, the circulation manager. That was double what the old *Western Catholic* had, but it was small consolation when the deficit hit $40,000 per year. This couldn't go on. The way Catholic newspapers in the U.S. survived was to go on the "parish plan," under which each parish subscribes and pays for a certain number. But I had wanted the paper to stand on its own. That was a mistake.

As we started the third year of publication, I told the board of advisers that the paper had encountered "the passive resistance of a large number of Catholics who are indifferent to what the paper stands for, and in many ways are indifferent to the Church itself, and the active resistance of a smaller but important group who have expressed opposition to the paper's progressive tendencies. In this latter group are both clergy and laity." I had learned the hard way that a Catholic paper concentrating on adult education in the spirit of Vatican II could not pay for itself. It had to be financed just as schools and charities are financed.

The board seemed overwhelmed by complaints from this or that person about this or that article. Finally, the chairman, Ed McManus, a straight-talking brewery manager, erupted, "I'm fed up with the bickering and penny-ante attitudes. We have to make up our minds whether we want a paper or don't want a paper." The paper was all about adult education, he said, "and any business worth its salt has a program of continued education." People wouldn't buy a religious paper that forced them to think about such things as abortion, contraception, family planning, medical care and responsibility to the developing countries until they were educated. He swayed the meeting to support parish plan coverage. Under this system, all families registered in a parish received a copy of the paper. But there was no coercion; if a family didn't want it, the name would be removed from the circulation list.

I set out for regular tours of the deaneries with Father John Spicer, who directed the Continued Education Office. Together we made a lot of friends among the pastors. The paper's finances stabilized, and the *WCR* continues to publish today. It is gentler, more pious than the product I turned out, in part because the Church itself has become more docile. And the editor, Glen Argan, is less "in your face" with controversial material than I was.

The *WCR* survived because of the tenaciousness of Archbishop Jordan. The paper was more than he bargained for, to be sure, but so was Vatican II. He was a man of vision: during that same period, he founded Newman Theological College, which prepares lay people, religious and ordained ministers for service and leadership in the Church in western Canada. Jordan was a bit brusque, but I always attributed it to shyness. He was reputed to be tough on his priests, but always gave me the support I needed. One time, he fired me, for insubordination, I guess, because I talked back to him in a salary dispute. But I wrote a note of apology and the chairman of the board came in on my side. When I was elected to Parliament, Jordan gave a dinner in my honour and made me a gift of a handsome chair with my name inscribed on it. In his farewell letter to me, he wrote, "For all that you have done, for your indefatigable industry, your wisdom and prudence, your constant loyalty to the Church generally and to me as your Bishop, your silence and calm in moments of criticism, your even temper, your fidelity to follow your ideal—and for much more, I offer you my deepest personal thanks." In 1977, when St. Stephen's College in Edmonton, awarded me an honourary doctor of divinity, he wrote to me again, calling me the counterpart of the great Catholic literary figures Wilfrid Ward and Frank Sheed. "You are one with them in your particular apostolate." Archbishop Jordan died in 1982 at the age of 80.

100 Years to Wait

In the latter part of the 1960s, every day was intense with the vibrancy of controversy. I was greatly helped in keeping my own balance by an interview I did with Cardinal Paul-Émile Léger, Archbishop of Montréal, whom Archbishop Jordan had brought to Edmonton for a round of ceremonies. Cardinal Léger gave me advice that I took to heart: don't try to push human beings into the post–Vatican II age faster than they are capable of moving.

"The great trouble with modern man," Cardinal Léger said, twisting his face as he reflected upon his thoughts before uttering them, "is that he forgets all that is natural takes time. It takes nine months to build a child in the womb of the mother, fifteen years to educate a person in school and even then the job is not finished, and 50 years for an oak tree to mature."

Because we have become so used to solving our problems mechanically—such as putting iron ore into one end of a machine and getting a car out the other end—"we think we can put a man in a changed institution and make him perfect overnight." It will be terrible, he added, "if the modern generation becomes so conditioned by automation that they think human beings are as adaptable as machinery." I wasn't sure whether he was just bemusing himself when he said that it might be 100 years before the full meaning of Vatican II became clear.

Shortly after our meeting, Cardinal Léger resigned his diocese and went to live the rest of his life as a simple priest working among African lepers. Was that act a statement by itself?

Meanwhile, I was living in the day-to-day turmoil and felt the need to get a better understanding of exactly what was going on in the Church. When the New York publishing company David McKay offered me a $10,000 contract to write a book about the crisis of confidence in the Catholic Church, I asked Archbishop Jordan for a short leave of absence to do the research and writing. I attended the 1967 Synod of Bishops in Rome and the World Congress for the Apostolate of the Laity, and travelled throughout North America and Europe, interviewing bishops, priests, former priests, sisters, former sisters, lay people who believed, lay people who didn't believe, college presidents, ecumenical leaders, blacks and other minorities and, of course, fellow Catholic editors. I went to theological conferences, priests' seminars, underground masses and discussions in living rooms where men and women talked frankly about their changing attitudes to the changing Church.

I titled the book *The Catholic Revolution*—not in the sense of overthrow but in the sense of activity or movement designed to effect fundamental change in an organization. *Evolution* was definitely too soft a word for what was going on: many priests were leaving their ministry, while others agitated about vows of celibacy; many religious women were emerging from the sanctuary of convents; progressive parishioners were insisting on a stronger role in parish affairs; experimental communities were springing up; and among the youth a massive alienation from institutional Christianity was underway. In short, the Catholic Church was in a state of revolution.

After a few weeks on the road, I returned to my editor's job. With the deadline for the book looming, I felt overwhelmed. I called my friend Gary MacEoin to come to Edmonton to help me sort out my research material and begin some early drafts. A canon (church) lawyer as well as a journalist, MacEoin can best be described as an Irish pixie, a cheerful, mischievous sprite of a man. While at the *Sign*, I had often hired him to write articles on the Church in Latin America, about which he was an expert. His encyclopedic knowledge of the Catholic Church was revealed in his own book on Vatican II, *What Happened at Rome?* (Holt, Rinehart and Winston, 1966). During the Synod of Bishops in Rome, when I had started the research for my book, we shared a room in a *pensione*. Gary came to Edmonton and showed me how to organize material for a book. When he left, I said to him, "Gary, will I ever be an author?" He looked at me and said, with a twinkle in his eye, "I'll tell you in 20 years." Forty years later, these memoirs are my nineteenth book.

Bishop and Layman: Man to Man

During the preparation for *The Catholic Revolution*, I came to know Bishop De Roo, who was one of the last bishops named by Pope John XXIII. De Roo was only 38 when he found himself a Council Father; from his Victoria diocese, he had established himself as a leading progressive. I felt relaxed talking with him; he was certainly more open than any other bishop I had met. Friendship and trust were quickly established. I don't remember who originated the idea, but we took on the project of a tape-recorded dialogue between a bishop and a layman to explore all the controversial subjects of a Church in revolution. I asked Gary MacEoin to be the editor of the book, whose title De Roo and I had already agreed on: *Man to Man*.

For a week in May 1968 the three of us gathered at De Roo's home on the southern shore of Vancouver Island, with its view across the

Juan de Fuca Strait to the cloud-capped Mount Olympus. In complete isolation from all other concerns, we lived, prayed and ate together. There were long days and late nights of discussion and evaluation. The temptation to score points did not exist. It was a discussion, an exchange of views and an effort at clarification between two people involved in a common search for truth and a common effort to make Christ more widely known and better served.

I began with an observation about authority in the Church. "As we get a better understanding of the meaning of Vatican II's idea of the equality of all the baptized, I believe we must find new ways to reconcile the authority of the bishop, an authority he receives from Christ, with democratic procedures in the Church."

"There is much confusion about the true nature of Church authority," De Roo responded. "When we compare it with social or political models, we should exercise great caution. Serious qualifications are required because the Scriptures show that Church authority is of an entirely different kind. Christ taught by word and example that his disciples' authority rested not on human prestige or power, but on service directed to his Father's kingdom."

I expressed the fear that the openness of Vatican II had created a rather messy situation, and that the bishops as a whole might be tempted to withdraw into a shell to protect the institution of the episcopacy. De Roo said, "I know there is a growing desire to bring the people into the consensus-making process." The discussion was stimulating and made for an interesting book. It was published in 1968 by the Bruce Publishing Company of Milwaukee, a Catholic enterprise, which went out of business shortly after because the Catholic market was drying up in the post–Vatican II upheavals. The *Sign* ceased publication for the same reason in 1982.

MacEoin presented me in his introduction as a "moderately progressive" layman. "He is certainly no far-out radical," MacEoin said. "He is, however, more than normally sensitive to the broadening credibility gap in the Church and the frustration of many young intellectuals who feel they are not being given a fair hearing."

The Birth Control Crisis

This credibility gap was fully exposed in the summer of 1968, when Pope Paul VI published his encyclical *Humanae Vitae* ("Of

Human Life"), which boldly declared: "Every marital act must remain open to the transmission of life." The Pope's ban on birth control provoked anguished reaction.

When the Vatican Council dealt with marriage in the Constitution on the Church in the Modern World, it treated the subject in a lofty manner. Marriage and conjugal love are by their nature ordained towards the begetting and education of children, the document said. At the same time, parents have a responsibility to verify the conditions that make procreation at a given time a correct decision. "The parents themselves should ultimately make this judgment in the sight of God." When it comes to implementing this decision, they "may not undertake methods of regulating procreation which are found blameworthy by the teaching authority of the Church ...."

But what was the teaching of the Church? Inasmuch as Pope Paul had, the year before the Constitution was adopted, established a papal commission to study disputed questions of birth control, the answer was unclear. In the new age of the pill, many Catholic couples desperately needed answers. The Council dodged any concrete answers but did not foreclose what a Jesuit editor gently called "new lines of development in Catholic understanding on the matter."

Since the Council did speak clearly of the dignity of moral conscience, fully informed and conforming to divine law, many married people expected the Church to, once and for all, make a theological distinction between contraception, which involves legitimate means to prevent conception, and abortion, which is the destruction of a life already conceived. The 1967 Synod of Bishops had wanted to deal with the issue, but the Curia insisted that it be removed from the agenda. So it was left to the papal commission, comprising eminent theologians and prominent married couples, to make its recommendation. The commission voted in favour of allowing contraception. Pope Paul overruled it. There is an "indissoluble connection" between the unitive and procreative functions of marriage, he said. "A moral birth control, therefore, does not allow the use of means which destroy even partly the finality of the marriage act."

Raw emotion exploded in the Church. A statement signed by 87 theologians across the United States said the Pope's encyclical "betrays a narrow and positivistic notion of papal authority." They declared that in their opinion, "spouses may responsibly decide according to their conscience." Moreover, they said, "it is common teaching in the Church that Catholics may dissent from authoritative, non-infallible teachings of the magisterium when sufficient reasons for doing so exist."

There was a great deal at stake in the Pope's birth control decision: the consciences of millions of parents, the ministry of priests, the development of collegiality, ecumenical relations, the social relevance of the Church in the modern world. With the shock waves reverberating around the world, I had to deal with the issue in an editorial. No other papal encyclical had ever aroused such controversy. I thought the Pope had erred in overruling a competent commission, which he himself had established, but I did not feel I could outright oppose him. I wanted to be loyal to the Holy Father but I was torn by a conscientious reaction of dissent.

There was much in the encyclical about the supernatural and eternal vision of marriage designed by the Creator, all of which needed to be heard. But the heart of the message was "no contraception." The furthest I felt I could go was to state, "One's conscience is the final arbiter in our actions; but conscience must be formed in a fully knowledgeable way and thus, as Catholics, we have the benefit of the teaching authority of the Church, of which the Pope is the highest spokesman."

The Canadian bishops faced the issue head on, publishing a courageous statement highlighting the importance of people following their conscience, fully informed.

Man to Man had not yet gone to press, allowing Bishop De Roo and me to do one last chapter, on the effects of *Humanae Vitae*. I argued that the encyclical was harmful teaching because it made the ill-informed feel guilty or "in sin" for doing something, the harm of which they either did not understand or did not agree with. Moreover, the encyclical was counter to the advances of science. People had all sorts of mechanical instruments and medications put into their bodies to keep them alive, yet could not use instruments or medication to prevent conception. I foresaw the peremptory use of papal power overwhelming the collegiality between Pope and bishops that was a cornerstone of the Constitution on the Church. Collegiality, while giving the final word to the Pope, should mean that the Pope does not act without the consent, or at least involvement, of the bishops. *Humanae Vitae*, in this light, threatened the integrity of Vatican II.

De Roo acknowledged that the encyclical presented almost insurmountable difficulties for many people versed in the sciences. But, he added, "We must get away from this hang-up over guilt, over mortal and venial sin, over worthiness for absolution or exclusion from the sacraments." Instead, he said, the encyclical calls for the compassionate attitude of the Redeemer, who does not make demands people cannot fulfill. As for authority and collegiality, De Roo was clearly of the view that authority should be used to clarify the consensus of the whole people of God. By this he meant a consensus of all the leaders who carry the collegial responsibility for the Church. This was his episcopal, and diplomatic, way of saying that the Pope should not have acted alone.

The World Beyond the Church

Neither De Roo nor I could resolve what we saw as the credibility gap of the Church, which Paul VI had opened. John Cogley, a leading and very thoughtful Catholic journalist in the U.S., quit the Catholic press on the grounds that the Pope had catastrophically misread the moral and human issues at stake in the birth control debate. I took the position that quitting was the wrong reaction, because highly informed people were needed to deal with the central challenge: the continuation of the reforms of Vatican II and especially the reconciliation of papal authority with the new form of collegiality legislated by the Council.

Just as the Pope had to follow his conscience in writing the encyclical, others should follow their consciences in expressing the opinions of the faithful for the Pope and bishops to hear. Besides, I argued in an editorial in the *WCR*, if contraception were approved tomorrow, it would not answer the chief social ills of humanity.

The most profound problem we face, I wrote, is the selfishness of the rich, not a lack of food or space. The failure to share the goods and space of this world is what causes misery. "The world is in the throes of revolution involving the black man's rights, the hungry people of Latin America, the helpless millions of Asia, plus war and nuclear annihilation. The reform movement in the Church is closely associated with all these issues. The reformers must work for the continued renewal of the Church so that a loving Christ can be shown in better ways to a suffering humanity. This is no time for the reformers to quit."

I went back to Rome for the 1969 Synod of Bishops, which was called to deal with the gathering crisis in the Church. While the bishops wrestled with how to implement authority and collegiality at the same time, 200 dissident European priests were on hand to protest the ecclesiastical fixation of the synod, which prevented it from dealing with the core issues of world population, hunger, poverty, war, the arms race and discrimination—all of which rob millions of their human dignity. Belgium's Cardinal Suenens gave an interview saying that the root cause of problems in the post–Vatican II Church was the rigidity of the Curia; 300 priests in Canada signed a statement supporting Suenens.

Working out the interplay of the Pope's authority and the collegiality of the bishops was certainly important in running the Church, but I took the position that achieving interior harmony would amount to little if the Church failed to be a vibrant witness of love and service among the millions of oppressed who daily became poorer while the rich got richer. The synod seemed to want to move the Church forward from its monarchical style of government. But immobilist forces, controlling much of the machinery, seemed to be digging in.

In *The Catholic Revolution*, I foresaw a new kind of Church. The days of the laity meeting on one side of the street and the hierarchy on the other would be ended, as the integration of the baptized, each with an infused priesthood, took hold. The consensus of the faithful would be sought before bishops issued declarations. Synods of bishops would take over the election of popes. Communion with other faiths would be common, married clergy permitted, the barrier against women priests dropped. As the 1960s—this turbulent decade of flower children and political assassinations—came to an end, I recognized that I would not likely see any of these changes in my lifetime. Maybe Cardinal Léger was right: it would take a century.

But in the one lifetime allotted to me, I came to realize, I didn't want to devote myself to Church governance questions. I had already seen the desperation of the millions of oppressed and the direction in which humanity was heading as the gap between rich and poor widened. My faith was no longer a comfort to me: rather, it had become a challenge. The outward message of Christ preoccupied me, and I found I had less time to think about the internal questions of the Church.

My grandfather, Thomas Roche, "The Patriarch of Killaloe,"
and my grandmother, Bridget Devine (circa 1875).

My father, Jimmy Roche, and my mother, Agnes Douglas, when they were teenage sweethearts.

The author at age six months.

Jimmy, a proud father, with his three children, Marion (left), Agnes and me.

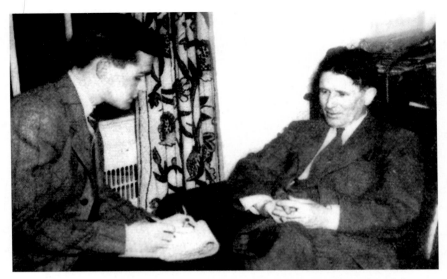

Interviewing Grattan O'Leary, editor of the Ottawa *Journal* and later a Senator, for the *Patrician*.

That's me sitting on the piano at the bachelor party that fellow Toronto *Telegram* reporters threw for me. Don Hunt (playing piano); clockwise from left: Tommy Williams, Ed Mahoney, Bob Crichton, Doug Creighton, Bob Vezina, Jack Dalrymple.

James Ibole, an Ibo teacher in Nigeria, presents a *kola* to me as a symbol of acceptance and friendship.

Aristides Bastidas, a Venezuelan communist labour leader, shows me the *favelas* of the poor.

"Mickey, Pretty Mickey," Eva used to sing to our second daughter.

My daughter Evita's sixteenth birthday. From left: Francis, Mary Anne, Eva, Evita, me, Tricia.

Archbishop Anthony Jordan, who brought me to Edmonton, dedicating new printing equipment at the *Western Catholic Reporter.*

Starting my political career with my nomination in 1971. Robert L. Stanfield,
leader of the Progressive Conservative Party, nearly became prime minister
in 1972.

Re-election campaign in 1979. Premier Peter Lougheed of Alberta visits my headquarters.

Three "St. Pat's guys" in Parliament together: me, John Turner (later prime minister), Hugh Poulin (later judge).

Chairing the P.C. "Foreign Policy for the 1980s" conference just before the 1979 election. John Holmes is at left; Joe Clark, the party leader, is at right.

Prime Minister Joe Clark invited me to accompany him to Africa in August 1979. This photo was taken in Tanzania just before we boarded a light aircraft.

Presenting a report of the work of the United Nations Association in Canada to the U.N. Secretary-General. From left: me, Javier Perez de Cuellar, Firdaus Kharas, Robert Muller.

Five nuclear disarmament leaders journeyed to both Moscow and Washington in 1982. From left: N.K.P. Salve, India; former President Luis Echeverria Alvarez of Mexico; me as International Chairman of Parliamentarians for World Order; Alhaji Idris Abrahim, Nigeria; John Silkin, U.K.

I brought the nuclear disarmament report of the parliamentarians' meetings in Moscow and Washington to Pope John Paul II.

After four successful elections, I stepped down from parliamentary life in 1984. Eva was delighted.

A new role as Canada's Ambassador for Disarmament. Here at the United Nations General Assembly: front row, from left, Foreign Minister Joe Clark, U.N. Ambassador Stephen Lewis, me; back row, Peggy Mason, Hon. Walter McLean, M.P., Reg Stackhouse, M.P.

As Chairman of the First Committee, I presented U.N. Secretary-General Javier Perez de Cuellar to the U.N. First (Disarmament) Committee.

As Ambassador, I brought Eva to a special dinner of the Consultative Group to hear an address by Prime Minister Brian Mulroney. The prime minister, right, seemed rather impressed.

II

The Parliamentary Years:
1972–1984

6

The Emergence of a Red Tory

One day in the summer of 1971, I sat on a bench on Parliament Hill in Ottawa and stared up at the Peace Tower. The Canadian flag fluttered gently in the breeze. My mind was on the future, even as I recalled my boyhood days lying in bed listening to the clock's reassuring chiming of the hours.

A few weeks before, Roy Watson, a politically active member of the *Western Catholic Reporter*'s board of advisers, had phoned to ask whether I would have lunch with Robert Stanfield, leader of the Progressive Conservative Party, who was in Edmonton. I duly arrived at the Macdonald Hotel expecting a room of a hundred people. Instead, the lunch was in Stanfield's suite. Besides Stanfield and me, there was only one other person: his executive assistant, Joe Clark. It was the first time I had seen Stanfield since my interview with him in 1967, when he was premier of Nova Scotia. I found him modest and earnest as he set out his views on the kind of Canada he wanted. To my surprise, he asked me to consider running for Parliament in my home constituency of Edmonton-Strathcona.

What would the future hold for me: stay with the Catholic press or try to get into Parliament, where I would have a larger stage for my ideas about extending social justice? Cardinal Léger's hundred-year prediction about Vatican II was haunting me. I could feel the Council reforms hitting the brakes as the bishops, fearful of divisions in the Church, started to retrench. Yet Vatican II, and especially its far-reaching Constitution on the Church in the Modern World, had aimed at putting more human values into government policies and, in doing so, had animated me. As a layman, I now felt much stronger. I sensed the growth in my own capacity to deal with public issues. Sitting on the bench that day in Ottawa, I weighed my role as editor and my possible role as a Member of Parliament. The challenge was irresistible, even though I didn't know the first thing about how to get elected to Parliament.

My next step was to see Joe Clark. Thus began a relationship that has coloured my entire public career. No other person in Ottawa so affected my political destiny. Clark came out of High River, Alberta, the son of newspaper editor Charles Clark, who had served on the *Western Catholic Reporter*'s board of advisers. Bright and ambitious, Joe Clark was one of the student leaders, with Brian Mulroney, in the Progressive Conservative Party, and jumped into Alberta politics early. His main interest was at the federal level and, in 1971, he was getting ready to run in Alberta's Yellowhead riding in the 1972 election. Clark was enthusiastic at the idea of my running in Edmonton. When I left his office I had at least the outline of a plan to get elected.

First, I had to talk to Eva. Her enthusiasm was a few degrees below mine. In the first eighteen years of our marriage, we had lived in four cities; now she had resumed her professional career as a social worker and was getting known in Edmonton. She had opened her own daycare centre in our home. The children were settled in school and she was not anxious to move again.

Another factor, of course, was our daughter Mickey. When she entered her teenage years, her condition worsened. We tried patterning exercises at home, with teams of volunteers coming in every day to give Mickey special massages. But there was no improvement. Mickey needed full-time care. We decided to place her in St. Joseph's Auxiliary Hospital, which was near our home. The day of the transfer was very hard for Eva and me, but we knew for the sake of the whole family it had to be done. We were consoled that Mickey was close by. For years, Eva would stop in to see Mickey when she drove by the hospital, which was often. We always went to visit on Sunday afternoons, and in good weather would take Mickey out to the park, where Eva would feed her. I would go to the store to get ice cream—"very berry" was Mickey's favourite—and I would read articles in the Sunday *New York Times* aloud to Eva. I used to joke that Mickey was the best-read patient in St. Joseph's.

We put out of our minds any thought of moving. "Let's stay in Edmonton," I had suggested. "I'll commute and be here on weekends." Eva gave me the green light to run. Once the decision was made, she helped me assemble a list of about a hundred people we knew in the constituency; I wrote to them asking if they would support my candidacy for the nomination.

My joining the Progressive Conservative Party was not an act of political ideology but pragmatics. It was true that I resented two policies of the Liberal government—to pay farmers not to grow wheat, and to fight inflation by allowing unemployment to rise—but the Progressive Conservatives, strong in Alberta, simply offered a better prospect for election. Stanfield and Clark were Progressive Conservatives. Why not me?

Edmonton-Strathcona was then held by Hu Harries, a Liberal and a highly intelligent man who was at odds with Trudeau. He had won in the Trudeau sweep of 1968, defeating a veteran Progressive Conservative, Terry Nugent. I did a random survey of the constituency and came to a twofold conclusion: the Progressive Conservatives wanted a new candidate, and that candidate would win the seat. About 30 people responded to my mail-out. One of them, Ruth Wallace, a friend of Eva's, gave the letter to Frank McMillan, a menswear salesman who had just arrived in Edmonton from Calgary.

"I'm Frank McMillan and I hear you want to run for Parliament."

The voice over the phone was strong and aggressive, and from that one sentence I knew the man would turn out to be dynamic. McMillan organized my political life while I wrote policy papers on the issues of the day. The former was definitely more important than the latter. What counts in nomination meetings is getting your supporters to show up. The quality of the candidate's speech has very little to do with the outcome, a fortunate truism in my case. Frank, understanding the psychology of politics better than I did, got the people to show up. We had 515 of the 799 voters on the first ballot. The Edmonton community was surprised that I had beaten the veteran Nugent, who was competing again for the nomination.

The election was delayed till October 30, 1972, and, since McMillan had to be on the road that fall, Darryl Smith took over my campaign. McMillan drove me hard, but Smith relaxed me. One day I introduced a woman to Darryl, thinking she was the convention manager of a Calgary hotel. She turned out to be Darryl's wife. "Well, now you know what a brilliant politician you have on your hands," I told Darryl with chagrin. Instead of making me feel more uncomfortable, he laughed at my gaffe. I felt so embarrassed that I later went out and bought Bernice Smith a rose.

I learned how to do door-to-door election canvassing (20 seconds per door), how to work the room at a crowded coffee party, and how to get off the platform fast at an all-candidates forum and shake everyone's hand at the back of the hall. I took pride in the fact that not a dime of my own money went into the $30,000 campaign budget, and took comfort in the assurance of my financial managers, Bob Lloyd and Woody Johnson, that the campaign would not owe a cent the day after the election. Fil Fraser, a television producer, shot a one-hour documentary on my campaign, which he (unbeknownst to me at the time) tentatively titled *Nice Guys Finish Last*. He had to do some revising on election night, when I collected 26,908 votes to Hu Harries's 16,625. Since Harries had won the previous election by 6,000 votes, the turnaround, the media proclaimed, was "astounding." Forty-five minutes after the polls closed, Harries phoned to say he hoped I would enjoy "all those Air Canada flights."

Trying to Prove Myself

Air Canada flights indeed became synonymous with my life. On Monday mornings, I would rise at 5 a.m. for a four-hour flight to Ottawa. With the two-hour time difference, it would be 3 p.m. by the time I reached Parliament. In those days, the House of Commons sat Monday, Tuesday and Thursday evenings. So I would end up working until 10 or 11 each night. Thursday meant a full day in the office and the House, then a long flight home in the evening. On Fridays I saw constituents in my Edmonton office. I was determined to spend as much time with Eva and the children as possible. There are many weeks of the year that Parliament does not sit; that compensated somewhat for all the time I was away. I started scheduling certain hours with the kids to be sure they had time with me, but Eva told me I was driving everyone crazy.

Because I felt insecure as a politician and guilty as a parent I worked harder on both fronts. Too hard, of course. I made mistakes. At the first provincial gathering of the Progressive Conservative Party, all the MPs were instructed to enter the hall one by one to great musical fanfare and applause, each with a curvaceous young woman dressed as a cheerleader by his side. It was supposed to be great "show biz." I looked for Eva a few minutes later, but couldn't find her. Finally, I located her outside walking by herself. I suddenly realized how hurt she was: good enough to be the MP's wife but not good enough to walk beside him in the spotlight. I felt terrible. Eva, God love her, recovered quickly. At the Alberta caucus meeting the following week, I said that this showmanship-with-blondes was dumb. I never did anything like that again. But I went on trying to prove myself.

The next summer, I was assigned to be a party representative at the Western Economic Opportunities Conference in Calgary, which was to be held just at the time we had scheduled a cross-Canada car trip with the family. I was so excited to be chosen that I told Eva to go ahead with the kids and I would catch up with them in Eastern Canada. On the day of my scheduled departure from the conference, a party media agent asked me to stay over and take part in a special television show the next day. Because I saw this as further recognition, I stupidly said yes. I phoned Eva to let her know. We had planned to meet in Quebec City but I told her to move on to Fredericton. When we met up there, one of the children told me how lonely their mother felt in the lovely room she had obtained in Quebec City, a city with undeniable romantic attraction to which I, wanting to advance my own career, had been completely oblivious.

Of course, there were many happy family moments in those early years in Parliament. Francis was an avid hockey player. Mary Anne and Tricia were busy with music and sports. One day, I flew across the country just to hear Mary Anne play the oboe in her school concert, then flew directly back to Ottawa. The children were growing up well and we seemed to be avoiding major crises in their teen years. But I knew they missed me, particularly at dinnertime. I had to keep telling myself that what I was doing was important, despite the fact that I often seemed to be accomplishing little in Ottawa. My political ambition weighed down my conscience periodically, but I kept up the life.

Since I had an apartment in downtown Ottawa, our daughter Evita, then a student at the University of Ottawa, lived with me and the children had a place to stay on their many trips to the nation's capital. Eva and I, in our Sunday evening cocktail-hour meetings, regularly weighed the ups and downs of my trans-Canada life and always came to the conclusion that the family was getting more out of it than they were losing. Yet it would be an understatement to say that Parliament plus a young family plus a 4,000-mile weekly commute equals stress.

My fate as a politician was determined the night of my first election, in 1972. The Progressive Conservatives missed forming the government by two seats. One of them was lost by four votes, the other by 32. A handful of people had decided that Pierre Trudeau would stay on as prime minister. Robert Stanfield, perhaps the soundest man I ever encountered in politics, did not become prime minister that night, nor again in the 1974 election. Thus, I spent my first seven years in Parliament in the Opposition benches.

The mark of a good Opposition member is how much he can bellow during Question Period. Bombast and feigned rage get you noticed by the media. I did my share of it, I suppose, but my heart was never in it. I did not enter politics to wake up in the morning and spend the day telling everyone how awful the government is. I wanted to work my ideas into the processes of public policy development. Had Stanfield been prime minister, I am sure that he would have found my value system compatible with his, and my career would have advanced. It was the unacceptable confinements of the Opposition that forced me to break out and find outlets for my ideas beyond Parliament Hill.

I spent a lot of my first year learning how to combine my purposes with the reality of parliamentary life. I made speeches on Alberta as the "New West" and joined the caucus committee on health and welfare to ground myself in domestic issues. I knew it was important to be noticed. Thus I welcomed the headlines at home when I accused the prime minister of playing patronage politics by inviting defeated Liberal candidates to dinner with the Queen and ignoring elected MPs from other parties. Even though I am a monarchist, having dinner with the Queen is low on my priority list. And although my outrage had a synthetic quality, protests like this build political capital at home. Publicity results in invitations to speak, which then enable you to put across your ideas. In the same way, serving constituents makes you a stronger politician as well as meeting genuine needs. I helped many constituents with their pension and unemployment insurance difficulties and succeeded in getting applicants with complex immigration problems into the country so they could be reunited with family members who were already here.

When I say "I" helped my constituents, what I really mean is my staff did. Pam Miles-Séguin entered my parliamentary life as a teenager fresh out of school. After six months, I began to wonder how I had ever functioned without her. She could delve through the mysteries of government departments with determination and charm, as well as handle all my logistics so I could operate in two cities at the same time. Pam stayed with me through all my years as an MP and rejoined me when I entered the Senate. I attended her wedding and watched her two daughters blossom into lovely young women. In Edmonton, Betty Mitchell and later Marge Brown kept track of all the constituents who came to see me and, with Pam, solved problems that would have overwhelmed me. This had the added benefit of building up my political capital. If politicians do not keep building political capital, what little they have quickly erodes. They need attention not just to feed their ego but to survive to do their job.

Capital Punishment: Black and White

I needed political capital to see me through the crisis surrounding the abolition of capital punishment. In 1973, I voted for a bill that removed the death penalty for capital crimes, except for the murder of a police officer or a prison guard. Such a bill had been passed five years earlier, in 1968, as a five-year trial; the 1973 bill would grant a five-year extension. This extension would expire in December 31, 1977.

A capital punishment debate touches the heart and emotions of the nation. It brings out deep feelings about the right to life, justice and the safety of society. The debate I entered in 1973 produced more mail, by far, than any other subject during my years as an MP. I argued then in favour of the extended trial period of partial abolition because it would help to develop the climate for acceptance of total abolition. But the mail, running four to one against my position, indicated that my constituents wanted Canada to retain capital punishment for all cases of premeditated murder. Acknowledging that I was not voting the way my constituents wanted, I said in a speech I gave during the debate:

> There is no way I can abdicate my responsibility to use my conscience in forming a decision as to how to vote. Some people think a Member of Parliament is a delegate to carry out automatically the wishes of the majority of his constituents, assuming the majority can be defined. But that is not my concept of the job. I believe a person is elected by constituents who possess a sense of confidence, for the time being at least, in his judgment and expect him to use it. The assurance that he will always vote according to his conscience is the best service that a Member of Parliament can offer his constituents.

When the *Edmonton Journal* carried a news story on my speech, the headline writer compressed my approach into these seven words: "Roche to buck voters on hanging issue." Another cascade of letters started, most of them blaming me for ignoring the desire of my constituents. "I would like an explanation of why you think you are better than your constituents who voted you into office to express their wishes," one voter wrote. Another said, "Please send me your reasons for voting exactly contrary to the wishes of the majority of your constituents ... These reasons will in effect tell me why you do not believe in the democratic system. Since you do not believe in democracy I think you should resign as an M.P. Your duty is to represent the wish of your voters, whatever it is."

Interspersed with the critical letters was the occasional letter of support for voting according to my own conscience:

> We do not have a vote in the House of Commons; you do, and we elected you to vote according to your information and beliefs. We consider you to be our representative, not a conveyor of our votes. You could not be sure how your constituents would vote without taking a referendum and this is obviously impossible on each issue. Perhaps the supporters of capital punishment are the most vocal because they are the most angry, but we are not sure they are even in the majority.

To everyone who wrote me, I replied that at almost every forum where I spoke prior to the election I was asked about my stand on capital punishment. I had clearly stated that I was in favour of extending the five-year partial ban: "Therefore, my vote was certainly no different from what I had indicated before the election. I do not like to offend people, but I must do what I think is right. Unless I am allowed to do what I think is right in any given issue, I would never remain a Member of Parliament."

The hard test of this view, I realized, would be the next election. As a Conservative in Alberta, I was not too worried about the outcome. In fact, in 1974 my majority increased by 1,188 votes over 1972. The voters had not held my viewpoint on capital punishment against me.

In the spring of 1976, the government took a chance that the group of Parliamentians, elected in 1974, contained more abolitionists than retentionists. Thus, Parliament would pass a total abolition bill to relieve the government of the nightmare of considering the applications by eleven men convicted of murdering policemen or jail guards to commute their sentences and to get this issue out of the way well before the anticipated 1978 general election.

When the government raised the abolition issue in the new Parliament, I studied the statistics. Violent crime in Canada had increased 90 per cent in the ten years between 1965 and 1974. In 1965, there were 243 murders in the country; in 1974, there were 545, and the murder rate had doubled from 1.2 per 100,000 population to 2.4. On top of this, the actual time served in prison by 42 murderers parolled between 1968 and 1974 averaged only 13.35 years. Was it any wonder the public was losing confidence in the government's willingness to enforce the law?

I wrote to Solicitor General Warren Allmand that the timing for the total abolition bill was all wrong. Bring in a crime control bill; enforce the partial abolition bill and repeat it for a third trial period. Only when the climate had improved would the public accept and respect a total abolition bill, I argued. Allmand responded, "You state that you will vigorously oppose any change in the law at the present time ... That is your right and a question for your own conscience."

The government presented two bills at once: a crime control bill and an abolition bill. The former, containing a controversial section on gun control, became tied up in committee. Nonetheless, the government rushed the abolition bill through because a deadline was looming for the commutation of the sentences of three murderers on death row. When my turn came to speak, there was barely a quorum of 20 in the House:

> It might seem that, as one who hopes that Canada will one day be an abolitionist country, I would welcome this bill. But I do not. The government's action in bringing in a total abolition bill now is an underhanded way of evading its responsibility in carrying out the present law. It will be impossible to build public support for total abolition while the public thinks that the enforcement of present laws, including the partial abolition law, is too lax. We must move forward slowly, surely, and honestly if real progress is to be made ....

Since I was prepared to accept an inferior law for the present for the sake of building the conditions for the acceptance of a better law in the future, I asked, what should the government do? Here was my answer:

> It should apply the crime prevention bill as improved in committee, and then extend the present capital punishment law for a third five-year period. Let the public judge, on the evidence of its application, whether it is a good law. Only then should we be asked in Parliament to make a definitive judgment on whether this country should live under an abolition or a capital punishment law. But free us from political machinations in such a deeply moral question. The common good demands that we take more time in coming to a final answer.

The next speaker was Ursula Appolloni, a Liberal with whom I had worked in the anti-abortion movement. "Mr. Speaker," she began, "I regret I should have to follow the speech of the Pontius Pilate on the other side of the House." Although I regard myself as reasonably hardened to criticism, the remark stunned me. Pilate had washed his hands of the blood of a man he acknowledged to be innocent. I was certainly not sentencing innocent men to death. Was my position so nuanced that no one would understand it? Tired and discouraged, I went back to my office. "Get the speech ready for a household mailing," I told my staff. "Let's hope people at home will at least read it before either damning or praising me."

The reaction started coming in quickly, especially with the *Edmonton Journal* carrying a front-page headline the following day:

"Anti-abolition stand by Roche a surprise move." The paper, in an editorial, dismissed my reasoning as "a tortuous explanation of an astounding about-face." My Edmonton secretary said the phone calls were in my favour, but as the mail started coming in it was clear that a lot of abolitionists were shocked and upset with me.

A constituent, Myron Johnson, wrote,

> What I find so despicable about your betrayal, what makes me ashamed to acknowledge that you are my M.P., is your utter hypocrisy and shameless opportunism in abandoning principle for short-term expediency.

> One would have thought that in your haste to abandon your unwarranted reputation for humanitarianism that you might at least have been ashamed enough to attempt to come up with some reasonably plausible explanation. But your reasoning was so specious and your excuse so pathetic that one hardly knows whether to laugh or cry.

The mail was not heavy, but the hostility expressed in letters like these indicated a belief that I was acting out of political expediency. Was it really impossible for an abolitionist to vote against Bill C-84 and maintain credibility? That became the central question in my mind. The *Calgary Herald* considered my position so unusual that the paper printed the speech. And in a follow-up article, Paul Jackson, parliamentary correspondent for both the Calgary and Edmonton newspapers, suggested that, despite my explanation, I was concerned about talk that unless I started paying more attention to the wishes of my constituents and less to the woes of the Third World I might be "either opposed for re-nomination or bumped off by a right-wing Liberal."

Some of the mail cheered me up. "Thank you," wrote Mrs. L. E. Burford, "and if more Members were so honest and straightforward with their constituents we would have a more honest government."

I continued to explain my position, but not many people seemed to understand. Abolition of the death penalty was a black-and-white issue; I had shrouded it in grey. Some thought I was afraid of my retentionist voters, yet that was the last thing on my mind. I may have been right on the principle of respect for the law that I was upholding, but I was too nuanced. The abolition bill passed 133 to 125.

I noted, however, that John Diefenbaker, a committed abolitionist, also voted no.

Justice, Not Charity

When Pierre Trudeau won a majority in the 1974 election (Robert Stanfield going down for a third time on a policy of wage and price controls, which Trudeau, after belittling the idea during the campaign, promptly implemented after the election), I decided to get away from an Opposition mentality for a while. I went to Europe for two back-to-back conferences: the United Nations World Population Conference in Bucharest, and the Second World Conference on Religion and Peace at the University of Louvain, in Brussels. The Progressive Conservative Party had no money for such research, so I financed the trip by writing a series of articles. The *Globe and Mail* gave full-page treatment to my report on the population conference under the headline "Canada: A Fat Cat in a Suffering World."

The population conference was held in the early stages of what became a series of global United Nations conferences on topics such as human security, food, water, habitat and energy. A conference on the environment had just been held in Stockholm in 1972. The world was beginning to understand the connections among development issues. In Bucharest, I learned that the world population problem has a double thrust: rapidly expanding numbers of people in the developing regions of the world, and the high standard of living in the developed regions. The vast majority of the increase in world population was occurring in Asia, Africa and Latin America, which already contained two thirds of humanity. In these countries, nearly half the population was younger than 15. The number of future mothers was doubling. But this was only part of the problem. The developed world, with a much greater per-capita environmental impact than the developing countries, was then, as now, a principal factor in the crisis. For example, a baby born in Canada, where the population problem is not visible, will grow up consuming 50 times the resources and energy that a baby in the heavily populated developing regions will consume.

In taking for granted ever-higher standards of living, which strain the resource and environmental capacities of the planet, the minority of rich people get richer at the expense of the multiplying poor. Delegate after delegate at Bucharest pointed to food, fertilizer, energy and capitalization emergencies to illustrate this point. Recent sharp increases in the prices of energy, fertilizer and food had demonstrated that international market mechanisms serve to direct scarce resources to those who can afford them, while denying them to the many others who need but cannot afford them.

The problem in the Third World, then, is not population as such. Rather, it is the extreme poverty perpetuated by the control the developed world exercises over the bulk of the earth's wealth and resources. The delegate from Bangladesh graphically depicted the point: "Our part of the world is sinking under the weight of population. Our growth rate is 3 per cent. We are short of food, short of education facilities, short of everything. Every flood sinks us."

In short, the minority of rich nations in the world were told bluntly by the majority of poor ones: stop thinking that expanded birth control programs will solve the population problem, because population is only a reflection of the overall unjust economic system that keeps the poor in bondage.

The plan of action that resulted from the Bucharest conference said that developing countries should certainly accept their responsibility to set population targets, but these targets could only be attained by making them part of a new economic and social system to deal coherently with worldwide problems of mass poverty, population growth, food, energy and military expenditures.

For me, the question was how to get the governments of affluent nations to change their priorities. Our priorities, I thought, are to make ourselves richer by increasing our own technological capacity, and then to exercise a modicum of philanthropy towards the poor. This attitude, based knowingly or unknowingly on greed, has backfired. Clearly, we need a new ethic by which to live.

Here, the World Conference of Religion for Peace made a special contribution by discussing a new global ethic at the Louvain meeting. More than 300 representatives of the world's great religions—Christians, Jews, Muslims, Buddhists, Hindus—appealed to the religious communities of the world to "inculcate the attitude of planetary citizenship, the sense of our human solidarity in the just sharing of the food, the energy, and all the material necessities of existence which our generous habitat, unlike any other yet perceived in universal space, will continue faithfully to provide only if it is well loved and respected by mankind."

The conference underscored the point that a social justice ethic leading to a new order was now imperative. Up until then, it had been assumed that the development of the poor countries could take place without any slowdown in the rate of growth of the rich nations. But shortages of petroleum, fertilizers and food grains pointed to the sobering reality that the demands of the rich for scarce resources to support wasteful and indulgent patterns of consumption and production were now severely impairing access by the poor to the supplies needed to meet their most basic development needs and in some cases to ensure their survival.

The World Conference of Religion for Peace put the case bluntly:

> It is these sinful consumption patterns of the rich societies (not excluding the extravagances of the small number of rich people within the developing countries) that we denounce. The affluent minority in the world, for example, feeds as much grain to animals as the deprived majority eats directly. We cannot in conscience stand idly by while fellow humans die from hunger. It is the task of religion to make this criticism and to encourage models of development based on justice.

> Good analysis and high-minded thoughts are not enough, unfortunately, to sway government policies. Governments operate on the principle of self-interest, an axiom that was on full display during the debate on a "new international economic order."

The very idea of bringing some order into the mix of cross-cutting economic and social policies appealed to me so much that I went to the United Nations the following year as a parliamentary observer at a special session of the General Assembly dealing with proposals for reform known as the New International Economic Order. The proposals comprised a wide range of trade, financial, and commodities- and debt-related issues put forward by developing countries. With good reason, these countries, which contain the great majority of the world's population, considered that the Bretton Woods economic system, set up after the Second World War, discriminated against them. They wanted to negotiate about the world's structural economic systems, in a new North-South dialogue.

The proposals for change were sweeping: they embraced international trade and tariff issues, industrialization, science and technology, transfer of resources, monetary reform and food production. Had the developed countries then entered into comprehensive negotiations to make the world economic system more equitable between nations— particularly between the developed and developing countries—much of the turmoil, not to mention the degrading poverty, social unrest and conflicts of the past three decades, would have been averted. But the governments of the powerful states, hit by oil price shocks and fearful of losing their advantage in world financial and trading systems, would have no part of it. The farthest they would go was to hold the negotiations within the framework of the international financial institutions, which they controlled. The developing countries wanted the negotiations to take place under the auspices of the UN General Assembly, in which they had numerical superiority. The result of this impasse, which went on for years, was that the New International Economic Order, though adopted by consensus as a framework document at the General Assembly, remained a piece of paper with diminishing meaning as time went by.

I began to write articles and give speeches in Parliament on this subject, which led to my appointment as the Progressive Conservative critic on international development (a post not hotly contested). I started to examine closely the performance of the Canadian International Development Agency. I was acquiring the label of "expert" on these issues, though, in parliamentary terms, even superficial knowledge is often enough to bestow expert status. The truth is, I enlisted Bob Miller of the Library of Parliament Research Branch to help me assemble mounds of facts.

The leadership of the six largest religious denominations in Canada at the time—Catholic, United, Anglican, Presbyterian, Lutheran and Disciples of Christ—invited me to write a book on the New International Economic Order for their members to use as a study document. Since they guaranteed to purchase the first 8,000 copies, McClelland and Stewart seemed happy to publish the book. *Justice Not Charity* appeared in early 1976, and nothing I have written since has evoked so much response.

The central point of the book was that charity consists of satisfying all our desires and then passing on some of what is left over; justice, on the other hand, requires adjusting our desires to the needs of others, so that there is a planetary sharing of what all have a right to.

Thanks to the new global crises, we have suddenly come up against a hitherto inconceivable prospect: maybe unlimited consumerism will have to come to an end. Maybe the rich of the world have over-reached themselves. Maybe a whole new assessment of how we live will have to be made. Exactly.

That is the message of the new economic order.

The new order, based on the expertise of an international array of political, scientific, and technical leaders, was arrived at through perceiving massive global disorder.

Thus, from two different streams of life—the moral and the pragmatic—there is a convergence on a common goal: a better system of sharing as stewards of the planet. This convergence—for the first time since the evolution of the modern world—is what gives me hope in an age that is still marked by frustration, despair and violence. It is a powerful convergence because it now makes possible a new global ethic.

Not in the Mould

The *Financial Times of Canada* called the book a "shocker" that broke "the stereotype of the safe vote-seeker concerned only with short-term goals and ready to seek immediate popularity with promises and smooth words." The *Financial Times* added, "Mr. Roche has succeeded very well in showing the folly, as well as the inhumanity, of shutting our eyes to the plight of more than half the world's peoples." A former moderator of the United Church, Ernest Howse, said, "Roche provides plenty of cause to rouse Canadians to troubled concern about the measures of their national response to their international responsibilities." But Peter Brimelow, business columnist of *Maclean's*, lambasted me for supposedly advocating the physical relocation of a large part of Canadian industries to "various deserving parts of the Third World as well as stripping us of capital through various schemes …." (I had done no such thing.) Said Brimelow, "The economic implications of his moralizing are appalling." Paul Jackson, the *Edmonton*

Journal's and *Calgary Herald*'s Ottawa correspondent, who was finding it hard to believe that I belonged to the Progressive Conservative Party, wrote, "Doug Roche has established himself as the Federal Progressive Conservative Party's social conscience in the plight of the Third World, while being written off by some as an unrealistic, foolish idealist and even as a 'professional Christian.'"

Inexperienced as I was in the machinations of caucus politics (a veteran MP once told me that your real enemies in politics are not your opponents across the floor but your supposed friends beside you), I instinctively knew that if I was going to be heard on the issue of international development, I had to talk about other things, too. A "one-issue" politician quickly gets marginalized. So I raised many other issues, particularly in Question Period, when a member more or less has the attention of the House. I talked about economic opportunities for the "New West," immigration and pension issues, the need for urban rapid transit systems, and the vicissitudes of the Post Office department. I succeeded in saving the old post office at Whyte Avenue and 105 Street in my constituency from demolition and having it declared a heritage building. I even made what I promised would be a "one-minute" speech on national unity. The *Edmonton Journal* was so impressed by my sterling example of brevity that the paper put the entire speech on page one.

I was not, therefore, a "one-issue" politician, but as time went on, my questions and speeches (which I like to think were reasonably well informed) about the need for more action to implement at least some of the tenets of the New International Economic Order defined my image as a politician. In the Progressive Conservative Party, filled as it was with many hard-liners on foreign, social and linguistic policies, I had all the markings of a "Red Tory."

Red Tories are characterized by a distinct concern for the common good, which they put above the unfettered protection of individual rights. This contrasts with Conservatives farther to the right who believe in individualism and pure capitalism. On the political spectrum, Red Tories are centrist to centre-left. They have a history of social concern and strong nationalism. Canada's first prime minister, Sir John A. Macdonald, was a Red Tory, as were John Diefenbaker and Robert Stanfield. Many others, such as Davie Fulton and Dalton Camp, have been influential cabinet ministers or strategists. It is erroneous to think that Red Tories are something of an aberration within conservatism.

Such a badge of honour should be worn with distinction. But somehow those with little time for problems beyond the shores of Canada had manipulated the political agenda so that people like me were considered "soft-headed." Some defined me as a "bleeding heart." A veteran MP in my own city was heard to refer to me, I am sure derisively, as a "Boy Scout."

Often, the caucus seemed dominated by a group of rough-and-ready MPs, who scorned enlightened international policies as pseudo-communism. I was but an irritation to them; the real object of their venom was Robert Stanfield, whose Red Tory stance went against the "me-first" style of politics and whose moderate views on public issues raised him to statesman status. Fortunately, the Progressive Conservative caucus also contained a number of national figures with whose progressive values I readily identified: Joe Clark, David MacDonald, Flora MacDonald, Gordon Fairweather, Heath Macquarrie and Walter McLean. They, too, were modern Red Tories, adhering to a political philosophy of deep social concern within a framework of conserving the best from the past. The progressives and the reactionaries somehow co-existed in the same caucus. It made for some explosive Wednesday morning meetings. The only way peace was maintained was through the frequent recalling of the attributes of birds, namely that they have two wings—a left wing and a right wing—both of which they need to fly.

Crossing Party Lines

With the cacophonous caucus meetings and bear-pit sessions in the House, I realized that I would have to reach beyond Parliament to be heard on the agenda that I thought was at the heart of Canadians' future security needs: our role in international development. I suggested to the Canadian Council for International Co-operation that it explore the idea of an MP from each of the three main parties travelling across the country to talk to Canadians about Canada's response to world development issues. Irénée Pelletier, a Liberal political economist from Sherbrooke, and Andrew Brewin, a veteran New Democrat MP from Toronto, had distinguished themselves in calling for Canada to do more to respond to the growing crisis of world poverty. In early January 1976, the three of us set out for ten days of public meetings from Halifax to Victoria.

The novel concept of three members of Parliament of different political stripes working as a team caught on, and we performed to packed halls. Pelletier opened with an overview of the interrelationship between the food, energy, population, industrialization, environmental and urbanization crises of the world, which amounted to a single crisis of world development. Brewin followed with a look at the New International Economic Order. I then focused on Canada's multi-dimensional approach, embodied in a new five-year (1975–1980) strategy for international development co-operation.

We didn't pretend to be united on every policy, but we did see eye to eye on the main approach Canada should take to meet the responsibilities of a planetary society. We agreed that Canada must begin implementing structural economic reforms as well as increase aid to the poorest countries. Recognizing all too well that Canada's new five-year strategy would only gather dust unless Canadians got behind it, we tried to awaken our audiences to the opportunities and obligations of Canadians in the years ahead.

The media covered the tour extensively, so we doubtless reached far more than the 2,000 people who attended the gatherings. When it was over, the *Globe and Mail* gave me almost a full page to report our findings: Canadians may not be cynical about the suffering in the world, but they were not in a sharing mood either; they wanted to know whether Canadian aid to the developing world was doing any good. "As a sign of hope for improved Canadian motivation," I wrote, "we noted individuals and organizations speaking and acting against the national trend of skepticism and self-concern. They are a creative minority reflecting a profound view that the people of the industrialized world must adopt new attitudes to consumption and stewardship of resources and the environment."

The peculiarities of the Progressive Conservative caucus notwithstanding, I felt I was beginning to have some impact—slight, perhaps, but not insignificant—on the political thinking of the country.

7

The Rise and Fall
of a Government

When the Progressive Conservatives went down to defeat again in the 1974 election, I wrote a piece for the *Globe and Mail* urging Bob Stanfield to stay on as leader, at least for a couple of years, to allow the Party to develop new public policies. But Stanfield, knowing better than I that politics, stripped to its essentials, is about winning, signalled that the Party should prepare for a leadership convention. Nothing taught me so much about the fierceness of politics as my experiences at the Progressive Conservative leadership convention held in February 1976 and the subsequent one in 1983.

If the Progressive Conservatives wanted a winner, I pointed out to a number of caucus colleagues, who better than Peter Lougheed, the popular and powerful premier of Alberta? An informal committee of about 10 MPs for Lougheed was formed. Lougheed sent me a message that he wanted to see me. I sat down to breakfast with him in his office. He said that he had thought about the matter a great deal and had come to the firm conclusion that he would not run. His commitment to Alberta was too strong. Nonetheless, shortly thereafter he went on a heavily publicized business and trade mission through Europe in which he displayed all the attributes of a national leader.

Meanwhile, Joe Clark invited me to a small meeting he was holding in Toronto to examine the viability of his candidacy. I was already out West and told him I couldn't go. Harvie André, a Calgary MP and Clark's closest friend, talked to me one day in the Parliamentary cafeteria about Lougheed. "We've got to get him," André said. We formalized the Committee of Ten for Lougheed and sent him a letter stating that, for the good of Canada, it was his "duty to run for the office of Prime Minister." André went to see Lougheed and came away with the impression that he was still open to the idea.

André and Clark came to my office a few days later; Clark said he was moving ahead with his plans because he was convinced Lougheed would not run. I could see Clark wanted our support. I told Clark I admired him for running, that he had the qualities of intelligence, drive and great political ability, and that his campaign would set him up beautifully for the next time around. He would come out of this race as an established national figure. Clark spoke clearly. He was not running for the next time; he was running for this time. I put his attitude down to the internal conviction politicians must have just to be able to do all the things demanded of a candidate.

I was in a difficult position. I liked Clark and believed in him, and yet I felt that he didn't have the experience to be a leader, especially of such a fractious caucus. Clark and I got along well: he had visited my home in Edmonton and I knew him as well as any MP. All this was going through my mind when he stopped into my Edmonton office a couple of weeks later. I was uncomfortable and wanted to talk, but Joe was in a hurry to catch a plane. We agreed to try to get together soon, but it was the last conversation I had with him until we met briefly the night the convention opened.

The Draft Lougheed movement was building up. The *Edmonton Journal*, which had criticized me a few weeks earlier for my "presumption" in pushing Lougheed to run, published a rare front-page editorial promoting our efforts. The *Globe and Mail* also urged Lougheed to run. Again, I went to see the premier. This time he said he would issue an irrevocable refusal. We shook hands and I walked out to my car where my son, Francis, was waiting to drive me to the airport. "I'm going to tell you something," I said. "Always do what you think is right. That way you can live with yourself longer. It was better to try to get Premier Lougheed and fail than not to have tried." We drove the rest of the way in silence.

My moment of decision about whom to support was nearing. One afternoon, during a development conference in Sainte Marguerite, Quebec, I went for a long walk through the Laurentian Hills.

It was a superb early winter day, and the scenery, flecked with light snowfall, had a calming effect on me. When I got back to my room, I got out my leadership file and read all the candidates' statements. Claude Wagner, a crime-busting attorney and judge from Quebec who had entered Parliament with me in 1972, had also asked me to support him. His first major speech on Canada's peace-keeping role in Vietnam had been a commanding performance and revealed a sensitivity obscured by his hard-line image. His colleagues looked on him as a leader. Wagner would often tease me about the "New West," and we developed an easy relationship that intensified as I gradually shifted my attention to the external affairs committee, of which he was caucus chairman.

When the committee set up a subcommittee on international development, Wagner asked me to take charge of it for our party. He promised to stand behind whatever I recommended. In a caucus in which I so often felt diminished because of my interest in world conditions that were not the bread-and-butter of retail domestic politics, Wagner's vote of confidence in my judgment and ability heartened me. When Wagner came west in the fall of 1973 on a speaking tour, I had a reception for him in my home and was glad to see the warm feelings he generated among my friends. It certainly didn't hurt our relationship when he showed that he was familiar with my book with Bishop De Roo, *Man to Man*. More important, I respected the patience and moderation he displayed when he spoke on bilingualism. He could easily have fractured an already polarized caucus, but he chose to be an instrument of unity. I liked that.

A Leader from Quebec

I was concerned about the handling of a $300,000 trust fund that key officials of the Party, including Stanfield, had set up for Wagner before the 1972 election. He was being asked to give up the security of the Quebec judiciary for the uncertainty of politics, and, moreover, to devote huge amounts of time to rebuilding the Party in Quebec. Former prime ministers Mackenzie King, Louis St. Laurent and Lester Pearson all had funds to supplement their income as politicians. These funds made it possible for all three to stay in politics, and no one has ever suggested that they acted improperly or gave special treatment to their benefactors.

In current-day politics, such political contributions must be disclosed, but in 1972 there was no requirement to publicize the fund; moreover, the fund managers decided it should be kept secret because they feared that opponents would charge the Progressive Conservative Party with trying to buy Quebec votes. But, of course, news of the fund leaked when Wagner started his campaign for election to Parliament. He was technically correct in his denial that he was benefiting: under the terms of the fund, he had first to be elected before receiving the $12,000-a-year interest from the fund. I decided that Wagner had not done anything wrong; I had received $10,000 in cash from party funds as a campaign contribution in each of my two elections and a subsidy for my constituency office. There was nothing unethical about this. Nobody was questioning my honesty. Why should Wagner's be questioned?

I turned back to the speech he made announcing his candidacy, in which he warned that Progressive Conservatives would remain in Opposition unless they raised their profile in Quebec. "I am a candidate set at winning, to enable the Conservative Party to carry out the dreams of so many generations of Quebecers to have the Progressive Conservative Party choose a Francophone leader, not merely because he is from Quebec, not for the mere sake of electoral calculations, but because I feel that more than anybody else, I am best able to help Canada survive in the unity and diversity our founders dreamed to be hers." I saw in Wagner a mediator. I thought he needed Westerners like me to exert an influence on him and who might, in turn, be able to help him in Western Canada. One other factor weighed deeply with me: Wagner was strongly anti-abortion, another issue that I knew was looming in my political career.

The afternoon was wearing on and the Laurentian Hills were already lost in the early darkness of December as I looked out the hotel window. Wagner or Clark? Quebec or Alberta? Experience or freshness? Which one? They both wanted me. Though I wished I had gotten a job as an election official so I would have to stay neutral, I hate fence-sitters. I wanted to stall. I couldn't. I tried to think of the country. But how did I know what was best for the country? Finally, I settled my mind. Clark next time. Wagner this time.

I wanted to tell Clark personally before he read my announcement in the press, but he was out West and wouldn't be back before the

Christmas recess. So I wrote him a long letter explaining my decision. When I arrived home, Christmas was in full swing and I didn't want to talk politics. The family had a five-day vacation to Jasper planned and we went off on the train in a happy mood, looking forward to being together, skiing, skating and playing bridge. When we arrived home, Eva read about my decision in the paper and was hurt that I hadn't discussed it with her. She favoured Clark and, although she would have respected (if not agreed with) my reasoning, she felt left out. I realized that I had handled this the wrong way. My mood was not brightened by a phone call from Frank McMillan, who had learned from his own sources of my letter to Clark. McMillan was furious with me for putting on paper thoughts that, he said, I should have only expressed verbally to Clark. But this was just one more instance of a trait, good or bad, of mine: I would rather write than speak something unpleasant.

Geoffrey Stevens, the *Globe and Mail* political columnist, interviewed me on why I was supporting Wagner. I found the right words, which he accurately conveyed to his readers: intelligence, strength and moderation. These were the qualities I sought, along with the ability to unify the Conservative caucus and the Quebec factor, Stevens reported. "When such a person comes on the national scene with a broad background of political, judicial and ministerial experiences, then I think to reject him would be to tell the people of Quebec: 'Look, no matter what your attributes are, you can't make it all the way in the Tory Party and the very best you can do is the Quebec lieutenancy'—which by its very nature implies a second-class citizenry." In short, the Wagner candidacy offered us a chance to repudiate once and for all the idea that the Conservative Party is the preserve of English-speaking commercial interests.

Wagner asked me to campaign with him through northern Ontario and western Canada. Unfortunately, the campaign went badly. Wagner was knocked off stride by new publicity on the trust fund that had been set up for him. The fund managers wouldn't speak of its origins, leaving the public spotlight on Wagner alone. He was accused of accepting money before the 1972 election. Finally, Eddie Goodman, a key party figure, said, "No money from the fund was ever given to anybody during the year 1972." But this statement was buried in media accounts. Wagner wanted to talk about the issues; the press wanted to talk about the fund. I pleaded with Stanfield on two occasions to publicly clear Wagner's name and reaffirm his integrity, but Stanfield was afraid of further escalation that might derail the Wagner campaign entirely. Flora MacDonald, also campaigning for the leadership, called for an investigation of the fund. Stanfield advised Wagner to stay cool, that the latest round of charges might produce sympathy for him. I understood Stanfield's wanting to stay outside the political fray, but I disagreed with his decision to hover above the ethical cloud also. We could sense an erosion of Quebec votes to Brian Mulroney. The internal conflict in Quebec mystified me. Mulroney had brought Wagner into the Party and was now locked in battle with him over Quebec delegates.

Clark's Strong Campaign

Though Wagner's confidence was weakened, he kept campaigning, and the media reports in western Canada were positive. Back at Wagner's campaign headquarters in Ottawa, I gave Paul Weed, Wagner's campaign manager, the pluses and minuses of the trip. Weed was buoyant, but I had already learned that if campaign managers aren't naturally buoyant they shouldn't be campaign managers. As the campaign entered the final week, the fund stories dropped off the front pages. Clark was campaigning strongly and picking up kudos for his knowledge of the issues. Eva and I gave a cocktail party in our Ottawa apartment for delegates. Mary Dantzer, wife of the former mayor of Edmonton, was an uncommitted voting delegate. "You're the most important person in town," I told her as I introduced her to the journalists at the party. My friend John Grace, by then editor of the *Ottawa Journal*, said he couldn't make up his mind about Wagner or Clark and predicted that they would both be on the final ballot. "That's the one scenario that bothers me most about this whole business," I responded. "It's one thing not to support Clark, but I never want to have to vote directly against him."

On the night of the candidates' speeches, I told Clark that he had run a great campaign and Alberta was proud of him. He was gracious enough—and professional enough—not to remind me that I hadn't been much help to him. Clark and his wife, Maureen McTeer, arrived at the podium in an open landau as a band played "I'se the b'y." A neat entrance, I thought, full of style. But his speech seemed hurried. Wagner had the attention of the entire crowd and rose to the occasion.

When I arrived at the arena Sunday morning for the vote, I was told that Harvie André wanted to see me. I had not seen much of Harvie since the Draft Lougheed movement had fizzled out. He had, of course, chosen Clark and was managing the Clark team at the convention. We went behind the stands to talk. If Wagner should falter, he wanted me to know I'd be welcome in the Clark camp. I decided not to press him. It seemed obvious to me that if Joe should fade, both Joe and Harvie would move to Wagner. It would be in both their long-term interests to do so.

Wagner's managers had said privately that he needed 600 votes on the first ballot to win, but could still make it with their predicted 555. But his first ballot count was only 531. Mulroney had 357—many, if not most, of these would otherwise have gone to Wagner. Clark surprised everyone with 277. The winner could now be identified as one of the top three: Wagner, Mulroney or Clark. Sinclair Stevens, a right-wing MP from Toronto who gathered 182 votes, astounded the crowd by marching straight to Clark's box; it had been anticipated he would move to Wagner. Paul Hellyer, who had 231 votes, did go to Wagner but so slowly that he missed the deadline to have his name removed from the second ballot, thereby acquiring 118 votes that would most likely have gone to Wagner. Stevens's and Hellyer's actions denied Wagner the big boost he needed on the second ballot and his vote total rose to only 667. Meanwhile, Clark's tally almost doubled to 532, establishing the needed momentum.

Though Jack Horner moved to Wagner, Flora MacDonald and other minor candidates went to Clark. On the third ballot, Wagner had 1,003, Clark was up to 969 and Mulroney was stalled at 369. Mulroney was off the ballot. The scenario I had dreaded was before me. Mulroney did not declare for either of the two remaining candidates. If his votes had split evenly on the fourth ballot, Wagner would have won. But Clark went over the top with 1,187 to Wagner's 1,122. Sixty-five votes. Thirty-three people had made the difference.

After it was all over, I bumped into Claude Ryan, editor of *Le Devoir*. Why he had given the support of his prestigious journal to Mulroney was a mystery to me, but I didn't feel like arguing. "I just hope, Claude, that you will tell your readers tomorrow that the

Conservative Party did not reject a French Canadian," I told him. "You know and I know that there was a cross-current of reasons why Wagner lost."

"How about your writing this for *Le Devoir*?" Ryan asked me.

"I'm too tired, Claude," I answered. "You write it."

Back at the apartment, I sank into a hot bath. My body was aching and I didn't want to go anywhere or do anything for a week. Eva brought me a drink and sat down; she knew I wanted to talk.

I told her that her political judgment was pretty good. She had backed Clark months earlier. In turn, she told me that she had developed a warm and favourable feeling for Wagner during the convention. We were trying to come together. The campaign, producing different viewpoints between us, had been a strain on us personally.

"Well," I laughed, "how would you like to be an Alberta MP who really likes Joe Clark but who worked not once but twice against him? I pushed both Lougheed and Wagner. It would be better for my career to be an Alberta opponent that he now needed to support him than an Alberta friend whom he doesn't need."

"Don't sell yourself so short," Eva said. "And since when did you start thinking politics was going to be your whole life?"

Bottom-up Development in China

Instead getting a week off, I was summoned by Wagner's office the next morning to come over immediately to formulate questions for him for Question Period. Although he had given a gracious concession speech, it was deemed necessary—by Clark's office, I think—for Wagner to be the lead questioner, to show party unity and, more especially, to show that he would serve under Clark. I drafted questions for Wagner and then went to see Clark. I congratulated him warmly, and Joe, once again displaying his considerate nature, said he understood why I had supported Wagner. We should put the campaign behind us and work together, he said. I agreed, and asked him whether he would consider going to Wagner's office that afternoon to show that he was personally reaching out to Claude. "He's bruised," I told Joe. Clark did so, and the salve helped. But, as the weeks and months went by, it became apparent to the caucus—and to Prime Minister Trudeau— that Wagner had lost his spirit to engage in political battle. Trudeau appointed him to the Senate in 1978. I attended Wagner's swearing in;

there was scarcely an MP to be seen. Shortly after, Wagner contracted a fatal illness and died on July 11, 1979, at the age of 54.

As the new leader, Clark retained Wagner as external affairs critic. I was content to stay on as the party spokesman on international development and decided I should settle down and deepen my knowledge of the subject.

In July, I finished writing *The Human Side of Politics*, a book that expressed my growing doubt of the ability of Canada's parliamentary process to face up to the global problems confronting society; the book would appear towards the end of 1976. "My early years in Parliament are over," I wrote. "Aside from flying half a million miles, what have I done?" Find a scandal and make a headline. Don't vote the wrong way. Don't offend. That's too stifling, I thought. I didn't want to be a political robot just so that some day I would get a Cabinet post. Practical politics lives by the short-term gain. I was interested in the long-term benefits to humanity. I was convinced that there was no hope for Western leadership in an explosive world if we did not base our political judgments on moral values. A long-range survivalist ethic was now imperative to protect succeeding generations from the dehumanizing force of population growth, the rich-poor gap, a runaway industrial order and nuclear dangers.

Every profession today requires creative courage to face up to a new kind of world, a global community. After my early years in Parliament, what I was left with was the thought that we cannot expect politics to plunge into deeply human concerns if creative politicians lose their courage.

The Canadian International Development Agency at that time was being criticized by the Auditor General for "the very unsatisfactory state of financial control." These management questions certainly needed to be attended to, but the real question—a simple one, but one that required deep analysis—was the effectiveness of the aid program as a whole: Does foreign aid help people lift up their lives?

China's ambassador to Canada, Chang Wen-Chin, had read my book *Justice Not Charity*. He sent me an official invitation to go to China to study development. I decided to accept, even though the caucus would likely frown on my spending time in a communist country. I thought it would be a good idea to combine a China visit with a tour of Indonesia and Bangladesh, two of the biggest recipients of Canadian aid. Comparing development models would be fascinating. Besides, it would get me out of Ottawa for a protracted period. I went to Clark with my idea. He not only approved it but "assigned" me to do this study, thereby opening diplomatic doors everywhere. I needed researchers: I selected Bernard Wood, executive director of the North-South Institute, and Clyde Sanger, associate director of public information at the International Development Research Centre. Wood and Sanger could get their airfare paid by their organizations, and CP Air gave my wife and me complimentary passes. Once in China, our expenses would be paid by the Chinese People's Institute of Foreign Affairs. I wanted Eva, who had become director of early childhood development at Grant MacEwan Community College in Edmonton, not only to have the experience of seeing China but also to do her own study of daycare facilities in that country.

I began by asking a set of questions: Why had a quarter century of foreign aid not closed the rich-poor gap in the Third World? Who is the chief beneficiary of aid? Why is China, the most populous country in the world, making great gains in development without any outside help at all? To ask these questions is to plunge beneath the superficialities and hypocrisy of much that passes for international assistance and to begin to distinguish between foreign aid and human development. They are by no means the same things, as China bears witness.

The four of us entered China through Hong Kong, travelling by train to Guangzhou (formerly known as Canton) and by air to Beijing, where my study began with a two-hour interview with Wang Hairong, vice-minister of foreign affairs and a niece of Chairman Mao. Following three days in Beijing, we travelled to Yan-Chuan and His-Yang to visit the Dazhai Brigade model agricultural community; to Shijiazhuang, Anyang and Linxian to study the economic effects of the Red Flag Canal's irrigation and electrification systems; and to Zhengzhou, Nanjing, Wuxi, Shanghai, Zhong Hua County and back to Guangzhou. We covered 4,000 kilometres by air, 3,000 by train and 1,800 by car, visiting communes, production brigades, factories, power stations, housing complexes, schools, nurseries and health stations. We met with Chinese in their homes and also attended several cultural performances. An official guide and two interpreters accompanied us. Often we took the opportunity to walk through the streets.

The trip, which had been planned long beforehand, took place two months after Mao's death on September 9, 1976; the Chinese leadership was still sorting out his legacy and the problems of party disunity, economic dislocation and labour discontent. Because it had been so insulated, so little understood from outside and so caricatured, China from afar seemed an island of stability. But it was clear that underneath the tranquillity brewed considerable turmoil.

It became apparent to me that China had followed a "bottom up" model of development, giving priority to meeting the basic needs of the people: adequate food, clothing, shelter, health care, education and employment. It would likely have been possible to find local cases of poverty in China, but in all my travels I hardly saw a beggar or a hungry child. On the contrary, there was a general atmosphere of purpose, accomplishment and self-fulfillment—a stark contrast to the customary Third World scenes of destitution, apathy and despair.

If there is one key to the egalitarian economic progress made by China since Mao's Communist Party secured power in 1949, it is water management. I saw massive water control projects built by the local people that have transformed life in entire counties. China is no longer subject to the worst caprices of floods or droughts. The availability of water for villages results in greater food production, better nutrition and improved personal hygiene—and therefore fitter people who are able to work harder on social goals in the community.

Our hosts wanted us to see Chinese altruism, but I thought I caught a glimpse of the future China when we met Granny Zhou, who became the unforgettable character of the trip. A kindly lady in her mid-50s, Granny Zhou lived in a two-room unit on her pension from her career as a teacher. She was the cadre, or leader, for fifteen families in her block and ran study sessions for the Sunflower Culture group, an after-school organization for seven- to sixteen-year-olds. For the first time, I saw books in a home (all political works) and even a piano.

"Before the Liberation, teachers were looked down on," she told us as she sat on the edge of her bed beside her friend Madame Ma, "but now we are honoured."

The standard questions having been asked and the standard answers given, I searched for something different to ask.

"What was the last thing you bought that was not a necessity?" I inquired.

"Oh," Granny Zhou said, whisking some lace off a bit of furniture, "this television set." It was a portable black-and-white set, for which she had paid $122.

"But why do you need a TV set when there are sets in the community rooms?"

"Well, it's nice to lie in bed in your own home and watch TV," she replied.

That was a universal statement if ever I heard one. Actually, she added, three of the fifteen families in her block had their own sets. Was this the beginning of Chinese consumerism, I wondered?

"Would you like a private car?" I asked.

Our travelling hosts blanched. Hadn't the Foreign Institute told us that, in the interests of conservation, no Chinese citizen would desire a car?

Granny Zhou, her neighbour Granny Zhen and Madame Ma all nodded their heads emphatically yes.

Top-down Development in Indonesia and Bangladesh

Eva, Bernie and Clyde returned to Canada the day after we left China. I went on alone to Singapore to attend meetings of the World Conference on Religion and Peace. As I listened to Asians talk about development, I realized that their idea of what development means extends far beyond economic progress, which is the criterion most Westerners use. I heard phrases such as "communitarian values of justice and sharing" and "harmony in human society." The conference president was Archbishop Angelo Fernandes of New Delhi, whom I had first met in India. "Besides inner tranquility," he told the assembly, "other Asian values of paramount importance to the process of humanization are simplicity and contentment, non-violence and compassion, cooperation, a spirit of adjustment and a deeply rooted communion with nature."

Ray Verge, administrator of the Alberta government's International Assistance Program, which provided matching grants to non-governmental organization programs in developing countries, joined me for my tour of aid projects in Indonesia and Bangladesh. We saw dozens of projects in both countries, which mainly followed a "top down" model of development: huge infrastructure projects. It was clear that Indonesia and Bangladesh did not have the egalitarian motivation that characterized development in China. To reach the Bangladesh Earth Satellite Station, a Canadian aid project, we travelled through villages where there was no clean water. Dysentery was rampant. This was the "top down" model gone mad. Canadian manufacturers benefited, since many of the satellite parts were made in Canada, but what about the people who needed the basics of life?

In Dacca, I learned a fact about life in Bangladesh. We climbed the steps to the National Mosque, stepping around and over beggars of every description: men, women, old, young, whole of body, deformed. Removing our shoes at the door (but carrying them with us), we entered a peaceful, almost elegant interior. Men, alternately prostrated on the floor or reaching out their arms beseechingly to Allah, were making their evening devotions. A Bengali brought us to the centre of the mosque to view the magnificent blue dome from directly underneath.

As we were putting on our shoes at the door, a couple of appealing young boys stuck out their hands in front of me. I gave them a couple of *takas,* about eight cents. Immediately we were surrounded by a clamouring group of 50 beggars. Money was in the air and they wanted in on the largesse. If I gave out any more *takas,* a riot might ensue. The only thing to do was to elbow our way quickly through the crowd. I lost Ray and headed for the rows of stalls that lined the square. After wandering for a while, I returned to the car. A few of the more persistent beggars had followed Ray, who was now sitting behind locked doors. A man looked at me with haunting eyes as I got in the car. Beside Ray's window was an emaciated woman carrying a naked year-old baby on her hip.

Neither of us could look at the faces anymore.

"We've come to help them, but we turn away from them," I grumbled.

"It's a hard lesson to learn that simple charity, without changing the conditions of their life, is hopeless," Ray said.

We continued on to old Dacca. The crush of people in the twisting streets was almost unbearable. When statisticians talk about density, they are referring to human waves, arms pushing against you, dirt underfoot, noise all around. The proprietors of tiny shops, selling jewellery and pots and shirts, sat cross-legged, hawking their goods.

Down by the river, the squatter camps—human jungles—gave off their distinctive odour, a blend of excrement and cooking food. A "home" consisted of a piece of earth less than three metres by two metres covered by a framework of bamboo that was filled in with cardboard and cellophane. In Bangladesh, it rains on and off for eight months of the year. All Bengalis seem to have sad eyes, but the expressions on these people's faces were desperate. All that can be said about a Dacca slum is that it is hell.

Kumu's Date Juice

We went into the countryside to meet Dr. Zafrullah Chowdhury, an internationally known physician who runs the People's Health Centre. With the help of Oxfam and Inter Pares, a small Canadian non-governmental organization specializing in aiding Bangladesh, he was training primary health workers in rural areas. Training paramedics in the field was far more beneficial, he said, than the centralized training the government was offering, since the latter produced skilled people who had nothing in common with village life. We walked through fields for a kilometre or so to one of the villages the clinic served. The huts were made of a mixture of clay and mud, with grass for a roof. There was no electricity. The nearest source of clean water was several hundred metres away. The cooking seemed to be done over small outdoor fires. Long sticks of cow dung were drying. Most of the children were naked. One child particularly caught my eye—a boy of about eight whose face was blackened on the right side. His mother, whose name was Kumu, told us it was a birth injury.

Because we were accompanied by a social worker from the People's Centre, Mrs. Ayesha Aziz, who was a grandmother herself, Kumu invited us into her hut. We sat on plain wooden chairs as her eight children gathered around her. Her husband worked the land as a sharecropper. There was enough food at the present time, she said, although the children's faces and bellies clearly revealed nutritional deficiencies. The date palm juice that flows from trees like maple syrup was very good for them, Kumu said, pointing to the fire outside where a pot of juice was being heated. She did not know how old she was but remembered being married at thirteen. Her eldest child was fifteen. Oh yes, the children go to school, she said. That is very important for them.

We circled through the village compound for a little while, talking to some of the elders sitting in the sun. As we were starting back down the trail, Kumu came running after us, carrying a pitcher. She wanted us to have a glass of the warm date palm juice. It was clear that through the date juice, which was all she had to offer, the woman was extending her friendship to these strange white Westerners who had dropped into her life for a moment. I knew it was a memory I would treasure.

I did not see a better use of Canadian aid than the project known as Proshika (a Bengali acronym for leadership training centre), in which villagers pool their labour in a self-financing co-operative. Pioneered by a CUSO leader, Raymond Courneyer (whose work was expanded by those he taught, the ultimate tribute to an aid officer), the program was based on the premise that the development of a society depends on the development of the men and women in that society. The start-up funds for training provided by Canadians produced far more development than big, glamorous capital projects, such as electronics equipment, generators, planes and trains. A serious effort to help Bangladesh, I concluded, would concentrate not on donating food but on improving the conditions for jute productivity. I went to the largest jute mill in the world, which employed 30,000 workers at that time, and saw the overwhelming importance of jute to the Bangladesh economy. But because of Western nations' discriminating quotas and tariffs that protect synthetic products, Bangladesh has not, even to this day, been able to earn what the jute is worth.

Development is a complex business, I told audiences on a cross-Canada speaking tour when I returned home, prior to writing *What Development Is All About*, which was published in 1979. "Development is top-down and bottom-up; it is aid and debt and high finance; it has economic, social and political and moral dimensions; it is humanitarian and self-interested; it is Kumu, the woman in the Bangladesh village, and it is myself."

A Geopolitical Movement of Historic Proportions

In 1978, Joe Clark named me acting critic for external affairs. Although the press focused on the mysterious meaning of the word *acting* in my job title, I didn't spend any time worrying about that. Instead, I decided to do the best I could to get the Party ready in the foreign policy field for the coming election. I always thought it highly unlikely that a prime minister from Alberta would have his foreign minister from the same province. My friend Duncan Edmonds, who worked for Clark as a foreign policy adviser, suggested that we go around the world together as a sort of trial run for a trip that Clark himself would make later on. Edmonds is a rare combination of academic and political scientist who also has business abilities. He had distinguished himself as a driving force behind the Miles for Millions marches of the 1960s that raised huge sums for people in developing countries, and had been campaign manager for the elder Paul Martin's leadership run in 1968. He later taught at Yale University.

Edmonds raised the necessary funds and we set off on a 30-day trip to Britain, Syria, Jordan, Israel, India, South Korea and Japan. We met Clark in London and arranged for Martin, then Canada's high commissioner to the United Kingdom, to give us a lengthy briefing on not only U.K. and European events but also world affairs. Clark absorbed such briefings well. I felt that, as prime minister, he would uphold a foreign policy built on United Nations values related to peacekeeping, development aid and human rights. To steer him in this direction, I had already introduced him to Robert Muller, assistant secretary-general of the UN. Muller, who was in my view (and that of many people around the world) one of the towering philosophers of the United Nations and revered as a prophet of hope. One Christmas, I gave an autographed copy of his book *New Genesis*, a blueprint for peace, to each of my children with the admonition that here is how the world ought to proceed. I arranged for him to brief Clark on a visit to the UN, much to the consternation of Canadian officials who, putting it delicately, said that Muller was not on their regular list of briefers. I liked the way Clark was opening his mind to viewpoints he had never heard before.

Edmonds and I went on to the Middle East. Crown Prince Hassem of Jordan spent an hour giving us an illustrated lecture on Middle East development plans to produce what he called a "Singapore-based economy." Then we went to the Macka Refugee Camp outside Amman to meet refugees who had never lived anywhere else. In both Jordan and Israel, we met businesspeople, academics and government officials who wanted compromise solutions to the Middle East crisis so they could get on with their lives.

In India, we met with Prime Minister Morarji Desai, who appealed for better understanding of human needs throughout the world. "Look at the baby who is just born," he said, "whether in India, Canada, Latin America or Africa. It is the same baby. It smiles the same, cries the same, responds the same to love. Let us learn from the baby how to live together on this planet." A simple and powerful message—one that dramatizes the fundamental unity of humankind, which I sensed once again on this trip.

My travels reinforced my view that achieving a proper balance between the world's security needs and development needs was now a top priority. The need for Canada to play a stronger role in building bridges between the two was obvious to me. In my report to Clark, I said that Canadian foreign policy in the 1980s should take a wider view of world problems beyond the traditional concerns of diplomacy. A partial list of these problems would include the escalating arms race, nuclear proliferation, food and energy shortages, the widening gap between the developed and developing countries, and worldwide inflation and unemployment.

I told Clark that I had concluded that Canada was not pulling its weight, that the world would welcome a more energetic Canadian role and that a total review of Canadian policy was necessary to meet the coming demands of the 1980s.

> There is a geopolitical movement of historic proportions taking place in the world today. Changes and developments in the world economy, in political institutions, in the environment, and in science and technology have combined to produce a world which, though composed of independent and sovereign states, is becoming more interdependent. The task for Canadian foreign policy in the 1980s is to reconcile independence with interdependence.

Clark's Minority Government

Later that year, Clark set out on his own round-the-world trip to Japan, India, Israel and Jordan. He took Sinclair Stevens with him. For some reason, they travelled west-to-east, which meant that their flight connections were not as good as they would have been had they gone east-to-west. Their luggage got lost; the press, or at least some self-important columnists, took it out on Joe, portraying him as a bumbler. In politics, image always triumphs over substance, as we had seen in the 1974 election campaign when Bob Stanfield's team had tossed a football around for some exercise during a refuelling stop at an airfield. Stanfield joined in and caught nearly all the passes thrown to him. He fumbled the ball once. From an entire roll of film, a Canadian Press editor selected the one picture of Stanfield fumbling; it was this picture that landed on the front pages of newspapers across Canada. The substance of what Stanfield was saying was lost. What people remembered was the image of him dropping the ball. Clark suffered from the same image problem. He may have been stubborn at times, perhaps vain (traits that Diefenbaker and Trudeau carried to extremes), but no one who ever dealt professionally with Clark would call him a bumbler.

When he returned from his trip, Clark asked me to organize a Progressive Conservative foreign policy conference to chart a new course for the 1980s. I enlisted John Holmes, a giant in the foreign policy establishment, as the keynote speaker, along with a number of leading analysts, including Denis Stairs, John Gellner, Margaret Doxey and Bernard Wood. Some 50 specialists with academic, research, business, church and non-governmental organization backgrounds from across Canada gathered at the Guild Inn in Toronto from January 26 to 27, 1979. Thirty-eight diplomats attended as observers, indicating how closely the international community was watching us. I was on crutches, having broken two toes in a fall on my way to watch the swearing in of Ed Schreyer as Governor General. Clark's speech at the conference, a comprehensive overview of the issues, was impressive. He pledged a full foreign policy review when the Progressive Conservatives formed the government.

Clark's fortunes began to rise. The Party smelled victory. Trudeau, now into the fifth year of his mandate, delayed the election as long as possible. Finally, it was called for May 22, 1979. Redistribution had shifted the boundaries of the Edmonton ridings, and I moved to the new constituency of Edmonton South. It comprised a good part of Edmonton-Strathcona, where I had won twice, but I no longer lived in the constituency where I was running. Still, I knew I would have no trouble winning. I polled 25,327 votes to Liberal candidate Alex Fallows's 12,065.

Clark had a rough ride to victory and succeeded in forming only a minority government. The seat breakdown was PCs 136, Liberals 114, NDP 26 and Social Credit 6. Nonetheless, Clark was prime minister. My days in the Opposition were over. Speculation about whether I would get a Cabinet post intensified. I thought I would make myself look foolish if I lobbied Clark only to be turned down (I had not supported him at the leadership convention, after all), so I stayed quiet. Wagner phoned, offering to intercede for me. But I told Claude, "*Que sera sera.*" The day before the Cabinet announcement, Joe phoned me to say that I would not be in the Cabinet. When he told me Flora MacDonald would be foreign minister, there was no need for protracted explanation. I knew instinctively why he had chosen a high-profile woman for the job. I thanked him for his courtesy and said that I would support him.

When I returned to Ottawa, the party whip, perhaps thinking he was handing out a consolation prize, offered me former Prime Minister John Diefenbaker's tiny but strategically located office directly opposite the Leader of the Opposition's Office in the Centre Block. Mr. Diefenbaker took up new prestigious quarters, but died that summer. For years tourists, especially from Saskatchewan, would come to my door and ask to see the office "just to be near Mr. Diefenbaker once more."

What I really wanted was for Clark to appoint me to be Canada's ambassador to the United Nations. I wrote to him suggesting that I resign my seat to free the way for an appointment, but Clark replied that, while he was amenable in principle, the political situation was too precarious to permit such a move.

When Clark got to the second-tier appointments a few weeks later, he offered me my choice of parliamentary secretary to the foreign affairs minister or chairman of the parliamentary committee on foreign affairs. By this time, I had three children in university, and I needed every cent I could find. The parliamentary secretary's job paid; the committee chairmanship didn't. The choice was easy: I became Flora's parliamentary secretary. I don't think she was thrilled about my decision, but because the prime minister also assigned me to be the chief Canadian delegate to the UN General Assembly that fall, she probably realized she would not see much of me. I don't think our relationship was improved when I went over her head to Clark to urge him not to accept her recommendation to fire Allan Gotlieb, then under-secretary of state for foreign affairs. I told Clark that Gotlieb had done a tremendous job and that Flora needed his expert advice. Clark retained him. In November, Clark called me again to say that a minor shift in the Cabinet was coming and I would be brought in. I thanked him and went back to work at the UN.

That summer, Clark journeyed to Africa to attend the Commonwealth Heads of Government Conference in Zambia. He asked me to join his party on the trip, which also included stops in the Cameroon, Kenya and Tanzania. He wanted to see the effects of Canadian aid projects for himself.

Our first stop was in the Cameroon. We landed on a Sunday morning in Yaounde, the capital; a delegation meeting was called for 6 p.m. I spent the afternoon walking through the city and eventually found myself on the outskirts, where I came upon a group of wailing women. As I stood watching, a man walked over to me and introduced himself as the father of a two-year-old boy who had just been buried. I expressed my condolences. The man invited me into his house to meet his wife and children. Although he was a civil servant, the man didn't have much. Finally, I said to him, "How did your little boy die?"

He pointed to his stomach. "Dysentery?" I asked. Yes, he said.

"Where do you get your water?" I asked.

The man led me down the street to a dirty mud creek where children were playing and women were washing clothes.

"You drink that water?" I exclaimed.

"Well," he said, "actually, up on the hill, there's a pipe with clean water. But you have to pay and it only works four hours a day. The kids don't have any money so they drink out of the creek."

When that man told me the story of his child, he spoke for the millions of parents who lose their children every year because of water-borne diseases, even today.

At the delegation meeting that evening, the officials briefed Clark, giving him statistics on the wonderful effects of Canadian aid to Cameroon. Finally, I spoke up. "Prime Minister," I said, "I would like to tell you what I saw today." Clark listened carefully. The officials tried to dismiss my story as mere anecdote.

When we arrived in Tanzania, Clark and I and one or two others got into a very small plane to fly to the highlands to see a wheat project that Canada had financed. When I saw the strip of grass the prime minister of Canada was landing on, I thought that he was carrying his inspection responsibilities a bit far. In retrospect, I would have to say that Clark probably should have stayed home shoring up his government that shaky summer when the polls started to dip. But he was determined to show that he cared about the human condition. Had his government survived, I think he would have grown with the job and become a great prime minister (just as he later became a great foreign minister).

But his hubris gave his political opponents the opportunity to bring him down. He said at the outset that, although possessing only a minority, he would govern as if he had a majority. This was a big mistake. He could easily have persuaded the Social Credit members to support him by offering their leader a Cabinet seat. He could easily have deferred having to fulfill his promise to move the Canadian embassy in Israel from Tel Aviv to Jerusalem by commissioning a lengthy study, during which the poisonous issue would have dropped off the political agenda. He could have deferred the budget vote of December 13, 1979, to the new year, when the Liberals might have lost their ardour to defeat him. But Clark was steadfast. Vacillation, the mother's milk of politics, was foreign to him.

On December 13, I was having lunch at the UN in New York when I received an urgent message from the party whip to get back to Ottawa immediately. The budget vote was called for that evening. We could win or lose by one or two votes. I headed for the airport and noticed the weather worsening. When I got to LaGuardia, sleet was in the air. The Air Canada flight to Montréal (there was no direct flight to Ottawa in those days) was delayed. Finally, the plane door closed. The pilot announced we were 25th in line for takeoff. I started to sweat. When the wheels finally went up, I calculated that we would land in Montréal ten minutes after the plane to Ottawa departed. I couldn't believe what was happening to me. The Clark government would go down by one vote—and Doug Roche would be blamed.

I wrote a note to the captain. "Dear Captain," I said, "I want you to know that I don't make a practice of talking to captains in flight, but I desperately need your help." Could he do something to get me on that Ottawa plane? A few minutes later, the captain came back to see me. "We're going to help you," he said.

When the plane landed, an RCMP officer rushed into the plane, calling my name. "Come with me," he said. He led me down the steps into an RCMP car, its red roof light whirling. We drove across the tarmac and I climbed the stairs of the Ottawa plane. "We'll send your luggage later!" the officer shouted as the plane door closed.

"We're going down," Stan Schellenberger, my seatmate, told me when I entered the Commons 30 minutes before the vote. "What do you mean, we're going down?" I said. "Don't we have the troops?" "No," he said, and he was right.

Every last Liberal and NDP member was present. The vote was 139 to 133 against the budget. The Clark government was over.

8

The Politics of Human Survival

The morning after the budget defeat, the House of Commons assembled to hear Clark announce that he had obtained the writ for an election from the Governor General. With the members dispersing, I spent some time on the floor talking to David MacDonald, one of the few MPs who seemed to understand me.

"I don't want to run, David," I said. "I'm fed up with this place."

"Stay," he said. "You'll undoubtedly go into the Cabinet. Besides, the Party really needs you. You lift us up."

We argued back and forth for fifteen minutes. I wanted to do something more with my life than go back into Opposition, which was where I feared we were heading. Still unsettled, I went back to my office. The Edmonton media were on the phone asking whether I would run. When I said I was still thinking about it, a headline appeared the next day saying that I was doubtful about staying in politics. I told Eva I would have to make up my mind fast or my right-wing opponents would brush me aside. Both Eva and I settled on the solution: one more time.

Gary Campbell, my constituency president, called a meeting of the executive for December 17. No one else had stepped forward to run and the executive thought the nomination would be by acclamation. Everyone was irritated that this political event was forced on us during the Christmas season, especially Campbell and I, who had both planned holidays. I was leaving with the family the afternoon of December 27 for five days in Jasper. The idea arose spontaneously that we would have the nomination at 8 a.m. that day in a downtown hotel. Then we could all go on our way. A notice went into the paper on December 18, providing the minimum ten days' notice the constituency constitution required. We didn't care that Christmas and a weekend fell within that ten-day period.

Only after the announcement did Elmer Knutson, a car dealer with extreme right-wing views, step forward to challenge me. He did not dispute the timing of the meeting, so it went ahead. A few days later, I realized an ambush was coming when I learned that Knutson was organizing every person he could find who thought that I was a "foreign aid do-gooder" who didn't care about the people of Edmonton. My supporters didn't believe the challenge was serious and organized listlessly. Darryl Smith, my campaign manager, told me not to worry; Knutson was just an irritant. On the appointed morning, 380 people showed up, and I won by only 50 votes. I thanked everyone and went skiing.

When I returned in early January, a full-blown controversy was raging. Knutson had challenged the legality of my win, protesting especially the early morning hour of the nomination meeting. He wanted a new meeting. Party executives outside my riding obliged him by conducting an investigation and declared the nomination valid. One of my supporters expressed regret that there would not be a heavily publicized new contest between Knutson and me because "Doug would have knocked him off four to one."

When the election was held on February 18, 1980, I had 14,000 more votes than the Liberal candidate, and 61 per cent of the popular vote, the same result as in 1979. Clark was not so fortunate. Trudeau had come out of retirement and, with new energy, swept to a majority government. He had only two seats west of Winnipeg, a very unhealthy situation for the country. I am told that Clark was in tears when his Cabinet gave him a standing ovation at their final meeting.

Not Serene but Calm

By this time I was 50. Because my father had died of cancer of the bowel, my doctor, watching me closely, decided I should have a colonoscopy. When I awoke from the anesthetic, a nurse handed me a note left by the doctor who had done the examination: "No abnormalities were found." It was at that moment that I suddenly realized, all my political difficulties notwithstanding, how much I was enjoying this time of my life. I felt so good that I wrote an article, "Free at Last at 50," for *Maclean's*. I increasingly felt a sense of wholeness, as if all the parts of my life—physical, spiritual, emotional—were fusing together. This recognition of wholeness was giving me a fresh sense of peace with myself and self-confidence to cope with ongoing frustrations. "If I have not yet reached a stage of serenity, I am at least calm in the storm," I wrote. I mentioned that Eva and I had found a new way to celebrate our liberation: going to the movies on Fridays at four o'clock. "That may not sound very exciting," I said. "But one of the pleasures of middle age is that you don't have to do wild things to enjoy yourself."

> When I see so many marriages breaking up, even among couples our age, it makes me especially grateful that my wife and I have survived together. Our own relationship has re-bloomed. We find we want to spend more time together, precisely when it is possible to do so. The first 25 years of our married life were full of babies and bills, teen-agers and tensions. There was time for fun, too, of course, but most of all it was a period of great responsibility to kids who were almost entirely dependent on us.

Our 25th wedding anniversary began with our daugher Evita "booking" Eva and me months in advance. The whole family gathered at St. Joseph's Hospital, where the kids had arranged a mass so that Mickey, then 22, could be present. An organist and a cellist played the wedding march and Eva and I stood before the hospital chaplain to renew our marriage vows. I kept thinking, "I know a lot more now about what is involved in this promise than I did 25 years ago," but I made it again eagerly. When I turned around and looked at the kids, their eyes were pretty misty.

The mass over, we took Mickey outside to the garden for family photos—and a lot of reminiscing. We left Mickey in peace and tranquillity and returned home for a family barbecue. No guests. Just us, crazy and uninhibited as we were when no one else was around. Then, of course, we had a round of family movies, with everyone clamouring to have their favourite shown.

Later, Evita and Francis drove Eva and me to a downtown hotel (it was called "rest and seclusion" on the schedule), where we found roses and a bottle of champagne in our swanky room.

We had strict instructions: be ready for the pickup at 7:30 p.m. the next evening—and be dressed for a party. When the car arrived for us as promised, it sported an amusing sign: "Just Married—25 Years." We arrived triumphantly home to find a huge crowd on the lawn.

I looked at the faces gathered—friends of Eva's and mine from so many aspects of our lives—all brought together by our kids. They had an accordion player outside, a pianist inside, a waiter and great strings of lights for a marvellous party atmosphere. Eva's father had made it all the way from Ottawa, despite an airline strike.

The kids got Frank McMillan to act as master of ceremonies; he read telegrams and messages from our friends throughout Canada and the U.S., which the kids had also arranged. I realized that if I tried to make a speech about how I felt, I would never be able to finish. Besides, when I looked into the faces of the guests, I knew that the statement I would have made about marriage, family, love, and solidarity had already been brilliantly expressed.

I said simply to the kids, "What you have done for Eva and me, especially in our private family celebration yesterday, will live in our hearts forever." Eva stole the show by singing her own rendition of "You'd Be Surprised," which brought gales of laughter.

When the last guests had left, we gathered in the dining room. "You know," I said, "Joe Clark's office asked me to go to Rome for the installation of Pope John Paul II. I would have had to leave right now to get there in time, so I said no, I want to stay with the family a little while yet."

We had all grown accustomed to my life involving so much absence from home. But that didn't make it easier, particularly on the two youngest, Mary Anne and Tricia, who legitimately wanted more time with their father. My work definitely had a price, paid not only by me but by the children. Gradually, they started moving out of the nest. Evita was already at the University of Ottawa on a scholarship, and she stayed in Ottawa to do her law studies and begin her legal career, specializing in family mediation. Francis, an entrepreneur, found his way to Harvard, where he spent four years before doing a combined law and MBA program at McGill, getting a master's in law at Laval, then setting up his own financial securities business. Mary Anne took time off after high school, but returned to attend the University of Alberta and later obtained a master's degree in adult education from the University of Toronto; she is now working in the not-for-profit sector. Tricia attended the University of British Columbia and went overseas for Canadian Crossroads International to work in community development in Africa before obtaining a master's degree in human rights at McGill. All of them are fascinating individuals; I leave it to them to tell their own stories.

Abortion: The Most Difficult Issue

I am sure that my strong opposition to abortion is rooted in my experiences with Mickey. Though she could not speak, I learned from her a meaning of life that's hard to get from textbooks.

No issue proved so difficult for me to handle in my entire career in Parliament as abortion. It brought together my faith, my powers of analysis, however limited, my sense of the common good of society and my belief that a Member of Parliament should never vote against his or her conscience.

The idea that abortion is exclusively a religious issue, let alone a Catholic one, is a myth. Whatever one's religious convictions, I believe the arguments against abortion as public policy can be cogently stated without resorting to religion. I'm not separating myself from religion here; of course, abortion is a religious issue. But it is much more than that. It is a human rights issue. In 1948, the World Health Organization urged respect for human life "from the moment of conception on." In 1959, the UN adopted the Declaration of the Rights of the Child, which includes this preamble: "Whereas the child, by reason of his physical and mental immaturity needs special safeguards and care, including appropriate legal protection, *before as well as after birth*...." The unborn child has a civil right to life.

Supporters of abortion often argue that the baby in the womb is not a human but merely a piece of tissue attached to the mother. If there were any scientific doubt of the humanity of the unborn— which there is not—surely the burden of proof would rest with those who would deny it. Even if there were doubt, it would have to be acknowledged that the wisest, most prudent policy would be to give the benefit of the doubt to those whose humanity is questioned.

In fact, the development of the individual in the womb is extremely rapid. The heart begins beating within 21 days of conception; blood vessels and circulating blood, a backbone, skeletal system and brainwaves are traceable at 43 days; then over the next few weeks rudimentary organs—liver, kidneys—and digestive tract, arms and legs, fingers and toes, eyes, ears and a mouth are formed. At the very moment of fertilization all the unique genetic characteristics are determined: eye, skin and hair colouring, height and bone structure, intellectual potential and inherited emotional makeup. From the time of conception 46 chromosomes are present, 23 from each parent. This is the chromosomal development defined by biologists as that of a normal human being. This small individual requires only nutrition and normal conditions in order to develop in the full pattern of human life.

When I settled into Parliament, I noticed that the number of abortions in Canada was climbing rapidly, from 11,152 in 1970 to 48,136 in 1974. The Criminal Code had been amended in 1969 to permit an accredited hospital therapeutic abortion committee to allow an abortion when the continuation of a woman's pregnancy "would be likely to endanger her life or health." But *health* was never defined. As editor of the *Western Catholic Reporter* at the time, I wrote that the new law was so loosely written that it would open the door to abortion on demand. But in the climate of 1969, a time of questioning of old values, the abortion section of the omnibus bill of which it was part passed easily. It was ludicrous to suggest that the state of health of pregnant women in Canada was five times worse in 1974 than in 1970. Yet there were nearly five times as many abortions. It was straining credulity to suggest that it was more dangerous to be pregnant in the three richest provinces of British Columbia, Ontario and Alberta, where the abortion rates were far higher than in any other province. It was becoming clear that many abortion committees interpreted an unwanted pregnancy as being a threat to health.

The Petition of One Million

Because I was becoming increasingly concerned that Canada was heading for abortion on demand, I gave my support in 1973 to the newly formed Alliance for Life, a citizens' movement, to protest the abortion escalation. The group presented to the government an anti-abortion petition bearing 350,000 signatures. A march on Parliament Hill was organized and I was invited to join the leaders.

On a bitterly cold November Saturday afternoon, 3,500 men and women carrying banners and white flowers marched through the streets and onto the Hill, where flowers were placed on the steps of Parliament in memory of the aborted. The occasion brought out a combative speech from me. "In fighting for the rights of the unborn," I said, "we are fighting for the rights of every person whose life might at some time be taken unjustly—the aged, the defective, the infirm." Then I threw out a challenge: "Go back to your homes across Canada and get one million signatures on another petition. Then let the government dare to say that Canadians want abortion on demand."

Alliance for Life took up the challenge. Two weeks later, I went to Toronto for a press conference to launch the drive. A rally was held in Edmonton, where I told the audience that Canadians must be told that abortion had become a social rather than a medical problem. "In fact," I said, "I now believe abortion to be the most alarming social problem in Canada today."

Several constituents wrote letters to me—and the local paper—criticizing my "distorted" sense of social values. One of my supporters insisted that "abortion is no more an issue for legislation than the religion which I choose to adopt." She was the mother of four children and said she would not hesitate to seek an abortion if she desired one: "I believe that I have the legal right to hold and to practice my opinion without interference from the government in this matter." There was, of course, plenty of mail supporting my position.

The development of the Petition of One Million proved to be a gigantic logistical job for a volunteer organization, but over the months about 90 anti-abortion groups sprang up across the country. On May 29, 1975, some 500 of their leaders converged on Parliament Hill with 35 packing cases containing a petition with 1,027,425 signatures. The petition said simply, "Over one million Canadians call upon Parliament to enact legislation providing for the child conceived but not yet born the same protection as is provided for any other person, and also urge Parliament to show leadership in fostering a life-sustaining society."

Altogether a crowd of 3,000 persons assembled beneath the Peace Tower to demonstrate their concern. Ten members of Parliament, one from each province, formally received the petition. The packing cases were left in the lobby as the House opened at 2 o'clock with a barrage of questions to Justice Minister Otto Lang. Robert Stanfield asked whether any proposed abortion inquiry would deal with the quality of the current legislation or merely its administration. All Lang would say was that the issue would be studied "with great thoroughness."

The pro-life delegates had jammed the galleries. I made an oblique reference to them as I rose to put my question: "My supplementary arises from the fact that the largest petition ever brought into Parliament was presented today signed by one million Canadians from the Atlantic to the Pacific, and asking for much faster action than the Minister of Justice seems to imply will be forthcoming." At this point the galleries applauded loudly, which is not allowed, joining the desk-pounding by MPs, who revealed a pro-life mood in the House as I had never before seen it. I continued, "I should like to ask the Minister, as he considers what kind of examination this question will be given and when, whether he would specifically consider the empowering of a committee to be set up to subpoena the records of hospital abortion committees to see whether cases are found in which abortions were permitted when the life or health of the mother was not in danger and if so, whether charges will be laid and by whom?"

"Mr. Speaker," Lang responded, "the power to examine how hospital committees operate was in fact put into the Criminal Code and entrusted to the hands of the provincial ministers of health in the various provinces. I am impressed that many persons who appear to applaud the last question, and might applaud any other question if they thought it appropriate to do so on a given day, apparently have not been pressing their provincial colleagues to take some action in this regard."

This was merely a dodge: blame the provinces. Nothing was done. The number of abortions grew to 65,000 per year.

Why I Opposed the Charter

In 1981, Pierre Trudeau, back in office with a comfortable majority, devoted himself to patriating the Constitution of Canada and drafting the Charter of Rights and Freedoms. In 1960, Diefenbaker had enacted the Canadian Bill of Rights, but because it was only a federal statute, as distinct from a constitutional document, it was easily amendable and had no application to provincial laws. Trudeau was determined to entrench the rights and freedoms of Canadians in the

Constitution so that it would flow from the Universal Declaration of Human Rights. The role of the judiciary in interpreting constitutional matters was greatly expanded. A huge battle to patriate Canada's Constitution from Britain got under way.

When I looked at the proposed Charter in terms of the abortion issue, I grew very concerned. Section 7 said, "Everyone has the right to life, liberty and security of the person and the right not to be deprived thereof except in accordance with the principles of fundamental justice." Section 15 said, "Every individual is equal before and under the law and has the right to the equal protection and equal benefit of the law without discrimination and, in particular, without discrimination based on race, national or ethnic origin, colour, religion, sex, age or mental and physical disability." I got up in Parliament and asked whether the words *everyone* (section 7) and *every individual* (section 15) would apply to the unborn child. The government responded that it did not intend the Charter to affect the abortion debate. In other words, the Charter would be neutral on the abortion question.

I then argued in a speech early in the Constitution debate that, since the courts had ruled that birth is the point at which the fetus becomes a person with full and independent rights, the fetus would not be protected under the Charter. The only rights and freedoms that would exist in Canada after the Charter became law would be those currently in existence. In effect, the government would be entrenching abortion. Moreover, I foresaw that section 251 of the Criminal Code, which restricted abortion to cases in which the life or health of the mother was threatened, would be attacked by pro-abortion groups as contravening a woman's right not to be discriminated against under the Charter. If the Supreme Court threw out section 251 because the Charter trumped it, we would then become a society of open abortion.

The issue became a focal point of hearings on the Constitution, with many arguing that unborn children are a link in the chain of life, so that their very weakness required special protection under section 7. But the opposite view, that the right to life of the fetus should not become an entrenched right in the Constitution, was vigorously promoted. The government held firm, stating again and again that the Charter's silence on the issue would not in any way alter the right of Parliament to legislate on abortion.

Joe Clark was determined that the Progressive Conservative caucus would support the Charter of Rights and Freedoms. How could the Party face the electorate otherwise? I argued vociferously in caucus that the Charter would lead to abortion on demand. I knew I had some support but not enough for a successful challenge. Clark made his own mark on the Constitution by introducing an amendment that locked in male and female equality in such a way that it could not be overridden by Parliament. I sent him a letter on November 24, 1981, arguing that this amendment, otherwise welcome, would further weaken the unborn child's right to life. Clark responded that same day, rejecting my legal reasoning. He left no doubt that he expected me to support his amendment: "I hope you will be able to vote for the amendment your Leader has introduced."

My dilemma on this point was resolved when the government suddenly accepted Clark's amendment without a vote. But he left the door open for an amendment I suggested: "Nothing in this Charter affects the authority of Parliament to legislate in respect of abortion." Caucus was by now meeting every day, and tensions, always high, were about to burst. Clark said the Party would introduce my amendment. To show my good faith with the Party, I then said I would vote for the Constitution if the amendment carried. That compromise was as far as I could go.

David Crombie, the former Mayor of Toronto and a prestigious figure in the Party, introduced the amendment. He said, "I ask the government to consider my motion. It is a simple one. It allows those who want to support this Charter of Rights and Freedoms to be able to support it once they have been assured that the Parliament of Canada, not the courts alone, will deal with the question of abortion." Prime Minister Trudeau rejected Crombie's amendment on the grounds that it was redundant and also that the approval of nine premiers would be required. They would consider further changes only after patriation. The amendment lost 129 to 61. I considered that the government's rejection invalidated its own claim that the Charter was neutral on abortion.

A few days later, on December 2, the fateful vote came. I worried all weekend. To oppose the Charter of Rights and Freedoms seemed inimical to what I stood for in politics. Eva told me to do what I thought was right. I went back to the final caucus and said

I would vote no. Clark was very unhappy but did not remonstrate with me. Sitting in my seat in the House waiting for the vote to be called, Erik Nielsen, Clark's deputy, and Jake Epp badgered me. I was accused of "betraying" the Party. I voted no. The vote was 246 to 24. Several other Conservatives and Liberals voted no on the abortion issue. Others voted no (as did my friend Senator Lowell Murray, one of Clark's closest advisers, when the issue came to the Senate) on the grounds that Quebec, which had dropped out of the negotiations because of Trudeau's heavy hand, was excluded from the great act of patriation. I issued an immediate statement to my constituents saying that a Constitution to which Quebec had not given its agreement opened the door wider to Quebec separation and severely threatened national unity. But my principal objection, I said, was that it opened the door to abortion on demand. "Throughout my parliamentary career," I wrote, "I have supported the rights of women to full and equal opportunity. I will continue to support women's rights. But we dare not extend those rights at the expense of the unborn, who need only time to become one with us."

The next day I invited Crombie to my office. I was worried that some members thought that simply introducing the amendment on abortion was sufficient to secure my vote. "Did I make it clear that the amendment would have to pass before I could vote for the Charter?" I asked Crombie. He said he had understood me perfectly.

Seven years later, on January 28, 1988, the Supreme Court of Canada, in a landmark decision, declared Canada's abortion law unconstitutional in its entirety, and in breach of Canada's Charter of Rights and Freedoms. Forcing a woman to carry a fetus to term unless she meets certain criteria unrelated to her own priorities and aspirations breaches a woman's right to security of the person guaranteed under the Charter, the Court ruled. A justice stated, "The decision whether or not to terminate a pregnancy is essentially a moral decision and in a free and democratic society, the conscience of the individual must be paramount to that of the state." Section 251 of the Criminal Code was gone; Henry Morgentaler, the physician who made a crusade out of performing and promoting abortions, had won. The Supreme Court did, however, encourage the government to introduce a new and improved abortion law.

The following year, the Conservative government put forth a bill threatening doctors with a two-year jail term if they approved an abortion when the woman's health was not in danger. The bill, inferior as it was, was passed in the House of Commons but was defeated in the Senate on a tie vote. After this failure, the government gave up on legislating abortion entirely. Canada now has no abortion law. By 2007, the number of abortions in Canada had grown to 110,000 each year, with a ratio of about 30 abortions to every 100 live births. That is a matter of conscience.

Canada's Stake in North-South Relations

With the 1980s under way, development issues started to at least get onto the world stage. Though the Cold War between East and West was about to turn much colder, a North-South dialogue was beginning, and I entered a short-lived period of satisfaction with my parliamentary life.

A UN high-level international commission led by Willy Brandt, former chancellor of the Federal Republic of Germany and a Nobel Peace Prize laureate, published a report on international development that linked North-South issues to the East-West conflict. Reshaping worldwide North-South relations, the commission said, was crucial to the future of humankind and equal in importance to stopping the arms race. This would be "the greatest challenge to mankind for the remainder of this century." The report, *North-South: A Programme for Survival*, stimulated an unprecedented North-South summit of 22 world leaders, co-chaired by President Lopez Portillo of Mexico and Prime Minister Trudeau, who met in Cancun, Mexico, in 1981. Although the summit produced a bland roster of good intentions, its chief value was in putting world poverty on the international political agenda.

Insisting that the world faced "much greater dangers" than at any time since the Second World War, Brandt's commission called for a fundamental change in relations between North and South as well as between East and West. The world is a unity, the commission said, and we must begin to act as fellow members who depend on one another. To promote genuine development and self-sustaining growth, the commission set out a program of priorities: a major initiative in favour of the poverty belts of Africa and Asia; measures for international food security; a fund to stabilize primary commodity exports; reversal of the trend of protecting Northern industries against competition from the Third World; improved international investment regulation to enable developing countries to benefit from the resources of transnational corporations; reform of the monetary system to related Special Drawing Rights to help meet the financial needs of the South; broadening of the international financial structure, and creation of a world development fund that would eventually lead to a system of international taxation. Brandt's commission also linked the high spending on arms with the low spending on measures to end hunger and ill health in the Third World.

When Brandt came to Ottawa, I brought him to a breakfast with the Progressive Conservative foreign affairs committee. Clark's attendance showed his continuing interest in the subject. As vice-chairman of the Parliamentary Task Force on North-South Relations, I wanted the Party's support for the recommendations we were about to make, which (except for international taxation) largely supported Brandt. Herb Breau, a Liberal MP from New Brunswick, chaired the task force, and my old friend Bob Miller from the Library of Parliament was the researcher. Together, we came up with 38 recommendations. I considered the most important one to be our proposal that Canada allocate one per cent of its Official Development Assistance to encourage awareness and involvement of Canadians in North-South concerns. Many non-governmental organizations were starting to get involved in development education and needed financial support.

In 1971, a commission headed by Canada's Lester Pearson had established an Official Development Assistance target of 0.7 per cent of the gross national product of the developed countries, but Canada was mired at 0.43 per cent. We charted a growth plan for Canada that would take that figure to 0.57 per cent by 1985 and 0.7 per cent by 1990. Spending a small fraction of this money to educate Canadians and maintain political support for Canada's active involvement in North-South issues seemed to us a good investment. We wanted aid to be concentrated on the poorest countries, and the government to play a more active role in resolving the structural crises of trade, investment, finance and energy. It was, I argued, good economics and good ethics at the same time.

I prepared a special report for the caucus, suggesting that Canada play a bridge-building role between North and South. Such a policy would flow from our recognition that Canada's strategic location and level of industrialization made us a highly developed nation, yet our natural resource and trading patterns are closer to those of the developing countries. Precisely because we are not a major power, I argued, we had a stake in ensuring international co-operation and could help bring North and South together by focusing on mutual interests. "To play a bridging role, we would have to strengthen Canada's credibility by taking steps towards sensible arrangements in North–South trade and monetary relations."

I chided Trudeau a few times in Question Period about why the government wasn't doing more, but he would usually obliquely refer to needing more support: from whom—his own party, the Opposition or the officials—was never made clear. The government rhetoric was always better than the action, but I would be hard-pressed to say that the Progessive Conservatives would have done any better. There was a constant refrain that we have to take care of Canadians first; since Canadians vote in our elections and foreigners don't, most of the political establishment stays focused on domestic issues.

But my political philosophy was turning global. I became preoccupied with a central fact of modern life: we were entering a totally new period of our planet's history. For the first time the opportunity existed to bring about a better life with larger freedom for the world's people. Yet the situation was tragically ironic: never before had we had the potential to free the world from the threats of hunger and war, but never was the world so hungry and the threat of war more monstrous. Yet we went on, seeking our self-interest, oblivious to the depths of the danger or the magnificence of the challenge. I found the words of the poet T. S. Eliot stunningly accurate: "*Here were decent godless people. Their only monument the asphalt road. And a thousand lost golf balls.*"

The foreign policy I sought would have as its goal the development of a world community in which diverse peoples live in peace, justice and freedom. Such a foreign policy could be created through the adoption of a public philosophy for the global community. We would have to drive straight to the central point: human beings must be seen as total beings, able to fulfill ourselves and to act with the full capacity of the qualities deposited in us by God. A public philosophy, underscoring foreign policy, would have to insist that every person, everywhere, has the right to life, to bodily integrity, to food, shelter, medical care and employment, and that every person has the right to freedom in searching for truth, the right to a basic education, and the right to be informed truthfully about public events.

From Development to Disarmament

I found parliamentary life in Ottawa to be not very conducive to the expression of such thoughts, so I looked elsewhere for the opportunity to do so. I wrote and gave speeches, as an outlet for my frustration as an Opposition backbencher.

Then I received an invitation that was to shift the focus of my entire public career. The Canadian Association of the Club of Rome invited me to give a paper, "Development in the Year 2000," at a conference to be held in Ottawa in 1982.

The Club of Rome, a global think tank, came to prominence with its report *Limits to Growth*, published in 1972. The report predicted that economic growth could not continue indefinitely because of the limited amount of natural resources, particularly oil. Continuing research showed that, with governmental action, economic and environmental catastrophes were preventable. I was a member of a similar organization, the North-South Roundtable, which concentrated on five priority areas for development: food, energy, technology, transfer of resources and the elimination of absolute poverty. Two of this group's leaders—Barbara Ward, the British economist and member of the Pontifical Commission for Justice and Peace, and Mahbub ul Haq, a World Bank adviser and later the first editor of the UN's *Human Development Report*—influenced me deeply.

As I got to know Barbara, who was a well-known author and one of the editors of the *Economist*, I admired the way she introduced a spiritual perspective into development issues. In one of her essays, she wrote, "On the one hand, we are faced with the stewardship of this beautiful, subtle, incredibly delicate, fragile planet. On the other, we confront the destiny of our fellow man, our brothers. How can we say that we are followers of Christ if this dual responsibility does not seem to us the essence and heart of our religion?" Mahbub, gentle and unassuming, was one of the giants at the UN. I visited him often.

I found both Barbara and Mahbub, who were both concerned with the state of the planet, much more interesting and visionary than the politicians I dealt with on a daily basis.

I brought the North–South Roundtable to Ottawa for a meeting and tried to get at least a few of my political colleagues to attend. I wanted them to hear that the ideas for a world with less poverty, less inequality, greater justice, greater respect for human rights and more equitable international relations had a sound basis. Though the New International Economic Order of the 1970s had been scuppered, the vision for a world of justice and greater humanity was still alive.

The Club of Rome's assignment challenged me. The Year 2000, on which my paper was to focus, was far in the future. How did I know what would happen by then? I decided to take a couple of months to research the subject as best I could. The more I pored over statistics and reports, the more I found the world painfully off balance: opulently rich in the forces of death, yet poor in providing for the needs of human lives. Behind the statistical shadows of income disparities, inflation and retarded growth were hundreds of millions of individuals trapped by shocking neglect. They suffered from hunger, illiteracy, illness and desperate poverty. I found this social deficit a threat to world security because the festering problems, neglected in favour of armed might, promised rising public anger and social upheaval.

No indicator more graphically showed the incredible destructive power loose in the world than the existence of 50,000 nuclear weapons, whose combined power was one million times greater than the Hiroshima bomb. At least five countries then possessed nuclear weapons; the capability of producing a rudimentary nuclear force was within the reach of 20 to 25 more countries. The nuclear spotlight was on Europe, where 572 NATO Pershing II and ground-launched Cruise missiles were to be deployed to offset 250 new Soviet SS-20 missiles and hundreds of older SS-4s and SS-5s currently aimed at western Europe. The "unthinkable" nuclear war had given way to "limited" options. I wrote:

> At this conference we are concerned with formulating the proper policies for Canada in the year 2000. But a higher and more urgent priority now demands the attention of everyone in the development field: ensuring global survival to reach 2000. The world has become such a dangerous place that *peace-making*

must become the foremost consideration of Canadian foreign policy.

I have come to the conclusion that the breakthrough development advocates seek in North-South economic and social progress will not come while East-West political and military tensions are so high. The power of war-making is clearly triumphing over the power of peace-making. It will little avail us to design the orderliness of the post-2000 era if we cannot first establish the survivability of world society to that beckoning milestone. For me, survivability has become the key to a future of economic and social justice. Development demands disarmament.

The paper, which was 29 pages, ran through a long list of actions Canada should take in both the development and disarmament fields. I called for the Canadian government to cut defence spending by 10 per cent and apply the savings to the United Nations Development Programme. "Would that not be a dramatic signal to the world that a turnaround in priorities can at least be started?" I also asked that Canada support the "freeze" campaign: a freeze on the testing, production and deployment of nuclear weapons and their carriers by the Soviet Union and the United States.

Nuclear Freeze and a Minority Report

The UN's Second Special Session on Disarmament, scheduled for June 7–July 10, 1982, was just around the corner. I urged the government to mandate Parliament's Standing Committee on External Affairs and National Defence to do a special study on security and disarmament to come up with proposals for action by the Canadian government. Many witnesses were called; there was strong support for Canada to support the 188 U.S. Congressmen who had signed a House-Senate Joint Resolution calling on the U.S. and the Soviet Union to achieve a nuclear freeze, to be followed by reductions in nuclear warheads. The U.S. administration (Ronald Reagan was in the early years of his presidency) was adamantly opposed to a freeze. The hawks who dominated the parliamentary committee were in complete support of the U.S. My own party would have no part of the freeze. Battles in the committee, points of order and parliamentary manoeuvering went on for days. It was clear that the final report would be full of bromides and that no honest evaluation of the merits of stopping the arms race was being made. I had had enough. But I wasn't alone. Five other MPs on the committee—my Conservative colleague Walter McLean; Paul McRae, a Liberal; and three NDP members, Pauline Jewett, Bob Ogle and Terry Sargeant—were also chagrined. I suggested a minority report; the others said yes, and I was commissioned to draft it for all of us to sign.

Our report, tracing the history of the conventional and nuclear arms races, pointed to the 7,770 nuclear warheads in strategic missiles, 6,340 nuclear warheads in strategic submarines, 2,790 nuclear weapons in strategic bombers and another 37,000 tactical nuclear weapons. "The development and deployment of still more fire power never ceases," the report stated.

Next, it outlined the horrors awaiting humankind in a nuclear exchange that had been detailed by the International Physicians for the Prevention of Nuclear War (an organization that was to win the 1985 Nobel Peace Prize): "Even a single one-megaton nuclear bomb explosion [80 times more powerful than the explosion of the bomb dropped on Hiroshima] over an urban area would cause death and injury to people on a scale unprecedented in the history of mankind and would present any remaining medical services with insoluble problems." People not immediately burned to death, blown apart or asphyxiated in shelters would find themselves in a nightmare world, populated by the dying, dead and insane. Food, crops and land would be contaminated, water undrinkable. The survivors would envy the dead. In an all-out attack, who would survive, as radiation swept across the oceans and into the atmosphere, depleting the ozone layer and releasing lethal ultraviolet rays? The collapse of the ecosystem would leave a global wasteland.

We recommended that Canada support the global nuclear freeze campaign, deny the U.S. permission to test the new Cruise missile system in Canada, press all nuclear powers to pledge never to be the first to use nuclear weapons, and devote one tenth of one per cent ($7 million) of its defence budget to disarmament efforts.

The report was, of course, hailed by disarmament groups across the country and denounced by U.S. supporters in Parliament, who insisted it had absolutely no status. I paid little attention to the attempts to discredit me.

Still, External Affairs Minister Mark MacGuigan named me a consultant to the Canadian delegation to the UN Special Session on Disarmament. I wrote a lengthy report, which McGuigan, in his memoirs, *An Inside Look at External Affairs During the Trudeau Years*, said "was better than anything produced by the department." MacGuigan went on, "It thus came as no surprise to me when Roche was appointed as Ambassador for Disarmament after the change of government in 1984."

The UN Special Session was road-blocked in trying to formulate a time-bound comprehensive program of disarmament by the intractability of the two superpowers of the day, the U.S. and the Soviet Union. It could do nothing but reaffirm the final document of the First Special Session on Disarmament in 1978. That document had acquired the status of "the Bible" on nuclear disarmament because it said, "Removing the threat of world war—a nuclear war—is the most acute and urgent task of the present day. Mankind is confronted with a choice: we must halt the arms race and proceed to disarmament or face annihilation."

Though the Second Special Session failed, it achieved folklore status when one million people marched past the United Nations Building, through the streets of Manhattan and into Central Park for the largest political demonstration in U.S. history. A petition for disarmament signed by 90 million people in nine countries was presented to UN Secretary-General Javier Perez de Cuellar. Ten thousand people crowded into the Cathedral of St. John the Divine, where prayers were offered in several languages for an end to the arms race. Seventeen hundred protestors, practising civil disobedience, blockaded the entrances to the British, French, Chinese, Russian and U.S. missions to the UN, and many were arrested. At the final non-governmental organization briefing, Inga Thorsson, the Swedish diplomat who had pioneered studies in the relationship between disarmament and development, urged expanded efforts to develop a worldwide international disarmament community "to continue our efforts until we succeed."

I took her seriously.

Rage was building inside me. World politics had become so distorted, anyone who advanced the cause of development and disarmament, the two great building blocks of the structure of peace, was seen as a radical. Anyone who pleaded for sanity in the use of the world's resources to build up humanity rather than the arsenals of war was considered idealistic. Anyone who urged rational positions in public policy was a voice crying in the wilderness of cynicism.

We weren't asking for unilateral disarmament but rather mutual, balanced and verifiable disarmament by first of all freezing further weapons growth. What nation would now take a step for disarmament and back up its words with deeds? "People have begun to march," I wrote, "and if that is what it takes to move governments, then let the marches continue to the point where the nuclear arms race is universally condemned as a crime against God and man himself."

9

Closing One Door
and Opening Another

"God never closes one door but he opens another," I can remember my mother telling me all the years I was growing up. Her words never proved more accurate than in the unfolding of my life following the 1980 election, when the Progressive Conservatives were unceremoniously shunted back into the Opposition.

The Liberal MP Mark MacGuigan, one of my close friends in Parliament, was surprised to find himself foreign minister in the renewed Trudeau cabinet. Two years earlier, while he and David MacDonald, who had urged me to stay in Parliament, were working with a few parliamentarians in half a dozen countries loosely affiliated through the World Association of World Federalists, they had drafted articles of incorporation for a new international organization, Parliamentarians for World Order. Since MacGuigan was now a minister and MacDonald had been defeated in the election, MacGuigan asked me to develop the fledgling organization. I began contacting key members, called a meeting for December 1980 in London, set out a program of action and was elected international chairman. Walter McLean, a Presbyterian minister with African development experience who had been elected to Parliament in 1979, came with me to the London meeting and was elected treasurer. He and I thus began searing experiences with the caucus that bonded our friendship. Like Frank McMillan at an earlier stage, Walter entered my life and stayed there through all the political ups and downs.

Surveying the bits and pieces of the organization, we found we had, on paper at least, 550 members in seventeen parliaments. Because Parliamentarians for World Order needed a presence at the United Nations, I enlisted the support of Brad Morse, a former American congressman who was then head of the UN Development Programme. He gave us an office around the corner from the UN Secretariat. MacGuigan helped to obtain some funding from the Canadian Parliament. I took Nick Dunlop, secretary-general of Parliamentarians for World Order, with me to see UN Secretary-General Kurt Waldheim to explain our plans. It was the first time I had been in the Secretary-General's mahogany-walled office, with its famous view from the 38th floor. I told Waldheim that I hoped I was bringing some help, not another problem, as I outlined our organization's plans to develop a UN-centred organization. The Secretary-General was both gracious and enthusiastic, and he offered full support.

We stepped up our fundraising efforts. A few weeks later I was startled when a woman in Boston sent us $20,000. Her donation enabled us to bring selected parliamentarians to our first major event, a three-day forum at the UN in September 1981. We titled the forum "The Politics of Human Survival," and built the program around the twin themes of disarmament and development. Out of the Forum, Parliamentarians for World Order adopted policies in support of the nuclear freeze campaign, a meaningful North-South dialogue on development issues, a standing UN peacekeeping force, and the establishment of a UN parliamentary chamber. These parliamentarians from widely different backgrounds all wanted the same thing: a change in direction, from the absurdity of armaments towards building the conditions for human security. I rejoiced in these new friendships that seemed a world away from the sterility of caucus discussions at home.

Dunlop and I felt that Parliamentarians for World Order could make a difference by bringing representatives from virtually every continent to Moscow and Washington to press the superpowers to stop the arms race. We made a quick trip to Asia, Africa and Europe to test the idea. We chose a number of representatives: from India, N. K. P. Salve, a deputy parliamentary leader of Indira Gandhi's Congress Party; from Nigeria, the deputy speaker of the House of Representatives, Alhaji Idris Ibrahim; from Mexico, former President Luis Echeverria

Alvarez; and from Britain, John Silkin, a former Labour minister. At first, we called the effort the Five-Continent Initiative, even though Mexico is part of North America. Later, when Argentina joined, the project evolved into the Six-Nation Initiative.

I wanted to be sure that the members of this group would not be perceived as diplomatic interlopers, so I went back up to the 38th floor, this time to see the new Secretary-General, Javier Perez de Cuellar. He listened with evident enthusiasm to my outline of PWO's work, and emphasized that it was an important expression of public opinion. He gave us a green light.

On the British Airways flight from New York to London the next morning, Dunlop and I talked about our action program for world security with Robert Johansen, the youthful president of the World Policy Institute, who joined the delegation as technical adviser and had drafted the 2,000-word document that set out the action program. We also speculated on whether the Soviet leaders might make a unilateral move towards a freeze for a period of, say, six months, and even withdraw some SS-20s from Europe to head off the NATO deployment of the Pershing 2 and Cruise missiles. We hoped to trigger some Soviet response, but were wary of being perceived as spokespersons for either superpower. Parliamentarians for World Order wanted mutual and balanced disarmament, with both superpowers involved.

To Moscow and Washington

It was a marvellous moment for me when all five members of the delegation met around a table in the council room of the Royal Commonwealth Society building near Trafalgar Square. The day before, I had met separately with each of them as they arrived in London, and had come to know a little about former President Echeverria over an extended lunch. When we were all gathered together, I could hardly believe we had pulled it off. Addressing them formally by title, I said that the moment was a historic one, and an opportunity for peace. I said we did not know each other well, and came from different cultures, races, religions and ideologies; uniting us was our desire to preserve life on the planet and our deep concern about nuclear arms. I asked them to rise for a moment of silent prayer and to reflect on what we were about to do on behalf of humankind. It was a poignant moment and it helped to bond us as a team from the outset.

During our three days in Moscow, we visited our respective embassies and moved by stages up the ladder of appointments: first to the Institute of World Economy and International Relations, then to the Soviet Peace Committee, and finally, on the last afternoon, to the fourth floor of the main Kremlin building, overlooking the Moscow River, for a meeting with Valentin Kuznetsov, first vice-chairman of the Supreme Soviet. I had sent our document to him ahead of time. John Silkin presented a verbal summary and Kuznetsov launched into a long answer from some notes. He insisted that the Soviet Union wanted to stop the production of all kinds of nuclear weapons and to reduce those weapons to the point of total elimination. It was the U.S. and NATO, he said, that were blocking progress; "The Soviet Union is willing to freeze the arms race." If the U.S. signalled its willingness to pursue a moratorium, the Soviet Union would enter into talks to this end.

For our arrival in Washington we had taken a wise precaution. Walter McLean had flown from Ottawa to supervise arrangements, and cars from the five embassies were waiting; to the Americans involved with our visit, there was nothing special about our delegation.

The program the following day also had to be cobbled together, and Silkin showed his political clout in nailing down appointments. Vice-President Bush had extended an Asian trip to go to China, but we finally organized meetings with Michael Guhin and Sven Kramer of the National Security Council staff in the White House and with Frank Carlucci, deputy secretary of defence, as well as with Eugene Rostow, then director of the Arms Control and Disarmament Agency. Just which of these people—senior staff in the Pentagon and Agency or less senior people on the White House staff—had the most influence we could not tell. The only possible choice was to cover all the bases.

It was a frustrating day. For a meeting at the White House, we all had to undergo a lengthy security clearance; then Guhin simply listened to the presentation of our action program and said, "The White House will study it." The discussion went on for another half hour, but our hosts had little of substance to add.

We met with congressmen, who seemed to support a nuclear freeze and a comprehensive program to end the arms race. But Rostow was categorical in his rejection: "We are not willing to enter into negotiations for an immediate halt." The reason, he said, was Soviet "superiority" in nuclear weapons.

Echeverria and I argued that, on the contrary, the superpowers had reached the stage of "rough parity" when all nuclear weapons are counted in, and this presented a rare opportunity to call a halt. That very morning, former President Jimmy Carter had been quoted in the *New York Times* from Stockholm as advocating a freeze because there was rough parity. But it was clear Rostow had rejected this argument many times before, including from his Arms Control and Disarmament Agency predecessor Paul Warnke.

He made one new point, however: the administration would soon be introducing proposals for strategic arms reductions. Although he did not say it, the proposals were to come in President Reagan's speech three days later at Eureka College, Illinois. Rostow had been called to the White House that afternoon for talks on the speech. He also expressed greater willingness than Kuznetsov had done to accept thorough forms of verification of any arms reductions that were mutually agreed, including on-site inspection.

After a reception at the Indian Embassy, our team gathered to work on a press release for the next day. This was a real test of our solidarity, for of course we all had different perceptions. Echeverria contrasted the interest about negotiations in Moscow with the skepticism in Washington. Silkin said we should not lose sight of the clear fact that neither side wanted a war and yet each believed the other could use the threat of war to achieve its political ends. Ibrahim thought we should be open about our problems in reconciling the attitudes of both sides. Salve felt we needed to emphasize that Moscow had accepted a freeze proposal for negotiating purposes while we had received mixed signals in Washington (because the members of the congressional committee had favoured it while the representatives of the administration had not).

These differences do not seem large, but they become magnified when people have to agree on every word of a text. What's more, we were all tired after the long journey the previous day and the frustrations of that afternoon. I felt that our late-night meeting was deteriorating into bad humour and eventually everyone headed off to bed. Before I slept, I wrote down the following summary of my thoughts about the mission. I dated it Friday, May 7, 1982, 2:30 a.m.:

What I learned was that political leadership in securing the world from nuclear devastation is shockingly deficient. Politicians, and especially bureaucrats, are enslaved by outmoded thinking that still considers nuclear war a possibility. It is time to wake up and realize that any kind of nuclear war will end in the destruction of the planet. The superpowers are playing Russian roulette with each other—and all humanity will be the victim. Why are there not serious negotiations—now—to rid the world of nuclear weapons and build a secure system through international institutions? In my view, people everywhere should rise up and demand that their leaders negotiate a halt and reductions in the nuclear arms race. If the people wait for the politicians to lead, they will wait a long time.

The next morning at breakfast, refreshed and energized, we were able to agree on a statement:

The Soviet government expressed readiness to negotiate on a complete halt to the nuclear arms race. The U.S. government has rejected this proposal, although many Congressmen have reacted favorably to the suggestion. However, whatever the public positions taken by each government, we are convinced that only concerted public pressure for comprehensive arms reductions will stop the present nuclear madness.

Both countries must start immediate negotiations for a halt in the nuclear arms race. Our delegation considers that the result of this mission is a positive one in the sense that we have communicated an urgent message on behalf of mankind to the leadership of both superpowers. This expression of public opinion must continue, and we pledge our best efforts to this end.

Journalists at the press conference understandably highlighted the negativism in Washington. The *Canadian Press* story began with this paragraph:

U.S. government authorities rejected an appeal by politicians of 26 countries for a nuclear arms freeze before disarmament talks, but crusade leader Douglas Roche of Canada vowed Friday to step up disarmament pressure on the superpowers.

Some might say that Parliamentarians for World Order was ahead of its time. In fact, we were carving out the future. I often spoke of the old idealism being "the new realism" and borrowed from Bernard Shaw and Robert Kennedy the phrase "Some men see the world as it is and ask why; others see the world as it might be and ask why not?"

A month later, we brought 50 parliamentarians to the UN for another forum, which featured the "Call for Global Survival," centring on the nuclear freeze and a world disarmament treaty: "We make this appeal on behalf of our constituents who, whatever their culture, whatever their ideology, whatever their nationality, share one desire: the desire for life." As the result of a mail-out, Parliamentarians for World Order collected the signatures of 910 parliamentarians in 55 countries representing 110 million constituents.

Where Should I Be?

During these early years of the 1980s, the mood in the Progressive Conservative caucus began to shift. I could feel the hard-right dominating the caucus and Clark's grip on the leadership loosening. Red Tories were being marginalized as what seemed to me to be a very unpleasant, selfish, narrow and definitely unintellectual conservatism took hold. Prime Minister Trudeau, pressured by the U.S., announced Canada's intention to allow the U.S. to test the Cruise missile delivery system in Canada. I vigorously opposed this decision, but the right-wing side of the caucus thought it was a good idea. They hated my open letter to Trudeau, in which I said I was "totally and irrevocably opposed." So did the *Calgary Herald*, which said, "Roche's comment is hardly patriotic; it is no less than shameful." I threw the paper aside. My interests had shifted beyond the internal fighting, yet I was constantly being pulled back into one internal dispute after another.

To sort out my thinking about what I wanted to do with my life, I went to Westminster Abbey in Mission, B.C., for a few days' contemplation. I have been there many times over the years, often with my son Francis. I love the serenity of the Benedictine life. The ambience of the monastery presents such a powerful, positive attraction that one should go there in search of positive values to rise up to the challenge God gives us, not to run away from daily life. I wondered if it was coincidental that the readings at night prayer were based on Vatican II's Constitution on the Church in the Modern World, which refers to the need for institutions to promote world order and end the arms race. It was striking how the aims of Parliamentarians for World Order, this organization that I was giving so much time to, were based in this document. It brought me back to the question I was starting to wrestle with. Where should I be? In Parliament or in a UN-related job? I read some of French philosopher Pierre Teilhard de Chardin's work on the convergence of all things on Christ. Teilhard de Chardin had been scorned by the religious establishment of his day, but the force of his ideas prevailed. I wrote in my journal:

> What is clear to me is my determination to work for peace and social justice. Perhaps 1982 will tell me, through the grace of God who has blessed me through my life, if politics is to be my continuing vocation or a part of my life, now ending, so that I can continue to build on my experiences in an evolving world. Through this week, Eva has been on my mind, as a loving and stabilizing force in my life. What is best for her? Could I just stop thinking of myself so much that I have more time for her? This is easy to say, but I feel the pressures within me intensely. That is one reason I am glad I cancelled January's activities—to give me some time at home to think and reflect and, most of all, be with her in some days of January hope and quiet. The waiting period.

A Warning from Clark

I was travelling so much for Parliamentarians for World Order that inevitably I missed some votes in Parliament. This became a particular problem when the Conservative House leadership started commando raids on the Liberal government, with votes called at the last minute. The idea was to catch the government off guard and defeat it on a piece of legislation, opening the door to a possible election. The party whip would suddenly call, even if I was in Europe, and say, "Get back quickly; there's going to be a vote." Walter McLean and I got so sick of this gamesmanship that, on a couple of occasions, we switched hotels so the whip couldn't find us.

The pressure on me to stay in Ottawa to be on hand for votes of spurious importance was intense. On the one hand, the Party was happy that my international commitments led me to give up my seat on the parliamentary foreign affairs committee to Sinclair Stevens, whose views were far to the right of mine; on the other, they wanted me around to vote. My journal reveals my nervousness:

> I'm worried about skating through the immediate political future. I explained the Task Force to Clark last week, gave him a letter to cover myself for absence in an anticipated big vote again. Clark was supportive, probably because he saw a chance of moving Stevens onto the Foreign Affairs committee. Anyway I'm going to try to make a deal with [Liberal M.P.] Paul McRae for a pair [so our absences cancel each other out].

Parliamentarians for World Order had another forum coming up at the UN in November, so I paired myself with Liberal Herb Breau, who also wanted to attend. The whip called, ordering me to return immediately to vote against a tariff bill, just as I was about to chair a panel on global economic negotiations featuring Luis Echeverria, the former president of Mexico. I said I was paired and refused to leave New York. When I got back to Ottawa, there was a letter waiting for me from Clark, reprimanding me for missing "a three-line whip."

He went on, "If I may say so, privately and personally, your action in assigning yourself a pair has increased criticism of you, in caucus, for Parliamentarians for World Order. Several colleagues have expressed to me their anger that you would give your attendance in New York priority over your attendance in Parliament." He also noted that some MPs wanted the funding we had received from the Canadian Parliament withdrawn, "since its meetings have twice led you and Walter to be absent at votes...." Clark added, "I believe I am not exaggerating the danger that the resentment at your missing two key votes escalate into an attack on the organization, and you will want to consider seriously the implications of that."

Clark's letter was very different from the one he had written only a few months earlier, congratulating me for leading the Parliamentarians for World Order mission to Moscow and Washington. "I consider it a signal honour for Canada that you have been selected to serve so prominently on this delegation," he wrote. It was also different from his letter thanking me for my help on the African trip when he was prime minister: "Your wise counsel on many issues was of great value to me personally."

I replied to Clark, telling him I accepted his rebuke, but said we should look at the larger picture. "Since the leadership of the Party has not found it possible to assign any serious responsibilities to me," I wrote, "gradually I have looked beyond the Party in order to make a constructive contribution to the global issues of peace, particularly in the fields of development and disarmament. That is how my involvement grew as International Chairman of Parliamentarians for World Order."

I told him I would be happy to put the same amount of effort into the Party's work (as I had done for the foreign policy conference of 1978), but I sensed that my views on the peace issue, so out of favour with the element that sought to dominate the caucus, precluded advancement into areas of responsibility.

I went on, "In my letter to you of July 27, 1981, in which I responded to your request to Members to outline preference for work, I set out my qualifications in the foreign policy field. I did not receive an answer to that letter. ... I think it fair to say that the main element of the foreign policy community in Canada (as well as the United Nations) is in accord with my views. My books, lectures and involvements have helped to strengthen the credibility of our Party."

I added that I was seriously concerned about the damage being done to the Party by those inimical to global realities: "The current attack on me, though precipitated by my absence at the vote, is really an assault on what I stand for in the wrenching issues of development and disarmament."

Since Parliamentarians for World Order had grown beyond being financially dependent on any one source, I added, it could not be intimidated by threats from a few parliamentarians in Ottawa. "Like our colleagues," I continued, "I stand committed to a new Progressive Conservative government for Canada (I went door-to-door in Edmonton South for eight days in September and I know what the people want). I also stand committed to peace—and to sensitive and sensible policies by our Party to advance true security, economic stability and social justice. I want to put these two commitments together."

Clark, always polite, responded that he understood the tensions in caucus and agreed that I was a special target when tempers were lost. He said he hoped that would diminish, "although Members whose interests and responsibilities carry them out of the country will doubtless remain vulnerable to criticism."

Clark was right in his prediction of a caucus attack on Parliamentarians for World Order. Some in the far-right wing were insisting the organization was subversive. I pointed out that the honorary president was the speaker of the House of Commons at Westminster, the Rt. Hon. George Thomas, MP, a figure of the highest standing in international politics. I recalled that William Wilberforce, the great British parliamentarian who ended the legalization of slavery, was a Conservative. I reminded them that it was John Diefenbaker, a Conservative prime minister, who had opposed Lester Pearson's acquiescence to the U.S. demand to place nuclear weapons in Canada. None of this mattered to the zealots of the right, who equated Canadian conservatism with lip-synch following of Ronald Reagan's and Margaret Thatcher's hard-line policies in the U.S. and U.K.

Clark was forced to assign John Crosbie, then the foreign affairs critic, to "investigate" Parliamentarians for World Order. It was galling, but I decided to give Crosbie, who carried a lot of weight in caucus, my complete co-operation by turning all the organization's records over to him. Crosbie gave a formal report to caucus: there was nothing in the organization inimical to either the Constitution of the Progressive Conservative Party or the Constitution of Canada.

A Party Divided

Clark had weightier matters on his mind: his own survival as leader. The same people who had gone after Parliamentarians for World Order were determined to bring him down. Their diminishment of the leader escalated when Brian Mulroney started organizing. Clark, who in my view was maturing in the intellectual demands on a leader, was increasingly perceived by the media as weak. High drama ensued as the Party moved into showdown mode at a convention in Winnipeg in February 1983, at which a leadership review vote would be held. In 2007, German-Canadian businessman and lobbyist Karlheinz Schreiber told the House of Commons Ethics Committee that he and other Germans had contributed significant funds to finance a planeload of Quebec delegates to fly to Winnipeg for the expresss purpose of voting against Clark. The convention was full of intrigue; I was disgusted by it.

On the night of the vote on a leadership review, Eva and I sat high in the stands of the arena. The announcer reported that Clark had received 66.9 per cent support. Clark then appeared on stage and said that amount wasn't enough; he was calling a leadership convention. I turned to Eva. "Tell me what I'm hearing is wrong. Clark should not be calling a convention. He's going to lose."

I returned to Edmonton and invited the members of my constituency executive to my home to decide whom I should support: Clark or Mulroney. In 1976, I had made my decision for Wagner on my own. This time, I wanted the views of my executive. We went around the room, with each person giving his or her choice: twelve were for Clark, and twelve were for Mulroney. Everybody looked at me to make the call. It was another agonizing moment in politics.

Clark had two big strikes against him: he had lost the government in the budget vote and he had lost the election to a revived Trudeau. But he was a decent man, maturing in his leadership, and he had the values in domestic and international matters that I thought reflected the best of Canada.

Mulroney was fresh, perceived as strong and came from Quebec; in 1976, the latter point had been a principal factor in my choosing Wagner. But I felt that Mulroney was too close to big business and would tie Canada too closely to the U.S. orbit. I didn't like the way he had started campaigning even before a leadership convention was called and was undermining Clark.

"Clark," I said. "He'll be better for the country."

But my heart was not in it. I felt Mulroney would win, and he did, on the fourth ballot on a hot, steamy day in the same Ottawa arena where Clark had triumphed in 1976. Clark pledged his "total support to Brian." I had now backed the loser (though runner-up) in two leadership conventions. What did that say about my abilities as a politician?

A Fragile World Near Anarchy

Immediately after the leadership convention, Eva and I set out on a seven-week round-the-world trip on behalf of Parliamentarians for World Order to meet with government leaders and senior parliamentarians to discuss new political initiatives to help stop the global arms race and promote economic development. It was also an opportunity to promote PWO's "Call for Global Survival." We started at the UN in New York, and then went to Britain, Ireland, Spain, Italy,

Romania, India, Singapore, China and Japan. I wanted to go to Sri Lanka because, through the work of Jayantha Dhanapala, that country was playing a leading role in nuclear disarmament. Eva and I got as far south in India as Madras, but the Canadian department of foreign affairs urged me strongly not to go to Sri Lanka because of the civil war raging at the time.

During the trip, I met with Shridath Ramphal, secretary-general of the Commonwealth; Dr. Garrett FitzGerald, prime minister of Ireland; Pope John Paul II; Prime Minister Indira Gandhi of India; Zhu Qizher, China's assistant foreign minister; and Takeo Miki, a former prime minister of Japan.

I came up with two major findings. On the negative side, the world was in the midst of a double crisis: the nuclear arms race and mounting international debt, both of which threatened the stability and security of the international system. On the positive side, development patterns were taking hold in many areas; new scientific and technological developments (such as solar power, desalination, the microchip and satellites) offered a promise of hitherto unknown abundance. The one word that summed up the current state of the interlocking global political, economic and social system was *fragility*. "Without an end to the arms race, without an end to the deepening poverty and human suffering," I wrote in my report, "the present fragility will explode as tensions mount. Militarism and deprivation are the principal threats to global peace." Everything I saw that summer confirmed the warning that had just been issued by Perez de Cuellar: "The world is perilously near to a new international anarchy." To turn the world towards more productivity for life and away from the menace of death clearly required political policies and decisions of a higher order than were now practised.

In Rome, it was arranged for me to present the Call for Global Survival to Pope John Paul II during a short private exchange following a general audience. The Pope, now recovered from his gunshot wound of 1981, appeared vigorous, his stride sure. I told him of Parliamentarians for World Order's efforts to seek world peace through world law and our concern for development and disarmament. The next day I asked Archbishop Achille Silvestrini, the official in charge of public affairs, for the Pope's active support of a mediation process for disarmament by the two superpowers that would implement UN principles for peace. This, apparently, was too much to ask.

Undoubtedly, the most powerful experience for me was our visit to Hiroshima. Walter and Barbara McLean had joined Eva and me for the China and Japan portions of the trip. We spent a long time in the museum in the Peace Memorial Park in Hiroshima, horrified at the scenes of human suffering. We interviewed some of the *hibakusha*, the survivors of the atomic bombing. The day was one of unremitting gloom. Back at our hotel, trying to cheer up, we hit upon the idea of going to a baseball game. Hiroshima was playing Tokyo. In the stadium, fans were cheering wildly. Life was going on. Hope for a better future was in the air. It was a lesson I never forgot.

The Six-Nation Initiative

During the trip, I explored an idea that Nick Dunlop and I had come up with to raise the nuclear weapons issue to the highest levels through the involvement of presidents and prime ministers. We wanted to stage a "middle power" summit to make the leaders of the U.S. and the Soviet Union listen. We felt that an active negotiating role by heads of governments from all regions of the world would help bridge the psychological abyss dividing the Soviet Union and the United States.

I knew if I could get Prime Minister Indira Gandhi to sign on, others would follow. Mrs. Gandhi received me in her office; I explained the PWO proposal. Without a moment's hesitation, she said yes. Then she reached for the phone and, in my presence, called her son Rajiv to tell him of our conversation and to say that she wanted him to meet "Mr. Roche from Canada." A chauffeur drove me to Rajiv Gandhi's residence. For an hour, we sat in his study and discussed what the nuclear arms race was doing to the world—especially India.

Olafur Grimsson, a social scientist and parliamentarian from Iceland (later elected president of that country) succeeded in bringing Prime Minister Olof Palme of Sweden into the initiative. Then President Miguel de la Madrid of Mexico joined, along with President Julius Nyerere of Tanzania and Prime Minister Andreas Papandreou of Greece. The Parliamentarians for World Order office started to prepare a joint declaration for the group members to sign, based on this premise: "We come from different parts of the globe, with differences in religion, culture and political systems. But we are united in the conviction that there must not be another world war."

I made a serious effort to enlist Prime Minister Trudeau in the initiative, bringing a delegation—including Echeverria, Grimsson, U.S. Congressman Tom Downey and Paul McRae, the Liberal MP who had signed the minority report on the nuclear freeze—to see him on September 20, 1983. We presented an extensive brief, asking him to join other heads of government to take on "a new role in a disarmament negotiating process which has so far been dominated by the superpowers."

Although we were political opponents, Trudeau was personally supportive of me. Only a month earlier, he had written me a candid letter expressing his frustration at the behaviour of the two superpowers. I had been awarded the Peace Award of the World Federalists of Canada for my work with Parliamentarians for World Order, which brought me into the company of distinguished former recipients, such as Lester Pearson, Maurice Strong and George Ignatieff. I sent Trudeau a copy of my speech for the occasion, making the point that Canada should be a pioneer in establishing "the permanent machinery of peace." That machinery would include an international inspection agency able to monitor disarmament, a world peace force recruited by the UN Security Council, an effective system of world courts to strengthen the rule of law, and a world development fund to transfer savings from disarmament to development. Trudeau said he was "impressed by the evident sincerity and depth of your convictions." Then he revealed his dilemma:

> It is, I know, anachronistic to the point of absurdity to have two blocs of highly developed nations devoting such enormous resources to armaments while so much remains to be done to improve the human condition. It is a scenario more suitable to the religious wars of the Middle Ages than to the space age. Human emotions, however, have not progressed at the same speed as man's technical prowess, and the fundamental problem at the moment is a lack of trust between the two superpowers. Re-establishing some degree of trust between them is essential to any progress in arms control talks, but that is probably going to be much more difficult to achieve than a creative manipulation of numbers at Geneva.

He concluded by suggesting that "we continue work, in a practical and realistic way, towards a safer and healthier world." The operative word there was "realistic." Trudeau's advisers told him that he could not join our initiative, which was centred on the nuclear freeze, because it would not be "realistic" to so counter U.S. and NATO policy.

The middle power initiative, of course, went ahead, with President Raul Alfonsin of Argentina joining at the last moment. The project's name became the "Six-Nation Initiative." On May 22, 1984, the joint declaration was publicly issued simultaneously in Athens, Buenos Aires, Dar es Salaam, Mexico City, New Delhi and Stockholm. The declaration began as follows:

> Today, the survival of humankind is in jeopardy. The escalating arms race, the rise in international tensions and the lack of constructive dialogue among the nuclear weapons states has increased the risk of nuclear war. Such a war, even using part of the present stockpiles, would bring death and destruction to all peoples.

Then it called for the freeze:

> We urge, as a necessary first step, the United States and the Soviet Union, as well as the United Kingdom, France and China, to halt all testing, production and deployment of nuclear weapons and their delivery systems, to be immediately followed by substantial reductions in nuclear forces.

I flew that night to Rome and presented the joint declaration to Pope John Paul, again meeting with him after a general audience. The Pope responded with a telegram: "I hope that this initiative and other similar ones will receive wide acceptance and be generously supported by those who have responsibility for promoting the cause of peace."

But it was not to be. The Reagan administration immediately spurned the approach. A state department spokesman said that a nuclear freeze would "perpetuate the dangerous disparities" between American and Soviet nuclear forces and undercut efforts to achieve arms reductions. In the House of Commons, Brian Mulroney questioned Trudeau about why Canada was not in the initiative. Trudeau said he supported the spirit of the proposal but refused to join because the Canadian government was committed to a NATO buildup of nuclear weapons defences in Europe. Canada's loyalty as one of

NATO's "faithful allies" committed to deploying new U.S. Cruise and Pershing 2 nuclear missiles in Europe made it impossible for the government to support the initiative, he said.

The madness of nuclear weapons policies was nakedly exposed. Yes, we share your goal to reduce the risk of war and nuclear annihilation. Yes, we recognize that nuclear weapons are an intolerable threat to humanity. No, we will not stop refining and producing new ones. Oh yes, and in Canada, we love peace, but we have to be loyal to U.S. and NATO nuclear policies. Madness.

The Six-Nation Initiative went on, but without me. I was about to enter a new phase of my life. In January 1985, the six leaders met in Delhi for their own summit. Indira Gandhi had been assassinated two months earlier by two of her security guards in the garden of her home. Rajiv Gandhi stepped into her place, and the Six-Nation Initiative issued a new call. The group held its second and third summits in Mexico and Sweden.

What did the initiative accomplish? The stepped-up nuclear disarmament negotiations of the late 1980s—including the Reagan-Gorbachev Summit in Reykjavik in 1986, at which the American and Russian leaders very nearly agreed to abolish all nuclear weapons, but instead listened to the paranoid opinions of their advisers—can be traced back to the Six-Nation Initiative. Mikhail Gorbachev referred to the urgings of the Initiative when he extended the test moratorium of the Soviet Union. The international conference in 1991 called to amend the Partial Test Ban Treaty of 1963 to a Comprehensive Nuclear Test Ban Treaty also had its origins in the Six-Nation Initiative. The work of Parliamentarians for World Order spawned future agreements, though it never claimed all the credit for this progress.

Olafur Grimsson and later Warren Allmand of Canada took over the leadership of Parliamentarians for World Order. The new executive realized that the word *order* was opening the organization to attack by right-wing extremists who claimed, absurdly, that we were surreptitiously working to bring about one government to dominate the world. The Canadian branch had had to put out a fact sheet stating that we did not support handing over Canada to a world government; we were not Marxists; we did not support unilateral disarmament; and we were not traitors. Even the first President Bush started using the phrase "new world order" in his speeches after the implosion of the Soviet Union, but his advisers quickly shifted his language when they saw the difficulties of the linguistic terrain. Parliamentarians for World Order became Parliamentarians for Global Action. By the time of the organization's 25th anniversary in 2002, its members included 1,350 parliamentarians from 105 countries.

Exposing Dirty Laundry

My stock in the Party seemed to go up considerably when I returned from my well-publicized meeting with the Pope. Members came up to me in the House of Commons lobby to congratulate me. I felt almost as popular as I had been the night a couple of years earlier when I stood up in the House of Commons and made a fiery speech defending the pay raise bill for MPs. My colleagues, most of whom did not want to go on the record, cheered me on. Now we were on the brink of an election and everyone was in a good mood.

This was a big change from a year earlier, when the regressive members of the caucus were throwing their weight around. The very week after Mulroney was elected leader, the New Democratic Party introduced a motion opposing Cruise missile delivery system testing in Canada. The House leadership (Mulroney hadn't even taken over yet) told Progressive Conservative members that we would have to oppose the motion—that is, vote in favour of Cruise testing. I said the day the Party made me vote to extend the nuclear arms race was the day I would leave the Party. With Walter McLean, John Fraser and Jack Murta, I stood to vote against the Party. Mulroney, to his credit, never held it against us; all four of us received important jobs in his government.

But the bitterness within caucus worried me. What would happen to Canada if the retrograde policies of the ideological right wing prevailed? I wrote an op-ed article exposing the two competing philosophies inside the caucus: the first giving strong support to UN values and programs; the second espousing the neo-conservatism of the Reagan administration. The centrepiece of what I called "the Canadian new right" was committing to massive military spending, slashing foreign aid and rejecting moves to restructure the world economy for the benefit of the poorest nations, seeing these activities as anathema to global capitalism. "The neo conservatives are determined to control foreign policy because they are genuinely committed to their viewpoint and because it is the one area where they can dramatically show their control of the Party," I wrote. "They label the adherents of traditional foreign policy as soft on communism, if not leftists, naïve and anti-American." I warned Mulroney that to be true to himself and to genuine conservatism, his foreign policy must expand international partnerships to reduce militarization and deprivation.

Having written the article, I then forgot about it as I departed on my world trip in the summer of 1983. It was several weeks before the *Financial Post* published it. The article might not have received much attention except that the *Toronto Star* made it front-page news at the very moment Mulroney was winding down his campaign in a by-election for a seat in the House of Commons. Mulroney was furious at me. He thought I was deliberately undermining his personal campaign for election. John Crosbie told me he had never seen Mulroney so angry. In fact, I wasn't even thinking of Mulroney's campaign when I wrote the article. But I realized, with a jolt, that what I had done was not very circumspect. I had hung the Tories' dirty laundry out for all to see, and a politician should never do that. At the next caucus meeting, I apologized for my indiscretion and said that, in future, I would be more careful with my "philosophical utterances."

Mulroney handily won his seat. But I suppose he felt he had to punish me. When he was forming his shadow Cabinet, he called to say he was appointing me deputy to Walter McLean, who would be the critic for secretary of state. I am sure this demotion was meant to be humiliating. But I said I would be glad to serve him in any way he wanted. He appointed Sinclair Stevens, one of the leaders of the neo-conservative band, as foreign affairs critic.

Clark's Buried Report

I was confident I would recover in my relationship with Mulroney. But my worries went deeper. One day, as I walked through the tunnel connecting the East Block to the House of Commons, the mélange of my frustrations and hopes suddenly came into sharp focus. Maybe I could get into a Mulroney Cabinet, but it would be in some minor post; the thought of having such a job as public works minister appalled me. I wanted to work full-time on the global issues of peace and development. At that moment I made the decision not to run for Parliament again.

I went to see Mulroney. The conversation was relaxed and pleasant; I told him I would be glad to serve in his forthcoming government, particularly as Canada's ambassador to the United Nations. He wrote me a gracious letter: "I cannot begin to enumerate the contributions you have made to your community, your church and your country. I cannot even attempt to set out in words the significant dimension you brought to our Party caucus since your election in 1972." He asked me to give him a report on Canada's role at the United Nations. A few weeks later, he appointed me his special representative to a new round of disarmament talks in Stockholm.

Then Mulroney did something that showed the masterful way he was bringing the caucus together. Since Trudeau was garnering headlines with his world peace mission to the capitals of the nuclear powers, Mulroney realized that he had to counter with his own peace move. He appointed Joe Clark to hold public hearings and write a report on nuclear disarmament policies for the Party. The idea was to out-Trudeau Trudeau. Clark asked Peggy Mason, a lawyer who was his personal assistant, and me to help him.

Clark wrote a report that would have lifted up the Canadian public—if they had ever seen it. But they did not, for Mulroney, fearful of starting a new controversy with the U.S. government on the eve of the Canadian election, buried it. The contents of the report have never been made public. For 23 years, the report has sat in my files. Now, for my memoirs, Clark has given his permission for me to reveal it.

He began by revealing his core beliefs:

- The nuclear build-up threatens the life of every Canadian and the existence of human society.

- The superpowers, left to their own devices, will continue to accumulate nuclear arms and endanger the world. Countries like Canada must use their influence to reverse the nuclear build-up. "That must be a constant, consistent, dominant priority of Canadian foreign policy."

- Canada is not neutral in the contest between open and closed societies, and defends the values of democracy and individual freedom. Canada's active contribution to NATO is a major source of our influence on allies and legitimacy in advocating arms control.

- Canada is more likely to inch the world away from nuclear destruction by specific, concrete initiatives, pursued consistently with international partners, than by solo dramatic gestures.

- The Canadian Parliament and people have a capacity to understand and a right to influence arms control policy, and must have both more influence on policy and more access to information.

Clark's first recommendation was a call for a limited nuclear freeze, cloaking this shift in Canadian policy by calling it a "pause." He said:

Canada should:

Propose, within NATO, that the Alliance advocate a reciprocal declaration by the Soviet Union and the United States of a one-year "pause" in deployment of nuclear weapons to open the way for the resumption of arms limitation talks.

He argued that a "pause" in deployment could let the superpowers see the suicidal risks they are running, and could give the non-nuclear states some hope that the spirit of the Non-Proliferation Treaty would be honoured.

He said Canada should associate itself with the Six-Nation Initiative's mediation role, support a Comprehensive Test Ban Treaty, reject the idea of a "winnable" nuclear war, get NATO to commit to a "no-first-use policy," review the Umbrella Testing Agreement (under which Canada allowed the U.S. to test the Cruise missile delivery system), and insist that the U.S. consult with Canada before proceeding to develop a space-based ballistic missile defence system. All of this was new and would have made headlines, committing the Party to progressive nuclear disarmament policies.

Clark emphasized that the new government should "assign a predominant priority in Canadian foreign policy to arms control and pursue that priority consistently." This would entail "informed public participation in making and implementing Canadian arms control policy," access by the organized peace movement to the councils of government, six "peace chairs" in Canadian universities to balance the government's funding of defence studies and putting "seed money" into the formation of a coalition of Canadian women's peace groups.

He wrote movingly about the peace movement. "During my public hearings, nothing impressed me more than the quality, tone and sophistication of most of the representatives of Canadian organizations working for peace and against nuclear arms." The "apocalyptic seed hatched at Los Alamos" has grown beyond the control of the experts and led to deep fears within the public. "The ordinary people are right." He scorned the disparity in government funding that allocated huge amounts to "strategic studies" programs sponsored by the Department of National Defence and little to peace studies.

> Strategic studies have to do with preventing wars; peace studies have to do with creating peace, and involve aspects of psychology, political science, history and anthropology. Programs range from the study of stress management, game theory and conflict resolution to global models of disarmament and development, and historical and anthropological studies of peaceful societies.

He insisted that peace *advocacy* groups ought to be able to publicly advocate changes in government policy without jeopardizing their tax-deductible status under the Income Tax Act. Fear of losing their charitable status through a Revenue Canada crackdown is a constant constraint on peace groups that know all too well that their revenue through donations would dry up if the donor cannot receive a tax credit.

The Clark report was, in short, revolutionary. Evidently, Sinclair Stevens feared publication of Clark's findings, for he prevailed on Mulroney to cancel a press conference at which Clark would announce its contents. Mulroney would not risk upsetting the Reagan administration.

Having decided to move on, I made my final speech in Parliament. Two-thirds of the 600 questions, motions and speeches I had made in twelve years in Parliament concerned domestic issues. But the work I had done as a parliamentarian undeniably cast me as an internationalist. "There is one dominant thought that I want to share with my colleagues as I prepare to depart," I said, "and that is the desire that I and so many people have today for collective security and economic and social justice in the world."

Allan Mayer, who later became editor of the *Edmonton Journal,* wrote a long article praising me. Eva, rejoicing that I was getting out of politics, wrote a letter to the editor saying that all this sounded "terribly somber."

"If I may be allowed one wifely comment," she said. "I would like to round out this profile by explaining that Doug enjoys musical comedy, cheering the Oilers, hot cannelloni on a cold winter evening, amusing friends with Ogden-Nash-type limericks, and lots of chilled white wine at the Bistro Praha. And I know some of his talents would be wasted as a priest." Then she added a post script: "I guess there is a kind of freedom that comes from being out of politics."

Eva looked at me nervously while I was reading her published letter, wondering if I would object. But I burst out laughing. I was free and it felt wonderful.

III

The Ambassador Years:
1985–1989

10

A Conflicted Ambassador

On September 3, 1984, the day before Brian Mulroney won his stunning victory and the largest majority in the history of Canada, the *Globe and Mail's* lead editorial was entitled "For Special Attention." Noting that I wasn't running and that I had spent all but nine months of my twelve years in Parliament in the Opposition, the paper said, "Mr. Roche ... emerged in his own right as one of Canada's most effective parliamentarians on North–South issues and nuclear disarmament. [He] is but one example of an M.P. outside the ministry, who made his own mark on national life." That's nice, I thought, but what about finding a job?

Eva and I drove to Clark's campaign office the night of the election to celebrate with him. There was no point in saying, "This could have been yours, Joe." The scale of Mulroney's win—211 seats in a 282-seat Parliament—was stupendous, and Clark's headquarters was happy bedlam. But what role would Joe play in the new government?

I flew back to Ottawa the next morning to clean out my office. The newspapers were full of speculation about who would get into the Cabinet. Joe was a certainty, of course, but would he get foreign affairs, where, in my opinion, he clearly belonged? The pundits were speculating that Mulroney, to placate the right side of his caucus, would name Sinclair Stevens as foreign minister. I sat in my office pondering this unpleasant possibility when an idea struck me. Without talking to Clark, I picked up the phone and called William Thorsell, an editorial writer (and later editor) at the *Globe and Mail*. I thanked him for the editorial on me and then got to the real purpose of the call.

"William," I said, "do you want Sinclair Stevens to be the foreign minister of Canada?"

"No," he said, "he's too right-wing."

"Well," I said, "you're going to get him unless the *Globe* comes out right away for Joe Clark. You've got to show Mulroney that there's strong support for Clark."

Two days later, on September 8, the *Globe's* lead editorial endorsed Clark. Discussing the merits of Stevens and Clark, the paper said Clark "would better serve the national interest" as foreign minister. "Foreign aid, the North Atlantic Treaty Organization, hemispheric affairs, Canada–United States relations all require mature, persistent attention. Canada's former Prime Minister would supply it."

Mulroney started to form his Cabinet, interviewing his picks in back-to-back meetings in different rooms of the Chateau Laurier Hotel. The day before the deadline for finalizing the Cabinet, he still had not interviewed Clark. Finally, the call came for Clark to go to the Chateau.

Clark's and my offices faced each other in the East Block. His wife, Maureen McTeer, nervous about what was happening, came over to talk to me. McTeer, a lawyer, was a controversial figure in her own right for her decision to keep her maiden name after marriage. I always admired her courage. On a couple of occasions when he had to be away, Clark asked me to escort her to a special dinner.

Maureen and I were chatting when Clark entered my office wearing a big smile. Recognizing the importance of this moment for both of them, I said I had to deal with some things with my secretary outside. "No," said Joe, "stay and hear this." He recounted his meeting with Mulroney and the offer to be foreign minister.

Immediately after the Cabinet was sworn in, the foreign affairs department gave Clark the draft of a speech he would have to make the following week at the United Nations General Assembly. Clark found the draft drab and asked me to liven it up.

I had just published a book, *United Nations, Divided World*. It was a fast-paced examination of the need for, and role of, a strengthened UN amid the global crises of the nuclear arms race and economic development. The book was timed for the 40th anniversary of the UN in 1985. Also, I had just become president of the United Nations Association in Canada.

I was convinced of the need for stronger Canadian government involvement in UN issues. I was not oblivious to the UN's defects, but I felt strongly that any serious criticism of the UN must place the blame for current disorders precisely where Secretary-General Perez de Cuellar had placed it: at the doorsteps of national governments that were resisting their own commitment to the UN Charter. Threatening mutual destruction as a way of life was not what the Charter fathers had had in mind. It seemed that everybody wanted to "tighten up" UN budgeting, but I took the position that it was ridiculous for UN critics to assume that tightening up a multi-faceted global operation that spent only $1 per year for every inhabitant of the planet was all that was needed to make the world a more secure place.

I went back to Edmonton and spent the weekend rewriting Clark's speech, trying to make it a blend of his own views, what the Progressive Conservative caucus would support, the basic stuff the bureaucracy wanted, and my own injection of a note of hope for the future. Clark did the final draft, and I was delighted to find these words in the speech he delivered: "We believe that the nuclear build-up threatens the life of every Canadian and that it threatens the existence of human society. Countries like our own must use their influence to reverse that build-up and reduce the danger of destruction. That will be a constant, consistent, and dominant priority of Canadian foreign policy."

A Travelling Ambassador

The foreign affairs department presented Clark with an immediate problem: whom to name as ambassador for disarmament.

This post had its origins in the 1978 appointment of Geoffrey Pearson, an external affairs diplomat and son of former Prime Minister Lester Pearson, as adviser on disarmament and arms control. Arthur Menzies was made the first ambassador for disarmament in 1980; he was succeeded by Alan Beesley. The post stood vacant for a while in 1984, just at the time the peace movement was becoming inflamed over the nuclear freeze issue and the deployment of Cruise and Pershing missiles in Europe. During his brief period as prime minister, John Turner, needing to make a high-profile appointment, chose one of the most prestigious ambassadors in Canada's foreign service. George Ignatieff, a White Russian (and the father of Michael

Ignatieff, who ran for the leadership of the Liberal Party in 2006), had been at various times ambassador to NATO and the UN and was then chancellor of the University of Toronto. Turner pulled him out of retirement (Ignatieff was 71) and dismissed his protests that he didn't want to do all the travelling the job required.

The department needed an ambassador in place for the fall sitting of the Disarmament (First) Committee at the UN, since the Canadian ambassador for disarmament chaired the weekly meetings of the Western ambassadors. The group was named the Barton Group, after Bill Barton, another distinguished Canadian ambassador, and it was considered an honour for Canada to chair it. But Ignatieff didn't want to spend the fall in New York. When Clark phoned him and offered him the post again, Ignatieff gave the same answer: yes, but no travel. Then he asked Clark what he would like to do. Clark said, "We're thinking of appointing Doug Roche." Ignatieff responded, "If you do, I will instantly issue a statement of support."

Clark called to formally offer me the job. The written mandate was exciting. I had three functions: to represent Canada at international meetings on disarmament and arms control, such as those held at the United Nations; to be a special adviser to the government on these matters, reporting to the deputy minister and having direct access to the foreign minister; and to be the point of contact between the government and non-governmental organizations interested in the subject in Canada.

Of course, the job I wanted was ambassador to the United Nations, because of the wider range of issues involved, but when Clark told me that Mulroney wanted Stephen Lewis in the post, I immediately comprehended what was happening. Lewis, the former leader of the New Democratic Party, had long been a critic of the Conservatives; just that week he had published a piece in *Maclean's* criticizing Mulroney for a trip to Washington to see President Ronald Reagan so soon after becoming Canadian leader. It was part of a "new fetish for America," Lewis wrote. Since Mulroney had scored heavily against Turner in the telecast campaign debate on the issue of Liberal patronage, what better way for Mulroney to signal to Canada that the "old patronage" was out the window than by naming Lewis to such a high-profile position? When Mulroney called Erik Nielsen, the deputy prime minister, to tell him he would be bringing the Lewis

nuclear weapons states "to agree to a freeze on nuclear weapons" that would stop further production of both nuclear weapons and fission-able material for weapons purposes. The Indian resolution went a bit further. It called for a comprehensive ban on the testing of nuclear weapons and their delivery vehicles, the complete cessation of their manufacture, a ban on any further deployments, and a stop to the production of fissionable materials for weapons purposes. The resolutions, which flowed from the work of the Six-Nation Initiative, were exactly what I wanted.

The officials sent a message to Clark stating that Canada should vote against all freeze resolutions because of "Canada's continuing strong support of NATO." They reminded Clark that during his government in 1979, Canada had signed on to NATO's "two track" decision, which authorized the deployment of Cruise and Pershing nuclear missiles in several European countries while calling for strategic negotiations at the same time. Canada's support for a freeze would have serious repercussions for our key European allies, they argued. Moreover, a freeze on delivery systems would contradict Canada's permission for the U.S. to test the Cruise delivery system over Canada. They also argued that a freeze could act as a disincentive to serious negotiations on reductions.

I talked this over with Stephen Lewis, who supported a freeze as ardently as I did. He had a personal stake in the decision. After the committee process, all resolutions go before the General Assembly for voting; thus, he himself would have to cast a vote he didn't agree with. We decided to send a joint telegram to Clark. "We feel duty bound to advise the government that it is our view that the security interests of the West are more than fulfilled by the existing level of the total number of nuclear weapons possessed by the U.S. and the NATO allies. Moreover, we are convinced that the future of life is clearly jeopardized by the present level of nuclear arms." We argued that the freeze represented hope for a beginning to the end of the arms race, which most Canadians wanted, and the widening peace movement would heavily criticize voting against the freeze. If Canada could not directly counter the U.S. by voting for the Swedish-Mexican resolution, let us at least abstain as some other NATO countries had done the previous year.

The department countered, "Despite the views advanced by Ambassadors Lewis and Roche, we recommend that Canada ... vote against all nuclear freeze resolutions." Clark agreed. The order came down and I was provided with an Explanation of Vote to be read to the committee before the voting. The statement said, "The government, reflecting the will of the people of Canada, wants significant, balanced and verifiable reductions in the level of nuclear arms in the world ... But mere declarations of a freeze are not a meaningful response to this danger. Rather we want immediate resumption of negotiations on reductions." The statement went on to give technical reasons why a freeze wouldn't work. The statement certainly didn't convince me or many states, for the vote on the Swedish–Mexican resolution was 127 in favour and 11 opposed, with 11 abstentions. Most of the NATO countries were in opposition.

The reaction from the peace movement in Canada was immediate. "Rather than betray your conscience, why don't you resign?" said one man in Winnipeg. Others asked how could I have advocated a nuclear freeze in my minority report for the parliamentary committee and voted against it at the UN. Some, of course, recognized that it was the government of Canada voting against the freeze, not Doug Roche personally. Nonetheless, I was the high-profile ambassador for disarmament, and the antipathy of the most ardent members of the peace community was directed against me.

At the morning meeting of the Canadian Mission the day after the vote, Lewis expressed strong moral support for me. I wrote him a private note:

> In this job, I have already discovered the full impact of the constraints: the bureaucracy/Americans on the one hand; the widening peace movement on the other. I must maintain a fairly wide field of maneuverability between them; days like yesterday reduce my space in which to operate. Of course, there are other battles and issues; the freeze is but a reflection of the frustration felt by so many. But what I feel so deeply is the hurt that I have given to so many in Canada who look to me with such hope. They truly do not understand the political constraints (on Mulroney and Clark, as well as you and me); but they do understand the essence: we must stop/halt/pause/freeze the upward momentum to total destruction. The reconciliation of this is my continuing

dilemma—and challenge. An increasing source of strength, and hope, for me is the quality of the Ambassador who serves here with me.

Lewis replied:

For you, voting against the freeze (as I will do in December) is a small compromise compared to the [Comprehensive Test Ban] Resolution, and chemical and biological weapons, and space wars, and nuclear winter, and immediate negotiations on arms reductions and the myriad of other interventions you'll make and initiatives you will take to contribute, with our voice, on the world's stage, in Canada's name, to the survival of the human species. Yes, the stand will cause hurt to some of your friends in the peace movement. But your sense of perspectives must not be thwarted by their dogmatism. So long as Doug Roche feels that the means he is pursuing, simultaneously on many fronts, are sufficiently extensive, just and workable as to shape the broadest consensus for world peace, he will never be compromised.

The U.S. Complains

The strength of U.S. opposition to the very idea of freezing the development of nuclear weapons was shown again a few weeks later. I gave an interview on CTV's national show *Question Period* and, of course, was asked about Canada's negative vote on the freeze. I responded by stating first of all that Canada had to work from within NATO, in concert with our allies, to build the conditions that can lead to productive results. A comprehensive freeze was a tough sell. But, knowing that Clark personally was in favour of some kind of pause in the nuclear buildup, I went on, "I believe there may be some prospect for a selective freeze on certain classes of weapons: for example, anti-satellite weapons or destabilizing weapons such as MIRVED missiles. Attention could now be given to a limited, selected kind of halt or pause...."

Even this cautious statement was enough to draw the ire of the U.S. government. An American spokesman told the Canadian embassy in Washington the next day that my comment was "decidedly unhelpful." In diplomatese, that is very strong language. A senior U.S. spokesman then called on External Affairs in Ottawa at the assistant deputy minister level to repeat his government's concern about my remark, which had the appearance of weakening NATO solidarity. He insisted that a freeze of any kind would have the "perverse effect" of preserving nuclear imbalances in favour of the Soviets.

It happened that two days later I was scheduled to meet with Prime Minister Mulroney to report on my work. He opened the meeting by extending his warm congratulations on the CTV interview, which he had seen. He observed that my work program was very full, and his general instruction to me was to keep "moving forward." It was, of course, ironic that the Canadian prime minister should praise me for remarks that the U.S. found objectionable. I am sure Mulroney knew nothing of the U.S. protest. The incident made me realize—and I saw this often in my career—that Canadian political leaders often personally wanted progressive disarmament policies but felt they had to, in their public utterances and votes, defer to the demands of the U.S. Trudeau's acquiescence to U.S. demands to test the Cruise missile delivery system in Canada is a case in point. Mulroney and Clark were both personally opposed to U.S. escalation of nuclear weapons. Nonetheless, they allowed Lewis and me to be instructed to vote against a freeze. I wanted to help Mulroney hold firm to his principles, which he had just reiterated in his year-end message: "There is no cause more urgent or more necessary for your government than to contribute to the reduction of the threat of war and to further the cause of peace."

No to Star Wars

One instance when Mulroney did not bow to the U.S. was on the U.S. request for Canada to participate in the Strategic Defense Initiative, otherwise known as Star Wars. This defence system was touted by President Reagan and his officials as a technological marvel that would shoot down incoming nuclear missiles in space, thereby rendering nuclear weapons obsolete. But a growing number of scientific and academic experts maintained that it would turn outer space into a new battlefield, spur a new nuclear arms race on earth and, furthermore, do nothing to stop the flight of nuclear weapons, such as the Cruise, that never leave the atmosphere and hence do not enter space. The inherent dangers of such a defence system were the very reason the U.S. and the Soviet Union both signed the Anti–Ballistic

Missile Treaty in 1972. But Reagan's ideological belief in the system was supreme.

Officials in External Affairs and National Defence prepared a memo for Cabinet and for Clark to sign: this document would agree to Canada co-operating with the U.S. on Strategic Defense Initiative research. The memo was in the same vein as material then working its way through the official system as part of the work to prepare a green (discussion) paper on Canada's foreign policy. Twice, I protested that the priorities of Canada's foreign policy were being surreptitiously shifted from the promotion of peace with collective security and economic development to increasing trade and the economic benefits Canada must claim in a world of competition. Arms control and disarmament matters were being marginalized by erosion.

Since Defence Minister Robert Coates had been forced to resign because of a security breach, Canada was temporarily without a defence minister. Clark was asked to sign not only in his own name, as foreign affairs minister, but also as acting defence minister. Alarmed that Clark was being stampeded by his own officials, I wrote a strong memo warning him not to inadvertently stumble. Only a few days earlier, he had told the House of Commons that Canada had "no plan, current, pending or anticipated, that would have the Government of Canada involved in any way with the Strategic Defense Initiative." Clark was now being asked to do a flip-flop. The memo was stopped, and I felt I had a little breathing room. I prepared another memo formally and strongly recommending that Canada not participate in SDI research "on the grounds that it is de-stabilizing and certain to escalate the nuclear arms race." I followed it up with another memo a month later, repeating my assertion that the Canadian public was being deceived by the so-called merits (such as safety and jobs) of SDI, and I made sure the Prime Minister's Office saw the memo. I urged that at least Canada argue within NATO for a study to determine what is permitted and not permitted in regard to ballistic missile defence research and testing under the Anti-Ballistic Missile Treaty. I was asked to join what Mulroney called "a collection of senior party members from the Red Tory spectrum," including Bob Stanfield, Lowell Murray, David MacDonald and Hugh Segal. After meeting secretly four times, we wrote a report to Mulroney, advising him to refrain from participation.

Mulroney appointed a distinguished public servant, Arthur Kroeger, who had previously served as Privy Council Clerk, to do a special study on Canada's involvement in the Strategic Defense Initiative. During his round of wide consultations, Kroeger came to see me. I handed him a lengthy brief and said, "Canada must have no part in a program which threatens to send the arms race reeling uncontrollably into the presently unweaponized region of outer space." I told him bluntly that the Initiative was not an economic question but fundamentally a strategic question with serious implications for Canada's national interest, sovereignty and security.

Kroeger recommended against Canadian involvement. The Cabinet agreed and Mulroney announced the decision in a politically adroit manner that reduced the possibility of U.S. retaliation. I then issued a statement that the decision was a clear reflection of the government's desire to continue to pursue a balanced and meaningful arms control policy within the context of our NATO commitments: "The decision not to participate in SDI research reflects and reaffirms the commitment made by the government one year ago that arms control and disarmament would be a dominant priority of Canadian foreign policy. As Ambassador for Disarmament, I can only welcome this decision."

The Machinery of Disarmament

On the freeze I had lost; on the Strategic Defense Initiative I had won. There were other issues, such as setting up new defence industries of dubious value in Canada, but I could not fight every battle. Peggy Mason, who became Clark's senior policy adviser, used to say, "We seem to spend all our time around here trying to keep bad things from happening rather than promoting good things." I had to be constantly aware of the question the columnist Richard Gwyn posed in writing about me: "Is he for real, or is he just a token? Even if he is for real, so what?" I certainly didn't see my job as adding up the wins and losses. I was concerned about moving ahead on the big picture.

Leading the Canadian delegation to the 1985 Nuclear Non-Proliferation Treaty (NPT) review conference plunged me into the "big picture." The NPT is the most widely supported international security treaty in the world. Its fundamental purpose is to stop the spread of nuclear weapons through the implementation of a bargain between the nuclear powers, which agree to negotiate the elimination of their nuclear arsenals, and the non-nuclear states, which agree not to use their guaranteed access to nuclear energy to build nuclear weapons. On the way to the month-long conference in Geneva, Eva and I stopped in France for a month's French immersion at the Institut de Français in Villefranche-sur-mer, a wonderful school on the French Riviera that gave me the confidence, finally, to speak French in social conversation. Geneva is principally a French-speaking city. Eva and I found an apartment hotel near Lake Geneva. We loved the charm of the city.

At that time, the NPT was fifteen years old. Already it was being undermined by the superpower rivalry that cast into the shadows their legal responsibility to enter into good-faith negotiations aimed at eliminating nuclear stocks. The 1980 review conference had been deadlocked. The redoubtable Mexican ambassador, Alfonso Garcia Robles, whose great prestige stemmed from his 1982 Nobel Peace Prize, threatened to introduce a resolution calling for negotiations to start in 1985 for a comprehensive nuclear test ban. Since the NPT operates by consensus, his action—well merited, in my personal opinion, but not in the Canadian government's—was deemed by the Western states to be divisive. I joined a small group of Western ambassadors who urged the U.S. to accept draft conference language calling for negotiations of a comprehensive test ban, as a matter of "highest priority," without specifying the year. The American representative, Lewis Dunn, accepted the argument that this would be better than seeing the U.S. almost isolated on a vote.

Was this progress? In the labyrinthine ways of diplomacy, it was. Though the conference final document gave the nuclear powers a loophole on the comprehensive test ban, it clearly reflected mounting world concern on the testing issue. This concern might at least lead to reductions in levels of armaments, or so we reasoned. But I was more influenced by the position of moderates from the Non-Aligned Movement (mostly developing states), such as Jayantha Dhanapala of Sri Lanka, Rolf Ekeus of Sweden, and the outstanding Egyptian scholar Mohamed Shaker, who was the conference president. They argued that the international community would be torn apart if there was no clear-cut progress or cessation of the nuclear arms race. Even with the comprehensive test ban issue papered over, the review conference could only achieve consensus by inserting an umbrella paragraph over the final text stating there was a consensus that some delegations believed this and other delegations believed that. Some consensus.

The Canadian delegation had strong officers who played important roles in the committees. I was struck by the influence that Canada had. In my report to Ottawa, I said that Canadian policies, reputation and contacts should not be underestimated. "The NPT process reaffirmed that Canada, modestly but firmly, is a player of some importance in multilateral work." Our set of core disarmament policies gave us strong ground to stand on.

The government had six main arms control and disarmament policies covering a wide canvas:

- negotiated radical reductions in nuclear forces and the enhancement of strategic stability;

- the maintenance and strengthening of the nuclear non-proliferation regime;

- the pursuit of a verifiable, multilateral Comprehensive Test Ban Treaty;

- negotiation of a global ban prohibiting the development, production and stockpiling of chemical weapons;

- the prevention of an arms race in outer space; and

- confidence-building measures to facilitate the reduction of military forces in Europe and elsewhere.

To flesh out what Canada was doing in these areas—and the work was considerable—I published a booklet, *Canada and the Pursuit of Peace*, which became a popular item, especially among parliamentarians who used it to answer their constituents' questions. The publication also dealt with Canada's professional work in UN peacekeeping and developing verification techniques. I felt that Canadians should understand that a realistic role for Canada to play on the world stage involved a long series of steps towards a nuclear weapons–free world, not reliance on a "quick fix" to make the world a safer place. Yet I recognized the anguish of many Canadians:

There is in the public today a puzzlement, a bewilderment, a frustration, a fear that the arms race may be out of control, that negotiations are impotent in curbing the relentless momentum of global militarism, that disarmament negotiators are not hearing the cries of anguish of those who sense that the future of humanity is threatened by nuclear peril.

I was involved in the machinery of disarmament. If I didn't stay strong, I knew I would be crushed. Staying strong meant fighting. Fighting would keep getting me into trouble with the officials, and eventually with Clark and Mulroney. They had a lot more to deal with than just my calls for disarmament steps. How far could I push them?

When Carol Goar of the *Toronto Star* interviewed me, the headline of her story caught the reality: "Doug Roche Catches Fire from Both Sides in Arms Debate." She wrote that some in the government thought I had turned into a promoter of the peace movement, while many peace activists wanted me to take more stands and make more noise. Goar concluded:

> The adjustment from life as a free-wheeling politician to life as a loyal government spokesman has not always been easy, he admitted.
>
> Is he glad he took the job?
>
> Roche nodded slowly.
>
> Always?
>
> "Those are tough questions. It's an important opportunity. But there is a heavy strain. It doesn't come from the work or the travel. It's because I take the damn thing so seriously."

11

Axes and Pillars

It wouldn't do for me to go around with a querulous look on my face all day long as if the world's problems rested on my shoulders alone. I had to remain upbeat if I was going to influence anybody. And, after all, I had a good life.

By 1985, the financial strain of the children's university education was behind us. Eva and I joked that we would now spend our money on the three R's—Rome, Raffles and the Russian Tea Room. Rome was a constant attraction, we had fallen in love with Raffles Hotel in Singapore, and the Russian Tea Room in New York was Eva's favourite restaurant. Mickey remained her placid self in St. Joseph's Hospital in Edmonton. Eva had fulfilled her long-held dream of acquiring a master's in social work, after which the children and I, proud to bursting, held a marvellous party for her at home to mark her accomplishment. She had even spent a fall with me in New York finishing her studies at Fordham University. We had a very pleasant suite at the Beekman Tower, a block from the UN, and Eva trod the streets of Manhattan in her sneakers. The Broadway theatre district was just across town. We frequented the famous Sardi's restaurant and one night found ourselves at a party with Tony Bennett and Lena Horne. There never was a more ardent "New Yorker" than Eva.

I travelled widely; my diary for 1986 shows that I was in Stockholm, Geneva, Vienna, Moscow, St. Petersburg, Bonn and London, and completed a thirteen-city speaking tour that took me to all ten Canadian provinces. I had a comfortable corner office on the eighth floor of the Pearson Building, the External Affairs headquarters in

Ottawa. Jim LeBlanc and Jill Sinclair, and later Jan Hansen, gave me tremendous backup and kept me out of trouble as much as they could. Simon Fraser University and the University of Alberta gave me honourary doctorates. I had developed an interesting set of friends in the diplomatic corps: Jayantha Dhanapala from Sri Lanka, Richard Butler from Australia, Yasushi Akashi from Japan and Sergio Duarte from Brazil. My life was full. Of course, there was loneliness when Eva was teaching at Grant MacEwan Community College and couldn't travel with me, but I was not suffering.

My sense of optimism increased as the 1986 International Year of Peace unfolded and a series of summit meetings between President Ronald Reagan and President Mikhail Gorbachev began. In declaring 1986 the International Year of Peace, the UN General Assembly had called upon peoples to join with the UN "in resolute efforts to safeguard peace and the future of humanity." The UN also sought to have member states focus on the multi-dimensional nature of peace— encompassing everything from human rights and the environment to the more traditional questions of the arms race. Clark told the House of Commons that the Reagan-Gorbachev Summit in Geneva, to be followed by regular high-level talks, would enlarge the common ground to improve East-West relations.

I took the position that a target date for the elimination of nuclear weapons was not the issue. What mattered was a genuine superpower effort towards radical reductions, which could unleash a renewed spirit of hope and inspire creativity that would lead to a more secure, equitable world. A lowering of East-West tensions would raise the prospects for global development. The cynics and naysayers had had their day long enough. The endless repetition of terrifying statistics on nuclear weapons and world hunger had worn down many people who had grown skeptical that the international political system could ever produce world security and social justice. Without denying the gravity of the world situation, it was necessary to look at the full picture to understand the solid reasons for hope.

Science and technology had made the world a dazzling place and offered the potential for every human being to enjoy a life of quality and quantity. Tremendous advances in food production and the tapping of new sources of food, such as the oceans, gave teeming billions the hope of adequate nourishment. Similar advances in medicine, energy, communications and a host of modern marvels all revealed that human civilization was raising itself to a higher level of existence. Although the positive benefits of modern technology were frequently obscured by strife in many areas and the massive buildup of arms, people were awakening to the recognition of their human selves, affirming their rights and clamouring for dignity and equality as well as bread and freedom.

The Consultative Group's Music

I was buttressed in my desire to look at the large picture by the members of the Consultative Group on Disarmament and Arms Control Affairs. In 1979, Geoffrey Pearson had established this group, comprising about 50 academics, activists and officials reflecting the wide spectrum of views on arms control and disarmament questions. When I took office as ambassador, the group had been dormant for a couple of years. Within a month, I brought it together for a two-day meeting, and Clark addressed the gathering. Mulroney addressed a subsequent meeting; that was followed by an appearance by Defence Minister Perrin Beatty.

Considerable money was spent to set up these meetings. Also, the government was contributing significantly to the education efforts of the World Disarmament Campaign at the UN and maintaining a disarmament fund at home to help groups hold seminars and peace events. The government was clearly engaged with the peace community across Canada. Several in the Consultative Group, such as John Lamb, Bev Delong, Ernie Regehr, Bob Reford, Joanne Harris, Bobbie Carrie and Jan Van Stolk, to name only a few, were kindred spirits. They understood what it was like to deal with the disarmament machinery of the government.

The Consultative Group became expert in its assessments. The 1984 meeting featured Franklyn Griffiths, a University of Toronto East European expert, who argued that we should switch from an over-preoccupation with the military-technical aspects of nuclear weapons to greater concern with the political relationships. We examined how to increase Canada's influence in Washington and Moscow and deepen the perspective of NATO, and looked at ways for the public to energize Canadian policy. The militarization of space, development of a ban on chemical weapons, strengthened verification and confidence-building measures to promote conventional disarmament preoccupied us. At subsequent meetings, I brought in the resident Canadian ambassadors at the Conference on Disarmament in Geneva, the Vienna-based Mutual and Balanced Force Reduction Talks, and the Stockholm-based Conference on Confidence and Security Building Measures and Disarmament in Europe.

I talked about Canada's work in sorting out the wide range of disarmament resolutions coming before the UN each year. Many members expressed concern that the North American Aerospace Defence Command (NORAD) was becoming more and more integrated into the comprehensive defence program of the U.S.; thus, there should be a firm decision that NORAD would not be linked to space defences or ballistic missile defence. Canada should also insist on strict adherence to the Anti-Ballistic Missile Treaty. Some suggested that the arms race was not a struggle for power between the superpowers but a defence of the privileges of power, and that Canada should distance itself from this struggle. Would not women bring more nurturing values to the global search for security? What could be done to stem the apathy and negativism among young people? Many wanted Canada to promote the themes of the International Year of Peace through strengthened peace education in the school system.

Interesting suggestions were made, including the following:

- Canada should urge the U.S. and the Soviet Union to extend a moratorium on nuclear testing to mark the International Year of Peace.

- Canada should take the lead in developing a comprehensive law of space similar to the development of the Law of the Sea.

- Canada should call for a special UN session on international security.

- Canada should sponsor an international competition to develop a model for a workable disarmament process.

The Consultative Group clearly wanted to be involved in helping Canada play a stronger role in peace issues. It was music to my ears.

Lifting Up, Dragged Down

As part of the government's program for the International Year of Peace, I set out to hold three-hour consultations with 198 individual Canadians in St. John's, Halifax, Charlottetown, Saint John, Montréal, Toronto, Waterloo, Winnipeg, Saskatoon, Edmonton, Vancouver, Victoria and Ottawa. With speeches to service clubs and schools, appearances before editorial boards, and a host of television, radio and press interviews, it was an exacting schedule, but I thrived on it. Firdaus Kharas, executive director of the United Nations Association in Canada, managed all the logistics in this and a subsequent Canadian tour I did at the end of 1987. His support of my work was heartening.

My opening speech at each event dwelled on the wide agenda. "The world needs the continued work of Canada in verification of arms control agreements, stopping the spread of nuclear weapons, fighting African famine, and speeding up economic development in the developing nations." No one, I said, expected these goals to be achieved by December 31, 1986. Rather, the International Year of Peace showed how the world must continue to evolve into a global community with increasingly closer relationships among all peoples. "It establishes peace as a system of values." The *Globe and Mail* printed part of my text:

> [The International Year of Peace] has served to remind us that peace without development is not peace, that peace without racial equality and harmony is not peace, that peace without a reasonable quality of life is not peace. It is, therefore, the fullness of Canada's programs—from development assistance and active support for human rights to the protection of the environment and the promotion of a better standard of living for people across the country and, indeed, around the world—that constitutes a meaningful contribution to peace.

Though I strove to lift up audiences, I was constantly brought back to the basic facts of the nuclear arms race and Canada's participation in it. Our UN votes shied away from freezing development and deployment of arms. We were testing the Cruise missile delivery system. We were not demanding an immediate Comprehensive Test Ban Treaty. We were building new defence industries. Once in a while, I heard demands for my resignation, but as a reasonably hardened politician I didn't pay too much attention. The recognition by many of the value of my work sustained me. Nonetheless, I felt obliged to report my findings to Clark and the officials.

I said it was my candid evaluation that in the view of a significant number of Canadians, the government's credibility on arms control and disarmament issues "is on a declining curve." Negative perceptions were outweighing positive actions. "What exacerbates the positive-negative Canadian imbalance is the U.S. factor." Canadians now recognize, though do not necessarily support, I said, the closer Canada–U.S. connection being developed by the government. Many Canadians perceive that the U.S. is not interested in vigorously pursuing arms control and disarmament agreements and is even hindering the prospects for progress, such as by investing in the Strategic Defense Initiative at such great financial cost, threatening non-compliance, maintaining nuclear testing, and ignoring Gorbachev's moratorium on testing. "Thus, these Canadians conclude that Canada, in pursuing good U.S. relations, is willing to adopt a more compliant and subservient attitude on arms control and disarmament than has traditionally characterized Canadian policy. In short, these Canadians accuse Canada of putting U.S. relations ahead of our duty to the world community, in terms of taking every step possible to stop the arms race."

I said that Canadians were not ignoring Soviet responsibility in the global arms race, but they sensed that Gorbachev was offering more than propaganda in proposals for cuts and that the negative response of the U.S. was a result of a resurgence of militarism in their foreign policy. "There is strong support for you personally [Clark] as a foreign policy leader; people sense your values in the African, Central American and UN theatres. They know that arms control and disarmament is so complex that it cannot be subjected to an instant fix. However, they are frustrated, fearful and angry. They see the arms race continuing (and Canada contributing to its expansion).... They see an erosion of Canada's traditional image and believe that the government is retreating from its initial pledge to make peace a centerpiece of its mandate and to make arms control and disarmament a constant, consistent and dominant priority."

I went to see Clark to urge him to make a couple of major speeches on disarmament. Appointments with him were getting harder to obtain. He was becoming more distant, more formal in his conversations with me. I don't think it had to do with our personal relationship; rather, the pressure I was putting on him ran up against Mulroney's enchantment with Reagan, the rightward resurgence of the Conservative caucus, and the determination of officials not to rock the boat themselves or to have Canadian policy interfere with the prime objective of good Canada-U.S. relations.

This last point could not be taken lightly. The North American Free Trade Agreement was coming into sight, and the economic prosperity of Canada, so dependent on the strong trade relationship with the U.S., was on the line. Mulroney and Reagan had become chums at the Shamrock Summit, and the sight of the Canadian prime minister belting out a chorus of "When Irish Eyes Are Smiling" struck many as being over the top. Clark had other major items on his agenda, not least trying to get the U.S. to stop blocking progress on ridding South Africa of apartheid and to help bring human rights and economic development to Central America. Lewis was pressuring both Clark and Mulroney to strengthen Canada's policies at the UN. Lewis, a politician to the core, worked all the strings in his private conversations with Mulroney (which Lewis would tell me about). Clark, always struggling to be loyal to Mulroney even when the prime minister was undercutting his authority as foreign minister, could only handle so many issues.

An Axe to Public Education

The Disarmament Fund was important to me, but I don't think it was to Clark. With a budget of about $700,000 a year, the fund did a lot not only to develop an informed public opinion but also to identify the government, in the mind of the peace community, with serious consideration of complex subjects. It funded some very creative projects. Four hundred women from across Canada and the world met at Mount St. Vincent's University in Halifax to discuss women's alternatives to negotiating peace and resolving conflict. Scientists at McGill University produced the elements for an international treaty regulating military space activities. Project Ploughshares developed material for Disarmament Week, linking the themes of disarmament and development. The Prairie Christian Training Centre in Fort Qu'Appelle, Saskatchewan, brought together church groups to discuss peace research and education projects. A wide range of projects tried to stimulate a balanced discussion of arms control and disarmament issues. Among the learning experiences provided by the fund were orientation tours in which members of the Consultative Group were brought to the UN in New York to experience first-hand Canada's diplomatic work. Clark himself had said that it was "essential" that Canadians involve themselves in these issues.

All this was public education at a very low cost to the government, yet when bureaucratic axes began to cut into Canada's deficit, the Disarmament Fund was an easy target. I protested a proposal to chop half a million dollars out of the fund, which would eviscerate it. Officials countered that the Canadian International Institute for Peace and Security, which started up just as the Tories were taking office, could handle grants. But the Institute was basically a research organization; it didn't interact with the public. This is the kind of argument bureaucrats love because it quickly becomes arcane and political eyes glaze over. The Disarmament Fund was slashed and, later, even the Peace Institute was killed in a federal budget deficit purge.

That the government needed more understanding, not to mention friends, in the peace community was readily apparent at a spectacular conference, "True North Strong and Free?" in Edmonton, the largest peace gathering in Canadian history. Despite -18°C temperatures, 5,400 people turned out for the two-day event. Star speakers Gwynne Dyer and David Suzuki assailed the nuclear arms race. George Ignatieff, my predecessor, stole the show when, assaulting the superpowers for endangering life on earth, he demanded, "No incineration without representation!"

The audience was reasonably kind to me when I opened the conference with an upbeat speech, but government officials who followed me were booed. National Defence had uniformed officers present, who were treated with respect. But hostility to government policies deemed pro-American, such as Cruise missile testing, was rampant. Canada's six arms control policies were given short shrift. What the conference demanded in resolutions was a stop to Cruise missile testing, a Canadian endorsement of the Soviet test moratorium and request to the U.S. to do the same, an international crisis centre to reduce the risk of accidental nuclear war, and an independent commission to study alternative defence policies, including non-alignment and neutrality. I found the event so stressful that, at the end of the first afternoon, instead of attending the cocktail party, I went to the gym to play basketball with my son.

Later, I found out that a departmental representative filed an unflattering report on my appearance at a Montréal event, where Stephen Lewis also spoke. The official recounted an academic asking him, "What is the government doing, letting these two ambassadors run all over the map on policy questions?" He referred to Lewis's support of Operation Dismantle, which challenged government policy, and my distancing myself from the Cruise missile testing policy. There is no doubt the department wanted to rein in Lewis and Roche. Increasingly, it perceived us as spokesmen on the part of non-governmental organizations to the government rather than the other way around. Lewis and I tried to have it both ways and maintained, for a while, a delicate balancing act.

Being Taken Seriously

Our work at the United Nations on behalf of the government was widely praised. The veteran Canadian diplomat John Holmes, who had achieved revered status in his retirement, came to the UN to assess the organization on its 40th birthday. It happened that the Canadian delegation, after several years of trying, had just won consensus acceptance of a resolution promoting verification procedures in arms control, despite the fact that neither the Americans nor the Russians liked it. Holmes, calling it the most successful consensus operation he had ever seen, wrote in the *Ottawa Citizen*: "The Canadian Ambassador for Disarmament, Douglas Roche, and his extraordinarily able team, did as professional a job of arm-twisting, cajoling, bargaining, and friendly persuasion as I ever saw in the so-called 'golden age.'" (He should have mentioned the work of Alex Morrison, a military officer representing the National Defence at the Canadian Mission, who worked alongside me at the UN.) Holmes noted how Lewis and I had established relationships of trust with colleagues from all the blocs. "Stephen Lewis and Doug Roche have become players of consequence in the Assembly," he said. The journalist John Best led off his piece with "Kudos to Douglas Roche and to Canada's United Nations team. The Canadian Ambassador for Disarmament recently got a U.N. committee to approve a landmark resolution on the verification of disarmament agreements."

The reason it was necessary to have some standing in the eyes of officials was so that they would take me seriously on big issues. There could hardly be a bigger issue than the emergence of Mikhail Gorbachev as the new leader of the Soviet Union. I first met him in 1983 when, as Agriculture Minister, he came to Ottawa and appeared before a lengthy meeting of the parliamentary foreign affairs and defence committees. It was apparent that here was a new kind of communist, a humanist. He was reaching out to the West.

In early 1986, shortly after becoming general-secretary, Gorbachev issued a fifteen-year plan providing for the stage-by-stage elimination of nuclear weapons by 2000. He wrote in his book *Perestroika*, published the following year, that this was not a propaganda move. "The move was dictated by a sense of responsibility about preventing nuclear war and preserving peace." World opinion was shifting this way, he said, adding that his move was, among other things, a response to the appeal made by the Six-Nation Initiative. A nuclear weapons–free world was not some slogan to stagger the imagination. "Security is a political issue, not a function of military confrontation. Failure to understand this can only result in war with all its catastrophic consequences."

Instead of welcoming this move, Canadian officials in Moscow threw cold water on it, dismissing it as an "extremely adroit propaganda thrust aimed at portraying Western nuclear policies in the worst possible light." The officials saw it as an attempt by Gorbachev to get onto the high moral ground occupied by President Reagan, who had justified his unwavering support for the Strategic Defense Initiative as leading to the abolition of nuclear weapons. They doubted that Gorbachev's pre-conditions for his elimination program—mutual U.S.-Soviet renunciation of development, testing and deployment of space weapons, and the U.S.'s joining the Soviet nuclear test moratorium—would work.

At that time, I was visiting the multilateral arms control and disarmament forums in Geneva, Stockholm and Vienna, where I talked to a wide range of international diplomats. I reported to Ottawa that there was "a strong current of thought that the Gorbachev proposals represented a fundamental shift into a new era of Soviet realism."

Gorbachev recognizes that he cannot keep up with the U.S. in nuclear technologies, now entering unknown fields of new physical principles, and also restore the Soviet economy. Not only can he not win World War III but too many Soviet guns are now getting in the way of the demand for butter. He has rushed out his visionary package to impress the forthcoming important Soviet Congress and to consolidate his drive for world opinion to put pressure on the White house. In this sense, he is as guilty of propaganda as any leader selling his policies, but it would be a big mistake to dismiss his moves as mere propaganda or to reduce the challenge to niggling points. What is at issue here is a move from military to economic priorities.

Since Clark himself had travelled to the Soviet Union not long after becoming Foreign Minister, I was confident that he would see for himself that the old rigidities of the Soviet Union were breaking up. Nevertheless, I continued to press him to ensure that Canada did not react "in a Pavlovian manner" to the new openings in the Eastern bloc. Canada had established a rapport with Eastern bloc countries, I said in a memo to Clark. "Can we not engage them in meaningful debates on resolutions and proposals in order to lessen the East–West divide and, in the case of the U.N., to work towards consensus resolutions?" Clark authorized me to visit the Soviet Union for a series of speeches and meetings with Soviet officials and scholars specializing in arms control issues as part of "Canada's ongoing dialogue ... with the Soviet Union."

On the Brink of Abolition

Before I could get there, Reagan and Gorbachev's historic Reykjavik Summit in Iceland occurred on the weekend of October 11–12, 1986. Gorbachev repeated his offer to eliminate all ballistic missiles. Reagan responded warmly. Suddenly, the two superpower leaders found themselves on the brink of a nuclear weapons–free world. But there was one stumbling block. Reagan offered to confine the Strategic Defense Initiative research and testing to ten years, during which time all ballistic missiles would be eliminated. Gorbachev insisted that such research had to be limited to the laboratory—in other words, no testing. Reagan would not give in. Some officials on both sides were horrified as the tense negotiations played themselves out. The idea of throwing away the strategy of mutual assured destruction was deemed too risky. American officials in particular were vehemently opposed, claiming it was U.S. nuclear weapons that held off the possibility of an invasion of Western Europe by Soviet conventional forces.

Though I felt devastated at the Reykjavik "failure," I came to realize that Reykjavik was actually a milestone, because it gave the highest political legitimacy to the concept of the complete elimination of nuclear weapons. Nuclear disarmament was now on page one.

Jim LeBlanc prepared my trip and came with me to Moscow, Leningrad (now St. Petersburg) and Kiev. I gave a lecture in each place and was careful to adhere to the texts Foreign Affairs provided. I simply couldn't afford to make a misstep by freelancing comments. My speeches were long, sweeping reviews of Canadian policy, even recounting how Trudeau's words that "a nuclear war cannot be won and must never be fought" had found their way into the communiqués issued by Reagan and Gorbachev. My sixteen-page Moscow lecture ended with this paragraph:

> The Reykjavik Summit revealed that the portents are more encouraging now than they have been for many years. The ideals of the International Year of Peace must continue to drive us forward. Results won't come without effort and the stakes are high. The task is clearly for everyone. Canada, for one, will continue to work in every way possible toward our common goal of a world of confidence, security, trust and peace.

I met with the Deputy Foreign Minister Alexandre Bessmertnykh, and representatives of the Institute of International Economic Relations and the Ukrainian Academy of Sciences. In addition to attending these formal meetings, I tried to talk to as many people as I could manage, given the language barrier. I found many encouraging signs that the Soviet leadership was in fact committed to a more open, re-energized society. Arms cuts were real, not just propaganda moves.

Gorbachev continued to stun the world with bold proposals. His comprehensive thinking about security was contained in a 1987 article he published in the Soviet publications *Pravda* and *Izvestia*, "The Reality and Guarantees of a Secure World." Here he called for a range of new international institutions: a multilateral centre for lessening the dangers of war, an international verification mechanism under UN auspices, a tribunal to investigate acts of terrorism, a special fund for humanitarian co-operation, a world space organization and a "consultative council of the world's intellectual elite." A central concept was a "system of universal law and order." He set the goal of the dissolution of military blocs, made possible by such steps as the elimination of foreign bases, the creation of zones free of chemical and nuclear weapons, and the wider use of peace-keeping forces.

In 1988, star billing awaited Gorbachev when he spoke to the UN General Assembly. I was seated at the Canadian desk when he brought the delegates to their feet with an electrifying speech. World progress, he said, is only possible through a search for universal human consensus. The principle of freedom of choice is mandatory. The world will find its unity in tolerating diversity. A more intense and open political dialogue is necessary for successful negotiations. One-sided reliance on military power ultimately weakens other components of national security. His renunciation of force won vigorous applause:

> … the use or threat of force no longer can or must be an instrument of foreign policy. This applies above all to nuclear arms …
> All of us, and primarily the stronger of us, must exercise self-restraint and totally rule out any outward-oriented use of force.

At the UN, the Soviets submitted a resolution that sought to establish a "comprehensive system for security." I argued with Canadian officials that this was the moment the world had been waiting for and that the international community must seize it to support and reinforce the superpower bilateral negotiations for arms reductions. After resisting it at first, Canada ended up voting for the resolution. Unfortunately, Gorbachev's holistic approach to peace lost ground in the aftermath of the Soviet implosion after the fall of the Berlin Wall.

From Guns to Bread

My desire to push progressive ideas yet get along with Foreign Affairs was tested again at the International Conference on the Relationship between Disarmament and Development. The very two themes that had propelled me out of Parliament and into full-time peace work were linked. The connection had first been highlighted by President Dwight D. Eisenhower, who said, "Every gun that is made, every warship launched, every rocket fired, signifies, in a final sense, a theft from those who hunger and are not fed, from those who are cold and are not clothed." A three-year study of the disarmament and development issues by 27 world experts headed by the formidable Swedish diplomat Inga Thorsson reported in 1981, concluding:

> The world has a choice. It can continue to pursue the arms race, or it can move with deliberate speed towards a more sustainable economic and political order. It cannot do both. ... The arms race and development are in a competitive relationship, both in terms of resources and also in the vital dimension of attitudes and perceptions. ... A compelling appeal can be made to the economic self-interest of states to reduce military expenditure and reallocate resources to development.

I welcomed grappling with the two issues. Lewis joined me in urging Clark to take the presidency of an international conference called at the UN for 1987. But Foreign Affairs was not enthusiastic. The U.S. said it would boycott the conference on the grounds that there was no such relationship. Besides, a group that the department termed "Third World radicals" was attempting to gain acceptance of the simplistic notion of transferring funds directly from weapons procurement, especially in the North, to development assistance. This didn't mean the department was not supportive of the conference; it was, but, like most of the Western nations, it wanted to resist the idea of a special fund being set up that would act as a conduit of money from guns to bread. It wanted to discourage initiatives that would threaten a consensus at the conference by injecting unrealistic prescriptions or unproductive political rhetoric.

Thorsson's approach was much more sophisticated than just the creation of a fund. By taking a broader approach to the problem of security, she defined a "dynamic triangular relationship" between disarmament, development and security. Security for all would be enhanced by vigorously pursuing disarmament and development in their own right, regardless of the pace of progress in the other. Although there would not be an automatic transfer of funds from disarmament measures to development, the possibility of reduction of public expenditures to social purposes, debt could be reduced and economic growth could be stimulated.

India was driving the conference, and the Indian delegation was led by a strong-minded economist, Muchkund Dubey. We became friends. Privately, I agreed with his demand that there be a tangible expression of even a slight shift of funds from armaments to sustainable development in the name of human security. Why official Ottawa deemed such a sensible move as "radical" was beyond me, but I knew the conference would founder if Dubey kept pushing. In between the preparatory meetings, I went to India, following a UN meeting in Pakistan, to urge him to back away from strident demands for the sake of obtaining a consensus in the final document, which would legitimize the disarmament–development relationship.

Dubey wanted the fund established. I warned him that continued insistence would jeopardize not only the conference but also international acceptance of the relationship. I backed up my views with a speech to the Indian Federation of U.N. Associations, and the Indian media took notice of what I was saying. I invited Dubey to Ottawa on his way to New York and gave a dinner for him in the Parliamentary restaurant. He came around to recognizing that his best interests were served by a consensus.

Clark decided not to accept the offer to preside at the conference, but did agree to be the first speaker. His emphasis that progress towards development and progress towards disarmament could both contribute to stronger security set the tone for the meeting.

The conference played itself out and the consensus final document described disarmament and development as "two of the most urgent challenges facing the world today … [and as] two pillars on which enduring international peace and security can be built." It said, "Security consists of not only military but also political, economic, social, humanitarian and human rights and ecological aspects." This sentence, giving the wide definition of security advanced by Gorbachev, was picked up at the 1992 Summit of the Security Council, the first time the leaders of all the countries on the Council had met, with the stated purpose of planning for the post–Cold War era. The world was coming to a new understanding of what security was all about. Security could not be obtained by large numbers of arms: rather it could only come about by attention to meeting human needs.

12

Applauded Abroad,
Sidelined at Home

Already in 1987, it was apparent that Mikhail Gorbachev was changing the defence policies of the Soviet Union. Though the Reykjavik Summit had failed, it had set in motion continued disarmament work, which culminated in the Intermediate Nuclear Forces Treaty that President Reagan and General-Secretary Gorbachev signed at their Washington Summit on December 8, 1987. Enforcing the destruction of all nuclear missiles with ranges between 500 and 1,500 kilometres, it was the first treaty to eliminate a complete class of nuclear weapons. Stringent on-site verification measures were included. The Soviets had three times as many such weapons as the Americans, yet Gorbachev cast them all aside. The treaty marked the beginning of the end of the Cold War.

I found it astonishing that, during the negotiation process for the treaty, the Canadian government issued a new defence policy laced with Cold War rhetoric and the promise to buy ten to twelve nuclear-powered attack submarines for the Canadian navy. When the National Defence White (policy) Paper was being drafted, I wrote to Defence Minister Perrin Beatty to urge the inclusion of a strong component of arms control and disarmament to reaffirm that Canada's security policy consisted of the elements of defence, disarmament, peacekeeping and conflict resolution. "The White Paper should dispose of the myth that defence and disarmament are two ships passing in the night," I said.

Far from recognizing the value of disarmament, the White Paper said Soviet bombers would gain even greater importance if the superpowers reduced or eliminated ballistic missiles from their arsenals. The paper claimed that little had changed in the Soviet Union under Gorbachev. "The new Soviet leadership continues to view the world as divided into two antagonistic camps. There is every reason to believe that its long-term aims continue to include the dissolution of NATO, the neutralization of non-communist Europe and the weakening of the West as a whole." The restructuring of Canada's land and naval forces was said to be urgent.

The Canadian Press called me for my view on this inflammatory paper. Using the diplomatic language I had learned, I said the harsh rhetoric was "unhelpful." I added that the paper's authors had not taken into account "this new moment that has arrived, in which East-West relations can be conducted not at ever-higher levels of arms but at increasingly lower levels." I tried to pass off the White Paper as but the opinion of National Defence but I knew that it would damage Canada's disarmament work, probably severely. The media and the Opposition in Parliament ridiculed the proposal to acquire a nuclear-powered submarine fleet as "rubbish" and "political posturing." Opposition Leader John Turner rose in Question Period to state, "The latest person to attack the White Paper on Defence … is Canada's Ambassador for Disarmament, Douglas Roche, who was, as Hon. Members know, a distinguished Conservative Member of Parliament and is the Prime Minister's personal appointee to this post." Why, asked Turner, had the government introduced a defence policy inconsistent—in the opinion of Ambassador Roche—with Canada's arms reduction policy? Nonplussed, Prime Minister Brian Mulroney replied that it is "quite normal and natural in a democracy" for a major initiative to provide wide-ranging comment.

Questionable Military Spending

I could not engage the prime minister in public debate, so I wrote to him, protesting the downgrading of disarmament work. The paper, I said, had gratuitously opposed "unilateral" disarmament, ignoring the substantive work going on in "mutual, balanced and verifiable" disarmament. I objected to the anti-Soviet rhetoric and the dismissing of Gorbachev's moves reducing East-West tensions. Why, at this new moment in world history, did Canada want "to use valuable resources for nuclear submarines, thus creating a disturbing precedent in weakening the non-proliferation regime as well as escalating military expenditures for a questionable goal?"

Leading figures across Canada concerned with these important issues with whom I have consulted, including the Steering Committee of the Consultative Group, are dismayed, and some are angry, at what they regard as the Defence Department subsuming the totality of foreign policy. Were I not to signal my dissent, I would be failing to do my duty to my post in not standing up for disarmament as a constant, consistent and dominant element of Canadian foreign policy. And my silence would be interpreted by those who know me as going along with a diminishment of my own function.

I attached to the letter a report of my activities during the 1,000 days I had been in office. "I would gladly do more for you and Canada, but I need Cabinet's support in strengthening the structural position of disarmament in the government's priorities."

Mulroney replied that, while a strong national defence would continue to be part of Canada's international security policy, the Defence White Paper was not a surrogate Foreign Policy White Paper. But the government had an obligation to meet "plausible threats." The most plausible threat came from the Soviet Union. "This basic fact of contemporary life does not in any way imply adoption of a Cold War view of the world."

The White Paper states—and I reiterate here—that a strong national defence is a major component—but only one component—of Canada's international security policy. Arms control and disarmament and the peaceful resolution of disputes are equally important. All of these activities are mutually supportive—both in terms of national policy and international security. I do not believe that we in Canada can have a credible voice in arms control and disarmament matters if we fail to meet our responsibility to our people and Allies for a prudent and responsible national defence. Nor do I believe that the East-West relationship can be improved in an enduring fashion if we in the West cease to maintain a robust defence.

He concluded on a slightly ominous note: "This is the policy of the Government of Canada, one which I hope you can continue to support."

The White Paper did not present a permanent problem for me because the idea of nuclear submarines vanished when deficit cutting became a new cornerstone of financial policy, and Canada's defence policy slid off the front pages as East-West relations eased. However, the continuing problem of Canadian acquiescence to the U.S. drive to maintain nuclear weapons primacy did not go away. It led to my severest wrench from the foreign affairs department.

Cruise missile testing in Canada had started under the Trudeau government, which felt unable to resist U.S. pressure at the peak of the Cold War. The Canadian government explained that testing in Canada demonstrated solidarity within NATO over the modernization of its nuclear deterrent; testing in winter in a 2,200-km corridor including the Northwest Territories, British Columbia, Alberta and Saskatchewan would provide conditions similar to the Soviet Union. Cruise was a Cold War weapon, but now the Cold War was winding down. Nonetheless, the U.S. came back to the Canadian government for permission to test the "stealth" advanced Cruise missile.

With each Cruise test, I felt Canadian credibility in nuclear disarmament work diminishing. The Umbrella Testing Agreement (under which Canada allowed the U.S. to test the Cruise missile delivery system), begun in 1983, was up for renewal in 1988. I pleaded that it not be renewed. Foreign Affairs, pressed by National Defence, did not agree with me and sent a memo to Clark recommending extension. I particularly objected to the communication strategy in which opponents of testing were described as the "anti-defence" movement. I sent a memo to Clark stating that it would be "absolutely fatal" to the government's credibility in disarmament to permit testing of the advanced Cruise missile at a time when the Cold War was ending. "There is no end to the advances of technology to 'refine' nuclear weapons and no end to the deceit advanced by the arms merchants that we will all be safer with the next round of escalation." Canada had no business aiding and abetting the U.S. to lock in nuclear weapons superiority, I insisted. Clark was able to maneuver through the political shoals and delay a decision on Canada's response.

Deepening Credibility Problem

Meanwhile, I had to concentrate on the disarmament and development conference in New York in 1987, then get ready for a second cross-Canada tour following the fall session of the General Assembly. Once again, with strong staff support, I travelled from St. John's to Victoria, speaking at public forums and high schools, giving background briefings to editorial boards, and doing radio and television interviews. My goal was to reaffirm Canada's role in the international arms control and disarmament process, discuss the implications of the Intermediate Nuclear Forces Treaty for the future of disarmament, and get public input into the preparations for the forthcoming UN Third Special Session on Disarmament.

I took, of course, a positive approach and found, generally, a higher level of optimism in the public about the turn of international events than on my previous tour. But despite my attempts to portray arms control, disarmament and defence as complementary elements of Canada's security policy, many people criticized the Cold War rhetoric of the Defence White Paper as being out of step with the world. There was widespread opposition to nuclear submarines and Cruise testing. I was frequently asked how I could be speaking about disarmament while the government was promoting the purchase of nuclear-powered submarines. I was exhorted to be firmer and more direct in my dealings with the prime minister and foreign minister. Listening to this advice, I thought wryly to myself, "If I go after Mulroney and Clark any harder, they really will fire me!"

I gave Clark a full report of the mood of the country as I found it:

> I think I can say with reasonable certainty that nobody emphasizes more than me the range of good work Canada is doing in the whole foreign policy field (which you are credited with) and yet nobody bears the brunt more than me of the skepticism in many quarters about Canada's commitment to help stop the arms race. What bothers me most is that the credibility of the Government is hurt in our proper effort to be a good ally of the U.S. In this sense there is (an increasing) political cost to the Government caused by the U.S.

"The Disarmament Game"

The reality of what Canada was up against in the international politics of nuclear disarmament was vividly on display during the UN Third Special Session on Disarmament, held at the UN in New York from May 31 to June 25, 1988. At the first Special Session in 1978, I had been just a casual observer. At the second in 1982, I spoke on behalf of Parliamentarians for World Order, where I had free rein to condemn the nuclear arms race as a crime against God and humanity. Now I was, excepting Clark, the head of the Canadian delegation and chairman of the Barton Group of Western ambassadors. I had to weigh every word in what, it was easy to predict, would be a clash of perspectives between Western states and states of the Non-Aligned Movement (most developing states) on the multilateral agenda for arms control and disarmament.

There was a huge turnout for a two-day meeting of the Consultative Group held six weeks prior to the Third Special Session. Although some members wanted Canada to reaffirm Trudeau's "strategy of suffocation," enunciated a decade earlier, it was clear that the government had moved into a more cautious mode, trying to avert confrontation at the very moment bilateral relations between the U.S. and the Soviet Union were yielding concrete results. Searching for compromise and consensus would be the Canadian approach. Canada would resist "unrealistic" proposals. It was considered realistic to work to strengthen the Non-Proliferation Treaty, support a step-by-step approach to a Comprehensive Test Ban Treaty and promote regional conventional disarmament moves. But it was deemed unrealistic to call for immediate negotiations to shut down the development and deployment of all nuclear weapons.

I considered it disingenuous to work for disarmament while supporting the modernization of nuclear weapons. The very concept of nuclear deterrence had to be discredited, in my view. But the official Western view, supported by Canada, was that nuclear deterrence was a cornerstone policy. It might be productive to adopt the step-by-step approach if all sides were sincere in trying to achieve the final goal. But the Western nuclear powers—the U.S., the U.K. and France—demonstrated time and again that they were not sincere. The Swedish Nobel Peace Laureate Alva Myrdal had titled her book on this old game of moving pawns around the disarmament chessboard *The*

Game of Disarmament. The book was a masterful explanation of why neither of the superpowers seriously tried to achieve disarmament. Underneath the debate over how many missiles each side could have, they actually institutionalized the nuclear arms race rather than stopping or reversing it.

One night at a dinner party at the UN, I was seated at a table of diplomats who enlivened the evening with stories about their children and grandchildren. The Soviet ambassador and the American ambassador proudly displayed photos they carried in their wallets. I sat in amazement at the antagonists by day becoming the proud parents by night, both expressing the same good wishes for each other's grandchildren. The next day, they were back in committee, reflecting their national policies, tearing each other apart. At the human level, these two men were ready for reconciliation, but their respective national policies forbade it. Another time in the Delegates Lounge, in a discussion with a high-profile Western ambassador, I raised the prospect of achieving better gains by getting more women diplomats into the process. "Don't be silly," he replied. "We don't want women here. They might actually *do* something." There is no shortage of cynicism in the diplomatic corps.

As the Third Special Session on Disarmament opened, the U.S., backed by the U.K. and France, said it didn't want to hear anything about the promises made at the first session ten years earlier in 1978. As far as the U.S. was concerned, this session would be a damage-limitation exercise. The U.S. and India occupied opposite ends of the spectrum. The U.S. pointed to the recently signed Intermediate Nuclear Forces Treaty to show the progress it was making; India wanted total nuclear disarmament on a time-bound schedule. Indian Prime Minister Rajiv Gandhi attacked the Western support of deterrence and outlined a proposal for the elimination of all nuclear weapons by 2010. The Western states virtually ignored Gandhi's plan. When Mexico's Alfonso Garcia Robles presented a special report on a comprehensive program for disarmament, it was brushed aside.

At one stage, I pleaded with the conference to build on the recent achievements and not to deny a consensus in those areas in which agreement existed. The chairman of the committee of the whole, Ambassador Mansur Ahmed, presented a draft report that reached out to all corners, but he lacked the dexterity to lead delegates through the storm, and the conference foundered. Although there was agreement on issues involving conventional disarmament, non-proliferation, verification and confidence-building measures, there was no agreement on the key issues of stopping an arms race in outer space, nuclear weapons–free zones, nuclear disarmament, and implementing the disarmament and development link. The conference went overtime with an all-night session the final evening, but the chasm was unbridgeable.

The West blamed India for overreaching. The Soviet Union blamed the U.S. for its intransigence. Both the West and the Soviets blamed the doctrinaire position of the Non-Aligned Movement. Privately, the Canadian delegation attributed the failure largely to the skepticism and inflexibility of the U.S., which wouldn't even extend the time for last-minute negotiations.

First Committee Chairman

The session's failure concerned me deeply because I was about to become the Chairman of the UN Disarmament (First) Committee. The chairmanship of all UN committees rotates annually among the five regions: the West, the Eastern bloc, Asia, Africa and Latin America. The only other time a Canadian had held the disarmament chairmanship was when Lester B. Pearson occupied the post in 1949. It was now the West's turn, and since all the Western countries supported my candidacy, the election in the fall would be automatic. I felt thrilled to be following in Pearson's footsteps. To prepare myself and to assess the mood after the failed third special session, I decided to hold First Committee consultations in key capitals around the world.

Eva and Jim LeBlanc joined me for what turned out to be one of the best trips I have ever taken. We started in Tokyo, where the Foreign Minister gave a dinner for us in a Japanese restaurant. Then we flew to Beijing and saw once more the Forbidden City, followed by a banquet at the State Guest House. Next was Moscow, where we were hosted at a spectactular luncheon by Deputy Foreign Minister Vladimir Petrovsky and his wife. Eva and I walked through Red Square at night, found a hotel dining room with a band and danced to "Midnight in Moscow." We took an overnight train to Leningrad (St. Petersburg) and toured the Hermitage, in my view the most elegant museum in the world. We flew to Stockholm, then to East

Berlin and made a visit to Potsdam. Paris, with the Tuileries Gardens, the Louvre and dinner at a sidewalk café on the Champs-Élysées, followed. We attended mass at Notre Dame Cathedral and strolled along the Left Bank. Next was Geneva and its charming "old city," then on to Harare in Zimbabwe and a short safari. We flew back to London, saw a couple of plays in the West End and had tea at the Savoy. When we arrived back in Edmonton, I rejoiced in having had such a world experience with Eva.

Though perhaps it seems hard to believe, all the sightseeing and attractions were a sideline to the business of the trip. The combination of being a Canadian diplomat and the incoming chairman of the First Committee gave me an entrée at reasonably high levels to governments' foreign ministries. I found that, despite the failure of the third session, government officials felt that a new opportunity had arisen to advance the disarmament agenda. There were three reasons for this. First, the Reagan-Gorbachev summits had dramatized the improved East-West relationship. Second, the summer of 1988 had seen the alleviation of several regional conflicts, such as the Iran-Iraq war, the Soviet invasion of Afghanistan, and the wars in Namibia, Cyprus and Western Sahara as the result of diplomatic activity. Third, there was renewed respect for the United Nations, which in turn generated a restored sense of self-confidence at the UN. In October 1988, the UN peace-keeping forces were awarded the Nobel Peace Prize.

In Geneva, home of the Conference on Disarmament, I took special care to do a round of consultations with the Western Group, the Eastern bloc, the Non-Aligned Movement, and China, and held special meetings with Ambassador Garcia Robles, a figure of great dignity, Miljan Komatina, the secretary-general of the Conference on Disarmament, and Jayantha Dhanapala, who had become director of the UN Disarmament Research Office. Alex Morrison, who worked with me at the Canadian mission, flew over from New York for these meetings; we were also joined by Serab Kheradi, secretary of the First Committee. All I really did was show everyone that I cared about what they thought and that I would try to run the First Committee in an efficient manner. For this, my effort was praised as the most comprehensive and organized set of consultations ever conducted by a First Committee chairman. The process instilled in me a sense of confidence in Canada as a leader.

I gave an upbeat speech at the opening of the committee meetings and established an open-ended "Friends of the Chair" informal group of ambassadors to advise me on ways to rationalize the work and merge competing or redundant resolutions. I drew attention to two new and important reports by experts of international standing. The first, *Study on the Climatic and Other Global Effects of Nuclear War*, stated, "The scientific evidence is now conclusive that a major nuclear war would entail the high risk of a global environmental disruption." The second, *Study on the Economic and Social Consequences of the Arms Race and Military Expenditures*, said, "During the 1980s, the arms race has continued, in particular in its quantitative aspect, unabated, in fact expanding in scale and accelerating in pace." Both reports, I said, showed in great detail the environmental and economic impact of the ever-growing accumulation of weapons. "These reports must not be put on the library shelf and left to gather dust. They should be acted upon, with a common understanding of their priority."

These reports did stir serious thinkers in the First Committee, but the ritual of resolutions, many of them repeated year after year, gave a mechanistic tone to much of the work. On soft resolutions, when not much was asked, it was easy to get consensus. Resolutions calling for action—stopping the nuclear arms race, for example—divided the committee. Most of the world wanted to take constructive and meaningful steps forward, but the U.S., corralling most of the NATO countries, resisted.

The U.S. intransigence became ludicrous when it was the only state in the entire committee to vote against Canada's resolution to launch a UN study on verification. Clark weighed in with a personal letter to U.S. Secretary of State George Shultz, asking that the U.S. join a consensus on "this important step forward in the process of enhancing international understanding of the importance of verification." Canada, over a number of years, had distinguished itself in developing the political and scientific aspects of verification. In the spring of 1988, I chaired a working group at the UN Disarmament Commission that had adopted, for the first time, sixteen principles of verification. Shultz gave his answer to Clark the next day when the American representative told the committee that verification was a treaty-specific activity and could not be studied in the abstract. The U.S. dismissed Canada's argument that it is important to examine general methodologies of verification independent of their application to specific agreements and to prepare a verification "tool bag" to help negotiators. Similarly, the U.S. maintained its opposition to the Soviet resolution calling for a comprehensive approach to international peace and security on the grounds that it did not want the UN's machinery for peace strengthened.

The progress in the First Committee was marked by slight improvements in the process (for example, more time for consultations on resolutions), not by a qualitative jump in disarmament action, which, unfortunately, was missing. It was certainly a pleasure for me to present UN Secretary-General Perez de Cuellar when he came to the committee to make a speech during Disarmament Week. And it was nice to receive the delegates' applause when the committee ended its work. But in what way, I asked myself, was the world a safer or more just place as a result of our work?

Stunned by Cruise

I returned to Ottawa in this conflicted state of mind. I thought my stock in Foreign Affairs was going up as a result of my performance in New York, but I was brought down to earth by a phone call late one afternoon in February 1989. A senior official told me that the Foreign Affairs department would announce the next day that Canada would permit the U.S. to test the advanced Cruise missile (AGM 129A) in Canada.

I was stunned. I had thought the issue would fade away when Clark obtained the previous delay in Canada's decision. But, unbeknownst to me, negotiations had continued, and now the deal was done. I had been shut out of the discussions. I told the official that this was a direct violation of my written terms of reference as a Cabinet appointee. I added that with President Reagan now gone and new nuclear arms negotiations starting up between President George Bush and Gorbachev, and the Cold War practically over, it was madness for Canada to take such a hostile stand against the Soviet Union. He merely said that "that was too bad."

When I put the phone down, I looked out the window. Darkness had descended. I sat immobile for several minutes. It was clear what had happened. The U.S. had put intolerable pressure on the Canadian government to test. Mulroney did not want good relations with the new Bush government ruptured. Clark, who would be personally opposed to more Cruise testing, was overruled. I had not been consulted because Foreign Affairs knew what my position would be and didn't want me escalating the fight.

Those who wanted me gone knew that this episode would do the trick. A memo had already gone up to Clark, requesting a change in the terms of reference for the next ambassador for disarmament. Foreign Affairs wanted a "line" ambassador, not a political appointee, someone who would go to the Conference on Disarmament in Geneva, stay out of the limelight at home and do what he was told. As an official once told me, "Doug, you're supposed to be just an actor spouting the lines written by the directors in the department."

Although I was angry, I decided it was not in my interests, nor in the interests of the peace community in Canada, to resign abruptly, storm out, call a press conference and denounce the decision. It would be a one-day story in the media and my detractors would doubtless paint me as a "hothead" who couldn't get his own way. I had to force myself to exit Foreign Affairs smoothly in order to be a continuing influence on the government and do it from a respected position in the peace community. I still had a lot of work to do.

I decided to finish my five-year appointment, which would be up in October. I let a few weeks go by. Meanwhile, the annual departmental appraisal of my work arrived on my desk. I shook my head in wonder at the "superior" rating of my performance. "Superior" was one grade less than "outstanding," but one more than "fully satisfactory."

> Mr. Roche is an effective chairman of any meeting, as he demonstrated in forums as diverse as UNGA First Committee, departmental meetings and the Consultative Group. He takes the task seriously and prepares carefully for each meeting. He is a persuasive public speaker and an effective promoter and defender of policies he espouses. He is tenacious and dogged in his pursuit of an objective, only occasionally crossing the line to stubbornness. Mr. Roche's highly developed writing skills were evident in the preparation of his many presentations in conference, Consultative Group meetings and international forums. His style of delivery is forceful and his tone optimistic.

I went to see Clark and told him I would be resigning. He seemed relieved. The conversation was relaxed; at one point he asked me whether I would like to take an ambassadorship to an African country. I had no hesitation in politely declining. I didn't want any more departmental instructions and I didn't want to uproot Eva from her successful career in Edmonton.

Over the years, I had struck up a friendship with Myer Horowitz, president of the University of Alberta in Edmonton. I went to see him to tell him that I would soon be leaving the ambassador job. To my surprise, he immediately offered to appoint me Visiting Professor. I would teach a weekly three-hour seminar to senior students. "Do you mean a credit course?" I asked him. "Yes," he said, and told me to write my own syllabus. That's when I knew he was serious. When I made the administrative arrangements, Vice-President Peter Meekison said the university would pay me at the same level as former Premier Peter Lougheed, who had also taken on a visiting professor role. I figured that was pretty good, given that I didn't know the first thing about how to write a syllabus. I got Duncan Edmonds, who is an academic, among his many qualifications, to help me, and called the course "Canada's Role in Global Peace and Security."

An Honour to Serve

On June 1, 1989, I sent Clark my formal resignation. I said it had been an honour to sit and speak at a desk labelled "Canada" at the United Nations. "Few Canadians have had the opportunity to bring into the international arena the values, policies, and aspirations that have given Canada its deserved reputation as a strong proponent for peace with security, stability and social justice," I said. I added that he himself continued to be "a great credit to Parliament, to the government and to Canada." I enclosed my final report, showing that, during my five years, I had chaired 106 meetings of the Barton Group and seven national meetings of the Consultative Group, given 165 addresses to public forums and 248 interviews to the media, and represented Canada at meetings in fifteen countries as well as at multiple sessions at the UN. I closed with a suggestion that the terms of reference for my successor should be reviewed, "because there are a number of problems that flow out of the present arrangement."

He named Peggy Mason, his policy adviser, as the new ambassador for disarmament, thus holding to a political appointment. But, in the next cycle, the job reverted to a "line" ambassador and the function disappeared from the public radar. Peggy was experienced in dealing with the bureaucracy, and I thought she would probably get along with the officials better than I did. She distinguished herself at the UN. The Barton Group of Western ambassadors took in their East European counterparts—in recognition of the end of the Cold War—and the expanded body was renamed the Mason Group.

During my final meeting with the steering committee of the Consultative Group, James Taylor, the deputy minister, gave a luncheon for me, where he read a letter sent by Prime Minister Mulroney, thanking me for having raised Canada's profile at the UN. Clark also sent a letter: "Your commitment, dedication and energy have been an inspiration to all," he wrote. Taylor called me "our esteemed colleague, friend and adviser." I gave a polite speech in return.

I wanted to leave Foreign Affairs with good feelings. I had learned long ago that harbouring resentments is corrosive. It is impossible to do peace work unless you are conciliatory in every aspect of your life. I have not to this day felt any antipathy to those in the government who did not see the world as I did. I had had special experiences that formed my view that long-term benefits to humanity require higher societal standards to protect the next generations from the dehumanizing force of endless nuclear arms buildup, the rich-poor gap, human rights violations and destruction of the environment. Short-range "practical politics" just cannot produce a long-range survivalist ethic. My fight was with the powers of greed and corruption in the world, not the people around me trying to respond to daily crises in the only way that seemed practical to them.

I used my accumulated vacation leave to go home, where I spent part of August and September writing a book, *Building Global Security: Agenda for the 1990s*, to serve as one of the texts for the course I would be teaching. Eva had a lawn party for my 60th birthday and gave me a bicycle as a present. I felt I had plenty of energy to use it.

IV

The Freedom Years:
1990–1998

13

Rejecting the Luxury of Despair

I pressed a coin into the concrete and a chunk of the Berlin Wall fell into my hands. Side by side, even without a chisel, Eva and I scraped away at the monstrous barrier for souvenirs to bring home. This was not tourism but history.

Immediately after I left the Department of Foreign Affairs, the *Toronto Star* asked me to write a weekly column on peace; the Canadian International Development Agency invited me to chair the new National Advisory Committee on Development Education; Global Education Associates, a small think tank in New York, appointed me president; and the Holy See Mission at the UN named me special adviser on disarmament—plus I had my weekly seminar at the University of Alberta to prepare. Juggling all my new commitments, I had never been happier. The combination of sources kept my income comfortable, and I could afford to do pro bono work. (I joked to a friend that "a heavenly accountant" was taking care of my pay from the Holy See.) My home office, the new age of the computer and the secretarial assistance of Bonnie Payne gave me the infrastructure I needed to take up my new "freelance" life.

The reviews of *Building Global Security* were starting to come in, and more than one reviewer noted that the book was my re-entry into Canada's peace movement. The book laid out an agenda for the 1990s to build on the "extraordinary moment" that had arrived with the end of the Cold War. At the top of the list was an end to the strategy of nuclear deterrence, a totally flawed policy that had to be replaced by a new global security system as called for by the UN.

Canada needed a "bold plan" to oppose all nuclear weapons modernization and get nuclear weapons out of NATO. The *Financial Post* published an excerpt from the chapter on Canada, in which I said that membership in NATO ought not to demand acquiescence in the war-fighting strategies of the nuclear powers.

I was careful not to use any classified information in the book. All my sources were public documents or reports, such as the Defence White Paper, the Consultative Group reports, and the analyses by Project Ploughshares and parliamentary committees. In his foreword to the book, Maurice Strong, the quintessential Canadian internationalist, wrote, "Douglas Roche describes the background to the historic opportunity we now face with the intimate knowledge and authority of one who has had a long and deep interest in issues of development, disarmament and peace as analyst, prophet and activist."

I had my mind so much on the future that I was surprised at the reaction to a comment I had made during an interview about U.S. influence on Canadian disarmament policies. I said, "In no field is pressure from the U.S. government as strong as in security." This was treated as news and led to a hubbub in Question Period. Maybe I had become so used to the heavy hand of Washington during my years as Ambassador that I took this pressure for granted. It was true that U.S. dominance put Canada in the contradictory position of working for nuclear disarmament while supporting the U.S. extension of the arms race. But my purpose in writing the book was not to harangue the Canadian establishment about its subservience to the U.S.; rather, I had hoped to stir Canadian discourse to help move the world forward to a new system of common security. Instead of better bombs, international peace would rest on a commitment to joint survival through structures to manage the planet.

Catholic New Times noted that for many years I had been "a conundrum" to the peace movement. "Roche has often been perceived as not forceful enough in protesting against his own Party's rigid dogmatism and Cold War attitudes," the paper said. Reviewing the book for *Peace Magazine*, Aaron Tovish said, "[Roche] does not indulge in self-pity over the strains that developed with many of his friends in the peace community. With dignity, he has laid his cards on the table, allowing others to draw their own conclusion. The experience has strengthened him for greater struggles. He can speak now with the authority of one who has seen things from the inside." Frank Ritter, a columnist for the *Vancouver Sun*, said, "Roche is just the sort of guy Canada needs running around the international community."

The Elusive Peace Dividend

"Running around" the world was something of an overstatement, but I did travel to Moscow in August 1990 for a UN conference that reflected the newness of the moment. Disarmers and arms producers mixed together to address the problem of how to rebuild Cold War economies that had grown overly dependent on military production. When conference participants finished their to-ing and fro-ing, it wasn't clear whether a peace dividend would ever exist. UNICEF officials called for five per cent of the $1 trillion arms bill, or $50 billion, to be devoted to alleviating the worst forms of poverty that killed fourteen million children every year. But industrialists from Rockwell and Westinghouse, along with the Pentagon brass, stiffened at resisting anything more than a two per cent cut in military spending over the next five years. As the conference was getting under way, Saddam Hussein invaded Kuwait, and the industrialists immediately argued that the U.S. could not afford to cut back on its military budget. The military-industrial complex, which would thrive anew with the two Iraq wars of 1991 and 2003, would not cease its never-ending promotion of the need for new weaponry.

UN representatives argued that the skills and technologies that had given the world intercontinental missiles, anti-missile missiles and the tools for Star Wars could be transferred to clean energies and technologies the planet was crying out for. But institutional pressures stood in the way: people wanted tax cuts and deficit reductions, while the dismantling of weapons was expensive and defence workers had to be retrained. Yasushi Akashi, UN under-secretary-general for disarmament, argued that steps towards the conversion of military industries to peacetime production were not utopian but realistic. "Governments, industries and societies ignore them at their peril," he said.

I talked to Russian economists and scientists, who revealed that the defence industries had been totally dependent on the state to be the sole buyer of their equipment, rendering them incapable of producing decent consumer goods at competitive prices. On a walk through the GUM, the famous Moscow department store, I discovered there were no men's shoes available. Food stores in a ten-block radius of Red Square had only pitiful supplies. Yet hard-liners were arguing that stepping up, not reducing, arms exports was the way to make fast money. Although Mikhail Gorbachev was drastically cutting Soviet military spending, and the armies of Eastern Europe were fading away in the sweep of democratization, the Western countries insisted on maintaining their high levels of military spending. And though the U.S. Joint Chiefs of Staff conceded that Western Europe could now be effectively defended without nuclear weapons, the U.S. administration insisted that nuclear weapons remain in Europe as part of the "flexible response strategy."

As Pierre Trudeau had said, it was anachronistic to the point of absurdity to have highly developed nations devoting such enormous resources to armaments while so much needed to be done to improve the human condition, at the very moment when a new ordering of world relationships had become possible.

Standing at the Berlin Wall, I felt this "new moment" for the world. I went to Berlin from the Moscow conference because I wanted to experience the wholeness, the recovered integrity of this seven-centuries-old city destined to be a shining jewel in the new Europe. During the previous 25 years, I had visited each Berlin separately: the energetic, even kinetic, West and the depressed but culturally deeper East. I resolved to absorb the Berlin integration as a deeply important symbol of how our world was coming together. It was a jumble of sights and emotions: East German soldiers selling their uniforms and medals on the west side of the Brandenburg Gate, Romanian gypsies huddled with their children on the Kurfustendamm, West Berlin's magnificent showcase street, and the art scenes depicting freedom painted on a mile-long stretch of the Wall on the East side where defacement was formerly forbidden.

Eva and I set out along the "Ku-damm," boisterous and crowded with a street fair, where champagne by the glass and beer in cups beckoned. We walked past the Kaiser Wilhelm Memorial Church, the bombed edifice that is a perpetual reminder of World War II, along Budapester Strasse and through the Tiergarten, the splendid gardens where families relaxed and cooked supper, and along the grand boulevard, renamed 17 Juni, and into Brandenburg Square.

Off to the left were the white crosses marking the deaths of so many who were shot as they scrambled over the wall or swam a 30-metre channel. I looked for a long time at the name Chris Geoffroy, who died on February 8, 1989. Had he waited nine months, he could have walked across the border as we were doing. But perhaps because of his sacrifice, freedom was purchased. We strolled down the great Unter den Linden in the former East Berlin, where Hitler had rolled his massive forces, and stopped for a glass of lovely German white wine at a sidewalk café. Thoughts of the war that raged when I was a boy, the resounding cry of U.S. President John Kennedy when the Wall went up that he was a Berliner, the new rush of freedom and democracy through Eastern Europe all filled my mind.

The reunification of Berlin and all of Germany was a vivid symbol that the world had become one. Everything was interlinked. In the nuclear age, no nation could achieve true security by itself. The new era demanded a new framework for security. But would the political structures everywhere seize the moment, opened up by the fall of the Berlin Wall, to build a system of common security? The question haunted me.

The next day, in a more normal tourist mode, Eva and I paid $25 for a three-hour bus tour of both East and West Berlin, our young German guide Daniela laughing as we drove through the old Checkpoint Charlie without a second's interruption. In perfect English, Daniela vividly described the history of Germany, spiced with details of construction to come. We went to the Pergamum Museum in East Berlin to see again the reconstructed Babylonian Way, an architectural masterpiece preserved through three centuries. Then back once more to the West and the "Ku-damm" for a final look at the bustling present and, of course, apple strudel with an unforgettable warm sauce.

In the oneness of Berlin 1990, where the past and present mingled, I felt the future—a future of the age-old mixture of joys and hopes, knowing that grief always gets in the way.

Iraq: "Not a UN War"

The grief of the first Gulf War—100,000 bombing raids over Iraq in a 43-day war that began January 17, 1991—quickly took hold. I was at the UN in New York the day the war started, but there was an eerie silence. The action was elsewhere. A friend wryly joked,

"The diplomats have been told to go home and explain war to their children."

The previous August, Saddam Hussein, the tyrannical leader of Iraq who spent nearly half of the country's oil revenue building up vast arsenals, invaded Kuwait and declared it a nineteenth province. Twelve UN Security Council resolutions demanded the immediate and unconditional withdrawal of Iraq, imposed sanctions and finally authorized the use of force. Operation Desert Storm, the largest assemblage ever of military power in the region, deployed 400,000 troops, with the U.S. as leader. After the war, a high-level UN team was dispatched to assess the damage. It reported that the conflict had wrought near-apocalyptic results upon the highly urbanized society. "Most means of modern life support have been destroyed ... Iraq has, for some time to come, been relegated to a pre-industrial age."

Could nothing have been done to avert this carnage? Of course it could. A number of states, led by Colombia, submitted a draft resolution to the Security Council calling for the unconditional withdrawal of Iraq and also stipulating that a UN peacekeeping force be set up to maintain law and order in Kuwait, that sanctions against Iraq be lifted, that foreign forces be withdrawn from the region, and that unresolved disputes be settled by the International Court of Justice. The U.S. opposed this comprehensive solution and, using coercive measures, secured passage of Resolution 678, which endorsed the use of force against Iraq. The multinational forces in the Gulf did not fight under a UN flag, nor was the Security Council given any role in the prosecution of hostilities. The U.S. ignored a last-minute diplomatic surge, led by Russia, to avert the launching of a brief ground war after weeks of air strikes. Pushed aside during the crisis, Secretary-General Perez de Cuellar set the historical record straight: "The victory of the allied, or coalition, countries over Iraq is not at all a victory for the United Nations, because this was not its war. It was not a United Nations war." A senior UN consultant, Erskine Childers, linked U.S. coercion with its economic power to buy or bully votes and military collaboration: "The war powers carried out a virtual coup against the Charter of the United Nations."

I hung around the UN for a few days. A conference aimed at converting the Partial Test Ban Treaty of 1963 into a total ban on nuclear testing was going on, but no one was paying any attention.

The "new world order" that President Bush had hailed after the fall of the Berlin Wall was, literally, going up in smoke. Bush's concept of "new world order," by the way, was far different from the one I brought to the development of Parliamentarians for World Order. We meant mutual, balanced and verifiable disarmament with a greater share of the world's resources devoted to the benefit of all peoples, not just those who were already rich. But Bush's concept revolved around Pax Americana, the very idea scorned by President Kennedy. For Bush, order meant the U.S. driving and enforcing the world agenda. When the U.S. decided on war, everyone was to get in line. Hence, Canada, in voting for Resolution 678 in the Security Council, put its foreign policy in lockstep with the U.S. Had Canada resisted and helped Colombia to muster the votes to demand a comprehensive solution to Middle East problems, the war could have been avoided, and the grounds for the subsequent Iraq War of 2003, which so destabilized the entire Middle East, never laid.

I returned to Edmonton and found the city a case study on how the Gulf War had deeply divided the Canadian people. Patriotism traditionally runs high in Alberta. There was also a strong peace community, and 2,000 people had turned out for a candlelight vigil on the eve of the war. Although the search for non-military resolutions to conflict was very much alive in Canada, this new maturity had not yet penetrated the political processes. The editorial board of the *Edmonton Journal* was so split that three editors each wrote a distinct viewpoint.

The contradictions in the madness of the Gulf War were agonizing for me. Overnight, the Canadian government had moved from sending Canadian forces to patrol the Gulf to participating in the bombing of Iraqis without a shred of parliamentary approval. At the same time, Mulroney proposed convening a UN conference of world leaders to mobilize the political will to stop the arms trade, which had armed Saddam Hussein in the first place. There it was: countries fighting the war ignored mounting calls for a ceasefire in the name of humanity, while at the same time calling for action to stop the spread of arms. The hypocrisy was stunning. In the strange alchemy of politics, the hatred unleashed by war was supposed to provide the co-operation for peace.

I decided to fall back on the aphorism I had heard so often from the great social justice activist Barbara Ward: "I do not have the luxury of despair." Barbara meant that we can't allow misguided politicians and their short-range policies, based on the primal instincts of greed and fear, to paralyze our actions in building a more human world community. The window of peace—opened so wonderfully by the fall of the Berlin Wall, Gorbachev's outreach to the world and the clamour for a "peace dividend" for the suffering poor of the world—was quickly closing.

It seemed to me that the world just couldn't stand the prospect of peace. That is an overstatement to be sure. Actually, it is the arms merchants, driving so much of what passes for public policy, who will not permit the processes of peace to develop naturally. But a complaisant public, manipulated by the media's incessant glorification of militarism as the solution to conflict, also bears responsibility. The war was costing Canada $60 million a month, forcing the government to strip money from development programs for the poorest people in the world. What was moral or just about a war that had such terrible consequences for the defenceless and dispossessed?

Everything I had worked for as a parliamentarian and diplomat—building a new global security that relies on international co-operation to meet human needs rather than the military confrontation that has produced so many wars—seemed to be evaporating. As I watched the horrors of war on television, my thoughts and prayers were with those who were dying or about to die. I was conscious of the stalwart qualities of Canada's armed forces in the Gulf but deeply critical of their political masters. Canada had a new defence minister who could do nothing but spout jingoistic gibberish.

I realized that I could not spend all my energy reacting to this latest episode in the march of folly. The only way I could help those personally suffering through the war was to get on with the pressing human security agenda: disarmament, international development, human rights and environmental protection. The route was education.

Excitement in the Classroom

My students at the University of Alberta had an animating effect on me. It was exciting to go into the classroom and grapple with young minds. I capped my seminar at 20 students and, for three hours every Monday, I took them, as I put it, "up a mountain" so that they could see the vistas of peace. The course soon evolved into "War or Peace in the 21st Century?": I told the students to take special note of the question mark at the end of the title. The world could go either way, depending on how much the new generation all over the world wanted peace. I said I was preparing a future prime minister of Canada, and I looked at the women when I said this.

The seminar was structured on three principles:

- War and violence are not inevitable and do not necessarily emerge inexorably from human interaction.

- The need to prevent deadly conflict is increasingly urgent.

- Preventing deadly conflict is possible through the early, skillful and integrated application of political, diplomatic, economic and military measures.

I told the students: "The sweeping power of technology has brought humanity to the point where a violent future must be avoided if humanity is to survive. That is the new *realpolitik*." Week by week, we reviewed the strengths and weaknesses of the balance-of-power system, the United Nations' strategies for human security and the challenges facing Canadian foreign policy. I had classes on such topics as "How the United Nations Works," "The Meaning of Interdependence: A New Definition of Security," "Equitable Standards in a Globalized World" and "The Ethical Basis for Peace." I devoted one class to "The Role of Women in Peace and Development," making the point that the participation and leadership of the female half of humanity is essential to assuring peace, security and people-centred sustainable development. I put the schema for each lecture on the blackboard so that students could see exactly the connections I was making. The students were deeply inspired by the outstanding book *GAIA: An Atlas of Planet Management*. The book, which I used as a basic text, shows what a complex and magnificent world we have inherited. I mixed vigorous discussion questions ("Should the sovereignty of nations ever be overridden by humanitarian considerations?") with the lectures and appointed students in turn to lead the discussion.

For the final session each term, I invited the class to my home for dinner and a long working session during which the students were divided into the five regional caucuses of the UN system. Each caucus

had to role model its UN counterpart and prepare a 20-minute presentation on the topic "The Priorities and Demands of Our Region
for a Common Security Agenda." The students entered this exercise
with zest and sometimes dressed in regional garb.

I could tell students liked the passion I brought to the class. I always interviewed them privately to see how they were getting along
and often informally counselled them about career selection. Many
went on to graduate studies and foreign service careers. Professors
must be evaluated by their students; my evaluations were consistently
high. One (anonymous) student wrote, "Professor Roche is extremely
well-versed in this area. He is an inspiration to his students. I will never
forget what this man has taught me. He has changed my perception
of the world in a fundamental and positive sense." I was thrilled when
the Students' Union selected me for one of the "Salute" awards to
outstanding professors.

The university asked me to give public lectures on what was
called the annual "Super Saturday," when the public was invited onto
the campus. After the Gulf War, the university sponsored a four-part
public lecture series I gave in a theatre in the Centennial Library in
downtown Edmonton. It was during these lectures that I began to see
what I have frequently observed since on the faces of my audiences:
an expression that said, "Give me hope." It was clear to me that people
want to be lifted up, to hope again that peace is possible. The lecturing
challenge was to do this without skirting around the obstacles of the
military-industrial complex and obtuse politicians.

Of all the things I have done in my life, I enjoyed teaching the
most. I stayed at the University of Alberta for thirteen years, and left
only because the demands of my Senate work started piling up and
I had to be in Ottawa for Monday meetings.

Global Education: A Perspective

At the end of the 1980s, the Canadian government adopted the
policy of devoting one per cent of Official Development Assistance
to development education, which had first been advocated by the
Task Force on North-South Relations at the opening of the decade. Lewis Perinbam, a vice-president of the Canadian International
Development Agency and one of the government's true visionary
leaders, realized this money had to be managed efficiently to head

off right-wing critics, who considered any intelligent discussion of the development process to be nothing more than leftist propaganda. He prevailed upon his minister to establish the National Advisory Committee on Development Education and suggested that, since I had been vice-chairman of the North-South Task Force and was now freed of my responsibilities as ambassador for disarmament, I should be the chairman. I took on a new role, guiding the committee of educators and activists in pursing our mandate, dexterously worded to stay out of the spotlight: "to examine the present funding structures and recommend policies, guidelines, selection criteria and evaluation methods for the outreach programs fostering development education." Our principal accomplishment was the creation of International Development Week, observed in universities and high schools across Canada.

The committee stimulated the development of programs to help teachers treat global education as a perspective, not just a subject. By helping students see themselves in a world context, they develop true values, knowledge, skills and attitudes to participate in a world characterized by many interdependencies. Most important, global education fosters in students curiosity, appreciation of diversity, concern for justice, tolerance of uncertainty and world awareness. *Global education* is a more comprehensive term than *peace education*, which suggests that the subject matter is the avoidance of war—a necessary pursuit, but too limiting. Rather, global education gathers under one umbrella the components of the peace agenda: disarmament, development, the environment and human rights. It extends these joint concerns into the community as a whole so that no bloc, interest or political party can claim ownership of the integrated agenda for security.

As valuable as the work of the committee was, it could not withstand the onslaught of the federal deficit-cutters. It was ludicrous to think that the tiny amount spent on the committee in any way affected Canada's deficit problems, but the Finance Minister accepted the argument that the government had to show it was serious in cuts. The committee, along with some comparable think tanks, was axed in the budget of 1992.

The work of the committee was compatible with what I did for Global Education Associates, a small non-governmental organization in New York headed by Jerry Mische. With his wife, Patricia, Mische had written *Toward a Human World Order,* which explored the need for ethical policies in the globalized world then coming into view. (I had written about the Misches's lay apostolate work in Latin America years earlier when I was with *Sign* magazine.) Global Education Associates acted as a catalyst for religious groups around the world, trying to inject world order perspectives into peace and development issues. Jerry asked me to be its president; I presided at a lot of meetings, but Jerry and Pat did the real work.

I was becoming more and more convinced that the holistic nature of the world, as revealed in the photo of the Earth sent back from space by the astronauts, needed to be understood much better throughout society. The long history of the world, characterized by the quest for domination, I thought, has reached a higher plateau where, for the first time, the mingling of intellectualism, technology and danger provides both motivation and means for common survival. I thought the birth of global consciousness provided people everywhere with a new kind of power for self-determination.

A Bargain for Humanity

These ideas were the basis of a book, *A Bargain for Humanity,* which I wrote to deepen my teaching at the University of Alberta. I also had a growing number of invitations to speak at teachers' meetings across Canada. My friend from Russia, Vladimir Petrovsky, now UN under-secretary-general for political affairs, wrote the foreword, supporting me in seeing "the magnitude and complexity of issues with great clarity." The bargain I envisaged between North and South would be more than a compact for survival and deeper than a commercial exchange. It would encompass the elements of logic, ethics and hope, and be rooted in necessity. The dependencies of North on South and South on North constituted a virtual demand for common management of the planet. The first part of the bargain would be to do away with nuclear weapons, move on to a fairer sharing of the resources of the world and instigate joint agreements to protect the environment. I conceded that it may indeed take a catastrophe to wake up the political systems of both North and South, "but fear is not a worthy human response to the challenges of planetary survival."

My own hope lies in the blossoming of intelligence about ourselves as a human community in a world that is interconnected in

every sphere of activity. I felt reinforced in these views by my participation in the Rajiv Gandhi Memorial Initiative for the Advancement
of Civilization, created to honour Rajiv who, like his mother, was
assassinated while serving as prime minister. I was invited to join a
group of international figures to develop an action plan for a nuclear
weapons–free and non-violent world order. I went to Delhi for the
inaugural meeting and met Sonia Gandhi, who spoke movingly about
her husband's vision of an alternative world system in which equality,
co-operation and co-existence replaced dominance, strife and deterrence. Non-violence was the governing principle of the Gandhi vision.
I called for India to get a permanent seat on the Security Council as a
non–nuclear weapons state, an aspiration that, sadly, went unfulfilled.
The group issued a declaration, the heart of which I repeat to this
day: "The elimination [of nuclear weapons] is the first pre-requisite
for the advancement of human civilization."

My spirits were lifted when I opened the mail one day to find
that I had been appointed an officer of the Order of Canada for my
work "as an active proponent of peace, ecumenism and justice for
oppressed peoples." Well, I thought, somebody's noticing my efforts
to promote awareness of the peace process.

Recipients were allowed only one guest for the ceremony at
Rideau Hall, but I inveigled two more tickets, and Evita and Francis
joined Eva to watch me, tuxedo-clad, receive the award from Governor
General Ray Hnatyshyn. Hnatyshyn and I had been colleagues in
Parliament. "There's no one I'd rather give this to than you," Ray
whispered to me as he draped the medal around my neck. I thought
the Order of Canada would increase my stature—and it did—in
pushing the Canadian government on peace issues. In fact, the medal
made me want to work even harder.

Retracing Bangladesh Steps

After so many years of attending conferences and participating in
abstract discussions, I realized it was time once again to come face to
face with the human condition. In 1993, the Canadian International
Development Agency (CIDA) asked me to go back to Bangladesh and
retrace my trip of seventeen years earlier to see what had happened
to the lives of the people in that time. Was Canadian aid effective?

As I did the first time, I found Bangladesh to be overwhelming: the sheer density of people, the magnitude of the poverty, the daily grind of existence assault the senses. Bangladesh then had 117 million people (the population reached 150 million in 2007) living in an area one quarter the size of Alberta. The population density in Bangladesh was 740 per square kilometre; in Alberta it is 3.8.

Recurrent floods, cyclones and tidal waves constantly impeded the development process, since so much of the country's resources must be devoted to emergency relief, reconstruction and rehabilitation. The 1991 Bangladesh cyclone, for example, killed 150,000 people and left three million homeless. Life is made worse by not only the vagaries of nature but also the effect of human-made environmental destruction. The flooding of its two huge rivers, the Ganges and the Brahmaputra, in recent years was caused in part by deforestation of the Himalayas outside Bangladesh. Flood waters in 1987 and again in 1988 caused catastrophic damage, dislocating 45 million people and causing 2,500 deaths. Crops were devastated, water systems polluted and diarrheal diseases swept a nation that has only one hospital bed for every 3,583 persons and one physician for 6,252.

Poverty was pervasive. Of the 72 million people living in poverty, 46 million were classified as destitute—that is, consuming fewer than 1,800 calories a day; moreover, the proportion of the extremely poor was rising. Health and education levels were low, and life expectancy at birth was 52, compared to the average of 62 for low-income countries.

Bangladesh has gained the image of a country with too many people, too much poverty, too few resources, too frequent disasters and too little ability to change for the better. Can such a country survive? Will it always depend on outside assistance? What is required for its economy to reach the "takeoff" stage?

Day by day, I thought about these questions as I met farmers and aid workers, teachers and officials, women and children. I found myself coming to the conclusion that, yes, Bangladesh will survive, yes, Bangladesh needs aid for some period of time and, yes, there is a potential for the economy to take off. Science and technology will not be strangers to Bangladesh in the 21st century.

My dominant finding was that Bangladesh, despite the enormity of its problems, *is* moving ahead. A chief factor was the education of women and their increasingly strong role in the life of the country. Another factor is the resilience of the people, who seem to be able not only to cope with repeated disasters but also to overcome them.

I found that CIDA's aid programs, when they were directed to health and education, helped to make people more self-supporting, to develop their own capacities and to make their own choices. This aid should be provided not because we feel sorry for a downtrodden people but rather because we recognize our solidarity with a part of the world that must be strengthened if the whole planet is to advance in peace and stability.

I visited Proshika (a Bengali acronym for a leadership training centre). When I was first there, it was a fledgling organization working in a few villages to introduce community development techniques. I was so impressed with this self-help project that I wrote an article about it for *Reader's Digest*. This time, I saw Proshika's twelve-storey building in which computer programmers were being trained for a global data exchange program. I looked up Dr. Zafrullah Chowdhury who, seventeen years earlier, had been frustrated at the lack of medical knowledge about local diseases. Now, with the help of Oxfam and Inter Pares, a Canadian non-governmental organization, he had opened a health centre that trained paramedics to go into villages to deal with scabies, worms and diarrhea, and to do immunizations. I interviewed Dr. Muhammad Yunus, the internationally acclaimed originator of the Grameen Bank, which lends money to the poor with no collateral. He was awarded the 2006 Nobel Peace Prize for this pioneering work in microcredit. I greatly admire him for his ceaseless campaigning for aid to the poorest so they can help themselves.

It was during my examination of the Rural Maintenance Program, an aid project implemented by CARE Canada and supported by CIDA, that I met Amana Bibi, a beneficiary of Dr. Yunus's pioneering work. Twenty women had gathered in Amana's house, a one-room clay dwelling with no water and no electricity but that did feature a corrugated iron roof. The women are part of a project embracing 61,000 women who maintain thousands of miles of rural, earthen, farm-to-market roads and thus earn a stable cash wage. The women in Amana's village had gathered for one of their regular sessions conducted by a field trainer, who taught them how to handle bank accounts and related expenses to income.

Seated on the floor, I watched the instruction and listened to their stories. The women work each day from 8 a.m. to 2 p.m. fixing potholes and repairing the sides of roads, which deteriorate quickly in Bangladesh's torrential rains. They earn the equivalent of about 75 cents per day; the bank deducts 12 cents of that per day and transfers it to their individual savings accounts. Some women had been able to buy poultry to earn extra money and increase their family income. One woman, previously a maid, said she had become independent and had even saved $200.

Amana, who now earned more than her husband, put her earnings and savings into the construction of their house. A few months previously, her 20-year-old daughter had died in childbirth. When their daughter became ill, she was taken to hospital, Amana said, but because the family could not afford the hospital charges, she was brought home to die. Now Amana looked after the daughter's three-year-old boy, who coughed repeatedly as he sat on his grandmother's lap.

I looked at the woman with her deep, dark eyes and shy smile. She wore a green flowered sari and delicate earrings. She proudly showed me a barrel filled with rice and corn. It was evident she was the strength of the family. She called Shahalam, her ten-year-old son, to meet me; the boy, in the local custom, bowed deeply before me, flicking the dust off my shoes. Shahalam had missed school for a year because of diarrhea. We talked about the three years of schooling he had before his illness and the difficulty of getting books. Although there was no radio in the house, he said he saw news programs periodically while watching entertainment on the village television. He saw his future as a rickshaw driver.

I could see Bangladesh in Shahalam: the crushing problems and hopeful attitudes of country and boy. Both had a potential to climb the ladder of development. Neither is doomed to poverty, though many think they are. A life of hardship and work awaits—and, perhaps, success. But they both, country and boy, needed the help of a political system and widening circles of humanity to care about them.

14

Of Nobility and Grief

S ome mornings I would wake up and scarcely believe that, on the
same day, I would deal with two extreme sides of the Catholic
Church—loftiness and sordidness. At one moment, I would be speaking with Archbishop Renato Martino, the Holy See's permanent
representative at the United Nations, on strengthening the Church's
stance against nuclear weapons. At another, I would be chairing a
process trying to help victims of sexual abuse in Catholic institutions.
The one was ennobling, the second enervating. There was a common thread—conflict resolution—running through both activities,
but often, I would have to strain to find it. Making peace has many
twists and turns. I needed to use a combination of my political and
diplomatic experience.

When I left the Canadian government in the fall of 1989, Archbishop Martino invited me to become a special adviser to the Holy
See's delegation to the UN General Assembly. He had just come to
the UN and wanted to expand the input of laypeople—men and
women—into the Holy See's work. The Holy See has observer status at
the UN and makes many interventions, especially in the committees. I
knew Archbishop Martino wanted to toughen the Holy See's opposition to nuclear weapons. We struck up a friendship and I remained his
adviser throughout his extraordinarily long tenure of fourteen years.
I helped him prepare his speeches and organized special luncheons
for key disarmament ambassadors. Martino was instrumental in my
being appointed a Knight Commander of the Order of St. Gregory
the Great. The order, founded by Pope Gregory XVI in 1831, is given

for meritorious service to the Church. In 2002, Martino was recalled to Rome to head the Pontifical Commission on Justice and Peace and was made a cardinal. I gently suggested to his successor, Archbishop Celestino Migliore, that he might want to get his own adviser, but he said he wanted me to stay on.

Throughout the Cold War, moral teaching on nuclear weapons was uncertain. While some ethicists condemned outright the concept of nuclear deterrence as a crime against God and humanity, others gave limited acceptance to the possession of nuclear weapons in the genuine belief that they were an aid to peace. Recognition of their evil took a back seat to the immediate gain of preventing nuclear conflict.

There was a great deal of twisting and turning, as religious leaders tried to reconcile the opposing demands of natural law and political realism. Moral constraints had to compete with "reasons of state." The tensions between them got caught up in the religious arguments about pacifism and the "just war." For centuries, Catholic thinking has been heavily influenced by the principles for a "just war" set down by Augustine of Hippo and Thomas Aquinas. The principles centre on limitation and proportionality in conducting warfare. But, of course, these principles were established long before modern means for averting war, such as the United Nations and its instruments, came into being. The "just war" concept is outmoded in the modern world. Yet some ethicists still cling to it. Their thinking has not caught up with the new reality that warfare in the age of weapons of mass destruction is fundamentally incompatible with the universal implementation of human rights. A moral consensus against the evil of nuclear weapons is impeded by those who think that war can still lay claim to being "just"—as long as not too many people are killed. This moral fuzziness has led some to conclude that nuclear weapons can possess some acceptability when they are used to deter "the enemy." Thus, during the Cold War, the barrage of propaganda about Soviet forces about to charge the Western gates led to public acceptance of nuclear weapons as a deterrent.

When the Soviets disappeared as the enemy, the nuclear establishment had to find a new one. The enemy became a political leader, now or in the future, who threatens the West with a nuclear weapon. This is the argument the George W. Bush administration used to start the Iraq war of 2003.

Grudging Acceptance of Deterrence

Definitive Catholic teaching on nuclear deterrence is found in the documents of the Second Vatican Council and in subsequent statements by Pope John Paul II. In its *Pastoral Constitution on the Church in the Modern World,* The Council taught that "any act of war aimed indiscriminately at the destruction of entire cities or of extensive areas along with their population is a crime against God and man himself. It merits unequivocal and unhesitating condemnation" (no. 80)

Though they elaborated their concern that a universal public authority be put in place to outlaw war, the Fathers of Vatican II rather grudgingly accepted the strategy of nuclear deterrence. The accumulation of arms, they said, serves "as a deterrent to possible enemy attack." Thus "peace of a sort" is maintained, though the "balance" resulting from the arms race threatens to lead to war, not eliminate it. Pope John Paul II restated the Catholic position on nuclear deterrence in a message to the UN Second Special Session on Disarmament in 1982:

> In current conditions, "deterrence" based on balance, certainly not as an end in itself but as a step on the way towards a progressive disarmament, may still be judged morally acceptable. Nonetheless, in order to ensure peace, it is indispensable not to be satisfied with the minimum which is always susceptible to the real danger of explosion.

Although this statement was not the full condemnation of nuclear deterrence I wanted, when one parses it carefully, it was saying that, to be acceptable, nuclear deterrence must lead to disarmament measures. Consequently, deterrence as a single, permanent policy is not acceptable. The U.S. bishops' Pastoral Letter on War and Peace, published in 1983, took up this theme. Though expressing strong opposition to nuclear war, declaring that a nuclear response to a conventional attack is "morally unjustifiable" and expressing skepticism that any nuclear war could avoid the massive killing of civilians, the bishops gave a "strictly conditioned moral acceptance of nuclear deterrence."

I began my association with Archbishop Martino with a long memo, written in 1990, making the point that even though the communist threat had collapsed, the Western countries insisted on maintaining nuclear deterrence. Not only had nuclear deterrence been overtaken by political developments but, by assuming a permanency in international relations, it had lost its limited moral justification. Consequently, the Church should now withdraw its limited acceptance of nuclear deterrence. I argued that a new ethical view of nuclear deterrence should come from greater recognition of what the "common ground" of our one planet means: "The end of nuclear weapons will not leave us with a perfect world, but will at least give the political order more room to deal with other imminent threats to peace caused by economic and social deprivation." Martino began a series of speeches in the UN Disarmament (First) Committee throughout the 1990s that stepped up the Holy See's opposition to nuclear weapons.

In 1993, I prepared a brief urging the Holy See to explicitly condemn nuclear deterrence and brought it to the Vatican, where Martino had opened many doors for me. Accompanied by Canadian Ambassador to the Holy See Theodore Arcand, I met with Cardinal Angelo Sodano, secretary of state. The meeting lasted much longer than I had expected as I walked the Cardinal through what each of the nuclear weapons states was doing to modernize its nuclear arsenals. On two occasions, I met the Pope. The first was when Eva and I attended mass in his private chapel and had a few words with him afterwards. The following day, Eva and I were seated in the distinguished visitors section for his public audience in St. Peter's Square. Again I spoke to him, handing him my brief and asking that he initiate a policy review.

Nuclear Weapons Deserve Condemnation

The next summer, I was called back to Rome for a Holy See seminar on nuclear weapons convened by Msgr. Diarmuid Martin, then a leading official of the Justice and Peace Commission and later Archbishop of Dublin. The meeting addressed the Church's statements on deterrence and the question of the abolition of nuclear weapons. Since the American representative at the panel, retired Admiral James Watkins, was holding for a continuance of moral acceptability of nuclear deterrence, the results of the seminar were inconclusive.

But the following year, Pope John Paul, speaking to Japanese bishops, began to move away from any support for nuclear deterrence. He called for the banishment of all nuclear weapons through "a workable system of negotiation, even of arbitration." This was more in keeping with the simple but direct statement he made while visiting Hiroshima in 1981: "To remember Hiroshima is to abhor nuclear war. To remember Hiroshima is to commit oneself to peace."

At the UN in 1997, Martino said that those nuclear states resisting negotiations must be challenged:

> ... for, in clinging to their outmoded rationales for nuclear deterrence they are denying the most ardent aspirations of humanity as well as the opinion of the highest legal authority in the world. Nuclear weapons are incompatible with the peace we seek for the 21st century. They cannot be justified. They deserve condemnation. The preservation of the Non-Proliferation Treaty demands an unequivocal commitment to their abolition.

Martino returned to the subject the following year when he called for "the abolition of nuclear weapons through a universal, non-discriminatory ban with inspection by a universal authority." His speeches occasioned a debate in the British House of Lords; the prestigious Catholic publication *The Tablet* noted that the Holy See's 1982 conditional acceptance had, in effect, been buried. I felt that my work, pushing the Holy See in this direction, had borne fruit.

In 1998, seeing the hardening of nuclear policies in the military doctrines of the major states, 75 U.S. Catholic bishops directly challenged U.S. policy. In a statement organized by Pax Christi, the Catholic peace and justice organization, the bishops said, "We cannot delay any longer. Nuclear deterrence as a national policy must be condemned as morally abhorrent because it is the excuse and justification for the continued possession and further development of these horrendous weapons." The Holy See still didn't go that far, but in 2005, Archbishop Migliore, speaking at the Nuclear Non-Proliferation Treaty review conference, made it clear that nuclear deterrence, in the modern context, cannot claim any moral legitimacy.

> When the Holy See expressed its limited acceptance of nuclear deterrence during the Cold War, it was with the clearly stated condition that deterrence was only a step on the way to progressive nuclear disarmament. The Holy See has never countenanced nuclear deterrence as a permanent measure, nor does it do so today, when it is evident that nuclear deterrence drives

the development of ever-newer nuclear arms, thus preventing genuine disarmament.

While this statement is admirable, it needs to be elaborated with the microphone available to the papacy. The shift in the Holy See's stance on nuclear weapons is a continuing story. As in politics, the Church faces obstacles to enlightened policies for the full reconciliation of peoples.

Staggering Sexual Abuse

When I entered Roger Tucker's legal office a few days before Christmas 1990, I knew virtually nothing about the complex psychological repercussions of sexual abuse. At the time, Tucker was my daughter Evita's law partner, and both believed strongly that in disputes, mediation is far more productive than litigation. Roger had with him David McCann, who had recently come forward with allegations of physical and sexual abuse when he had been a student many years before at St. Joseph's, a residential school at Alfred, Ontario, run by the Brothers of the Christian Schools. McCann was stirred to speak out by the memories evoked by the publicity surrounding spectacular cases of sexual abuse at the Mount Cashel Orphanage in Newfoundland. When McCann went public, he was inundated with calls from other former students of St. Joseph's and a companion school, St. John's, in Uxbridge, Ontario, claiming that they, too, had been abused. McCann formed an association of former students at the two schools called "HelpLine." Though they did not recruit, membership developed spontaneously through word of mouth. By the time I met McCann, 300 people had joined. The Ontario Provincial Police began a widespread investigation: when it was over, sixteen Christian Brothers, eleven from St. Joseph's and five from St. John's, were convicted of criminal charges of assault, buggery or indecent assault relating to incidents spread over three decades. There were at least 10,000 "incidents" at the two schools, the police said. The scale of abuse was staggering.

McCann wanted the kind of redress the courts could not provide: healing. He wanted a process to empower the victims to deal on an equal basis with the institutions involved and to address the emotional and spiritual needs of the victims. In other words, redress required more than mere compensation. Healing, in its many dimensions, was to be at the forefront of the process. The process required a convenor, known and respected by all, to bring all parties to the negotiation table to design a detailed dispute resolution model. I asked Tucker and McCann why they wanted me. "Because you are a prominent Canadian Catholic layman with experience in Church questions combined with diplomatic experience on behalf of the Canadian government," they replied. I said this wasn't the kind of work I did in life. They responded that this was, indeed, an issue of peace in the hearts of the victims. It would be an opportunity to have a positive influence on the lives of hundreds of victims and their families. Also, there was the challenge of creating an innovative process for healing, unfettered by the confrontation of litigation. The model might be adopted elsewhere.

Searching for an expert view on the wisdom of trying to launch a reconciliation model in sexual abuse cases, I met with Paul McAuliffe, a social worker who headed a committee of the Canadian Conference of Catholic Bishops on the long-term pastoral needs of sexual abuse victims. When I asked him for the strongest reason for the Church to be involved in mediation, his answer was unambiguous: "the regaining of trust in the Church by the People of God." This revealed a profound understanding of the Second Vatican Council, which delineated the Church as a community of persons equal in baptism rather than merely an institution of hierarchical personages.

McAuliffe cautioned that many victims, brutalized by the abuse of power, would not be able to respond and function well in life; for others, it would be too late to enter "the uncharted waters of treatment." The majority of victims would be lost in the legal process because they did not have the physical, emotional, spiritual, cognitive or financial resources to stand up to it. Moreover, McAuliffe admitted, "whether we wish to admit it or not, the rich and powerful most often win in a legal forum." The Church, which had betrayed trust once, ought now to be a model of trust in its response to HelpLine, he said.

The Benefits of Reconciliation

I took on the challenge. Six years later, when the Reconciliation Process Implementation Committee file was closed, 595 Helpline claimants had been validated, $14.5 million in cash benefits awarded, counselling, educational, vocational and medical benefits provided, and institutional and personal apologies issued. Ben Hoffman, an alternative dispute resolution expert who advised me, memorialized the incidents at the schools in a 298-page report.

Sexual abuse is debilitating. It produces trauma. It destroys trust. The abuse of power in a religious setting is a desecration. Diocese after diocese in North America has been infected with it. The Church—not just Catholic, but other denominations as well—has paid out millions upon millions of dollars in compensation, sometimes to the point of bankruptcy. The residue of scandal, shame and mistrust is palpable. The sordidness of some (albeit a small percentage of the total) members of the clergy, both priests and brothers, is a blot on the Church. This repeated exploitation, often of young boys, is so far from the teachings of Jesus, let alone the strictures of civil law, that the perpetrators must be living in their own private world of evil fantasy. When I listened to the stories of the victims, I saw the damage done to their sense of self-esteem and their ability to consider themselves as normal people. It was not just money they needed to repair their lives but professional counselling, and most of all, I think, to hear their victimizer say, "I'm sorry." During the years I worked on the file, I also mediated sexual abuse cases for the Jesuits. I saw first-hand the incalculable harm done by one priest in a First Nations community in northern Ontario.

I started my work by meeting with officials of the government of Ontario, which had jurisdiction over the St. Joseph's and St. John's schools. They agreed to take my recommendation for mediation to Cabinet. I next met with the Archbishop of Ottawa, Marcel Gervais, and his auxiliary, Brendan O'Brien. I wanted their pastoral involvement, even though the provincial government and the Christian Brothers had legal responsibility for the conduct of the schools. I made the same argument to Msgr. Edward F. Boehler, designated by Cardinal Aloysius Ambrozic as his Judicial Vicar in sexual abuse matters, and Peter D. Lauwers, legal counsel. They suggested that the Toronto Archdiocese might enter the process if it were seen to be doing so willingly, to join in the moral reparation, as distinct from being forced into an unwanted legal process.

I met with Brother Jean-Marc Cantin, then the provincial of the Ottawa District of the Christian Brothers, his colleague, Brother Maurice Lapointe (who later became provincial) and their counsel,

Ron Caza. I found them defensive but open to mediation. Unfortunately, their counterparts in Toronto, who were also defensive, were not open. The refusal of the Toronto Brothers to enter the process vastly complicated the process we were starting, for the St. John's students wanted the same benefits the St. Joseph's students would receive. Complicated formulas for sharing were developed, followed by recriminations. More former students came forward and a second group had to be processed to ascertain validity. The process dragged on. At times, the atmosphere was toxic. Through it all, McCann never lost his determination that some sort of reconciliation be achieved.

I was with McCann in Notre-Dame Cathedral in Ottawa when Archbishop Gervais gave a formal apology to the HelpLine members arrayed before him at mass. Some could not contain their anger and shouted at him. The Archbishop invited them downstairs for coffee afterwards. McCann and Gervais hugged in a gesture that said the apology was given and received. Under the agreement, the premier of Ontario, Mike Harris, was supposed to stand in the Legislature and apologize. Harris fobbed this off on his attorney general and McCann felt betrayed again. He threatened to sue the government. Years later, Harris did issue an apology of sorts. But it was left to his successor, Dalton McGuinty, who rose in the Legislature in 2004, and said, "As the Premier of Ontario, it is my duty and responsibility to apologize unreservedly today for the neglect and abuse suffered by the children in these schools many years ago." McCann, sitting in the gallery with his family, said, "This brings closure for me."

It could not be said that such a file is ever closed. But I think that, however volatile the atmosphere, a reconciliation process, even with its defects, offers a greater prospect for human healing than does civil litigation. Many HelpLine members were helped to rebuild their lives; however, others were not able to overcome the trauma. Suicides, alcoholism and broken marriages were common. Reconciliation for most is not so much an accomplished fact as an ongoing process. When I told McCann I would write about this episode in my memoirs, he wrote me that "the work we did together is one of the proudest things I have ever done ... The memories are there every day and I am at peace because of what we tried and what we actually did accomplish."

Man to Man to Woman

The turbulence of sexual abuse and nuclear weapons—and what the Catholic Church was doing about both—led me to think again about the state of the Church in the world after Vatican II. My years in Parliament and as a diplomat had not left me much time to dwell on the affairs of the Church. But on one of my visits to Bishop Remi De Roo, now living in the new Pastoral Centre in Victoria, the conversation got around to our book *Man to Man*, the dialogue we had held 23 years earlier. What about a reprise? I wondered. Remi's eyes lit up.

"You know, Remi," I said, "if we do this again, it can't be called *Man to Man*. A dialogue today would not be complete without a woman. Who?"

There was about a five-second pause. Then both of us said, almost simultaneously, "Mary Jo Leddy."

Then a Sister of Sion, Mary Jo Leddy was a founding editor of *Catholic New Times*, and had been a CBC commentator during Pope John Paul's 1984 Canadian tour. She was a highly articulate social activist, specializing in refugee problems. She would be perfect in a new dialogue that would have a deeply concerned woman's perspective. I went to see her in Toronto, and she and I agreed to clear a week in our schedules several months later for the three-way conversation that would be published in book form.

When Mary Jo and I arrived in Victoria in January 1991, the city was buried in two feet of snow. It was practically impossible to venture out even for a walk during the first three days, so almost without interruption Remi, Mary Jo and I sat around a table in Remi's apartment mornings, afternoons and evenings conducting a tape-recorded dialogue. With an eye on the weather outside and also on the turbulence in the Church, we called the book *In the Eye of the Catholic Storm*. As editor, we brought in Michael Creal, an Anglican professor of humanities and religious studies at York University in Toronto. There was no script, only an outline of subjects to be covered, such as "Vatican II: Fading Dream or Enduring Hope?" "Women in the Church: Unfinished Revolution," "The Hunger for Spirituality" and "War and Peace Today: No Middle Ground."

We didn't pretend to settle all the contentious questions in the Church. As Creal put it in his introduction, "When people struggle with such questions in genuine dialogue, they don't achieve perfect clarity on every issue. But ... this book addresses those matters in a way that offers a pattern for continuing Christian inquiry and debate." At the end of each afternoon session, we would celebrate the Eucharist around Remi's dining room table. We were happy, exploring the fullness of the Church, and there was lots of laughter during and between work sessions.

We were, we thought, voices of reason. But a frank look back at the failed promises of Vatican II and ahead to the challenges and opportunities for the Church in the 21st century was too much for the *Catholic Register*, the newspaper of the Toronto Archdiocese. The editor at the time, a priest, rejected an advertisement for the book, an action that, of course, produced headlines in the *Toronto Star* and bounced the book onto the bestseller list. "This is a very loving book about the Catholic Church," I said in an interview. "It is a very honest and sincere effort to come to terms with the challenges the Church faces internally and how it can be present in the world in a loving and caring manner." The priest editor of the *B. C. Catholic* also refused an ad. I thought this was a direct slap at De Roo, whose efforts to implement Vatican II in Victoria were downgraded by the Vancouver authorities. Deafness by authorities was one of the things wrong with the Church, as we pointed out in the book.

Stephen Scharper, an editor at the now defunct *Catholic New Times*, wrote a thoughtful review for the *Montreal Gazette*. "Given the character and commitments of the interlocutors," he wrote, "this is, not surprisingly, a rich book, filled with divergent but stimulating reflection. It is an important resource for engaged Catholics who want to give meaning to their faith experience in light of the 'Catholic storm' of the past 25 years but have lacked the words to do so."

The year after the book was published, a new publisher, Bernard Daly, took up duties at the *Catholic Register*. Daly, a highly competent journalist who had written extensively on Vatican II, brought in Joe Sinasac as editor. The paper, which improved dramatically, is an excellent religious journal.

Peace, Equality, Justice, Development

When I was writing *United Nations: Divided World* for the 40th anniversary of the UN, I included a short dialogue with Robert

Muller. His 36 years at the UN, during which he was a close adviser to three secretaries-general, were devoted to planning the ways in which nations could overcome their narrowness and work for true peace. With the 50th anniversary in 1995 looming, and the eve of the third millennium practically upon us, I thought it would be interesting for the two of us to collaborate on a book-length dialogue to meld our common philosophy with the urgent political issues to offer a roadmap for finding safe passage into the 21st century. Muller had just retired as chancellor of the University for Peace in Costa Rica. I had become chairman of the Canadian committee for the 50th anniversary of the UN, a sprawling network of Canadian non-governmental figures across the country organizing programs to educate Canadians on the value of the UN.

The University for Peace, established by the UN in 1980, provides higher education for peace and also promotes understanding, tolerance and co-operation among peoples. The university projects the values of Costa Rica, the first demilitarized nation in the world. The university's motto is *Si vis pacem, para pacem* (If you want peace, prepare for peace). Located on a vast hill, it overlooks tropical-forested valleys in the central plains of Costa Rica. Flags of a number of nations fly at the entrance near a monument erected to Mahatma Gandhi. The setting provided serenity for the week-long dialogue I had with Muller. I felt free of much of the daily clatter that often prevents me from taking a long view of how we can proceed with the development of God's planet. Muller and I called the resulting book *Safe Passage into the Twenty-First Century*.

The UN provided the framework for our discussion. In its deliberations aimed at producing a declaration for the 50th anniversary, a steering committee determined that the Charter needed to be applied to a new agenda under four headings: peace, equality, justice and development. We examined how each of these elements could be advanced in terms of common values. The long history of the world, characterized by the quest for domination, we said, has reached a higher plateau at which, for the first time, the mingling of intellectualism, technology and danger provides both motivation and means for common survival. It is this very ability to assess situations that provides the human family with its new power.

We knew only too well how slow political structures are to change and how sluggish they are in finding agreement on ways to move forward. Our vision of peace, equality, justice and development recognized political realities, but we felt the UN Charter gave us a compass to find the way forward.

This passage captures the vision of the dialogue:

RM: The Agenda for Peace of the Secretary-General was considered to be great progress. It was great progress because, in addition to peacekeeping, it pointed out that we should also be active in the work of prevention and peacebuilding. On prevention, I would have liked the United Nations to create what NATO has, namely a NATO room, but this would be a United Nations "Peace Room" on the thirty-ninth floor, where we would get information on every potential danger in the world. I would like to see a telecommunications system between all heads of state in their offices and their homes to be in direct contact, instead of listening to their diplomats who often complicate things to render themselves important and indispensable.

DR: We are beginning to learn that war is a barbarian system of resolving conflict, but it has not yet seeped into public consciousness, at least at the public policy level. It is sweeping horizontally through the world. There is a resistance to war, a recognized horror to war. Nobody sings anymore about troops going off to war, as they did in my own childhood. That being said, there is still a public recognition that war is inevitable because the alternative instruments are not understood or trusted. Here is the Secretary-General of the U.N., through the Agenda for Peace, trying to prevent hostilities but, when the prevention is insufficient, favouring a military intervention. The very debate that the world is now having about the proper uses of intervention—Bosnia, and Somalia being cases in point—and where the U.N. has not been successful, scares people about the United Nations. They don't realize that what needs to be done is to strengthen the U.N.'s system for peacemaking and peacekeeping to obviate the recourse to war.

We included a blueprint for action with dozens of proposals, among them setting up a UN arms reduction agency with the goal of lowering national armaments to the level required for domestic order;

holding a parliamentary assembly of elected representatives at the UN; giving the International Court of Justice compulsory jurisdiction over disputes between nation-states; and reprioritizing the lending practices of the international financial institutions towards sustainable, community-based projects. We concluded with a number of education priorities to promote the advancement of a new global ethic based on an understanding of the evolving unity of the planet.

A Family in Mourning

The interplay of joys and griefs in life hit me hard in this period. In the summer of 1994, Eva and I had a wonderful couple of weeks together in Greece. We flew back to Toronto; Eva went straight to Edmonton and I went to New York for a meeting of Global Education Associates. Early the next morning, Eva called me to say that Mickey had become very ill with pneumonia during our absence. Francis had been carefully monitoring her condition. Mickey was now on a respirator in an active treatment hospital. Eva said she would have more information in a few hours. I went to the conference, but just before I was to speak, I was summoned to the phone.

"Come home immediately," Eva said.

I cancelled my speech and headed for the airport. In Toronto, Tricia was waiting for me at the gate for the Edmonton plane. When we reached Edmonton, Evita, Mary Anne and Francis were already there. Mickey had been anointed and was sinking. The doctors said she would not get better. I knew an agonizing decision would have to be made. I went to see Father Martin Carroll, our pastor at Assumption parish. "God help me in the decision I have to make," I said. He reached out and held my hand. Later, the family talked. Eva and I returned to the hospital and gave permission to take Mickey off the respirator. The doctors said she would not be able to live more than six hours. But Mickey fooled them. I think a strong heart is one of the characteristics of the Roche clan, for Mickey's kept beating for three weeks. We maintained a vigil by her bedside. Eva obtained a tape of the softest music, like a waterfall, and played it for Mickey, who was in a coma. Everyone was at peace with what was happening. Mickey died on August 2, 1994, at the age of 38.

Mickey's death bonded the family once again. Not much was said, but everyone was nervous about Eva's health. In 1991, she had been diagnosed with cancer of the lymph nodes. It was her dentist who first spotted the problem during a regular checkup. Surgery was required, followed by a long recuperation, then radiation therapy. She recovered her energy and returned to work at Grant MacEwen College. We continued our active life, and the summers of 1993 and 1994 were full of travel. Eva and I had taken a special trip for our 40th wedding anniversary in 1993. The hotel room she liked best in the world was a special suite in the Gore Hotel in the Kensington area of London; we encamped there for several days, seeing plays in the West End and listening to Mike McKenzie, her favourite pianist, at the Dorchester Hotel. Then we went to Rome for our meeting with Pope John Paul and long walks through the Eternal City. Stockholm followed, where I had meetings featuring wonderful receptions and a boat tour. The next summer we were on the idyllic island of Crete.

Eva continued her heavy teaching schedule through 1995. I remember her dashing home after work for her dancing shoes and rushing off to tap-dancing class, where she earned her Level II certificate. When the college term was over, she came with me to New York for the month-long Nuclear Non-Proliferation Treaty review conference. During that trip, I noticed her energy slipping. But on her return to Edmonton, she felt well enough to go to Calgary for a conference of her own. I finished the draft for a new book, *An Unacceptable Risk: Nuclear Weapons in a Volatile World*. We had a UN flag ceremony in the park across the street and Eva helped to entertain the guests. Her energy went down again.

Eva's surgeon, who had been keeping track of her, said the cancer had recurred. Her specialist at the Cross Cancer Institute told me we should spend quality time doing the things we wanted to do. Eva invited our close friends Bernie and Kay Feehan for a visit. I was hesitant about taking her to San Francisco, where I was to participate in meetings around the UN 50th anniversary celebration, but Eva insisted that she wanted to go. We flew to San Francisco and stayed in an apartment hotel. On the third day, though again not feeling well, she was determined to go to hear Robert Muller speak at a gala dinner. It was her last public function.

The next day, I phoned Eva's doctor in Edmonton to report her condition; he said to bring her home. We arrived back in Edmonton and I took her straight to the hospital. Emergency surgery was performed. The doctors called me in for a palliative care conference. I brought all the children home. Evita, Francis, Mary Anne, Tricia and I gathered around Eva's beside while she was anointed.

Eva came home and we brought in nurses round-the-clock. On her 65th birthday, July 4, she summoned up the energy to come out to the porch for a bit of a family celebration. Irish black humour prevailed. Her brother Michael Nolan played the piano for her, and Eva smiled as Francis and Tricia danced to one of her favourite pieces, "Moonglow." Three days later, she went into crisis.

Eva died at 3:17 p.m. on Tuesday, July 11, 1995.

15

When Hope Became a Verb

The *Edmonton Journal* interviewed Evita for a story on Eva. There were many tributes to Eva's professional work as an outspoken advocate for quality childcare. Only the year before, she had been awarded the Grant MacEwan Medallion, the college's highest honour. But Evita brought out Eva's fun-loving side.

"My mother was a hoot," she said. "She took her work very seriously but not herself. She was full of life and did crazy things." Evita recounted that, at the 50th birthday party for Gerry Kelly, president of Grant MacEwan, Eva decided to recreate the famous image of Marilyn Monroe leaning over President Kennedy to sing "Happy Birthday, Mr. President." "She got a blonde Marilyn Monroe wig, poured herself into a gown with the cleavage and all and sang a perfect imitation. She brought the place down."

Eva left instructions that, at her funeral, the recessional "hymn" was to be "When the Saints Go Marching In." Everybody said Eva would likely be tap dancing her way into heaven. I was astonished to see all three of her doctors at the funeral. A second funeral was held two days later in Ottawa, so that Eva's mother could attend with Eva's two brothers, Michael and Terry Nolan.

Eva's death hit our housekeeper, Edel Maran, hard. When Edel had immigrated to Canada from Germany as a single parent in 1973, she could not speak English. Eva hired her anyway and said she could bring her small daughter to work. A number of years later, Edel remarried. Eventually, she and her husband decided to return to Germany. We gave a farewell party for them. Six months later, the phone rang one day at 6 a.m. "Mrs. Roche," Edel said, "we want to come back to Canada and this time we're going to stay. Can I have my job back?" Eva said, "Get on the next plane." Edel has now been in the Roche household for some 35 years. It would be impossible to find a more devoted, trustworthy friend of the family.

Even though I wanted just to stay home and be by myself, I knew I needed help to deal with grief. I had once pinned to the door of my study the cover of the playbill from the Broadway show *The Me Nobody Knows*. Sometimes I felt there were two sides of the same me. The professional me goes into a crowded room and "works it," projecting myself to an audience and shrugging off any rebuffs. The personal me would rather spend a week in a monastery, read a book or go for a solitary walk. I'm outgoing when I have to be, introspective when I want to be. The latter gives me the strength to put myself out on the edge. With Eva gone, I was off balance.

Fortunately, I found a grief counsellor, Dr. Ronna Jevne, whose patience and understanding enabled me to recover not only my balance but also my wholeness. She showed me that the heart is a very big place. Dr. Jevne made me conscious that my life and Eva's had very much been one of celebrating life. Now I would have to find a way to go on celebrating life.

Celebration was the theme of a memorial Evita and I held for Eva in New York. We called it "Eva at the Beekman" and invited a host of friends to our hotel for an evening of storytelling and reminiscing. Champagne toasts abounded. Barbara and Joe Calnan, close friends of Eva's and mine for 30 years, were there. So were Peter Mann and Joan Boyle and Father Bob Kennedy, S.J., all of whom had played important roles in our lives. That evening, recapturing the New York that Eva loved, was part of my healing.

But more deaths of people close to me kept occurring. Only a few days after Eva's Ottawa funeral, which Jerry and Pat Mische had attended, Jerry suddenly died. Jerry and I had grown close during the years I chaired Global Education Associates; I immediately flew to New York to speak at his funeral, and then at a second one in his birthplace in Minnesota. Then Barbara Calnan died after a relatively short illness. Next to die was Lenore McHardy. We had become close friends; Lenore had often driven me out to the countryside to see her horse, Racalla. Those were peaceful afternoons. Lenore had seemed to understand the grieving I was going through.

Reeling from so much death, I found myself becoming angry. I lashed out at people, a trait foreign to my normal self. I sought ongoing help from Dr. Jevne. She talked often about hope. "What is this thing called hope?" she wrote in an essay. "It weaves itself like an essential thread through thoughts and experiences that speak of the human condition ... The choice is ours: we can open ourselves to the mystery of hope or maintain our illusions of certainty. Yet somehow we must come to know hope, to be intentional about it, to claim its power."

Ronna was instrumental in having me join the board of the Hope Foundation of Alberta. As I began to study hope, I saw it as a verb, not a noun. In other words, I had to use the blessings in my life to find my way out of grieving—not just my personal grieving, but my sorrow and anger at the stupid political policies that continually brought the world war instead of true human security. I found my deepest solace and strength in Christ. He suffered so much, yet ultimately triumphed. Thinking about Christ energized me. Often, when I was in New York, I would sit and contemplate a huge statue of the risen Christ over the altar in Holy Family Church, near the United Nations. I wanted more and more for my life to be a reflection of his teaching on peace. And in that desire, I found my own peace.

In 1996, immediately after the first anniversary of Eva's death, Francis and I went on a "root-tracing" expedition to Ireland. In Westport, County Mayo, the Westport Heritage Centre found the marriage certificate issued when Michael Roche, my great-grandfather, married Ann Keenan. They even located the sharecropper's certificate issued to Michael's father, Thomas, in the last years of the eighteenth century. Was it authentic, given the paucity of records from that period? I didn't ask too many questions. Francis and I were having a good time driving down the back lanes of rural Ireland and staying at bed and breakfasts on picturesque farms. Like the pilgrims who come from all over the world to climb the mountain where St. Patrick fasted for 40 days in 441 AD, we climbed the famous Crough Patrick, in two hours and 20 minutes; I felt I was doing something Michael Roche himself might have done. We found a wonderful Benedictine monastery, Glenstal Abbey, and stayed in the guest house for three days. Then to Limerick, Cashel, Cork, Ardmore and the famous Waterford Crystal Factory. Ireland was bliss. I suppose there cannot be a time when Ireland is not good for the soul.

I needed the rest in Ireland, for ten hours after arriving home, I was off again to speak in Worcester, Massachusetts, at a conference of the International Physicians for the Prevention of Nuclear War. The overarching problem of nuclear weapons was becoming the centrepiece of my professional life. I had come to the conclusion that the abolition of nuclear weapons is *the* indispensable condition for peace in the 21st century.

Exposing Nuclear Incoherence

Because the Canadian government had not undertaken a public and comprehensive post–Cold War review of its security, defence and international relations policies, a number of peace and disarmament advocates generated a public debate through an unprecedented Citizens' Inquiry into Peace and Security, a two-year effort (1990–1992) that produced a report entitled *Transformation Moment: A Canadian Vision of Common Security*.

The Inquiry, conceived by the Canadian Peace Alliance, brought together fourteen major non-governmental organizations representing a wide range of interests: labour, academic, religious, Aboriginal, environment, disarmament and development. The Inquiry took the form of public hearings in nineteen communities across Canada. The hearings were conducted by me along with four other commissioners, including Iona Campagnola, former president of the Liberal Party of Canada, who later became Lieutenant-Governor of British Columbia, and Johanna den Hertog, former president of the New Democratic Party. Our report called for a comprehensive view of security: the abolition of the war system itself, starting with the abolition of nuclear weapons and other weapons of mass destruction and the substantial reduction of conventional weapons and forces. "It is not enough merely to attempt to balance the world's arsenals of nuclear and other weapons from now until the end of time," we said. "'Balancing' these forces only perpetuates their existence. If nuclear weapons remain, they will eventually be used."

The Canadian government brought out a new foreign policy paper, *Canada in the World*, which included environmental, demographic, health and development issues in a broader concept of security. That was a good start to finding security in the post–Cold War world. But the paper retained the continuing contradiction of Canadian foreign policy. On the one hand, it said that "the U.N. continues to be the key vehicle for pursuing Canada's global security objectives." On the other hand, it said that NATO and NORAD "remain key guarantees of our military security." This contradiction centred on nuclear weapons, a subject on which the UN and NATO had long been at odds. The government came out strongly for the indefinite and unconditional extension of the Nuclear Non-Proliferation Treaty (NPT) as the instrument to stop the spread of nuclear weapons; it would uphold the NPT. What the paper did not say was that the NPT requires the total elimination of nuclear weapons, whereas NATO continued to call its possession "essential" and maintained stocks of them deployed in European countries. This is more than a contradiction; it is incoherence.

The actions of the government, which put U.S. interests ahead of those of the UN, weakened the NPT. Four preparatory meetings over two years showed clearly that the 1995 NPT review and extension conference would be a difficult exercise: the nuclear weapons states were determined to keep their nuclear weapons, while the leading states of the Non-Aligned Movement (Mexico, Egypt, Indonesia and about a dozen others) were equally determined to hold the nuclear weapons states to their promise to negotiate both nuclear disarmament and general disarmament.

The length of extension of the NPT became the central issue. The nuclear weapons states held that "indefinite and unconditional" extension was the best route to world stability in the post–Cold War era. Many non-nuclear states argued for fixed periods, taking the form of a "rolling 25-year extension," which would maintain pressure on the nuclear weapons states to demonstrate compliance with the Treaty, particularly Article VI.

Furious with Canada

Attending the review and extension conference as a Holy See delegate, I saw the political gymnastics first-hand. The Canadian government insisted that indefinite extension would enshrine permanently the legal commitment to dismantle all nuclear arsenals. But the countries of the Non-Aligned Movement and most representatives of the non-governmental organization community feared that an unconditional indefinite extension would be regarded by the nuclear powers as permanently legitimizing their possession of nuclear weapons while denying the nuclear option to everybody else. Mexico and Indonesia submitted draft resolutions calling for specific disarmament steps within time frames. Had they been accepted, indefinite extension of the NPT would have been a good idea. But Canada countered with a resolution calling for indefinite extension without any conditions. Canada lobbied hard for its resolution, thus undermining the efforts of the conference president, Jayantha Dhanapala, to get effective commitments to disarmament steps.

Trying to avoid a decisive vote, Dhanapala held out for consensus by crafting a package deal with three elements. First, in addition to review conferences every five years, there would be annual preparatory meetings. Second, the Conference on Disarmament would complete a Comprehensive Nuclear Test Ban Treaty by 1996; a ban on fissile materials would be negotiated; and nuclear weapons states would make "systematic and progressive efforts" to reduce and ultimately eliminate nuclear weapons. Third, the Non-Proliferation Treaty would continue in force indefinitely. The package would not have been approved without Dhanapala's deft massaging of an Arab-sponsored separate resolution calling for a Nuclear Weapons Free Zone in the Middle East.

Dhanapala did not dare ask for consensus. Rather, having obtained assurances from the dissenters that they would not ask for a vote (which they would lose), he quickly declared that the package was "adopted without a vote" and banged his gavel down.

The Canadian delegation led the applause, but in the statements that followed, thirteen states denounced the action. Nigeria said, "The decision to extend the NPT indefinitely without a time-bound program of nuclear disarmament measures attached to such a decision poses grave security risks for the present as well as future generations." Indonesia said it was "dismayed" by the policies of some nuclear weapons states with regard to the fulfillment of their obligations. The decision, it said, "will deprive the sense of urgency from the obligations under Article VI."

The conference staggered to an end, unable even to agree on a generally worded final document. In 2008, thirteen years later, a Comprehensive Test Ban Treaty, though achieved, has not yet entered into force. Negotiations for a fissile material ban have not begun. And, with 25,000 nuclear weapons still in existence, the nuclear weapons states have made a mockery of their 1995 commitment to "systematic and progressive efforts" to nuclear disarmament. The powerful states wanted the NPT extension on their terms, and they got it. I sat with Dhanapala during the final hours of the conference. He was furious with Canada's action and plainly worried about the future viability of the treaty.

The Ultimate Evil

Another effort to strengthen the NPT was made a year later, when the International Court of Justice unanimously ruled that negotiations to eliminate nuclear weapons must not only be pursued, as ordered by the NPT, but concluded. Often called the World Court, the court is the principal judicial organ of the UN and the highest legal authority in the world. But, in acknowledgment of the fact that global civilization still has some distance to go to reach full development, its rulings are not mandatory. The court has jurisdiction in disputed cases only when the parties involved agree to it. Would it be tolerable to have the rulings of the Supreme Court of Canada issued on an optional basis? The World Court, holding that the use or threat of use of nuclear weapons would contravene every aspect of humanitarian law, could only put its view into an advisory opinion.

The court was divided on the question of whether a nuclear weapon could be used "in an extreme circumstance of self-defence, in which the very survival of a state would be at stake." In effect, the Court delegitimized using nuclear weapons as a war-fighting strategy but left open the question of their use in an extreme circumstance of self-defence. This was just what the nuclear states needed to bolster their claim that nuclear weapons are intended only for defence purposes and, accordingly, these states would not alter their nuclear war policies to reflect the court's advisory opinion. But the President of the court, Judge Mohammed Bedjaoui of Algeria, in his lengthy dissent, stated that the vote could in no manner be interpreted to mean that the court was "leaving the door ajar" to legalizing nuclear weapons. "It would be quite foolhardy," he wrote, "to set the survival of a state above all other considerations, in particular the survival of mankind itself."

I was greatly impressed with Judge Bedjaoui's powerful argument:

> The very nature of this blind weapon ... has a destabilizing effect on humanitarian law which regulates discernment in the type of weapon used. Nuclear weapons, the ultimate evil, destabilize humanitarian law which is the law of the lesser evil. The existence of nuclear weapons is therefore a challenge to the very existence of humanitarian law, not to mention their long-term effects of damage to the human environment, in respect to which the right to life be exercised.

Bedjaoui's phrase *the ultimate evil* appealed to me. That is exactly how I feel about nuclear weapons. I wanted to use the phrase for the title of a new book. I wrote to the judge to ask not only for his permission but also if he would write the foreword to my book. Much to my surprise, he agreed. I sent him the manuscript. He wrote an elegant plea to free the world from the fear of nuclear devastation. "Fear and madness may still link arms to engage in a final dance of death," he said. "Peoples are still subject to perverse and permanent nuclear blackmail. A way has to be found of delivering them from it."

I found the technical aspects of nuclear weapons were mesmerizing people. A combination of historical amnesia about Hiroshima and Nagasaki, combined with the incessant projecting of nuclear weapons as necessary for deterrence, led to a state of either denial or apathy. The sheer horror of nuclear devastation was veiled from people's minds. Media and political processes ignored the centrality of the nuclear issue: evil.

In my book *The Ultimate Evil*, I used the description of the effects of nuclear weapons emphasized by another judge of the World Court, Christopher Weeramantry of Sri Lanka, who went on to become a powerful advocate for total elimination. Nuclear weapons, he wrote:

> Cause death and destruction
> Induce cancers, leukemia, keloids, and related afflictions
> Cause gastro-intestinal, cardiovascular, and related afflictions
> Continue for decades to induce health-related problems
> Cause congenital deformities, mental retardation,
>   and genetic damage
> Could cause a nuclear winter

Contaminate and destroy the food chain
Imperil the eco-system
Produce lethal levels of heat and blast
Produce radiation and radioactive fallout
Produce a disruptive electro-magnetic pulse
Produce social disintegration
Imperil all civilization
Threaten human survival
Wreak cultural devastation
Threaten all life on the planet
Irreversibly damage environmental and other rights
     of future generations
Exterminate civilian populations
Damage neighbouring states.

Moral Bankruptcy of Nuclear Weapons

A close and unvarnished examination of the multifarious effects of nuclear weapons must lead any decent-thinking person to abolition. I wanted to be part of the abolition movement seeking to open the eyes of society to this evil. Society is not impervious to evil: the Holocaust, AIDS and genocide have all been recognized as the evils they are. But the ultimate—last, final, most removed in time or space—evil appears to be too far removed from daily life to engage our attention.

It is almost as if the issue is too big to handle. Nuclear weapons assault life on the planet. Indeed, they assault the planet itself, and in so doing they assault the process of the continuing development of the planet. This is an affront to God, the Creator of the universe—an affront to the mysterious process of creation that connects us to an unfathomably distant past that the present generation has no right to interrupt. Nuclear weapons rival the power of God. They challenge God. They lure us into thinking we can control the destiny of the world. They turn upside down the natural morality that ensues from the relationship between God and humanity. Nuclear weapons are evil because they destroy the process of life itself. They invert order into disorder.

Nuclear weapons are supposed to be governed by the covenants of humanitarian law. In fact, a nuclear war would destroy the very basis of humanitarian law. The structure of our civilization would disappear.

Nuclear weapons, with no limitation or proportionality in their effect, make a mockery of old "just war" theories. How can self-defence be cited as a justification for the use of nuclear weapons when their full effect destroys the "self" that is supposed to be defended?

I came to the conclusion that nuclear weapons would be abolished only when the moral consciousness of humanity was raised, just as it had been raised by the moral reassessment and rejection of slavery, colonialism and apartheid. Moral constraints on nuclear weapons have always had to compete with "reasons of state." But the World Court tried to tell us that "reasons of state" can never justify breaching of humanitarian law by using nuclear weapons. Humanitarian law is based on natural morality. Yet the moral challenge to nuclear weapons remains weak.

It is almost as if moralists are afraid to moralize, as if the argument of immorality loses its impact in a secular world, as if stamping out evil can't compete with scientific advancement. I did not regard speaking out against the immorality of nuclear weapons simple "moralism." It is rather the reassertion of the human conscience distinguishing between right and wrong. The nuclear powers must be challenged from a moral basis, because, in clinging to spurious, self-serving rationales, they are deliberately deceiving the world. The doctrine of nuclear deterrence cannot claim the slightest shred of moral acceptance: it is morally bankrupt. The nuclear powers will doubtless turn a deaf ear to a clear-cut moral condemnation of nuclear weapons. But the force of morality and law cannot long be ignored if the peoples of the world build their case for abolition on these twin bases.

Nuclear weapons are no longer about the enemy. Nuclear weapons *are* the enemy. They do not prevent evil: they *are* evil, in its most devastating form.

Cross-Canada Roundtables

At the 1995 NPT extension and review conference, a group of non-governmental organizations launched a new network called Abolition 2000. The goal was to secure the political will and commitment of the world's governments to complete negotiations by the year 2000 on an international convention setting a firm timetable for the elimination of all nuclear weapons. Undaunted by the failure of the nuclear weapons states to move, the group retained its name after the year 2000 because 2,000 groups had signed on. Several of them were in Canada; out of this nucleus grew the Canadian Network to Abolish Nuclear Weapons. The Network now comprises some fifteen leading nuclear disarmament groups, including Project Ploughshares and the Canadian Pugwash Group.

When Lloyd Axworthy took over as foreign minister of Canada in 1996, I sensed a window of opportunity was opening to toughen Canada's policy. Ernie Regehr, executive director of Project Plough-shares, felt the same way. He took up my suggestion that Project Ploughshares sponsor me on a cross-Canada tour to hold community roundtables to raise Canadian awareness. From September 10 to October 1, 1996, I held eighteen roundtables attended by 404 community leaders with diverse occupations, including members of Parliament, members of provincial legislatures, mayors, city councillors, bishops, clergy, university professors, teachers, physicians, lawyers, judges, journalists, editors, First Nations leaders, directors of foundations, peace activists, school board trustees and students.

By engaging a wide range of community leaders and activists, including people and constituencies not usually associated with disarmament advocacy, the roundtables were intended to make the point that all levels of communities (from the international to the local) have an opportunity and responsibility to face the reality of the nuclear threat and to demand concrete action.

The roundtables answered a number of questions Axworthy posed to the public upon taking office. For example, when asked to give their views on Canada's "step-by-step" approach, the roundtable participants said that "step-by-step" without a comprehensive program and a definable end goal would allow the nuclear weapons states to carry their nuclear weapons well into the 21st century. Participants were able to see that the resulting disparity between nuclear haves and have-nots would sow dissension and mistrust and would risk unravelling the NPT. There was considerable puzzlement, even resentment, that Canada still maintained a high defence budget, which had been cut only 16 per cent from its Cold War peak, whereas Canada's Official Development Assistance program had been slashed 31 per cent.

It was noted at the roundtables that the ambiguity in Canada's position on nuclear weapons reflected, in some ways, the ambiguity in Canadians themselves. While professing to scorn violence, we have become inured to violence—on the streets, in our institutions, in our entertainment. It is little wonder that we give so little thought to the violence we share in being part of a system that threatens to use nuclear weapons, thus killing countless individuals who have every bit as much a right to life as we do. Several participants thought it unlikely that we can root nuclear weapons out of our military system until we root violence out of our society.

These discussions led to the general recognition of nuclear weapons as the pinnacle of a system of violence that increasingly has economic as well as military overtones, and the further recognition that the subject of nuclear weapons and violence constitutes the supreme moral issue of the day. Many participants (not only clergy) called upon the churches, temples and mosques of Canada to do much more to sensitize Canadians to the effects of the toleration of violence.

The roundtables made three recommendations:

The Canadian Government should put its commitment to international law ahead of allegiance to NATO, and it should follow the World Court's admonition to conclude negotiations for the elimination of nuclear weapons.

Canadian support, with that of like-minded nations, for a U.N. resolution calling for immediate negotiations on a Nuclear Weapons Convention may help the U.S. Administration overcome domestic elements hostile to nuclear weapons elimination.

The step-by-step approach to nuclear disarmament must be incorporated into a comprehensive program—or framework— based on an unequivocal commitment by the nuclear-weapon states to total elimination of nuclear weapons.

Regehr and I took the report to Axworthy, who used it as the basis for a mandate the government gave the parliamentary foreign affairs committee to review Canada's policies on nuclear weapons.

Hiroshima and Nagasaki Messages

In 1997, I returned to Japan to speak at peace rallies in Hiroshima and Nagasaki. Because Regehr and I were about to testify to the parliamentary committee in Ottawa, I asked the mayors of the two cities that had suffered such devastation from nuclear bombs to give me a message for the parliamentarians. Mayor Takashi Hiraoka of Hiroshima wrote, "We, the citizens of Hiroshima, who have suffered a nuclear bombing, deeply believe that the development and possession of nuclear weapons is a crime against humanity and that nuclear weapons and humankind cannot coexist." His counterpart in Nagasaki, Iccho Itoh, said, "Based on our experience, the people of Nagasaki have been appealing to the world that nuclear weapons are lethal, that they could annihilate the human race, and that genuine world peace cannot be attained as long as nuclear weapons exist on this planet."

In presenting these letters to the committee, Regehr and I appealed for a fresh examination of the moral and strategic arguments against nuclear weapons: "the risk of disastrous war that they pose (through accident, miscalculation, madness, desperation or deliberate terrorist act), the immorality of potential participation in mass murder, the repercussions of the continuing disparity among nuclear haves and have-nots."

Before the committee could finish its work, Prime Minister Jean Chrétien called an election. All parliamentary work was suspended while Chrétien went about securing a second majority government. I had voted for him when he came to power in 1993. I truly felt that I wasn't leaving the Progressive Conservative Party; rather it was the Party, with its right-wing bent, that had left me. I was sure that Robert Stanfield, the leader I had so respected, would not have supported Canadian involvement in the Iraq war. Chrétien had not only opposed the war but supported Axworthy's move to strengthen Canada's nuclear policies, so I felt comfortable voting for him again in 1997.

The foreign affairs committee resumed its examination of nuclear weapons in 1998 under the chairmanship of Bill Graham, and I was invited to testify again. By now, I had taken on the chairmanship of the Canadian Network to Abolish Nuclear Weapons, and had also become chairman of the Canadian Pugwash Group.

The Pugwash Conferences on Science and World Affairs takes its name from the location of group's the first meeting, held in 1957 in the village of Pugwash, Nova Scotia, birthplace of the philanthropist Cyrus Eaton, who hosted the meeting. The stimulus for that gathering was a manifesto issued by a group of world figures headed by Bertrand Russell and Albert Einstein, two of the towering figures of the

20th century, who launched a famous appeal for the end of nuclear weapons. Their appeal ended with these stirring words:

> There lies before us, if we choose, continual progress in happiness, knowledge, and wisdom. Shall we, instead, choose death, because we cannot forget our quarrels? We appeal as humans beings to human beings: Remember your humanity, and forget the rest ....

The youngest signer of the Russell-Einstein manifesto was Joseph (Jo) Rotblat, a Polish nuclear scientist who quit the Manhattan Project when he realized the terrible human carnage nuclear weapons would bring. Rotblat became the driving force of the Pugwash movement, and in 1995 Rotblat and Pugwash were jointly awarded the Nobel Peace Prize. Rotblat became a hero of mine, and I will say more about him later in this book.

A Lesson in India

It was at a Pugwash workshop in New Delhi that I learned an enduring lesson. I took as my theme that India has a vital role to play in the campaign to eliminate nuclear weapons. Mine was the high-road approach. "I make this statement conscious of the controversies swirling around India's position on nuclear weapons, conscious also of India's history of seeking global nuclear disarmament, and conscious of India's own potential for leadership as it enters its second half-century on the eve of the New Millennium." The workshop participants were invited to meet with India's prime minister, Shri I. K. Gujral, who received us in his residence. As we sat around the prime minister's living room, each of us was given the opportunity to make a short remark. I gave him my lofty India speech and urged him to occupy the moral high ground by refusing to test a nuclear weapon and thus lead the world by example. The prime minister looked at me without making any comment. As we were filing out, one of my Indian friends put his arm around me. "Nice speech you made in there, Doug. Now go and make the same speech to the American President."

Taking his words to heart when I appeared for the second time before the foreign affairs committee, I said that Canada must exert itself to influence a change in U.S. policies:

... the heart of the issue for this Committee and for the Government of Canada is how to influence the United States. They are our friend: they are our ally ... The U.S. administration needs help, because they have their own recalcitrant elements within the United States itself. They need help from like-minded states. They need help from public opinion.

I drew a parallel between the campaign to ban land mines and the efforts to abolish nuclear weapons. Ottawa was then basking in the success of the "Ottawa Process," by which the Canadian government had simply called an international conference that produced a treaty to ban the production and deployment of land mines. I reminded the parliamentarians that the media, awakened by the celebrity intervention of Princess Diana, focused intensely on the 26,000 deaths and maimings per year from land mines. "So too must the deaths of millions in minutes that would result from the explosion of a nuclear weapon." I made my own appeal to the parliamentarians: "I ask you to register the horror, the deaths and the desolation, and the inhuman and incalculable after-effects of nuclear weapons. Nuclear weapons must be seen for what they are: weapons of mass murder."

The committee's report turned out to be a progressive document. It urged the Canadian government to "play a leading role in finally ending the nuclear threat overhanging humanity," and backed up this sentiment with a call for Canada to "argue forcefully" within NATO for a change in its nuclear weapons policies. Also, the report said Canada should work with NATO allies and pro-nuclear disarmament states to "encourage the nuclear weapons states to demonstrate their unequivocal commitment to enter into and conclude negotiations leading to the elimination of nuclear weapons." Since these recommendations were precisely what I had been arguing for, I hailed the report. Bill Graham sent me a note expressing appreciation. "Your work has, of course, been a considerable inspiration to us all and served as a foundation for much of our deliberations."

I didn't know whether to be shocked or amused at a minority report issued by the Reform Party that was opposed to any curtailment of U.S. power to use nuclear weapons as deemed necessary. Fifteen years earlier, I had led the production of a minority report by the same committee but for exactly opposite reasons. At least the first minority report took principled positions and gave detailed recommendations. But Reform's report merely dissented "from the broad conclusions of the Report." Reform's knee-jerk reactionary views were swept aside by Axworthy, who used the committee's main report (signed by parties that had gained 80 per cent of the popular vote in the 1998 election) to get the government formally to call for a review of NATO's nuclear weapons policies. Axworthy demonstrated political bravery, and later paid a price for his courage.

Birth of the Middle Powers Initiative

During the long and truncated process of the foreign affairs committee's hearings, I wrote a memo, the results of which took over my life and defined my work for peace. The Middle Powers Initiative (MPI) was conceived in that document.

The memo, dated October 27, 1997, was addressed to my fellow executive members of the Canadian Network to Abolish Nuclear Weapons: Ernie and Nancy Regehr, Bill Robinson, Dr. Alan Phillips, Debbie Grisdale and Bev Delong. I said the nuclear weapons states were turning their backs on the World Court, the NPT was jeopardized and negotiations for nuclear disarmament were paralyzed. A new Canadian campaign led by non-governmental organizations (NGOs) was urgent. I proposed that the Network construct a new network of NGOs to work with key middle power states to use their access to the nuclear weapons states to press them to fulfill their commitments to the NPT.

Defining and working with middle power states was by no means a sudden inspiration. In my 1989 book, *Building Global Security*, I recalled that the British development economist Barbara Ward once argued that middle power states can lead the way in new experiences of co-operation. "The superpowers," Ward said, "are too vast, too unwieldy, too locked in their own responsibilities. The great mass of states are too poor and too shaky. It is the middle powers ... who occupy the right position on the scale of influence." The Six-Nation Initiative (Argentina, India, Greece, Mexico, Sweden and Tanzania), which pressed the superpowers in the mid-1980s to move towards disarmament, demonstrated the influence that middle-range states can have when they act together. The role of middle powers seemed to me to be in the ascendancy.

The Network executive was excited about the idea, but said such a group ought to be run by an international steering committee, not a Canadian one. They encouraged me to take the idea into the international arena. I began contacting key leaders of non-governmental organizations: Rob Green, Kate Dewes and Alyn Ware, who had played prominent roles in the development of the World Court; Jonathan Granoff, a Philadelphia attorney representing Lawyers Alliance for World Security; David Krieger, director of the Nuclear Age Peace Foundation in Santa Barbara, California; Dr. Ron McCoy and Michael Christ, of the International Physicians for the Prevention of Nuclear War; and Alice Slater, director of Global Resource Action Center for the Environment in New York. They proved to be a dynamic team, filled not only with commitment but knowledge on how to get the job done. "The Middle Powers Initiative will require immense staying power," I warned them. As ardent abolitionists, they knew all about staying power.

We held our first meeting on March 19 and 20, 1998, in Alice Slater's boardroom on Madison Avenue in New York. Ron McCoy nominated me chairman. I looked around the room. There didn't seem to be anyone else looking for the job, so I accepted. We set out our purpose:

> MPI will urge the leaders of a number of key Middle Power States to form a new coalition to press the nuclear weapon states for an unequivocal commitment to complete nuclear disarmament as demonstrated by the immediate commencement of negotiations leading to the elimination of nuclear weapons and by practical steps such as de-alerting and pledging no-first-use.

We decided to ask prominent nuclear disarmament organizations to co-sponsor MPI: International Physicians for the Prevention of Nuclear War, the International Peace Bureau, the Women's International League for Peace and Freedom, the International Association of Lawyers Against Nuclear Arms, the International Network of Scientists, Scientists for Social Responsibility, the Global Security Institute, the State of the World Forum, and the Nuclear Age Peace Foundation. The first three had won the Nobel Peace Prize.

We debated what kind of governments we wanted to work with, settling on states with strong track records on nuclear disarmament issues, access to the nuclear weapons states, credibility in the area of human rights and leaders who could work together. The initial list of countries that we would try to establish a relationship with included Australia, Brazil, Canada, Costa Rica, Egypt, Iceland, Ireland, Japan, Kazakhstan, Malaysia, Mexico, New Zealand, Norway, South Africa, Sweden and Ukraine.

International Physicians for the Prevention of Nuclear War offered us quarters in their office in Cambridge, Massachusetts. In the midst of a long session on delegations, budgeting and staffing, Jonathan Granoff went outside to phone his friend, Senator Alan Cranston of California, who was then starting the Global Security Institute. Granoff returned to the meeting, a big smile on his face.

"Senator Cranston just donated $5,000 to the Middle Powers Initiative," he said.

"What do you mean?" I asked. "We haven't even done anything yet."

"He believes in us," Jonathan replied.

At first, money was not hard to raise. Dr. Jennifer Simons, president of the Simons Foundation in Vancouver, whom I invited to join us for the second day of our meeting, pledged financial support. Tom Graham of the Rockefeller Brothers Fund heard about what we were doing and pledged $100,000 for a seminar to get us off the ground. We could afford one full-time staff member; I hired Suzie Pearce, a well-known Boston activist and the sister of the outstanding writer Jonathan Schell, author of *The Fate of the Earth*.

Surmounting the Ifs

Three months after the first MPI meeting, an announcement by Ireland and Sweden caught us by surprise. Unbeknownst to us, a group of countries had drawn up a joint declaration to revive the international drive against nuclear weapons. Besides Ireland and Sweden, the countries involved were Brazil, Egypt, Mexico, New Zealand, Slovenia and South Africa. They called themselves the New Agenda Coalition. (Slovenia later dropped out, fearing its application for coveted NATO membership would be rejected if it were part of such a group.) Their opening statement signalled that they would apply political pressure on not only the five traditional nuclear weapons states but also on the newcomers, India, Pakistan and Israel.

Here were a group of countries now doing what the Middle Powers Initiative had established itself to do as a non-governmental organization. Should we stay in business? I decided to go immediately to Ireland and Sweden and find out. On the evening of July 1, I left a Canada Day lawn party of Francis's friends to fly overnight to Dublin. I met Rob Green and Alyn Ware at the hotel. The three of us went to the Irish ministry to meet with Darach MacFhionnbhairr who, it later became clear, was the inspiration behind the New Agenda Coalition.

I put the issue plainly to Darach. "We don't want to interfere with your work. Would it be better if we disbanded so we don't muddy your waters?"

He replied, "On the contrary. The New Agenda Coalition needs your help. You have credibility. You can send important delegations to countries. Please continue and develop your work."

He arranged invitations for us to the U.S. Ambassador's July 4 cocktail party to give us the opportunity of meeting officials and politicians in Ireland. Since the U.S. Ambassador was Jean Kennedy Smith, a sister of former President John F. Kennedy, the turnout for the garden party was impressive. It gave us the opportunity to talk to the Irish Taoiseach (prime minister) about MPI's work.

Alyn, Rob and I flew to Stockholm for similar meetings, where the response was the same: full speed ahead. An immense program of work loomed: sophisticated briefing materials, coordinated political strategies and generating support from other non-governmental organizations.

I saw the Middle Powers Initiative as a tender shoot that had just poked its head above ground. It was very vulnerable to being trampled on. But, nourished and given time, its roots would spread and the stalk become stronger. If enough people believed in it, if we at all times conducted it professionally, if we could raise enough money to sustain it, if the nuclear weapons states would listen to the voices of reason, MPI could make a significant contribution to building a nuclear weapons–free world. Of course, that was a lot of "ifs."

But I knew that a responsible political organization, capable of entering foreign ministries to talk business and building civil society support at the same time, was critically needed. MPI would work inside governments and simultaneously put pressure on them from the outside. It would be a delicate balancing act. I didn't have a textbook to tell me how to do it. But I knew that my political, diplomatic, academic and activist experience was a rare combination, enabling me to find a sustainable structure. I felt a great strength spiritually in being part of God's plan for the continued development of the planet. All the facets of my life were coming together in this one, last great exertion for a cause I believed in.

I plunged in. Just around the corner lay an offer I never expected.

V

The Senate Years:
1999–2004

16

An Independent
in the Red Chamber

On Friday, September 4, 1998, I was sitting at my computer, preparing for a second tour of Canada for Project Ploughshares to keep developing public support for stronger Canadian policies against nuclear weapons. The first tour in 1996 had produced the parliamentary hearings that were now drawing to a close. Ploughshares executive director Ernie Regehr and I wanted to keep the pressure on the government. I was in a rush to finish preparations because I was scheduled to fly to Victoria for the Labour Day weekend to see Tricia and my two grandchildren, Isabelle and Nicholas. (When Isabelle was born, I was so excited at becoming a grandfather that I dedicated the book I was working on at the time, *The Ultimate Evil*, to "my granddaughter, Isabelle Eva Roche Hurley, and all the grandchildren in the world." A strange book to dedicate to a tiny baby, I suppose, but her birth reinforced my commitment to try to spare future generations the horror of nuclear war. The arrival of Nicholas Nolan Roche Hurley strengthened my resolve; I dedicated my following book, *Bread Not Bombs*, to him.) I was anxious to see them. Just then the phone rang.

"Is this Doug Roche, who used to be a Member of Parliament?" the voice asked.

"Yes, who's this?" I replied, irritated at being interrupted.

"This is Percy Downe in the Prime Minister's Office. Prime Minister Chrétien wants to know, if he appoints you a Senator, will you accept?"

"Are you sure you're not playing a joke on me?"

"No, no, this is legitimate."

"Well," I said, "you certainly know how to upset my workday."

In some shock, I told Downe I needed to think about it and consult my family.

"Make sure it doesn't leak out," Downe said. We agreed to talk the following week. When I told my children, they were all supportive and encouraged me to accept, because the Senate would be a wider platform for me to present my views. I was told later that several people were campaigning for the Senate seat left vacant by the resignation of Jean Forest on account of her husband's illness. While I had noted in the paper that Jean was resigning, I hadn't given the matter any thought. Now I said to myself, why not me? I have the background for this job.

I went to Victoria, played with my grandchildren, and started the speaking tour on the West Coast, moving on to Calgary, Saskatoon and Winnipeg before returning to Edmonton for my opening class of the new term at the University of Alberta the following Monday. When I got home after class, there was a message to call the Prime Minister.

Jean Chrétien and I, though political opponents, had always gotten along well. One time when I was Ambassador for Disarmament, Chrétien and his wife Aline and I found ourselves on the same early-morning plane from Ottawa to New York. Chrétien was then in Opposition, after having served as Canada's foreign minister when John Turner was prime minister. Flights from Canada to the U.S. are now pre-cleared in Canada for the most part, but in those days the flight to Kennedy airport was not. We had to pass through U.S. immigration and customs after landing. Unfortunately, two big planes had arrived just before us and there were 400 people in line. It didn't bother me because I had a diplomatic passport, but Chrétien had forgotten his passport at home. He winced as he saw the length of the lineup, which would make him late for his first meeting. "Don't worry," I said, "I'll get you through." Aline spoke up, "Doug, we don't want to create an incident." I left them at the back of the lineup and went up to the officer in the diplomatic channel. I showed him my passport and said I had Canada's former foreign minister and his wife with me. Would he let them through? Sure, he said. I went back to get the Chrétiens. Two minutes later, they were in a taxi headed for New York City. A few years later, I led a delegation from the United Nations Association in Canada to present to Chrétien, then prime minister, the report of the Canadian committee for the 50th anniversary of the United Nations. So we had a friendly relationship.

"Doug," the prime minister said when I reached him on the telephone, "I want you to go to the Senate."

"Thank you very much, Prime Minister," I said. "It would be an honour."

"I want you to use the Senate to expand all your work on disarmament, development and the other themes of the United Nations. This is the work that has brought you to the Senate."

"I'll do what I can to speak out effectively," I said.

"Now we have to decide where you'll sit in the Senate. As a Liberal?"

"Prime Minister, if I sit as a Liberal, everyone in Canada will say I sold out the Conservatives so that you would appoint me. You know that's not true, and I know it's not true, so I don't think we should do it."

"Yes, you're probably right. What about sitting as a Conservative?"

"Well, Sir, that party left me years ago. I've had enough of the Tory Whip telling me how to vote and I don't want to go through that again."

Chrétien chuckled. "Well, it doesn't leave much else. Independent?"

"Will you let me sit as an Independent?"

"Doug, in your case, I think I will."

"Well, Sir, in that case, I'll take the job."

The prime minister said the announcement would be made in a few days. Meanwhile, I couldn't tell anyone. I headed for the airport to resume the speaking tour in Toronto. Downe caught up with me in Kingston.

"You've got to get back to Edmonton immediately," he said. "We're going to announce your appointment tomorrow and you've got to be home to handle the media."

I was due to speak in Peterborough, London and Waterloo on the following days. I called Regehr and he agreed that he and Walter McLean would substitute for me without telling anyone why I hadn't shown up.

Impeccable Credentials

On Thursday, September 17, the storm broke. The announcement was made at 9 a.m. Eastern time, which is 7 a.m. in Edmonton. At 7:01, the phone rang. For the next five hours I handled two lines non-stop. It was a media frenzy.

It was not about Doug Roche. It was about Chrétien appointing a senator while an election was taking place for "senators-in-waiting."

Senate reform has been an issue in Canada since Confederation in 1867. The stately Red Chamber, as it is familiarly called because of its dominant and regal red decor, is most often in the news when one plan or another for its rejuvenation is pressed upon the public. Both the Senate and the House of Commons must approve bills separately before they can become law. The Senate thus is an integral component of Parliament. Media attention, however, focuses almost exclusively on the House of Commons. Attention is paid to the Senate only when it balks at a piece of legislation. Even though both the Senate and the House of Commons inhabit the Centre Block of Parliament, they seem to operate in two different spheres. Of the historical total of 4,019 members of Parliament and 875 senators, 311 Canadians have served in both the House of Commons and the Senate. Of this number, only three have had the further opportunity of serving as an ambassador for the government of Canada (Paul Martin Sr. and

Eugene Whelan are the other two). I found it astonishing that I would be in such select company.

The Constitution says that the Governor-in-Council "shall summon qualified persons to the Senate." This has evolved to give prime ministers the power to appoint their personal choices. In the course of history, some selections have been outstanding and Canada has been the richer for the parliamentary presence of a number of individuals, particularly representing minorities, who might never be elected. Other appointees have been of dubious quality. It should not and could not be said that being a prominent fundraiser for a political party is incompatible with being qualified for the Senate. But there have been a few too many cases in which this seemed to be the only distinction a Senate appointee carried. The drive in western Canada for an elected Senate was sparked, not by an assessment of the quality of the persons already there but by anticipation that elected persons would fight more doggedly for western interests. A "Triple-E Senate" became the rallying cry: equal, elected, effective.

The "equal' provision of the Triple-E is inextricably intertwined with "elected" because, when Confederation occurred, Alberta had a very small population but was given six seats, more than it deserved at the time. By the mid 1990s, the population had grown to three million, more than the four provinces of Atlantic Canada combined; yet these provinces had a total of 30 seats. Nova Scotia, with fewer than one million residents, had ten seats. To achieve "effectiveness," a rearrangement of seats is vital. It would take constitutional change to bring this about. Various efforts have been made through the years; all have failed. In frustration, the Reform Party proposed holding an election, even though it would not be binding, and pressuring the prime minister to appoint the person "elected." This worked in 1989 when Brian Mulroney appointed the "elected" Alberta Senator Stan Waters. When Waters died soon after, the Reform tried again. It succeeded in getting a slot for "senators in waiting" on the municipal ballots of 1998. Although the Conservative government of Alberta approved the procedure, no political party other than Reform nominated any candidates; the others all regarded the procedure as a transparent attempt to circumvent the Constitution. Chrétien was having no part of such a strategy and was determined to follow the Constitution. He appointed Doug Roche.

Chrétien's political opponents in Alberta—principally Premier Ralph Klein, leader of the Conservative Party, and Preston Manning, leader of the Reform Party—immediately attacked the appointment. Klein fumed it was a "slap in the face" to Alberta and that Chrétien had set back national renewal. Manning said the appointment was "illegitimate." But they couldn't get any traction because, as the *Edmonton Journal* commented, the appointee had "impeccable credentials." Dave Hancock, Alberta's Intergovernmental Affairs Minister, who started his political career putting up signs in my first election campaign, got himself in trouble by phoning to congratulate me, even though, officially, he was supposed to be attacking me. Deborah Grey, the first Reform MP, after expostulating to the media why the appointment was so terrible, called me "a class act." I felt I didn't need any defence, especially since the *Edmonton Journal* ran a feature on me, describing me as a "compassionate crusader." Alberta's Liberal Cabinet Minister, Anne McLellan, was quoted as saying, "I have always been struck by his inherent decency and integrity. He's a man who has always taken the high road. That's the kind of person we should be putting in the Senate."

Nonetheless, the storm raged for days. The letters in the Calgary and Edmonton papers dissected the issue as if the fate of Canada hung in the balance. Some praised the quality of the appointment; others urged me not to take my seat. I found it hilarious when Reform workers phoned to offer their support if only I would resign and run in the election. The *Calgary Sun* started a mail-in campaign to "fight back." I thought political commentator Dalton Camp, who seemed bemused by the Alberta spectacle, offered a calmer and certainly more astute response. Roche "will be an adornment to the Senate," he wrote. "In politics he was considered insufficiently combative and overly idealistic. People like that puzzle fellow politicians and baffle bureaucrats, but he will be a useful Senator and a civil one."

I decided to reach out immediately. Even before going to Ottawa for the swearing-in, I went to see Edmonton's mayor, Bill Smith, to pledge my support in bringing Edmonton's interests to the floor of the Senate. Smith welcomed me and told the media he agreed with my observation that "there's too much polarization, too much alienation" between western Canada and Ottawa.

I brought the same sentiments to Reform leader Preston Manning when I paid a courtesy call on him on the day of my swearing-in. Preston's father, Ernest Manning, was Alberta's longest-serving premier before ending his career with several years' service in the Senate. Flying with him regularly on the Edmonton–Ottawa route, I got to know him well and respected him enormously. Preston was somewhat reserved when I sat with him in his office for a few minutes, offering my help in advancing the cause of Senate reform with the required constitutional change. I refrained from quoting his father's views on this controversial subject. "As Senators," the elder Manning wrote, "we occupy a position uniquely different from that of the elected members of the other house. We constitute more than a chamber of sober second thought. We have been appointed to represent our respective provinces in this house. We have been selected in order to provide the necessary checks and balances on a parliamentary structure where representation by population results in imbalances that invite the kind of abuse of parliamentary majority power that we are witnessing today."

Preston told the media afterwards that he had "dismissed" my offer; that, of course, made the headline. But I thought this was more a reflection on him than me. Reconciliation does, indeed, carry a price. The reception I received when I called on the other party leaders—Gilles Duceppe of the Bloc Québécois, Alexa McDonough of the New Democratic Party, and Elsie Wayne, interim leader of the Progressive Conservative Party—was warm and gracious. Duceppe seemed pleased that I opened the meeting speaking in French, though he kindly replied in English. I called formally on the Leader of the Opposition in the Senate, John Lynch-Staunton, who didn't seem to hold it against me that I wouldn't be sitting in his Progressive Conservative caucus.

Full Circle with Clark

My reception, or non-reception, from Joe Clark was another matter. My appointment came in the midst of his own campaign, his third, for leader of the Progressive Conservative Party. When Brian Mulroney left office in 1993, with the Progressive Conservatives' reputation in the country in tatters, Kim Campbell was left to pick up the pieces. It couldn't be done. The Party was humiliated, reduced to two seats in the election. Jean Charest, who became leader, held one of those seats. He fared not much better in the 1997 election; in 1998 he departed, to lead the Liberals in Quebec. In 1998, Joe Clark came out of retirement to contest the leadership of the Party once again. When my Senate appointment was announced, this mattered to Clark because he would be seeking a seat in Calgary, where the Reform trumpets blew the loudest. He issued a statement: "Mr. Chrétien's appointment of an Alberta Senator was cynical, provocative and wrong. This controversy has little to do with the qualities of Douglas Roche, who is a sincere and able person. I regret that he has been used by the Chrétien government." He embellished this comment by saying that the government's actions showed "clear contempt" for Alberta's "senator-in-waiting" elections.

The media, of course, played up the angle that Clark was attacking his old friend Doug Roche. Clark's aides spun the story that Clark didn't want to be perceived as attacking me personally. Nevertheless, it stung me that Joe would suggest I was being "used" by Chrétien, as if I was some political neophyte who didn't realize that just as my appointment served Chrétien's desire to give the back of his hand to the Reformers, it served my interests in getting a wider platform to discuss peace issues, not to mention getting my phone calls to important people returned. Politics, if it's about anything, is certainly about symbiosis. I was the right man for Chrétien. The Senate was the right place for me.

Then the media asked me whether I would support Clark in his campaign for leader. In the absence of credible opponents, I thought Clark's election would be virtually automatic. But I hadn't been involved; Clark had never approached me. I merely said: "I am giving this very serious consideration." I should have immediately jumped onto the high road and said, "Yes, of course I'm supporting him." But in the heat and haste of the moment, I let an opportunity to extend a hand of reconciliation slip by. Clark, of course, went on to victory.

I sent word to his office in Parliament that I would like to see him. I wanted to explain that my decision to sit in the Senate as an Independent had nothing to do with my continuing respect for him personally. No appointment was forthcoming. I talked to Clark's two closest political friends, Senator Lowell Murray and Harvie André. Both said they would get me an appointment. But it never happened.

Time went on. Several months later, I ran into Clark at a social event on Parliament Hill. He greeted me warmly and we chatted about the events of the day. This happened on two or three other occasions when we bumped into each other.

Cordiality. Pleasantness. Professionalism. We have recovered at least those. But I would like, before I depart public life for good, to embrace Joe Clark. I would like to say, "Joe, there have been a lot of ups and downs over four decades, and intolerable pressures in both our lives. We've both made mistakes. But both of us unquestionably stand for integrity in politics. Let us close out our lives in complete reconciliation."

There is no doubt in my mind that Clark is crushed by the sad fate of the Progressive Conservative Party, to which he devoted his life. Through a string of political finagling, the Party was absorbed into a new Conservative Party dominated by the former Reform Party of Western Canada. Red Tories are anathema to this right-wing political amalgam, which, under Stephen Harper, won the election of 2006. Harper's foreign policy, centering on U.S. interests and Canada's combat role in Afghanistan, has undermined the UN values that Clark spent a lot of time building up. Clark has spoken out against Harper's policies, trying to restore Canada's "long, proud, bipartisan history of international initiative." This is what I want, too. Joe Clark and I have come full circle.

Honeymoon is a State of Mind

My personal life took an upward turn when I accepted an invitation in the late 1990s to attend a meeting of the Quality of Life Commission in Edmonton. The commission was formed by a group of citizens who came together to express their concern about the effects on Alberta's poorest citizens of the provincial government's social spending cutbacks. Its best-known report was *Listen to Me*, which recounted the stories of people who felt trapped in a cycle of dependence and powerlessness with regard to decisions affecting their lives. At the meeting, I noticed a blonde woman, four seats down. During the coffee break, I spoke to my long-time friend Betty Farrell, a social activist.

"Betty, who's that blonde woman?"

"Why, that's Pat McGoey," she said.

"Do I know Pat McGoey?"

"I don't know. She was one of the founders of the Quality of Life Commission."

"Is she married?" I asked.

"No, she's a widow," Betty said.

On the way out of the meeting, I managed to find myself walking beside Patricia McGoey on the way to our cars.

I let a little time go by before phoning Pat to ask whether she would have dinner with me. As we chatted, I was surprised to learn that she had known Eva. In fact, the two of them were colleagues at Grant MacEwan Community College and had had lunch when Pat returned after working in St. Lucia for two years. A social worker, Pat is a specialist in alcohol and drug addiction counselling. Her husband, Sylvestre McGoey, a crown attorney, had died in 1992. Pat and I found we had a lot in common: our religion, our political viewpoints, our social justice concerns. Her four children and my four were about the same ages. The dinner was successful. It led to more social occasions. I took her to Ottawa to meet my family and friends; she took me to Winnipeg to meet hers. I don't think anyone was surprised when we announced our engagement. I felt that Eva, who herself had a very big heart, would be fully supportive.

Pat and I had to decide where to live. I had a house, Pat had a house and I had bought a condo. I suggested that Pat make the choice. They say you shouldn't bring your second wife into your first wife's house. But Pat said she favoured my house. Could we do renovations? We hired a contractor and I went to Ottawa for a month to concentrate on writing *Bread Not Bombs*. Pat supervised the renovations; when I returned, the house was livable again.

A special feature of the wedding, on July 24, 1999, was the mingling of adult children and a variety of grandchildren. Francis was my best man; Pat's daughter, Mary, was matron of honour. Pat's sons, Tom, Richard and Kevin, all took part in the ceremony, as did Evita, Mary Anne and Tricia. Pat's grandchildren, Christine and Michael Fulsom and Tom and Kim McGoey, all had a role. Tricia and her husband,

Michael Hurley, shepherded Isabelle and Nicholas. Bishop De Roo attended, as did Archie Daley. Walter and Barbara McLean came from Waterloo, and Peter Mann from New York. Pat's and my close friend Father Mike McCaffery performed the ceremony. Everyone gathered in a circle around Pat and me. It was a blessed moment.

Pat and I drove to the Chateau Lake Louise, where Pat had worked as a summer maid during her college years. Then we drove from Banff to Jasper on the Colombia Icefields Highway with its magnificent view of the Rockies. The honeymoon was short because our major trip, a few days later, was to Japan, where I was to speak at an international symposium on nuclear weapons sponsored by the Japanese newspaper *Asashi Shinbum*. We flew to Tokyo and took a train to Osaka to rest. Our hosts put us up at New Otani Hotel, a grand hostelry that rather impressed Pat. A formal welcoming banquet awaited us in Hiroshima. I took Pat through the Peace Park with its vivid reminders of the terrible suffering the people of that city had endured.

Tadatoshi Akiba, a young mathematician who had spent 20 years in the United States and spoke perfect English, had just been elected mayor. He received us formally at City Hall. After a few days, Pat and I moved on to Nagasaki for similar meetings and graphic reminders. It was the Christian area of Nagasaki that took the full force of the atom bomb. Pat cried when she looked at the charred statues outside the Catholic Cathedral. We returned to Tokyo and meetings with the Japanese government. I was in the midst of planning a Middle Powers Initiative (MPI) delegation to Japan. Rob Green joined us; I made presentations to two major religious groups, Soka Gakei and Risso Kosso-kei, for funding for MPI.

Pat was amazed to find that when flying back from Asia to Canada, with the peculiarities of world time zones, you can start the same day all over again. All this was not your average honeymoon experience. But it seemed to me that Pat coped very well with my lifestyle. I told her that a honeymoon was not a time-bound experience but a state of mind. I found the honeymoon continuing as I settled in for the weekly commute to Ottawa during the weeks the Senate was sitting. My Ottawa apartment was long gone, the furniture having been dispersed to various children, so I began staying at the centrally located Cartier Place Suites Hotel, whose chief feature as far as I was concerned was the swimming pool. I needed to swim every day, even for only a few minutes, to keep my back in shape.

Right after Christmas, Pat and I took a decent holiday in St. Lucia, a southern Caribbean island 27 miles long by 14 miles across, where the weather, except for the odd hurricane, is glorious. It was Pat's turn to show me around all the sites that had been an important part of her life. I quickly saw how much she meant to the people whom she had counselled in alcohol and drug addiction. Pat invited Lira, one of her former clients, to lunch in our apartment. Lira arrived with a present for Pat. Then she handed a present to me, a sport shirt with the name St. Lucia emblazoned on it.

"Lira," I said, "I can understand why you brought a present for Pat. But why one for me?"

"Oh, Mr. Roche," she said, "I just wanted to thank you for bringing Pat back to us."

Michael Douglas and Nuclear Weapons

In the midst of the bedlam on the day my Senate appointment was announced, I answered the phone one more time to hear a familiar voice on the line. It was Pam Miles-Séguin, my secretary from my days as an MP. When I left Parliament in 1984, Pam easily switched to other MPs offices and then went to Paris for several years when the Canadian Security Intelligence Service (CSIS) posted her husband there. They had just returned to Ottawa. Pam said she heard the announcement on the radio.

"I figured you need an administrative assistant right away, and I need a job," she said.

"Can you get right up to the Senate and get me a decent office?" I replied.

That's the way I lived for the next six years. Pam handled my entire administrative life, including ensconcing me in Jean Forest's old office in the Victoria Building, with its lovely view of the Parliament Buildings. Overnight, I was back in the familiar parliamentary routine.

My Senate colleagues were rather impressed (I intended them to be) when, during my first week in the Senate, I walked the actor Michael Douglas through the splendid Senate foyer at its busiest time of the day. Douglas had recently been appointed a UN Messenger of Peace, with a mission to focus worldwide attention on nuclear disarmament and human rights. I had asked him to join a Middle Powers Initiative delegation to the Canadian government to give it some "star power." Douglas had flown from New York to Ottawa in his private jet; when the Oscar-winner walked through the corridors of Parliament, flashbulbs popped and TV cameras pursued him. Secretaries rushed out of their offices to catch a glimpse of the star of *Fatal Attraction*. It was, as one journalist noted, "Hollywood on the Hill." When Prime Minister Chrétien heard that Douglas was in town, his office called me to invite the MPI delegation in for a visit. Coming out of the Prime Minister's office, Douglas was assailed by a dozen assistants, usually very sophisticated people used to dealing with presidents and foreign ministers, who called out, "Michael, Michael, come over here for a photo with us!" Douglas, relaxed and charming throughout, obliged. Pam put a photo of herself and Michael on the wall of her office.

I am of two minds when it comes to using the services of celebrities to push causes. On the one hand, the media coverage of the issue tends to be trivialized ("Bureaucrats Go 'Ga Ga' for Star" was one headline after Douglas's visit). On the other hand, at least there is coverage, which gets the attention of the political system. The landmines issue, for example, became a household topic when Princess Diana became involved. Ordinarily, the media ignore the urgent questions in the nuclear weapons field. The critical findings of the International Court of Justice received almost no attention. I have come to the conclusion that, since human beings are attracted to stars (not necessarily from Hollywood; the Dalai Lama and Nelson Mandela are also stars), MPI should use celebrities to open doors so we can push the political systems.

In Michael Douglas's case, it is a pleasure dealing with him. He has a genuine interest in the issue. His concern about nuclear issues dates back to when he produced and starred in *The China Syndrome*, a movie about the failure of nuclear power.

"I personally feel that nuclear weapons are the greatest danger for the future of our planet, of our life, of civilization," he told the Ottawa press conference. "I'm committing my energies and my notoriety— the fact that people recognize the face around the world—to this particular cause."

I have been with him in several locations and have always found him courteous and self-deprecating. One night, after he appeared at the MPI dinner at the Carter Center in Atlanta, I found him sitting alone at the back of the bus waiting patiently to go back to the hotel. In Ottawa, he joined with the rest of us filming promos for the "I Said No Nukes" campaign, organized by Dr. Mary-Wynne Ashford, which showed on television across Canada.

When the MPI delegation, including U.S. Senator Alan Cranston, assembled in Chrétien's office, Michael neither dominated the conversation nor sat silently. The Prime Minister said he doubted that zero nuclear weapons was in the cards because of the U.S. position. Michael responded that the U.S. government would listen when the nuclear message reached larger audiences. On the way out, Foreign Minister Lloyd Axworthy quietly asked Jonathan Granoff and me whether we could bring a second MPI delegation of senior American officials to Ottawa. Michael Douglas had certainly opened the doors for us.

Roche Rocks the Boat

With media attention still on me, I decided to make my maiden speech in the Senate early. A few days after Douglas left town, I rose in the Senate to give a three-part speech. I was amazed—again—at the pettiness that so often infects the political process.

The speech was based on the need to counter the disaffections of our time with a concentrated political effort to end the shocking economic and social disparities in our midst, correct the inequality of representation in the Senate, and foster a more dynamic role for Canada in building the conditions for peace and security.

"These three themes—equitable economic and social development, reform of the Senate, and setting out a forthright Canadian policy to support the abolition of nuclear weapons—are central to my views on the healing processes needed to rebuild Canadian unity, and advance a human security agenda for the 21st century," I said.

I complimented the leadership of the government of Alberta, which had produced the fastest-growing economy in Canada: "The Alberta advantage continues to draw more and more people to our province." I credited the Alberta government for achieving a balanced budget and deficit and debt reduction.

"However, fiscal management has come at a cost," I continued. "Cuts in health, education and social spending have had a deleterious effect on our society, particularly the most vulnerable people: those in low-paying jobs, the aged, the ill, children, and single parents ... Now that our fiscal accounts are in order, on behalf of the disadvanged in our society, I call for a restoration of health and education spending as an investment in the continued development of our people."

Turning to the Senate, I made the case that changing the distribution of seats has to happen in addition to instituting a constitutional process to elect Senators in order for there to be equal representation. And I concluded with a call for Canada to work to get nuclear weapons out of NATO and to take a leading role in working for a nuclear weapons–free world.

I ended with the kind of rhetorical flourish they love in the Senate.

> There is no land more blessed than Canada. The United Nations regularly attests to that fact. I love this country. I love Alberta, my home province. I love Quebec, the province of my birth. My children live in four different cities across Canada. I love St. John's and the whole of Newfoundland. I love Victoria, British Columbia, and the whole of Vancouver Island. I want this country to stay together. I want our people to work together. I want our political process to come together. There is too much alienation in our society, too much polarization, too much confrontation. I want to contribute to a spirit of reconciliation, an atmosphere of healing, a new basis of hope, as we prepare for the third millennium.

Shouts of "Hear, hear!" greeted my peroration. I knew that I had given, if not a great speech, at least a notable one.

That, however, was not how the *Edmonton Sun* saw my effort. A front-page banner headline screamed, "Roche Rocks the Boat." Underneath was the line "Alberta's newest Senator pans high cost of economic progress." The story led off with my presumed "swipe at Premier Ralph Klein's Tories yesterday, suggesting economic progress has come at the expense of the poor and weak." That was followed the next day with another banner headline: "Ralph Raps Roche: Premier responds to new Senator's criticism with stinging rebuttal." The *Sun* quoted the Premier: "I am concerned that a Senator from Alberta would use his maiden speech to damage his province's national reputation with disparaging and inaccurate remarks."

Premier Klein then wrote to chastise me for my "shocking lack of knowledge" about significant health and education reinvestment already happening in Alberta. He also took umbrage at my dismissal of the Senate elections under way as piecemeal reform. The full guns of the Alberta government were levelled at me in a quick succession of letters from the ministers of health, education and intergovernmental affairs.

Since this unexpected controversy showed signs of getting out of hand, I decided to seek a meeting with Premier Klein. He received me cordially.

"Mr. Premier," I said, "when you issued your blast at me to the *Edmonton Sun*, had you actually read my speech in the Senate?"

"No," he said. "I was just reacting to the part the *Sun* reporters quoted."

Since it doesn't do to laugh in a premier's face, let alone dress him down in his own office, I replied calmly that the speech had actually praised the government of Alberta while stating the indisputable fact that the poor were suffering from social spending cutbacks. All the figures I had used about the Alberta situation, I said, had been verified by the Edmonton Social Planning Council. Klein held his ground, stating that in the interval between the *Sun's* phone call and writing his letter to me he had read the speech. "And actually," he said, "it wasn't too bad." On that note of being damned with faint praise, I decided to let the matter rest.

It was clear to me what had happened. The *Sun*, waging its campaign against me for having accepted the Senate appointment, seized on my perceived insult towards Alberta and fed a piece of red meat to Klein, who reacted like a starved puppy—anything to undermine the credibility of the new Senator. The *Edmonton Journal*, a responsible paper, showed its disdain for this artificial controversy by ignoring it. I was never able to take Ralph Klein very seriously afterwards, but, since he remained the Premier throughout my term in the Senate, I made it my business to get along with him, at least minimally.

'Discover the Real Doug Roche'

Right-wing adherents (Klein and the *Edmonton Sun* would be at the top of the list) do not like to hear that cutbacks on social spending further marginalize the poorest people. They certainly find unpalatable the statistics showing that the number of children under the care of the province's child welfare programs had grown by 10 per cent a year for the five years preceding my Senate speech. The persistence of child poverty, not only in Alberta but also throughout Canada, remains a national disgrace. Supply-side economists need to be reminded—as the Edmonton Social Planning Council and the Quality of Life Commission try to do—that depriving poor families of the means to sustain themselves by cutting welfare benefits too often leads to desperation and deprivation. Poverty in the midst of plenty is an ugly reality resulting from misplaced government priorities. The Klein incident stiffened my determination to use my Senate post to speak out for social justice.

The *Globe and Mail* took an entirely different view of my speech, singling out the passage in which I said, "Good order and stability in this country demand that constitutional change be brought about through due process involving the federal government and provincial and territorial governments. The Constitution cannot be changed by piecemeal acts in any one province. Such attempts will surely lead to other provinces also attempting unilateral acts. National unity would then give way to disorder." The paper called this an "eminently reasonable" approach, adding that Klein was "spouting nonsense" in criticizing me. "Mr. Roche has all the makings of a good Alberta Senator. He knows the difference between standing up for his province and defending a Premier's political agenda. He has also shown he respects and understands the Constitution. You have to admire that in a politician."

In all the hullabaloo about my speech, no one commented on the nuclear weapons section. That disturbed me far more than Premier Klein's huffing and puffing. However important the subjects of poverty and Senate reform, they are eclipsed by the global calamity threatened by the use of nuclear weapons. The media cannot seem to get hold of this issue in a coherent way. In politics, it's much easier to attack someone than to try to understand what he or she is saying.

I am used to being attacked, and in my political career I usually just shrugged it off. But a line was crossed when George Koch, a right-wing columnist in Calgary, wrote an op-ed piece for the *Globe and Mail*, calling me "the consummate appeaser" for opposing NATO's deployment of nuclear weapons in Europe. It was a standard attack in some ways, since he criticized me for being "far out on the left on almost every political issue, from nuclear weapons policy to homosexual rights." But Koch went too far. "For years [Roche] consorted with Bishop Remi De Roo, one of the most left-wing senior clerics ever to inhabit the Roman Catholic Church in Canada."

I wrote a letter to the editor, which was published, stating that, of course, I expected the slings and arrows that go with the Senate job, "however outrageous and distorted."

"But the line of decency was crossed when [De Roo] was attacked in the tirade. As history will reveal, Bishop De Roo is one of the great Canadian Roman Catholic bishops of the 20th century."

I decided to give Koch a little jab by closing the letter with this offer: "As for myself, my record over 40 years as a journalist, author, parliamentarian, diplomat and educator is an open book—in fact, fifteen of my books. I will be glad to send you a list so that you can dip into them and discover the real Doug Roche."

17

Stop the Bombing!

"Stop the bombing!"

Those were the first words I uttered at a peace rally attended by 350 people in Vancouver on April 10, 1999. The crowd leapt to its feet. NATO's bombing of Serbia and Kosovo had commenced, ostensibly to stop the brutal aggression against the Kosovars by the forces of Slobodan Milosevic. For 78 days, NATO, using 700 aircraft and 20 ships, dropped 20,000 bombs on 600 cities, towns and villages. There were 13,000 civilian casualties, including 2,500 dead. Utilities, roads, bridges, hospitals, clinics and schools were destroyed, along with military targets. Bombing for peace is an oxymoron, I kept saying. Once more, the positive work of building the conditions for peace was interrupted by having to protest, which appears a negative thing to do.

The Kosovo War plunged me into one of the deepest Senate debates in years, jeopardizing my association with Lloyd Axworthy, still Canada's foreign minister. For a while, I was practically the only politician on Parliament Hill publicly opposing the bombing and Canada's role in it.

The day after the bombing began, I rose in the Senate to ask why Canada was now participating in a military action not authorized by the United Nations. Since the reason given for bombing was to stop the killings in Kosovo, what about slaughters in other parts of the world, notably Africa? Did that justify bombing, too? The Government Leader in the Senate, Al Graham, responded that Canada "stands

by its allies in participating in NATO's military actions in Kosovo."
Milosevic must co-operate with international authorities and then the
bombing would stop, he said. I replied that Canada had campaigned
hard for a seat on the UN Security Council because we wanted to
make a difference. "Is NATO going to be the determining factor in
Canadian foreign policy, or will it be the United Nations?" Graham
fobbed off this key question by saying that "decisions were made after
very long and thoughtful consideration of the consequences."

Then he added the riposte, the appeal to patriotism that is supposed to flatten all debate: "Senator Roche should support our troops."
I intervened immediately to respond to that red herring and make it
clear that my support of Canada's troops was not the issue: "The issue
is what will be the criteria upon which to build conditions for world
peace." I could see Graham, who was obviously uncomfortable having to defend a government policy he did not personally agree with,
slinking down in his seat. I could not hear his mumbled response, but
Hansard quoted him saying, "I accept that."

I spoke at rallies and press conferences in Ottawa, Toronto, Edmonton and Vancouver. I even spoke on Easter Sunday at a pro-Serbian
rally of 250 protestors on the steps of the Alberta Legislature in
Edmonton. "My stand is not pro-Serbian or pro-Kosovo," I said. "It is
pro-humanitarian." I made my central point: "The NATO bombing
is morally outrageous, a violation of international law, and it is causing untold human suffering." I called for the UN to send Secretary-
General Kofi Annan to Belgrade to negotiate a political and humane
solution to the dispute.

At the Ottawa press conference, I joined a number of prominent
and respected Canadians, among them David Orchard, former candidate for the Progressive Conservative Party leadership, Buzz Hargrove,
national president of the Canadian Auto Workers, and Debbie Grisdale,
executive director of Physicians for Global Survival. But in Toronto, I
wasn't careful enough in examining beforehand who would appear on
the platform with me. I guess when I saw that the historian Michael
Bliss and the respected peace activist Ursula Franklin would also be
appearing, I thought everything would be fine. But it wasn't. After
I gave my standard denunciation of the bombing, David Jacobs, a
Toronto lawyer whom I did not know, launched a much more strident
attack, demanding that the political leaders who made the decision to

bomb Serbia be indicted for crimes against world peace. He named President Clinton, Prime Minister Chrétien and other NATO leaders as war criminals. I had to wait till my next turn at the microphone in the question-and-answer session to defuse this serious and, in my opinion, misguided allegation.

To brand someone as a "war criminal" is to surmise that a leader has intentionally sought to kill people, as happens in genocide. My contention was that the NATO leaders were guilty of bad political judgment, which resulted in deaths, not that they had deliberately set out to kill. I have always thought that extremists within the peace movement, with their inflated rhetoric and venomous charges, undermine the central arguments against using violence as a means to peace. I prefer to fight the proponents of war by telling them they are wrong in their thinking, not that they are malicious or evil. But the damage was done. The next day's *Globe and Mail* featured a photo of me at the press conference. I was quoted accurately, but the very linking of me and the other panelists with Jacobs conveyed the impression that the group as a whole supported the "war criminal" charge.

I knew how Lloyd Axworthy had agonized over his decision to support the bombing. He would react fiercely to any implication—especially from me—that he was a war criminal. In *Navigating a New World*, the book he wrote four years later, Axworthy traced the dilemma he faced in reconciling his reticence to use force with the "just war" theory. He recounted visiting his United Church minister for guidance. "Finally," he wrote, "it simply came down to what I felt in good conscience—that without the willingness to use military power to enforce the rule of law, there could be abuses that would violate many innocent people."

While I don't agree with bombing for peace, I certainly respect Axworthy's argument. He displayed throughout his tenure as foreign minister a determination to use "soft power" to resolve conflict. He was the driving force behind the Ottawa Process, which produced the anti-personnel landmines treaty. And he was certainly courageous in challenging NATO on its continued possession of nuclear weapons.

It was on this latter file that I was most engaged with Axworthy. When I tried to see him following the Toronto incident, his office said no. I went to Heidi Hulan, his policy adviser, and explained that I dissociated myself from the "war criminal" charge and wanted to get on with business. Heidi arranged an informal "encounter" for me with Axworthy following a speech so that the appointment would not show on his schedule. Axworthy and I talked briefly about current events. We met a few times after that, and he did give a ringing endorsement of the Middle Powers Initiative, which helped us in fundraising. I praised him at a public dinner in his honour. We got over this bump in our relationship, but we were never as close afterwards as before. As for Chrétien, I doubt that he ever spent a second thinking about what Jacobs said, and if he did, he would dismiss it as just another bee buzzing around him.

Clearing up Muddled Thinking

At first, the mail and phone calls were heavily against my Kosovo position. "Shame on you, Senator Roche," Louis Schmittroth wrote in his letter to the editor in the *Edmonton Journal*. "I'm a 74-year-old veteran of the Second World War and I'm glad NATO has finally taken a stand. I applaud the efforts by NATO planes, including our own CF–18s to hit military targets and avoid civilian casualties …." Luigi Rossotto, a retired major in the Canadian Forces, took me to task for "muddled thinking." After questioning my intellectual capabilities, he devoted his guest column in the *Edmonton Journal* to asserting that the UN has repeatedly proven itself unable to perform the role I would have it perform. "What NATO is doing may be horrific … but should one not ask oneself if it were preferable to simply sit aside and view the slaughter of hundreds of thousands as happened in Rwanda?"

I decided to respond to Major Rossotto in my own letter to the *Journal*. "Permit me to say what muddled thinking in this instance really is," I wrote. "It is muddled thinking to consider that NATO can violate the international law provisions of the UN charter and NATO's own charter without serious negative consequences for the whole world. It is certainly muddled thinking," I added, "to believe that we can help the people of Kosovo by destroying their economic and social infrastructure and those of the people of Serbia."

After the first three weeks of public debate, I noticed a shift in public opinion in my favour in my mail. Of 185 letters and emails I received, 71 per cent supported my criticism of the NATO bombing while 29 per cent backed the Canadian government's actions. Norm Ovenden, the *Edmonton Journal*'s Ottawa correspondent, expressed interest in this development, so I turned over the whole file of correspondence for him to examine. He wrote a lengthy article depicting me "as both the darling of the peace movement and a 'stomach-turning' traitor after becoming Canada's most prominent opponent of NATO bombing strikes." He quoted Mr. D. MacIntosh of Vancouver: "I suggest you leave Canada and apply for Yugoslav citizenship. You don't belong here. You're disgusting. You turn my stomach." Fortunately, Ovenden also quoted an opposite view from Judy Haiven of Saskatoon: "Keep up the good work ... We now have the worst of all worlds—a violated United Nations, people homeless and bombed civilians." Michael Bahniuk of Bow Island, Alberta, wrote: "Your wisdom in this situation is needed desperately ... We need 100 more Senators of your caliber."

I don't know how many senators sided with me, for there was never a clear-cut vote on the issue. But I sensed that more than a few were coming to the view that bombing was not only wrong but also futile.

I gave a major speech in the Senate detailing all the reasons for my opposition to the bombing. Senator Jerahmiel Grafstein of Toronto, a proponent of NATO, immediately challenged me. What should the world have done to stop the ethnic "cleansing" of Kosovo? Strengthen the UN by creating peacemaking forces as called for by Boutros Boutros-Ghali when he was Secretary-General of the UN, I responded. "Will we continually have recourse to military action and bombing to deal with despots and dictators? We must build an architecture that will guarantee peace and security."

I stayed on the issue and raised questions on it almost every day in the Senate. I quoted former President Jimmy Carter, who had criticized his own government, declaring, "The decision to attack the entire nation has been counter-productive, and our destruction of civilian life has now become senseless and excessively brutal." The Government Leader threw back at me the NATO line that it was the Milosevic government that had deliberately killed and injured thousands of civilians. "They have burned hundreds of villages and they have driven over one million people from their homes ...."

Milosevic was, in fact, indicted in a Yugoslav tribunal for the horrors he committed. But, when the facts came out after the war, it turned out that Carter was right and NATO was wrong. Though there was brutality, there was no genocide in Kosovo. Most of those who fled did so to escape the bombing, not the Serb forces.

The bombing was not about humanitarian concern; it had to do with U.S. determination to maintain NATO as an essential military organization. That was the argument I carried into the Senate after the bombing ended and the UN was brought in to be an interim administrator of Kosovo. Senator Grafstein and I locked horns again, Grafstein arguing that NATO came to the aid of international law when it was degraded and abused by Milosevic's egregious conduct. I stuck to my contention that NATO, including Canada, subverted international law by war. Several Senators joined in the debate, with Senator Noel Kinsella, later to become Speaker, holding that "there have been fewer [more] important debates in this chamber."

What are the lessons to be learned from this experience? Kinsella asked. The question evoked my sense of the tremendous responsibility Canada has in the modern world. I spoke from the heart.

> We are the second largest piece of real estate in the world, a country which the United Nations called the number one country for our social indices. We do not know how blessed we are in the capacity we have … I am only pleading here that Canada, having gone through this unfortunate experience in the Kosovo War, now redouble its efforts to build the conditions for peace and work with the like-minded states … to strengthen the U.N. capacity to deal with international peace and security questions in every region of the world.

Grafstein thought so much of the Senate debate that day that he published a booklet containing the speeches.

The Place of an Independent

It was a good debate—and there ought to be a place in Canada for high-minded, non-partisan discourse on the nation's problems. That is what the Senate does when it is operating at its best. Though it is reputed to be a more civilized place than the House of Commons, a characteristic I found generally to be true, it has had its moments of pandemonium. One such moment was the Liberal attempt to quash the legislation the Mulroney Conservatives brought in to establish the Goods and Services Tax. This took place long before I entered the Senate, but—as an Independent Senator—I felt the effects none-theless. As a result of the venomous debate in the early 1990s on the GST, both the Liberals and the Progressive Conservatives sought to jealously preserve their rights to membership on Senate committees. Hitherto, independent senators were allowed to sit on committees and, in one instance, an independent senator, Hartland Molson, even chaired the Senate Committee on Transport and Communications. Suddenly, the Selection Committee informed independent senators that neither the Liberals nor the PCs would yield a place to make room for an independent. Since independents do not have access to caucus research facilities, they were given a few thousand dollars extra in their office budgets to pay for research assistance.

In the history of the Senate, there have been only eleven inde-pendents among the total of 875 senators. With my arrival and that of Senator Lois Wilson, former Moderator of the United Church of Canada—we joined my old colleague from the House of Commons Marcel Prud'homme—there were now three independent senators who each wanted a place on at least one committee. Of course, all senators have the right to attend all committee meetings and receive all information, but only officially appointed senators may vote in a committee.

I rose one day in the Senate to protest this "second-class member-ship." I asked, "Are we not all appointed by the same constitutional process?" To show my good faith, I started regularly attending meet-ings of a subcommittee studying palliative care, headed by Senator Sharon Carstairs. I suppose I insinuated myself into the process, but I played a full role in the development of the committee's report, which Sharon acknowledged in the introduction. I was genuinely interested in the subject because, to the extent that palliative care facilities are improved in the country, the pressure for the legalization of assisted suicide, which I absolutely oppose, will diminish. The government took the committee's report seriously and she herself led Liberal gov-ernment programming to extend palliative care, until the subsequent Conservative government cut the funding.

A Close Vote for Clarity

Breaking down the barrier against independent senators involved a circuitous route—although I didn't know it at the time. The 1995

Quebec referendum, in which Canada came perilously close to break-ing up, scared Prime Minister Chrétien, who became determined that any future referendum on separation would have to be based on a clear-cut question to the electorate and a clear-cut majority vote. Out of that thinking came the *Clarity Act*, which stipulated that, in any future referendums, the House of Commons would be called on to decide whether the question was clear and whether a true majority existed for separation. Nationalists in Quebec were up in arms and Chrétien was pilloried, but he stood his ground and the bill passed in the House of Commons.

Although the Liberals held a healthy majority in the Senate, sev-eral of their members opposed the bill. Since the Conservatives also opposed the bill, its passage was unpredictable. I was torn because, while I wanted the unity of Canada protected, I opposed the part of the bill that lumped the Senate into a category with other national bodies so that the Senate could only give its views to the House of Commons on the clarity of a referendum, rather than being able to be decisive. Since the Senate is a constituent part of Parliament, I op-posed the downgrading of the Senate. I argued that the Senate "must be inextricably involved in such a political decision," and called for an amendment to make it clear that the Senate must share equally with the House of Commons in the determination of clarity.

Before any amendments could be considered, the bill had to pass second reading in the Senate. When the vote came, I was at the United Nations in New York, attending the Nuclear Non-Prolifer-ation Treaty review conference. The vote was 38 in favour with 30 opposed. Since seven Senators abstained (signalling their unhappiness with the legislation), the vote turned out to be perilously close. Had I been there, I would have voted in favour in order to send the bill to committee. Even so, the chances of an amendment passing had greatly increased.

A special committee was struck to fast-track the bill. I attended as many of the hearings as I could and saw the continued divisions among the senators. Every vote was going to count. The Liberal Senator in charge of the bill, Marie Poulin, sat down beside me in the Chamber one day and asked me what I was going to do. She was obviously counting heads. "I just don't know," I said. "I want the bill but I don't like the diminishment of the Senate."

Two days later, Prime Minister Chrétien called me.

"Doug," he said, "I need your help. The Clarity bill is very important for Canada."

"I know, Prime Minister," I said, "but I'm worried about the role of the Senate."

"Well," he replied, "I think the bill is better the way it is. Besides, if there are any amendments and the bill has to be returned to the House, it will die."

"O.K., Prime Minister, I'll review my position." Then, on an impulse, I added, "By the way, it would certainly be nice if independent senators could become official members of Senate committees."

"You mean they aren't now?"

"No, sir, there's some kind of stupid rule against it."

"Well, Doug, I'll look into it."

I thanked him and got out my file on the Clarity bill. Recognizing that my vote conceivably could be determinative—and that the prime minister was watching me—I studied hard.

I came to the conclusion that the bill was constitutional (some had argued that it wasn't) and that a vote of support for the bill was a vote of confidence in the government's dealings with the threat of separatism in Canada. On the point of the downgrading of the Senate, several witnesses in committee had made the point that if the views of the House and the Senate on giving the government permission to enter into negotiations for a constitutional amendment for secession were given equal weight, the Senate would be seen to have an indirect veto over constitutional amendments. It became clear to me that the bill could not give the Senate a power it does not already enjoy under the Constitution. In other words, the Senate must accept the fact that it is in a junior position to the elected House of Commons on constitutional matters.

Moreover, if the Clarity legislation were amended to give a new and controversial power to the Senate, the House would surely reject it. The Senate would find itself in the centre of a raging storm, which would distract from the issue at hand, which was supposed to be a clear question on separation in any future referendum. Chrétien was right. The legislation would die. I concluded that it would be much better for the country to have the legislation as it stood.

I picked up the phone and reached Bruce Hartley, Chrétien's executive assistant, who was travelling with the prime minister. "Tell the prime minister that I'm going to vote against amendments and fully support the bill on third reading," I said. "He'll be glad to hear that," Bruce replied.

On June 29, 2000, the last day before the summer recess, the Senate held final votes on the bill. There were several amendments. The first to be voted on—with the best chance of passing—would require a joint resolution of both the Senate and the House to determine the legitimacy of a referendum vote. Two Liberals, Jerry Grafstein and Serge Joyal, were pushing the amendment, and they could be sure of Conservative support. The galleries were full. The Senate was tense. Nobody could predict how the vote would go.

On the way to her desk, Lois Wilson stopped to ask me what I was going to do. She indicated she was in favour of the amendment, but didn't feel strongly. I told her why I thought it should be defeated. "O.K.," she said, "I'll vote with you." The vote was 46 in favour of the amendment and 50 opposed. Three Liberals abstained. Had they voted for the amendment, it would have been defeated by only one vote. Hence, my vote, and that of Senator Wilson's, did turn out to be crucial. The final vote on third reading of the bill was 52 in favour and 34 opposed with nine abstentions. The *Clarity Act* was law.

Immediately after the last vote, the Liberal Whip, Leon Mercier, crossed the aisle to shake my hand and thank me for my vote. "Now," he said, "I'll make certain you'll get on a committee." There was nothing to do but smile and silently wonder once again at the mysteries of the political process.

When Parliament resumed in the fall, Senator Carstairs, now the Government Leader in the Senate, called to say I would be appointed to the social affairs committee. I really wanted the foreign affairs committee, but since the lineup for that committee was already long, I quickly settled for my second choice. I knew I needed to get more deeply into domestic issues to balance my work on peace issues. I was already seen as caring mostly about nuclear weapons and war issues. There was a certain truth in that, since I have long taken the view that if the nuclear weapons problem blows up in our faces—literally—nothing else will matter. However, as I had found out years before in the House of Commons, the media generally ignored my statements and actions on domestic issues; what I did internationally was noticed.

Impact of Two Senate Motions

While I was going about my daily routine, I was apparently being monitored by Bert Brown and Ted Morton, the two "senators-in-waiting" who had been elected in the spurious Alberta election of 1998. One day when they were visiting Ottawa, I invited them for tea in my office. The conversation was cordial as we discussed a range of current issues. But a little while later they issued a statement saying I should resign because I was more interested in the poor and disarmament than changing the Canadian Senate.

"What the hell's he doing for Alberta?" Morton asked the *Calgary Herald*. "He's interested in nuclear disarmament, or whatever, but the impact of what he does through that is virtually nothing," Brown added. "Unless he has the whole Senate on his side, his impact is going to be zero." My work, in the eyes of the erstwhile Senators, was "trivial."

I didn't have to say a word. The public reaction was instantaneous. Brian Bechtel, executive director of the Edmonton Social Planning Council, said their criticism was "incredibly narrow and one-dimensional." Patricia Hartnagel, in a letter-to-the-editor, said "their myopic view of the world would be laughable were it not such a horrifying reflection of their insularity." Ray Martin, leader of the New Democratic Party in Alberta, wrote, "They are the poster boys for narrow-mindedness and inward thinking. As an Albertan, I am embarrassed that their comments received national exposure." (In 2004, Ted Morton was elected to the Alberta Legislature and later was appointed Minister of Sustainable Resource Development. In 2007, Prime Minister Harper appointed Bert Brown to the Senate.)

Brown's comment that I would have to have the whole Senate on my side, or my impact would be zero, was interesting. I don't think he was paying close enough attention, because on two important occasions I did have the whole Senate on my side. Twice, the Senate unanimously adopted motions I had put forward on nuclear weapons. I was doing exactly what Chrétien had encouraged me to do—use the Senate to further the UN agenda for disarmament and human security that had brought me there.

The first of these motions was debated March 23, 1999, shortly before NATO's 50th anniversary summit. My motion would have the Senate recommend that the Government of Canada urge NATO to begin a review of its nuclear weapons policies. The House of Commons Foreign Affairs Committee, in its examination of Canada's nuclear weapons policies, had recommended the same thing. Since the origins of the parliamentary committee's study on nuclear weapons could be traced back to the 1996 Project Ploughshares report on my tour of Canada, I felt it only fitting that I use the Senate to propel the idea of a NATO review. This was certainly not a brave motion, but if I had made it any more challenging, it would never have been accepted. As it was, Senator Grafstein expressed skepticism about "a careful and deliberate strategic overview of Canadian and NATO objectives and capacity." He warned me not to confuse collegiality with consensus.

Senate rules make it easy for a Senator to derail a private motion by "taking the adjournment of the debate" and then never speaking on the item. It is very hard, if not impossible, for the proponent of the motion to force a vote that one or more senators, let alone the government itself, opposes. I found that out when I tried to get motions through calling on the Canadian government to stay out of the U.S. missile defence system.

Even though Grafstein wasn't blocking my motion on NATO, it appeared stalled until, during a quiet day in the Senate when the mood seemed agreeable (political experience enables one to take the temperature of the Chamber on any given day), I jumped up when the item was called. I appealed to the Speaker to find out if any senator really wanted to speak, since time was running short before the NATO summit. Luckily, I escaped a procedural debate when Senator Kinsella, deputy leader of the Conservatives, rose to call for "thoughtful consideration" of the evolution of NATO's policies. "Speaking for my colleagues who discussed this matter in our caucus, we are prepared to support the motion." The Speaker looked around and, not seeing anyone else who wanted to speak, called for the vote. The motion went through on the nod.

The second motion occurred a year later, shortly before the 2000 Nuclear Non-Proliferation Treaty (NPT) review conference. It called for the Senate to recommend that Canada urge the nuclear weapons states to "reaffirm their unequivocal commitment to take action towards the total elimination of their nuclear arsenals." I argued, "Honourable Senators, it is critical to global security that the NPT survive until a comprehensive plan for eliminating all nuclear weapons is negotiated. This means that the nuclear weapons states, recognizing the importance of the NPT to their own security, must be committed, without equivocation, to fulfilling their Article VI obligations."

Senator Sheila Finestone, speaking for the Liberals, praised me for bringing the motion forward. "That he would ring the alarms bells is very much in keeping with the kind of role he has played as a conscience for Canada and the world in these areas." Again, Senator Kinsella spoke for the Conservatives, and drew from the words of Martin Luther King to embellish his support: "I refuse to accept the cynical notion that nation after nation must spiral down a militaristic stairway into the hell of nuclear annihilation." No senator challenged the motion and it was adopted.

Deliverables for Funders

I wondered what actually happened to Senate motions. Was anyone listening? Did anyone care? One day, in Question Period, the Government Leader in the Senate, Senator Graham, responded that my motion "has been dispatched directly to the Prime Minister and the Minister of Foreign Affairs with my notation." Well, that's not bad, I thought. You can't always make the horse drink the water, but leading it to the well is an important step. In fact, in the case of both my motions—Canada calling for a NATO review of nuclear weapons and pressing the nuclear powers for an unequivocal commitment to elimination of nuclear weapons—both events occurred. NATO did conduct a review and the nuclear powers did make an "unequivocal" commitment. I am not under the illusion that my motions alone were responsible; that would be ridiculous. There are too many political currents running through any given issue to be able to isolate one and point to it as the father of a good event. When the government wants to do something, it will do it, and when it doesn't, no amount of Senate advisory opinions will overcome opposition. But it is also true that a formal expression of opinion from the Senate encourages action that might otherwise not take place.

Similarly, in my work with the Middle Powers Initiative (MPI), I have always been careful to position the organization as a credible, forward-minded body encouraging states to take constructive measures towards nuclear disarmament, but never to say afterwards that we were responsible for the action. Others are also working in this field. It is impossible to ascribe success to any one group. What counts is cumulative pressure on governments from several sources to overcome the lethargy and downright obstinacy that mire governments in the status quo. My own nature is not to attempt to claim credit when good things happen. I'm more comfortable simply making the effort and letting it go at that.

Personal reticence, however, runs up against the need for a politician to be seen to be accomplishing something, lest he or she be written off as being a mere bit player in the drama around life's major issues. Modesty, if that is what it is, becomes a fault, however, when it comes to fundraising. In all the presentations my colleagues in the MPI and I have made to funders and potential funders, I have learned that it is essential to trumpet the "deliverables." Tell us what you have accomplished, the funders demand. Why should we give you money?

When the funders apply the word *deliverable* to nuclear disarmament work, I sometimes feel that I am supposed to "deliver" the remnants of a nuclear weapon that I have personally disassembled. This frustrates me, because nuclear disarmament is all about changing the mindset of governments so that they no longer rely on weapons of mass destruction for their security. The dismantling of weapons will follow only when governments recognize that the weapons involved are not needed for security.

This is what happened with land mines. An intellectual rejection of their utility was needed before the land mines treaty was achieved. In the case of nuclear weapons—the ultimate evil—the case must first be made that they are actual impediments to security before governments will shift from reliance to dismantlement. This process requires a historic shift in thinking to accept a growing truism in a globalized world that the use of massive violence is not the route to peace. I am engaged in fostering an attitudinal shift in societal thinking. I cannot produce "results" overnight. The subject is far too complex. Not even the Secretary-General of the United Nations or the Pope has a magic button to push to rid the world of its proclivity to violence. What counts is working from whatever station of life we occupy to change public policies so that they become based on equity, justice and true human security.

Patience and Resilience

How the subject matter of my two motions involving NATO and the NPT played out illustrates why patience and resilience are but two of the attributes needed to persevere in the nuclear disarmament field.

With Lloyd Axworthy as foreign minister, Canada argued forcefully at the summit to mark NATO's 50th anniversary for a re-examination of the nuclear component in NATO's Strategic Concept. For a long time, the Strategic Concept has held that nuclear weapons are "essential to preserve peace" and are "the supreme guarantee of the security of the Allies." NATO's nuclear forces based in five European "non-nuclear" states—Belgium, Germany, Italy, the Netherlands and Turkey—"provide an essential political and military link between the European and North American members of the Alliance." Axworthy challenged this thinking but, although the NATO leadership began a review, Axworthy felt his efforts diminished when Canada was called a "nuclear nag."

I led an MPI delegation to five key NATO states—Norway, Germany, Italy, the Netherlands and Belgium—and also to NATO headquarters in Brussels during this review. Accompanied by Rob Green and Scilla Elworthy, two of the most knowledgeable people on nuclear weapons in the civil society movement, I brought an MPI brief detailing how NATO's policies directly contradict the commitment NATO states had made to the NPT. Government officials, particularly in the defence departments, time and again denied there was any contradiction between calling nuclear weapons "essential," on the one hand, and making an "unequivocal undertaking" to eliminate them, on the other. NATO officials themselves saw the review under way as merely examining safety provisions and the possible advance-

ment of confidence-building measures. As for examining the core
doctrine of possession, this was ruled out of the question. "Mission
impossible!" was the repeated response.

We found NATO and its backers to be in a state of denial that
its determination to keep nuclear weapons is a primary stimulant to
proliferation. Those few, usually in the foreign ministries, who would
contemplate a full review stated that such a process would indubitably
upset the U.S., the U.K. and France and thus break "cohesion," which
NATO proclaimed was an end in itself. That the non-nuclear weapons
states (the overwhelming majority) of NATO might be able to exert
their will on the other three for a nuclear review in the name of that
self-same cohesion seemed not to have occurred to officials.

While it was undoubtedly true that the U.S., the U.K. and France
dominated NATO, it appeared to the MPI delegation that the non-
nuclear members were their willing accomplices. Canada, seeing the
stone wall of resistance to its original ideas, eased up on its demands
and, after Axworthy left Foreign Affairs, fell silent.

In the end, NATO did not change its Strategic Concept. Nuclear
weapons remained "essential." But a crack in NATO's conviction
showed. The report on the review stated that, while nuclear weapons
must be kept up to date as a "credible deterrence," the role of NATO's
nuclear forces in today's environment "is fundamentally political." Was
this gobbledygook or constructive ambiguity? The one bright light
in the report was the recognition of the need for "a more vigorous,
structural debate within NATO—leading to a strengthened common
understanding among allies…" Also included was a paragraph committing NATO to "meaningful public outreach" and more dialogue.
MPI was ready to take up that challenge.

In my double role as a Holy See adviser and MPI chairman,
I attended the entire 2000 NPT review conference and carefully
watched Canada's performance to see how much "urging" of the
nuclear weapons states occurred, as called for in the Senate motion.
The sprawling month-long conference got caught up in numerous
issues and, of course, the countries of the New Agenda Coalition,
deeply committed to nuclear disarmament, played a starring role.
The Canadian delegation performed creditably, though not flashily,
in helping the Coalition secure from the nuclear weapons states an
"unequivocal undertaking to accomplish the total elimination of

their nuclear arsenals." The Canadian Ambassador, Chris Westdal, performed brilliantly in negotiating compromise language to keep the conference from collapsing over the Middle East problems centred on Israel's possession of nuclear weapons. When the landmark final consensus document was achieved, I felt Canada could well share in the praise.

The Senate motions played a role, however modest, as the nuclear disarmament issues took centre stage in the large world arenas. It was the government of Canada that determined this country's actions. I was but one advocate. But, as I have said, if enough advocates exert their will, marvellous things can follow. Just look at what happened when a critical mass of advocates raised the level of action against slavery, colonialism and apartheid.

Holy Year Modern Pilgrimage

With the pressures of the Clarity bill and the NPT review conference behind me, I was overjoyed at the arrival of the summer of 2000. I needed to unwind, and what better place to relax than the Eternal City? Besides, Patricia had never been there. I seized the opportunity presented by the Jubilee Year, marking 2000 years since the birth of Christ, to make a modern pilgrimage to celebrate not only the Holy Year with its special blessings but also humanity's entrance into the third millennium. For the past seven centuries, Holy Year pilgrimages to Rome have been a significant part of the life of the faithful, assuming different cultural forms in different eras. During the Middle Ages, the journey was incredibly arduous and dangerous. What a contrast for us to fly in comfort at 39,000 feet, all the preparations made by email and fax.

On July 28, Pat and I set out on our journey. In Rome, we stayed at the Hotel Forum, an ex-convent whose rooftop restaurant boasts a spectacular view of the ruins of the Roman Forum and the Coliseum, where gladiators fought wild beasts. Since we had only four days, we decided to concentrate on the four principal basilicas, each with its own holy door, and spend at least two hours in quiet contemplation amid the architectural and cultural splendour.

Our first stop was St. Mary Major, one of the patriarchal or major basilicas. Pope Sixtus III built it immediately after the Council of Ephesus in 431, which had proclaimed the dogma of Mary's maternity.

Later, Byzantine-style mosaics were added to illustrate episodes connected to Mary and the childhood of Christ.

It was an easy walk to the second basilica, St. John Lateran, built in the fourth century. Pope Gregory I consecrated the basilica to St. John the Baptist and St. John the Evangelist; it houses relics of the two saints. In 1370, when the remains of the heads of saints Peter and Paul were brought here, the church acquired great prestige. We spent an hour of reflection in the adjoining cloister, a masterpiece of mosaic art.

Next was St. Paul Outside the Walls (definitely too far for this modern pilgrim to walk), a basilica rebuilt many times over the tomb of the Apostle Paul. Until St. Peter's was built, St. Paul's was the largest basilica in Rome. Its thirteenth-century art is both stunning and peaceful. We spent a long time in silent prayer there.

Since this was Pat's first experience in Rome, I had deliberately saved St. Peter's, which is so overwhelming that it takes your breath away, for last. There is simply nothing else like it in Christendom.

Long lines of people waited to enter the basilica, whose monumental dome designed by Michelangelo can be seen from miles away. Michelangelo's *Pietà*, possibly the most exquisite statue in existence, stands near the Porta Santa behind bulletproof glass. Baroque art on a heroic scale dominates the basilica, which was first built 1,700 years ago on the tomb of St. Peter. We descended to the crypt to see the tombs of 20th-century popes, including John XXIII, who changed the Church with Vatican II.

We saw the recently renovated Sistine Chapel, which is dominated by Michelangelo's disturbing "Last Judgment," one of the milestones of European culture. The images of the resurrected and the damned, and the raging battle between angels and devils vying for souls, are haunting. Next door, the Pauline Chapel, featuring two of Michelangelo's paintings of the conversion of St. Paul and the crucifixion of St. Peter, was more peaceful.

The next day we returned to St. Peter's for the regular Wednesday audience with Pope John Paul. The Holy Father flew over the throngs in St. Peter's Square in his helicopter before arriving in his Popemobile. Pilgrims from dozens of countries called out to him and serenaded him in several languages. It was blazing hot in the square, so his assistants kept the Pope, now aging and stooped, in the shade for the 90-minute audience. Speaking in Italian, he spoke of how God reveals himself in human nature and called on us to work for the common good. Then he gave the papal blessing.

The Pope received and blessed many people with disabilities. Then Pat and I were brought to him. There was time only for a greeting. Though obviously tired from the long morning, the Pope seemed determined to meet as many people as possible. He even posed for pictures with newlyweds.

The papal audience was the high point of our jubilee year pilgrimage. Other wonderful moments included strolling through Piazza Navona and viewing artists' work, listening to the chimes of St. Mary's Church in Trastevere, and marvelling at Bernini's lifelike statues in the museum of Villa Borghese.

Half a century had passed since my first visit to Rome for Archie Daley's ordination. Dozens of visits over the years have never dulled my excitement at savouring the fullness of the city. Eternal and ever fresh, noisy and sublime, Rome embodies all the vistas of the human journey. The vibrancy and hope of the 2000 jubilee year were etched in my mind. Sometimes there are wonderful, ecstatic moments when we can just enjoy being alive, being happy, forget our cares, have fun, rejoice in the grandeur of God's creation and our part in it. The summer of 2000 was a moment to remember.

18

Battle for the Planet

On Tuesday, September 11, 2001, when I stepped out of the shower at 7 a.m. Mountain Time, Pat said her daughter, Mary, had just called to tell us to turn on the television. With a towel wrapped around me, I stood staring at a replay of a lone plane smashing into the World Trade Center in New York City. Then the second plane. Then a third plane hitting the Pentagon. Then a fourth plane downed in Pennsylvania. Terrorists had struck the United States with full force. With the collapse of the Twin Towers, I saw my hopes for a culture of peace shatter.

There wasn't much to do at first except stare transfixed at the horror unfolding on the screen, to lament the political chaos, and to be bewildered by it all. Since the Senate wasn't sitting, I was in Edmonton, and since flying in Canada was immediately banned for several days, I wasn't going anywhere. Within a 20-minute period that morning, all my children—Evita in Ottawa, Francis and Mary Anne in Toronto, and Tricia in Victoria—called to see whether I was all right. Knowing how often I travelled to New York, their first thought was that I might somehow be near the disaster. I found their care about their father comforting. I was, in fact, scheduled to be in New York in two weeks' time.

In times of crisis, politicians put out a statement. That's what I did. "The New York/Washington attacks were attacks against humanity," I said. "They require a humanity-centred response." Revenge is unworthy of the solemn obligation we have "to end violence by getting at the root cause of violence." That meant, in my view, that Canada had to help the U.S. to combat terrorism with comprehensive strategies that included the economic and social development of peoples around the world. I doubt anyone paid the slightest attention to the press release.

My best statement was simply attending a Muslim service at the El Rashid Mosque in Edmonton to show my solidarity with the Muslim community, which had felt a backlash because the suicide terrorists were young Muslim men. My friends Rev. Bruce Miller, a United Church Minister, and Rabbi Neil Loomer of Beth Shalom Synagogue and I stood with hundreds of men in their prayer. Imam Shobau Sheriff told the assembly to remember that Islam stands upon the pillars of justice and peace. With tears in their eyes, Muslim men came up to shake my hand and thank me for coming. It was evident that they were trying to find ways to show their abhorrence of violence.

The following week, the first order of business when the Senate reconvened was the swearing-in of a number of new senators, including Mobina Jaffer, a distinguished immigration lawyer in British Columbia. I found it prescient that Jaffer, the first Canadian senator of the Muslim faith, arrived just at the moment that Islam was being unfairly and inaccurately blamed for motivating the September 11 attacks. The Senate immediately launched an emergency debate on a government motion expressing condolences to the victims and determination to bring to justice the perpetrators of the terrorism. I was the seventh speaker. I urged the government to uphold the principles of international law in responding to the terrorists and shun the language of war, which suggests that only militarism can combat terrorism. "It is not a war that we should seek, but justice. It is not the rule of war that should predominate but the rule of law."

In calling for Canada to use the catastrophe as a wake-up call to energize the political systems to provide more social justice, I could, I knew, be perceived as being insensitive to the thousands of lives lost in the terrorist attacks. So the following week in New York, I took the subway down to the financial district and saw the World Trade Center wreckage with my own eyes. The devastation at Ground Zero was overpowering. Mounds of debris, six storeys high, assaulted the eyes. People were stunned looking at this grotesque sight. I then went to the United Nations and talked with Jayantha Dhanapala, now the Under-Secretary-General for Disarmament Affairs, who said that, bad as the tragedy was, it could have been even worse. "Consider if weapons of mass destruction had been used by these terrorists," he said.

By another twist of fate, Kofi Annan and the UN were awarded the Nobel Peace Prize that fall at just the moment the UN was trying to resolve the terrorist threat without recourse to more violence. Annan expanded on Dhanapala's point: "While the world was unable to prevent the September 11 attacks, there is much we can do to help prevent future terrorist acts with weapons of mass destruction."

But these thoughts about preventive diplomacy were swept aside in the U.S. rush to start bombing Afghanistan, the presumed home base of the terrorists. Though the hijackers did not come from Afghanistan, some of them were trained there. Afghanistan had to be punished. Pushed by the U.S., the UN Security Council gave its assent to "take all necessary steps" to respond to the September 11 attacks. The bombing of Afghanistan started. I got up in the Senate several times to argue that the Security Council had not given its assent to a bombing campaign that would kill innocent Afghan civilians in their villages and force thousands of refugees to flee along the Afghanistan-Pakistan border and try to survive in unspeakable conditions.

The Silence of the Peace Movement

After the bombing had gone on for three weeks, I made another plea:

> The bombing of Afghanistan, one of the most desperate and vulnerable regions of the world, is producing an international catastrophe. The bombing is immoral, unproductive, and only by the most dubious logic can it be said to possess even a shred of legality ... It is the utmost folly to think that we can end terrorism by trying to bomb terrorists out of existence.

The alternative to bombing was to send in ground troops to comb the countryside and all the caves to find Osama bin Laden and his fellow plotters. This was not done; the U.S.-led coalition feared that troops would be killed by the mines planted throughout Afghanistan. Yet later, the U.S. and NATO did deploy ground troops for combat operations in the country, to take out the Taliban warriors. Canada, without any hard thinking about the matter, found itself fighting a war in Afghanistan.

I found the bombing raids, chosen as the first response to terrorism, unconscionable and unworthy of nations that pride themselves on upholding human rights. As the Kosovo bombing two years earlier had shown, even "smart" bombs cannot distinguish between military and civilian targets. The human misery left in the wake of a bombing campaign is horrendous. Kofi Annan was immensely frustrated. He kept stressing political, legal, diplomatic and financial means to fight terrorism. He got money for humanitarian relief. But it was disingenuous for the states doing the bombing to couple it with drops of food and medicine. This was a chaotic and ineffectual way of meeting humanitarian needs. I thought the international community should have mounted—with the same vigour displayed in the bombing campaign—a massive assault on poverty. It is the inhuman conditions that so many millions of people are subjected to that breed the conditions that terrorists exploit.

I went to a press conference in Toronto with Senator Lois Wilson, Ursula Franklin and David Orchard (I was careful this time about who I appeared with in public) to call for a halt in the bombing so that humanitarian aid could get through to the desperate people of Afghanistan. We hardly made a ripple in the national media. I did receive one email from a man who said that the U.S. "has every right to go after those terrorists with everything they have, wherever they are ... This is war and innocent people will die." He said that I had no support from the people of Canada and stood alone.

This was not exactly true, for I did have letters of support, but it wasn't far off. In fact, the peace movement in Canada went silent after 9/11. I found it a deafening silence. The terrorist attacks cowed many people who would otherwise have taken to the streets to protest the wanton breach of humanitarian law that the incessant bombing represented. They swallowed the pontificating of supposedly erudite columnists who claimed the Afghan bombing was a "just war."

A "just war" requires proportionality and limitation; the bombing raids were neither proportional nor limited. In any case, the "just war" theory was formulated at a time when humanity did not possess the diplomatic, political and legal tools that we have today to overcome violence and conflict with forceful means that do not involve war. What was "just" about killing innocent civilians and ruining the infrastructure of a country?

I was in personal turmoil. I could raise my voice, but who was listening? I could write statements, but how many would read them? The only way I could live with myself, the only way I could find some peace in my own heart, was to take a personal action. "Showboating" the action would be ridiculous. Patricia and I talked this over. Appalled at the suffering caused by this new "war on terror," she felt as I did. We decided simply to forgo our winter holiday in St. Lucia and to send the money for Afghan relief. In the great scheme of things in life, this was an insignificant action, but it enabled us to express, in our own way, our concern for the human condition.

No to the Iraq War

As the bombing gave way to ground combat in Afghanistan, and the spectre of a U.S. war against Iraq loomed, I tried in the Senate to promote three lessons to be learned from 9/11. First, endemic poverty, the dark side of globalization, is fanning the flames of violence and extremism. Such poverty must be eased. Second, the UN must be enabled to protect the rule of law. Third, nuclear terrorism must be averted through binding norms to shut off the development of nuclear weapons and negotiate their complete elimination.

But the drums of war in Iraq drowned out calls even by eminent world leaders to take a comprehensive approach to stamping out terrorism. On October 10, 2002, fearing that war in Iraq was coming, I tabled a motion in the Senate:

> That the Senate notes the crisis between the United States and Iraq, and affirms the urgent need for Canada to uphold international law under which, absent an attack or imminent threat of attack, only the United Nations Security Council has the authority to determine compliance with its resolutions and sanction military action.

By this time, many Canadians were becoming alarmed at the belligerence of the Bush administration. Not satisfied with the retaliation wreaked on Afghanistan, it had branded Iraq as part of the "axis of evil," and was deploying U.S. military forces in preparation for a strike on Iraq. I joined a group of 100 prominent Canadians, including Pierre Berton, Margaret Atwood and David Suzuki, in issuing a public statement that an attack on Iraq would be profoundly immoral and "would almost certainly result in destabilizing repercussions that would endanger the whole world."There was no connection between the al Qaeda terrorists and Iraq; nor was there credible evidence that Iraq currently possessed weapons of mass destruction. In my speech, I made a plea to the Canadian government: "Go on the offensive for peace! Stand up in the international community and provide an alternate beat to the drums of war."

Over the next few weeks, several senators spoke on my motion. I was pleasantly surprised when Tommy Banks, an outstanding professional musician who became a star performer in the Senate, said he agreed with me. Banks was a self-described hawk on military matters, but to join in a war on Iraq, he said, "would be out of kilter with the history, traditions and values of Canada."

Canada then began a high-wire act of diplomacy. With the deadline for the U.S. war closing in, Canada's Ambassador to the UN, Paul Heinbecker, tried to delay military action. In an astute move, he proposed that the Security Council authorize war on Iraq in three weeks only if it concluded that Iraq was not in compliance with disarmament demands. This would give the Council time to conclude whether Iraq was co-operating actively on substantial disarmament. If Iraq was found within three weeks to be co-operating fully with UN inspectors, further deadlines would then be set for verification and monitoring work. In other words, there would be no war. The Canadian government knew the current inspections were working. All the relevant figures—chiefly Hans Blix, chief UN inspector, and Mohamed ElBaradei, Director-General of the International Atomic Energy Agency—had said so. These professional inspectors and their teams could not find anything that would give Iraq even the slightest power to launch an attack using weapons of mass destruction. Canada was gambling that continuous inspections would show that, however heinous a regime Saddam Hussein ran, it did not pose an imminent threat to peace in the region that would justify war against Iraq.

This was Canadian diplomacy at its finest. It would give Bush the credit for winning the war without firing a shot while preserving the unity of the UN. But it was not to be. Bush was fixated on war. Jean Chrétien says in his memoirs, *My Years As Prime Minister*, "I think we came close, because Canada was one of the few countries with the courage and credibility to try, but the clock was running out too fast."

On the morning of March 17, 2003, Canada received a note from the British government asking whether Canada was willing to "provide political support for military action against Iraq." The U.K. wanted a yes-or-no answer before noon. Chrétien had already laid out his position: No UN approval; no war. At 2:15 p.m. he rose in the House of Commons during Question Period and said:

> Mr. Speaker, I want to set out the position of the Government of Canada. We believe that Iraq must fully abide by the resolutions of the United Nations Security Council. We have always made clear that Canada would require the approval of the Security Council if we were to participate in a military campaign. Over the last few weeks, the Security Council has been unable to agree on a new resolution authorizing military action. Canada worked very hard to find a compromise to bridge the gap in the Security Council. Unfortunately, we were not successful. If military action proceeds without a new resolution of the Security Council, Canada will not participate.

The next day, I rose in the Senate and asked the Government Leader to express to Prime Minister Chrétien and Foreign Minister Bill Graham "the deep appreciation that many Canadians feel for the government having made a correct and courageous decision in deciding that Canada would not participate in the war in Iraq." Senator Carstairs said she would be delighted to do so. But the Senate amity was quickly broken when Senator Michael Forrestal rose and stated, "Please assure the Prime Minister that Senator Roche's observations are not the unanimous observations of this Chamber." For several days, right-wing senators attacked Chrétien, claiming that many Canadians were "appalled" that he would not join in the U.S.'s "noble endeavour." Senator Laurier LaPierre, the famous Canadian broadcaster, had the last word on my motion with some profound words:

> The contribution of a nation to the people of this planet, and that nation's influence in the world, depends more on the value system that resides at the very core of the identity of that nation. In our name, the Prime Minister of our country proved that our values are not dead, they are not marginal and they are part and parcel of each and every Canadian.

The Human Right to Peace

With that, the motion dropped off the Order Paper. I was deeply grateful that Chrétien had had the courage to stick to his overarching regard for the authority of the UN. In his memoirs, Chrétien decries reliance on "vision" in making political decisions. He prefers to present himself as "*le petit gars de Shawinigan.*" I do not agree. In the most momentous Canadian decision made since the end of World War II, Chrétien did indeed display vision.

But the Iraq war started and there is no doubt in my mind that Canada found itself in the combat quagmire of Afghanistan precisely because it had said no to participating in the war in Iraq. We had to prove we were good allies and so took on fighting operations in Afghanistan. But we took them on by stealth, since there never was a full debate in either Parliament or the media.

Once again in my political life I felt powerless to stop the onslaught of war. In the 20th century, at least 110 million people were killed in 250 wars. The 21st century was already scarred with new conflicts. The terrorist attacks of 9/11 revived the culture of war, yet the UN stood for a culture of peace. How to move from one to the other? I turned inward and forward at the same time. To cope with the oppression of war in the modern world, I had to think about the future. To get my mind off the hourly news, I plunged into the voluminous literature of the United Nations and began to see that, wars notwithstanding, a human right to peace is actually coming into view. The view was certainly obscured by the wars in Iraq and Afghanistan, but for those who would see beyond the commanding heights of power occupied by the military-industrial complex, a culture of peace agenda was already coming into focus. By thinking and writing about the world as it could be, I was able to cope with the stupidity of the present.

Soon I was immersed in writing *The Human Right to Peace*. I think it has been the most important of my books, for it showed that, in a world in which our destinies are increasingly held in common, a culture of peace can bring genuine hope to the lives of the many millions who need and want to be lifted up from the horrors of daily life. Using UN documents and actions as my guide, I made the case that the very agonies of war and the dark night of suffering that has lasted for centuries are awakening civilization to a new understanding: the peoples of the Earth have a sacred right to peace. The object of the book was to explore and animate the concept of peace as a human right so that it could finally take its place among the other human rights recognized by the international system.

The book caught on and briefly appeared on a bestseller list. It received an award from the *Canadian Book Review*. An edition was published in India. Khalid Yaqub, my former student whose expertise in computer graphics had long helped me, created a vibrant Power-Point presentation of the book, and I lectured widely on it, particularly to teachers' groups. Clyde Sanger wrote a lengthy review in the *Literary Review of Canada*, which showed that at least the book was being taken seriously. As satisfying as that was, I was more concerned that the idea of a culture of peace be taken far more seriously by the media, academics, governments and the public.

A culture of peace is an approach to life that seeks to transform the cultural tendencies towards war and violence into a culture in which dialogue, respect and fairness govern social relations. The culture of peace uses education as an essential tool to foster attitudes supportive of non-violence, co-operation and social justice. It promotes human rights and sustainable development for all, and stresses equality between men and women. It requires genuine democracy and the free flow of information. It leads to disarmament. The culture of peace recognizes the human crisis of our time: in our journey through time, we have reached the point where we are capable of destroying all life on earth just at the moment when the recognition of the inherent human rights of everyone is beginning to take hold.

Sanger quoted one of my favourite lines in the book. I had cited the words of the U.S. delegate during the UN debate on the Declaration and Programme of Action on a Culture of Peace: "Peace should not be elevated to the category of a human right, otherwise it will be very difficult to start a war." Whether intended or not, the speaker had put his finger precisely on why a human right to peace is needed.

Nourishing the Seeds

It was in 1984 that the UN General Assembly adopted the Declaration on the Right of Peoples to Peace, which states that "the peoples of the planet have a sacred right to peace." Although 92 states voted in favour of the resolution and none opposed it, the 34 abstentions (mostly from key states) rendered it virtually inoperable. At the end of the Cold War, UNESCO, under the driving leadership of Federico Mayor, revived the idea. Drafts UNESCO prepared emphasized that war and violence are "intrinsically incompatible" with the human right to peace. It is the "duty" of all global actors, including individuals, to "contribute to the maintenance and construction of peace." And the implementation of a culture of peace—rooting peace in people's minds through education, communication, and a set of ethical and democratic ideals—is the means by which the right to peace would be achieved. The Western states attacked this concept and, since a consensus could not be achieved, Mayor did not press further.

In 1999, the UN did adopt a more softly worded Declaration and Programme of Action on a Culture of Peace, establishing 2000 as the International Year of the Culture of Peace. A group of Nobel Peace Prize laureates issued a list of principles that could guide practical actions and public awareness campaigns: respect all life; reject violence; share with others; listen to understand; preserve the planet; and rediscover solidarity. A surge of activity culminated in a General Assembly resolution designating 2001–2010 as the International Decade for a Culture of Peace and Non-Violence for the Children of the World. The beginning of this promising movement was shattered by 9/11 and the new "war on terrorism."

A deep sense of fear has now pervaded the general populace. The media continually propound the old ideas of war for peace. In this environment, the culture of peace can hardly be heard, let alone gain the political attention and government funding to make an impression on electorates. In 2002, the UN Social, Humanitarian and Cultural Committee adopted a resolution calling for the promotion of the right to peace, but the hostility shown by the dissenting Western states revealed the naked war fever the terrorists had provoked.

I am the first to recognize that the right to peace is still but a seed in the ground. But it has been planted. The idea and the struggles of Gandhi, Martin Luther King, Archbishop Oscar Romero and a host of other valiant defenders of the core ideas of peace, many of whom gave their lives for the cause, live on. True, they need a better political climate in which to thrive and blossom, but active work to nourish the ideas will help to produce that better climate. If there is a core to my political life, it is to go on—despite the wars of our time—nourishing the seeds of the human right to peace that are found throughout the planet.

Gorbachev's Continuing Influence

My thinking was strongly reinforced when I attended a remarkable meeting of Nobel Peace Prize laureates convened by Mikhail Gorbachev in Rome in October 2002. I was then a vice-president of the International Peace Bureau, a recipient of the Nobel Peace Prize in 1910. The Bureau had asked me to represent the organization; I brought Jonathan Granoff with me. The meeting was held in the Piazza Campidoglio, overlooking the ruins of the Roman Forum. The session provided a good perspective on the war culture in the modern age. Not even the might of the Roman Empire could prevent its collapse, yet the human spirit soared again and again through the ages to create the vibrancy of today's Rome.

Though the topics of the meeting were weighty, it opened on a light note with the presentation of the Man of Peace prize to Italian actor-director Roberto Benigni who, seizing the baton, conducted a children's choir, to the delight of the astonished singers. The moment captured the hope that animated the meeting. The Nobel laureates quickly asserted that they refused, the war clouds notwithstanding, to accept the cynicism and despair that crush hope and vision. In fact, they began their final statement by affirming "our common humanity and capacity to work cooperatively, informed by compassion and inspired by love. Our humanity demands this."

Gorbachev eloquently and firmly outlined the crisis of our civilization brought about by war, violence and the instability caused by poverty. The status quo of dominance by a few could not be allowed to continue, he said. He warned about the overabundance of power in NATO, which was expanding once again and possesses 70 per cent of the military power in the world. Quoting President John F. Kennedy's famous address to the American University on June 10, 1963, Gorbachev said that it was not a Pax Americana that was needed today but rather the cooperation of all to overcome the tendencies of unilateral domination. He noted that 31 countries now have the ability to develop a nuclear weapon, which is a terrifying situation. He excoriated governments for pleading that they do not have enough money to cure poverty while at the same time spending enormous sums on arms. He especially criticized the development of nuclear weapons—this will go on and on, he said, unless the world community is energized to stop it. Certainly, new weapons were not needed to fight terrorism. A principled position against nuclear weapons should be taken so that we can get on to the next stage of civilization.

The speech—like the one he gave many years before at the UN, where he renounced force as an instrument of foreign policy—won him a standing ovation. Because the U.S.-Iraq crisis loomed, the meeting featured an extraordinary session, "Overcoming Unilateral Militarism: Responding to Threats to Human Security." Granoff and I were asked to co-chair it. With the Nobel laureates and the representatives of Nobel organizations grouped around a table, the discussion ranged from the urgency of the Iraq crisis to the need to preserve human rights while fighting terrorism.

At the end, the Laureates agreed: "The problems of poverty, suffering, the humiliation of millions of people and the growing gap between North and South represent a time bomb. These problems are a source of conflict and are fertile soil for terrorism." The "battle for the planet," they said, required at a minimum the abolition of nuclear weapons. They concluded, "A culture of peace must overcome today's culture of war." At the conclusion of the final dinner, in an impromptu moment, Gorbachev began to sing Russian songs. The joy on his face spread around the room.

Star Wars Redux

While I recognized that achieving peace is a long-range goal, short-term political imperatives kept yanking me back to the turmoil of the present. An issue that preoccupied me during my years in the Senate was the pressure the U.S. was putting on Canada to join the ballistic missile defence system. I thought I was finished with the issue when Prime Minister Mulroney rejected Canadian participation in the Strategic Defense Initiative (Star Wars). But, under George W. Bush, the issue was back. The President pledged to deploy a rudimentary missile defence system during his first term of office. He showed his seriousness by starting a process to withdraw the U.S. from the Anti-Ballistic Missile Treaty, the very purpose of which was to prevent defensive systems from being created. It was long recognized internationally that defence systems act as a spur to new offensive arms development. I regarded Bush's act as igniting a new nuclear arms race. The thought of Canada participating in this escalation of tensions upset me deeply.

On February 1, 2001, I tabled a motion in the Senate recommending that Canada avoid involvement and support in the U.S. system on the grounds that the system countered the Treaty, "which has been a cornerstone of strategic stability and an important foundation for international efforts on nuclear disarmament and non-proliferation for almost thirty years." I wanted the motion dealt with before the actual date of U.S. withdrawal would occur. But I ran into a combination of apathy on the part of most Senators, and opposition from a few. After several months, it was suggested that the issue be studied in committee before a determinative vote was held. Then, opposition was raised on the grounds that my motion was not neutral, thus potentially prejudicing the committee's study. More procedural wrangling followed. Senator Nick Taylor summed up the situation aptly: "The subject has now become extremely obscure and convoluted, especially with terrorism thrown in." I offered to withdraw my original motion and substitute it with a new, neutral one as long as it would go to committee. More delays. This went on until Parliament was prorogued and the legislative slate wiped clean.

By 2003, the issue was starting to heat up, particularly when Paul Martin, as a candidate for the Liberal leadership, said he favoured Canada joining the U.S. program. His fellow Liberal, Lloyd Axworthy, challenged him in an op-ed piece in the *Globe and Mail*, "Say No to Missile Defence," co-authored with Michael Byers, an author and professor at the University of British Columbia.

I introduced a new motion in the Senate that would have Canada refuse to participate, and the debate started all over again. I knew there was nothing to be gained by submitting a neutral motion because it would again get caught up in procedural blocking. But because an increasing number of Liberals were becoming apprehensive about ballistic missile defence, I tried to muster the ranks of the Liberal opponents in the Senate. "Honourable Senators, Canada must not compromise its values by joining this imprudent U.S. military plan that scientists say will not work; that analysts say is destabilizing; and that ethicists say is distracting the world from investing in true human security."

Paul Martin became the Liberal leader and prime minister, and Canada moved closer to agreeing to participate as the pace of official U.S.-Canada meetings picked up. Many non-governmental organizations spoke out in opposition, including Project Ploughshares, the Group of 78 and the Liu Institute at the University of British Columbia. Steve Staples, a young and dynamic activist who would later start the Rideau Institute, and Debbie Grisdale came to see me about strengthening the campaign. I suggested that they form a non-partisan coalition of civil society groups and get it up and running before the anticipated 2004 election. They should get a coherent message out to the public before the election, I said, adding that I would be glad to work with them. The Canadian Campaign to Oppose Missile Defence was formed. Ernie Regehr, Peggy Mason and Michael Byers joined the team. Staples led the campaign, bringing U.S. military experts to Ottawa to speak out against ballistic missile defence and organizing rallies across Canada.

Martin started a new session of Parliament and, once more, I introduced in the Senate a motion to oppose the ballistic missile defence system. I tried to make it both comprehensive and biting:

> That the Senate of Canada recommend that the Government of Canada not participate in the U.S.-sponsored Ballistic Missile Defence (BMD) system because:

> It will undermine Canada's longstanding policy on the non-weaponization of space by giving implicit, if not explicit, support to U.S. policies to develop and deploy weapons in space;

> It will destabilize the strategic environment and impede implementation of Article VI of the Nuclear Non-Proliferation Treaty;

> It will not contribute to the security of Canadians, and Canadian non-participation will not diminish the importance of Canada-U.S. defence cooperation under NORAD in addressing genuine threats to Canadian security.

At the end of a long speech, I concluded, "I ask you to consider that I am not standing alone in my opposition to BMD. Important voices and votes show the rising concern that Canada not make a terrible mistake. Thirty Liberal MPs in the House of Commons voted against Canada continuing discussions on, let alone participation in, missile defence." Senator Jane Cordy of Halifax adjourned the debate,

The green marble podium in the U.N. General Assembly is world famous.
I found it a distinct honour to speak there representing Canada.

From 1989 to 2008, I was an adviser to the Holy See delegation to the U.N.
Here, I am at a Non-Proliferation Treaty conference.

For a week in January 1991, Bishop Remi De Roo, right, Mary Jo Leddy and I dialogued about the troubling issues affecting the Catholic Church of the day from the perspective of a bishop, a woman and a journalist. The book was called *In the Eye of the Catholic Storm*.

Another dialogue partner was Robert Muller. Our joint book, *Safe Passage into the 21st Century*, dealt with the U.N.'s quest for peace, equality, justice and development. The dialogue took place at the University for Peace, Costa Rica.

In 1993, I returned to Bangladesh to see the effects of Canadian aid projects and became captivated by the sparkle and hope of these young students.

My family on September 22, 1998, the day I was sworn in to the Senate. From left: Tricia, holding infant Nicholas, Evita, me, Mary Anne, Francis.

My assistant, Pam Miles-Séguin, organized the details of my life as an M.P. and Senator.

In the Jubilee Year of 2000, I introduced my new wife, Patricia McGoey, to Rome. We were both received by Pope John Paul II.

My wife Pat took this photo of me outside the A–Bomb Dome in Hiroshima. I have used it in all my PowerPoint presentations to establish a personal connection with nuclear devastation.

Jo Rotblat, who became a principal world leader against nuclear weapons, was a hero of mine.

With Mayor Tadatoshi Akiba of Hiroshima, President of Mayors for Peace, which has mounted an international campaign to rid the world of nuclear weapons by 2020.

Film star Michael Douglas appeared as part of the Middle Powers Initiative's first delegation to Canada in 1998. From left, Dr. Mary-Wynne Ashford, Foreign Minister Lloyd Axworthy, Jonathan Granoff, U.S. Senator Alan Cranston, Prime Minister Jean Chretien, Michael Douglas, Dr. Jennifer Simons, me.

Michael Douglas is a U.N. Messenger of Peace. He has strongly supported the Middle Powers Initiative.

This is the scene described in the Prologue, where I spoke at the Carter Center, Atlanta, in one of the Middle Powers Initiative's first major consultations. From left: Jonathan Granoff, former President Jimmy Carter, Harry Barnes, me, U.S. Senator Alan Cranston.

A Middle Powers Initiative delegation to Canada in 2003. From left, former Prime Minister Kim Campbell of Canada, U.S. Ambassador Tom Graham, Alexa McDonough, M.P., Jonathan Granoff, me.

I was privileged to speak at a meeting of Nobel Peace Laureates in Rome. From left: me, the Dalai Lama, former Soviet Union President Mikhail Gorbachev.

It was a dinner to remember when the three men closest to me in my life –
but all at different times of it – gathered in my home for the first and only
time. From left, Frank McMillan, Jonathan Granoff, me, Walter McLean.

Part of the Middle Powers Initiative team met in 2007 in New York. On couch: from left, Jonathan Granoff, Alice Slater, me. Rear: Kim Kroeber, Armin Tenner, Alyn Ware, Hiro Umebayahsi, John Burroughs, Ron McCoy, David Krieger, Miguel Marin-Bosch, Rhianna Tyson, Tony D'Costa, Jim Wurst.

"The four kids," as we were known in our youth, gathered for my sister Agnes's 80th birthday in 2005. Agnes and Marion in front; Archie Daley and me in rear.

The new generation emerges. Nicholas, 9, and Isabelle, 11, with their mother, Tricia, and grandfather.

Peace and Protest in India in 2008. Pat and I at the majestic Taj Mahal, and joining in a peace march at the New Delhi Congress of the International Physicians for the Prevention of Nuclear War.

The author meets Pope Benedict XVI during his visit to New York in April 2008. In the centre is Archbishop Celestino Migliore, Permanent Representative of the Holy See to the U.N.

but never spoke. The motion languished on the Order Paper until, once again, Parliament was prorogued for the election of 2004. By now, I had become accustomed to the frustration of seeing a motion of critical national importance just sit on the Order Paper, the victim of those who disagreed with it. I complained several times about the anti-democratic nature of the Senate, in which it is almost impossible for a private member to force a vote on a motion that others are opposed to. Had I been a parliamentary scholar, I might have launched an extended discourse on this arcane subject, but I had, and still have, too many other things to do.

Instead, I used an Open Letter to Prime Minister Martin, published in the *Hill Times*, to exert the very limited influence I had on Parliament Hill. "You will hear arguments that 'the protection of Canadians' requires participation in missile defence and that we must join in with the U.S. to maintain good Canada-U.S. relations," I wrote. "These are false arguments." I urged him to demand facts from his officials. The facts would show that ballistic missile defence, even if it worked, would have no capacity against short-range ballistic missiles fired from ships and would be completely impotent against warheads smuggled into shipping containers. Ballistic missile defence was the first step to weapons in space. "Why abandon Canada's steadfast course in nuclear diplomacy to satisfy the momentary desire of a hard-core element in Washington?"

I had left the Senate when Martin took his decision: No. On February 24, 2005, Martin, in a shaky political position (the Liberal majority had been reduced to a minority in the 2004 election), cloaked his answer with abundant praise of the U.S. "However, ballistic missile defence is not where we will concentrate our efforts." The victory belonged to Staples and his team in the Canadian Campaign and to those Liberal MPs who stood against their own caucus. But even when champagne was being downed, there was foreboding about the future. Opposition Leader Stephen Harper vowed that the Conservatives would return to the negotiating table if his party won the next election. Harper did win. For good reason, Staples titled his book on the campaign *Missile Defence: Round One*.

The Demands of the Clock

For me, the Senate clock was winding down. Age 75 means automatic retirement. It's probably a good rule; without it, I would likely have hung around, my efficiency more or less waning. As in the House of Commons, I never lost the feeling that it was an honour just to be able to walk onto the floor of the Senate Chamber. I was often in awe in that mahogany-panelled room with its brilliant red carpet and the huge paintings of First World War scenes on the walls. True, I was frustrated with the apathy and opposition I encountered, but there were times of great satisfaction and pride that a boy from Sandy Hill, of decidedly modest means, could debate as an equal among the senators of the land. It was fun to take Patricia, who came to Ottawa for special occasions, to the receptions and balls at Rideau Hall.

One night at a party, we wandered through the Governor General's residence out to the greenhouse where our close friend Lois Hole, Lieutenant-Governor of Alberta and a renowned gardener, was giving gardening tips to a host of admirers. That was a scene straight out of the best of Canada. In 2002, Lois came to my house in Edmonton to preside at the awarding of the Golden Jubilee Medal, marking the 50th anniversary of Queen Elizabeth II's reign as Queen of Canada. Senators were allowed to choose a number of recipients for outstanding service to the country and the community. I selected fourteen individuals I knew had given tremendous service to Edmonton: Patricia O'Brien, Betty Farrell, Kay Feehan, Chinwe Okelu, Stuart Lindop, Bob McKeon, Sister Teresa Devine, Kathleen Quinn, Msgr. Bill Irwin, Ronna Jevne, Don Mayne, Patricia Hartnagel, Father John McNeil and Jim Gurnett. The Lieutenant-Governor gave a hug to each honoree.

Again, as I had during my years in Parliament, I often felt the loneliness of working alone in the office at night and walking by the deserted Centennial Flame on the way to my hotel. For every night there was a reception somewhere, there were ten spent in solitude. I worried about more than nuclear weapons as I grappled with the intricacies of health care, corruption of political values, and how postal increases were penalizing religious newspapers.

Yet I certainly had more than my share of public recognition during this time. York University and Royal Rhodes University gave me honourary degrees. And in a wonderful interfaith moment, the

Canadian Islamic Congress and the Catholic Focolare Movement of North America both gave me awards for my work for peace. Also, the Nuclear Age Peace Foundation and the Canadian Pugwash Group gave me lifetime achievement awards. I had nothing to complain about in my Senate years.

I decided to devote my last major speech to the historical role of women in the Senate and the challenges modern women legislators faced to advance peace and human security. The "Famous Five" women of Alberta—Emily Murphy, Louise McKinney, Nellie McClung, Henrietta Edwards and Irene Parlby—had successfully petitioned to have women declared "persons" so they could serve in the Senate. I talked about the great women senators of the past and pointed to those still in the Senate leading the way on a variety of issues: Mobina Jaffer, Sharon Carstairs, Landon Pearson, Joyce Fairbairn, Thelma Chalifoux, Raynell Andreychuk, Lucie Pépin, Ione Christensen, Elizabeth Hubley and Marjory LeBreton. I looked at them as I made my final plea:

> Raise your voices against hunger and AIDS, against weapons and against the great injustices that drag down so many people around the world.
>
> Raise your voices for an end to poverty, abuse and discrimination. Raise your voices for a nuclear weapons–free world. Raise your voices for the full application of human rights for all women and for our children and men, too. Take the high moral ground in the struggles ahead to obtain true peace. You stand on the foundation of what the women who have come before you have built. You hold up half the sky. The future is yours.

The Senate gave me a standing ovation. I was glad Patricia was in the gallery.

I'm Still Here

The tradition in the Senate calls for nice things to be said about a departing senator. The Government Leader, Senator Jack Austin, led off the tributes: "He possesses a faith in the potential of his fellow human beings that is a true inspiration to those of us who watch him work on our behalf. More than that, he believes in the goodness of creation, in the beauty of this world and that it is worth protecting." As the tributes went on, I found it both soothing and somewhat embarrassing to be praised by the very senators who had dragged their feet on the ballistic missile defence and nuclear disarmament issues. But, as I had long ago learned, that's politics. When my turn came at the end, I expressed gracious thanks for the opportunity to serve in the Senate and for the many courtesies I had received. "I personally, as long as God gives me the strength, will never rest until nuclear weapons, the ultimate evil of our time, are abolished." I found it energizing when the senators applauded that line.

Senators who belong to political parties are given a farewell dinner by their respective caucus. Since I was an Independent (I used to joke that when I wanted to go to a caucus meeting I would take a bath), there would be no such dinner. It didn't bother me a bit. I organized my own dinner of 40 family members and friends and titled it "Peace: The Future, Not the Past." The evening, chaired by Patrick Boyer, a former MP who shares my world view, was filled with fun and laughter. Speakers addressed the compartments of my life: Senator Carstairs on the Senate, Ernie Regehr on the non-governmental organizations, Jonathan Granoff on the Middle Powers Initiative, David MacDonald on the political dimension, and Walter McLean on my religious involvement. MacDonald, alongside whom I had fought so many political battles in earlier years, struck the note I wanted to hear: "Doug, far from being over, your most important work lies ahead."

I knew the occasion was no time for one of my ponderous *tour d'horizon* speeches. So I had prepared an adaptation of the great Broadway composer Stephen Sondheim's song "I'm Still Here." I didn't sing it, but my heart was in the words:

Good times and bad times, I've seen them all in my years
and I'm here.

I've been through the dirty 30s, the swinging 60s,
joys and hopes, griefs and anxieties
and I'm here.

I remember Gandhi, Churchill and JFK.
Tony Bennett records still make my day.
Judy Garland's rainbow made me glad
that I'm here.

I've been through Trudeau, Mulroney, Martin Sr.,
and MacKenzie King
and I'm here.

I've been through four elections in the Commons
and no elections in the Senate.
I've logged a million miles on Air Canada
and I'm here.

I've been through the U.N. and around the world
seen the shanties and the flags unfurled.
What a blessing in Canada that
I live here.

I was 50 years old only last month, 60 about a week ago,
75 this evening
but I'm here.

The Senate will replace me, my students outpace me,
I'm a senior senior,
but I'm here.

I can write, I can lecture, I have a new PowerPoint presentation.
So find me an audience and I'll be there because
I'm still here.

VI

The Concluding Years: 2005–

19

When the Flower Blooms

The mild euphoria over the "unequivocal undertaking" to total nuclear disarmament achieved at the 2000 Nuclear Non-Proliferation Treaty (NPT) review conference faded quickly when U.S. President George W. Bush took office in 2001. Before the end of the year, the Bush administration had issued the revised Nuclear Posture Review, outlining an ambitious plan to replace the entire U.S. arsenal with a new generation of nuclear weapons and to revitalize the U.S. nuclear weapons production complex. Nuclear weapons, the review said, would "continue to play a vital role." The old Cold War policy of maintaining nuclear weapons for deterrence gave way to a new policy in which the U.S. claimed the right to use nuclear weapons pre-emptively against nations that do not possess them. The Second Nuclear Age was born with that document. The notorious double standard—nuclear weapons are fine for some but bad for others—had become entrenched.

With some apprehension, I attended the annual two-week preparatory meetings for the 2005 NPT review conference. The 2002 meeting at the UN in New York was an exercise in frustration, with the U.S. stating that it "no longer supports" two of the most important of the 13 Practical Steps listed in the final document from the 2000 NPT review conference: the Anti-Ballistic Missile Treaty, and the Comprehensive Test Ban Treaty agreed to in 2000. The wrangling over procedures was a surrogate for the deep divisions persisting in the international community on the future of nuclear weapons. The next year in Geneva, despite Mayor Tadatoshi Akiba of Hiroshima's warning that "we stand today on the brink of hyper-inflation and perhaps of repeating the third actual use of nuclear weapons," and the New Agenda Coalition countries complaining that there was "no sign" of efforts to involve all nuclear weapons states in nuclear disarmament, a desultory mood prevailed. I remarked to Jayantha Dhanapala, "They're just going through a ritualistic façade." He shook his head sadly.

Back in New York for the 2004 meeting, the delegates could not even agree on an agenda for the 2005 NPT review conference. The U.S. insisted that NPT priorities should be directed at stopping the proliferation of nuclear weapons and that the problem of their own compliance with Article VI, which calls for good faith negotiations towards the elimination of nuclear weapons, is non-existent. The leading non-nuclear weapons states claimed the exact opposite: the proliferation of nuclear weapons could not be stopped while the nuclear weapons states limited the possession of nuclear weapons to themselves and refused to enter into comprehensive negotiations towards elimination as directed by the International Court of Justice.

I reported to my Middle Powers Initiative (MPI) colleagues that the crisis was the worst in the history of the NPT. Goodwill and trust were gone, largely because the nuclear weapons states, led by the U.S., had tried to change the rules of the game. At least before, there was a recognition that the NPT was obtained through a bargain, with the nuclear weapons states agreeing to negotiate the elimination of their nuclear weapons in return for the non-nuclear states shunning acquisition. Brazil put the issue tartly: "One cannot worship at the altar of nuclear weapons and raise heresy charges against those who want to join the sect." The patience of the more aggressive members of the Non-Aligned Movement snapped. They saw, accurately, a two-class world of nuclear haves and have-nots becoming a permanent feature of the global landscape.

The members of MPI returned to the Carter Center in Atlanta in January 2005, almost five years to the day since our first consultation there. Former president Jimmy Carter was again on hand. "It is disturbingly obvious," he told the 75 participants and observers, "that there has been no improvement over the situation as it was described in our previous meeting. In fact, proliferation and the behaviour of the nuclear weapons states with regard to disarmament have worsened over the past five years." It was evident that the representatives of the middle power governments wanted to move ahead but felt blocked by the intransigency of the Bush administration. The MPI report, based on the two-day consultation, addressed the issue as diplomatically as possible. Backtracking from previous disarmament commitments was eroding the integrity and credibility of the Treaty, we warned.

Robert McNamara's Indictment

The day before the opening of the 2005 NPT review conference, Patricia and I joined a march of 40,000 people through Manhattan to Central Park to protest the continuing presence of nuclear weapons in the world. Akiba and his fellow mayor, Iccho Itoh of Nagasaki, who would be assassinated in Nagasaki a year later, led the way. Though this was but a fraction of the one million people who had protested in the famous 1982 walk at the height of the Cold War, the marchers showed the resilience of a hard core of civil society that has never given up on nuclear weapons abolition. Representatives from nearly 2,000 non-governmental organizations were on hand at various stages of the review conference, the largest number ever.

The next day, Kofi Annan opened the review conference on a note of urgency. He asked delegates to "imagine, just for a minute," the consequences of a nuclear catastrophe on one of the great cities of the world. "Tens, if not hundreds, of thousands of people would perish in an instant, and many more would die from exposure to radiation." But the conference could not rise above petty disputes; at times, the mood became acrimonious. The U.S. rejected any reference to the commitments made by the nuclear weapons states at the 1995 and 2000 review conferences. Iran blocked proposals to limit access to the nuclear fuel cycle by non-nuclear states. Egypt blocked a weak text on universalization of the NPT because of the Western states' failure to take action against Israel, which is not a party to the NPT and whose nuclear facilities are not safeguarded. As a result of the failure to agree on anything, North Korea remained unpunished for leaving the NPT and announcing its possession of nuclear weapons. Fully fifteen days of the 20-day conference were consumed by procedural battles, which was an abuse of democracy, and left the majority the victim of an obstreperous minority that hijacked the proceedings. Excessive devotion to consensus, in which a dissenting state exercises a virtual veto, derailed what would have been decisive steps forward had a vote been taken. Political will to isolate the U.S., on the one hand, or Iran, on the other, was not strong enough to counter the constant subverting.

Early in the conference, copies of the magazine *Foreign Policy* were prominently displayed on the literature tables. The cover caught the attention of many delegates. It showed a mushroom cloud with the title of the lead article superimposed: "Apocalypse Soon: Why American Nukes Are Immoral, Illegal, and Dreadfully Dangerous." The author was Robert McNamara, who was U.S. Secretary of Defense from 1961 to 1968. Since *Foreign Policy* is published by the prestigious Carnegie Endowment for International Peace, the article was read with respect. McNamara, then 88, had become an outspoken critic of nuclear weapons in his later years. He came to the conference during the fourth week for an event sponsored by the Global Security Institute to present his case personally at a noon-hour panel. Other presenters were Ted Sorensen, former special counsel to President John F. Kennedy, and Ambassador Thomas Graham, who had led the U.S. delegation to the 1995 NPT review and extension conference; both men were critical of U.S. behaviour.

McNamara characterized current U.S. nuclear weapons policy as "immoral, illegal, militarily unnecessary, and dreadfully dangerous." Because 2,000 of the 8,000 active or operational U.S. warheads were on hair-trigger alert, ready to be launched on 15 minutes' notice, "the risk of an accidental or inadvertent nuclear launch is unacceptably high," he said. The average U.S. warhead, he added, had a destructive power 20 times that of the Hiroshima bomb. But far from reducing these risks, the Bush administration was keeping the U.S. nuclear arsenal as a mainstay of its military power. It refused to ask the Senate to ratify the Comprehensive Test Ban Treaty, had ordered the national laboratories to begin research on new nuclear weapons and was preparing the underground test sites in Nevada for nuclear tests. In short, the Bush administration assumed that nuclear weapons would be part of U.S. military forces for at least the next several decades. McNamara scorned U.S. policy:

> The statement that our nuclear weapons do not target populations per se was and remains totally misleading in the sense that the so-called collateral damage of large nuclear strikes would include tens of millions of innocent civilian dead.

... This in a nutshell is what nuclear weapons do: they indiscriminately blast, burn, and irradiate with a speed and finality that are almost incomprehensible. This is exactly what countries like the United States and Russia, with nuclear weapons on hair-trigger alert, continue to threaten every minute of every day in this new 21st century.

The Union of Concerned Scientists, not given to hyperbole, corroborated McNamara's testimony: "Current U.S. nuclear policy is outdated, dangerous and misguided."

Birth of the Article VI Forum

I wrote a lengthy report, *Deadly Deadlock*, which MPI circulated widely to governments and non-governmental organizations. The report called for a reinvigoration of the process if the NPT was to survive. Instead of accepting the roadblock thrown up by the nuclear weapons states, a group of like-minded states could, in a non-combative atmosphere, start new work to identify the legal, political and technical requirements to eliminate nuclear weapons. Out of this report, MPI's Article VI Forum was born.

I had been inspired by the original and optimistic working paper submitted to the conference by Malaysia and Costa Rica, which pointed to the Model Nuclear Weapons Convention submitted to the UN General Assembly in 1997. Such a convention would prohibit the development and deployment of all nuclear weapons. While the model convention had languished for want of support by major countries, the underlying ideas were still very much alive. The 13 Practical Steps of 2000 were clearly a route to a nuclear weapons–free world. The Malaysia–Costa Rica paper considered the step-by-step approach to nuclear disarmament too limiting, yet a comprehensive approach by itself did not offer much possibility for success because it was so strongly opposed by the nuclear weapons states. An "incremental-comprehensive" approach—incorporating step-by-step measures within a comprehensive framework—offered the best route to the final destination.

The work of the Article VI Forum, convening diplomats, decision-makers and experts, would start at first among like-minded states, because working in forums with the nuclear weapons states is, as the 2005 NPT review conference experience and the continuing paralysis at the Conference on Disarmament showed, debilitating. I felt that those states that really believe in Article VI of the NPT needed to work together for a while to allow their creativity and commitment to surface. Of course, nuclear weapons cannot be abolished without the active consent and participation of the nuclear weapons states, but that does not mean that productive work cannot start without them. In fact, the international atmosphere is so bad because of their truculence—as demonstrated once again by the U.S.'s blocking of references to nuclear disarmament in the documents that came out of the 2005 summit to mark the UN's 60th anniversary—that working around the nuclear weapons states in a confidence-building environment may well be the only way to produce an outline of how negotiations could proceed. At some point in the Article VI Forum deliberations, it was planned that members would reach out to the nuclear weapons states. In the interim, the U.S. could be expected to resist any progressive steps.

The U.S. proved this once again in 2007 by voting against a resolution in the UN Disarmament (First) Committee calling for initial steps to take nuclear weapons off alert status. In fact, the U.S. voted against every substantive nuclear weapons resolution. The U.S. spokesperson kept denying that U.S. nuclear forces are on "hair-trigger alert." But Bruce Blair, an eminent U.S. expert, rebutted this falsehood, warning that terrorists could one day exploit weaknesses in the control systems.

New and Creative Thinking

Starting the Article VI Forum was a high-risk venture. Although by this time, MPI had established a formidable record of high-level delegations to key middle power countries, such as Germany, Canada, Japan, the Netherlands, Italy, Belgium and Norway, and had held several consultations attended by the leading middle power states, it could still fail to generate political interest. While it was true that many states were tired of being dominated by the recalcitrant nuclear weapons states and needed to be liberated, would they, in fact, have the courage to liberate themselves? Also, because of the dampening effect Bush administration policies had on U.S. foundations, which had previously been a major source of MPI funding, we had very little money. But the MPI executive felt we had to take a chance that we would get sufficient political support and funding. We prepared a briefing paper inviting "like-minded countries into an initiative that would send out a positive message to a waiting world that, despite the great obstacles we face, serious work is being done to help humanity attain a nuclear weapons–free world."

We called a noon-hour meeting on October 3, 2005, at the UN; I was surprised that so many states accepted our invitation. In the course of four meetings, a total of 30 states participated: Argentina, Austria, Belgium, Brazil, Canada, Chile, Costa Rica, Egypt, Germany, the Holy See, Hungary, Indonesia, Ireland, Italy, Japan, Jordan, Lithuania, Malaysia, Mexico, Mongolia, the Netherlands, New Zealand, Norway, Poland, Republic of Korea, Samoa, South Africa, Sweden, Switzerland and Turkey. Nobuyasu Abe, UN Under-Secretary-General for Disarmament Affairs, welcomed the Article VI Forum as an example of "new and creative thinking," and Ambassador Choi Young-jin of Korea, Chairman of the First Committee, called it "timely and valuable." Other diplomats made the point that business as usual was no longer acceptable and that the time had come to stop waiting for results from the other disarmament forums, which had become laden with confrontation.

Filled with encouragement, we set a two-day meeting of the Forum for the following March at the prestigious Clingendael Institute in The Hague. Frank von Hippel of Princeton University, one of the outstanding nuclear physicists in the world, phoned me to say that a new group, the International Panel on Fissile Materials, had been formed to do professional work on advancing a ban on the production of fissile materials. Von Hippel and his panel wanted to work with MPI because we could provide a political outlet for their work; at the same time, the panel could provide the technical expertise that MPI lacked. Von Hippel brought his team to The Hague, and the diplomats listened closely to explanations on how a fissionable materials ban would work.

The stars of the meeting were two former prime ministers, Kim Campbell of Canada, and Rudd Lubbers of The Netherlands. Following her defeat in the 1993 election, Kim Campbell had struck out on a new career working with international bodies on governance issues. I got to know her and invited her to be a member of MPI's international steering committee. On two occasions, she led MPI delegations to the

Canadian government. I thought it might be awkward for her entering Prime Minister Jean Chrétien's office with the MPI delegation, but the graciousness of both Campbell and Chrétien prevailed. After the Conservative leader Stephen Harper was elected prime minister, she led another MPI delegation to Ottawa. Harper (unlike Chrétien, who met with MPI four times) would not meet with the delegation but he did receive Campbell privately in his office.

The third meeting of the Article VI Forum, held in Ottawa in September 2006, focused on five measures that the previous meeting had deemed urgent: the Comprehensive Test Ban Treaty; a Fissile Materials Cut-off Treaty; de-alerting and reduction of U.S.–Russian nuclear dangers; negative security assurances; and verification of the reduction and elimination of nuclear forces. Expert panels probed each subject in depth. The Department of Foreign Affairs hosted the event in the Pearson Building, its headquarters, and Foreign Minister Peter MacKay spoke. I told the participants I was proud to bring them to my own country.

The consultation opened with a public lecture by Hans Blix, the former UN inspector who led the Weapons of Mass Destruction Commission, a team of world experts that produced a report containing 60 recommendations on what the world community—national governments and civil society—can and should undertake. The two final speakers were Ambassador Yukiya Amano of Japan, who in 2007 would chair the first preparatory meeting for the 2010 NPT review conference, and Ambassador Sergio Duarte of Brazil, who later became UN Under-Secretary-General and High Representative for Disarmament. There was no doubt that the Article VI Forum was embracing the key international players.

The fourth meeting, under the auspices of the government of Austria and the International Atomic Energy Agency, was held in Vienna in April 2007. It delved into fuel cycle and proliferation challenges, steps towards implementing the 1995 Middle East resolution (aimed at getting Israel to join the NPT), steps non-nuclear weapons states can take to enhance prospects for nuclear disarmament, and strategy for the NPT review process.

Out of the Forum's deliberations with such a good cross-section of states, MPI identified seven priorities, the implementation of which before or at the 2010 review conference would save the NPT:

- verified reduction of nuclear forces;

- standing down of nuclear forces (de-alerting);

- negotiation of a Fissile Materials Cut-off Treaty;

- bringing the Comprehensive Test Ban Treaty into force;

- strengthened negative security assurances;

- regulation of nuclear fuel production and supply; and

- improved NPT governance.

These measure are valuable in and of themselves, for they would decrease the risks of use of nuclear weapons, reinforce the NPT and enhance the rule of law. They would make the world much safer than it is now. MPI recognized that the powerful states would balk at some if not all of the steps. Also, non-nuclear states, which wanted access to nuclear energy, would oppose multilateral regulation of nuclear fuel production and supply, but they would likely agree if there were a "visible intent" by the nuclear weapons states to implement the "unequivocal undertaking." In other words, individual steps stand a better chance of being accepted when they are manifestly part of a global plan for the elimination of nuclear weapons.

MPI put all our findings into a report, *Towards 2020: Priorities for NPT Consensus*, which I presented to Ambassador Amano at the first NPT preparatory meeting later in April 2007. The Canadian embassy in Vienna hosted a reception for me to make the presentation in front of the assembled ambassadors. Several governments vocally supported MPI's policy priorities later that year when the First Committee met in New York during the General Assembly. Indonesia, coordinator of the Non-Aligned Movement's disarmament efforts, lauded the Forum's work. Needless to say, the powerful states have been less than effusive in their praise.

Life with a Purpose

When David MacDonald said that my most important work would be done after I had turned 75, I thought it was a nice rhetorical flourish for the dinner gathering. But David turned out to be right. Freed of responsibilities in the Senate (not least showing up for votes on matters of questionable importance), I have been able to concentrate on the one matter of overriding importance in my professional life: helping to build the conditions for peace, particularly through ridding the world of nuclear weapons. It has become not only a cause but also the purpose of my life at this stage, when I am told "normal" people retire.

I want to make it clear that I do not consider myself to be a superman, nor am I so obsessed that I can think of nothing else (I still love going to movies on Friday afternoons), but I am determined to use every day that God continues to give me good health to work for at least a better measure of stability, security and social justice in the world. I think I owe this to my grandchildren, Isabelle and Nicholas, because I know the dangers facing them as they grow up. I have political and diplomatic experience, the intellectual capacity to understand the great themes of globalization, and the energy to address the issues. I like doing this work.

Sometimes, I think I can hear Frank Sinatra singing "September Song" just to me. "*It's a long, long while from May to December; but the days grow short when you reach September ... Oh, the days dwindle down to a precious few, September, November ...*"

For me, it's no longer September. But it certainly doesn't feel like December. I prefer to think of myself as ... mid–October. The leaves of autumn are flaming in their colour and have not yet fallen to the ground. The days are warm, but the nights are cool. We know what is ahead, but we revel in the softer sun. Each day is increasingly precious. Time is racing. Life is full.

A swim every day, my iPod with 2,000 of my favourite songs at hand, my laptop as my roving office—all these are the stuff of my life. I've got my health, my wife, my family, my friends, my Church, my work, my country and my world. As Tony Bennett would sing, "I've got everything I need." Or as Gershwin would put it, "Who could ask for anything more!"

Since leaving the Senate, I have written two books, *Beyond Hiroshima* and *Global Conscience*. The first makes the case for the elimination of nuclear weapons as a precondition of peace in the 21st century. The second describes the awakening of concern about how we humans treat one another and the planet; this has tremendous possibilities for moving the world forward to a new era of peace. With Senator Claudette Tardif, the Alberta senator who succeeded me, I co-chaired a world conference, "Building World Peace: The Role of Religions and Human Rights," sponsored by the John Humphrey Centre in Edmonton. We dealt with the need for all religions to rise above their denominationalism and speak out to press the political systems for better policies for peace and social justice, and especially to reject the exploitation, abuse and misuse of religion as justification for hate, oppression and terrorism.

I also organized a workshop, "Revitalizing Nuclear Disarmament," which brought some 20 experts to Pugwash, Nova Scotia, to mark the 50th anniversary of the first conference at the Thinkers' Lodge there and the founding of the Pugwash movement. I now work closely with Stephen and Dennice Leahey as they develop the Pugwash Peace Exchange into a vibrant, interactive centre that gets out the message of peace and nuclear disarmament.

A Strong MPI Team

But most of my time these past few years has been devoted to the Middle Powers Initiative. MPI's track record of working, credibly, with governments, always pushing them to go a bit faster than they think they can, would not have been possible without Jonathan Granoff. When funding for nuclear disarmament dried up shortly after the Bush administration took office, the International Physicians for the Prevention of Nuclear War informed me the group could no longer subsidize the MPI office. We would have to move out of our quarters in Cambridge, Massachusetts. Without an infrastructure, I would not be able to carry on MPI's work.

I looked at our co-sponsors. The only one in a growth mode was the Global Security Institute, which had been started by Senator Alan Cranston of California to build concern and action on peace issues among U.S. congresspersons. On New Year's Eve in 2000, Cranston died suddenly. The board elected Granoff, a lawyer and social activist living in Philadelphia, as president.

To describe Granoff as indefatigable, tenacious and demanding in his quest for peace would be to considerably understate his personality. His mother, Kitty Kallen, was a star pop singer of the 1940s; his father, Budd Granoff, was Frank Sinatra's media agent. Jonathan comes from a show business family and has all the qualities of an impresario. A Sufi, he is at home in Jewish synagogues and Muslim mosques as well as being comfortable when he attends Catholic Mass with me. He brings a high moral sense as well as finely honed legal standards to nuclear weapons issues. He was the right man to develop the Global Security Institute into an important non-governmental organization in the Washington establishment. He saw immediately how MPI, with its international expertise, could broaden the Institute's impact, and I saw how the Institute could take MPI's ideas and recommendations to the heart of Washington, which would solve the biggest problem of all for nuclear weapons abolitionists. We established a symbiotic relationship between the organizations and, later, enlarged it when Granoff opened a New York office close to the UN.

While the Institute houses MPI, providing our structural and financial base, its board was wise enough to leave the direction of MPI in the hands of the MPI international steering committee and the executive. I am particularly sensitive that MPI, as an international non-governmental organization, not be seen as U.S.-driven just because we are located within an American organization. As long as a national of a middle power heads MPI and we ensure the active presence of non-Americans on the steering committee working alongside American activists, I think MPI can continue to develop as a key international player.

Also at the heart of MPI is Alyn Ware, a multi-talented New Zealand activist, who heads the parliamentary wing of MPI, Parliamentary Network for Nuclear Non-Proliferation and Disarmament. With more than 500 members in 70 countries, it provides material to parliamentarians in several languages, helping them to introduce questions and motions in their own legislatures. Alyn is the co-author of *Security and Survival*, a primer on the Model Nuclear Weapons Convention, which, if ever enacted, would prohibit the production of nuclear weapons. He has accompanied me on many MPI visits to European capitals. Jim Wurst, a veteran journalist, manages MPI's programs; John Burroughs, a legal scholar who leads the Lawyers Committee on Nuclear Policy, writes authoritative and penetrating MPI briefs; Rhianna Tyson, a graduate of the London School of Economics, is a prime example of why I place such hope in the best of today's youth.

The team that surrounds me—David Krieger and Alice Slater of the Nuclear Age Peace Foundation; Michael Christ and Xanthe Hall of International Physicians for the Prevention of Nuclear War; Karel Koster of The Netherlands; Jean Du Preez of the Monterey Institute in California; and Aaron Tovish, international coordinator of Mayors for Peace—has truly enriched my life. As expert consultants, Jayantha Dhanapala and Rebecca Johnson, a veteran British activist, have enabled MPI to deepen its outreach. These and the other members of the international steering committee are experienced and passionate advocates for nuclear disarmament. They are certainly more knowledgeable on the intricate points of the agenda than many of the diplomats I have dealt with. Leading these people in MPI's work has been a privilege for me.

Rotblat, Epstein, Akiba

Three men have had the greatest influence on my work as a nuclear disarmament campaigner. Joseph (Jo) Rotblat, a Polish-born nuclear physicist, was a member of the Manhattan Project, which first developed the atomic bomb. When World War II ended in Europe and he saw that the bomb was no longer necessary to defeat Germany, he quit the project on moral grounds. The bomb would cause catastrophic human suffering, he said, and should not be used against the Japanese. He was ostracized by the scientific community for his actions. Undaunted, he went on to found the Pugwash movement and became a formidable campaigner against nuclear weapons for the rest of his life. He and Pugwash shared the 1995 Nobel Peace Prize. His conscience told him that one should be loyal to civilization, not just to a nation-state. In so doing, one's service to the state is enriched by helping it to reach out and embrace global strategies for survival and peace. Rotblat became a mentor to me. He shared his knowledge and convictions and gave me the confidence that I had enough knowledge of the subject to speak out also. He died in 2006 at the age of 96.

Bill Epstein, also one of the great figures of the Pugwash movement, joined the fledgling UN immediately upon his discharge from Canadian military service in World War II. He worked in the UN disarmament office and became a walking encyclopedia on nuclear disarmament. When he retired from the UN, he took up a new advocacy career, which centred on pestering the life out of the Canadian government to beef up its anti-nuclear weapons policies. I was often

on the receiving end of his needling for not doing more for abolition. When he was 89, I decided to give a dinner for him in Toronto
to honour his 90th birthday. Unfortunately, when the day arrived, he
was too ill to travel from his residence in New York to Toronto, but
we held the dinner anyway. A few days later, I brought a video of the
proceedings to him. There were tears in his eyes when he saw the
outpouring of love for him. He died a few days later.

I met Tadatoshi Akiba, Mayor of Hiroshima, just after his election
in 1999, when he received Pat and me in his office. His commitment
to work for a nuclear weapons–free world was palpable, and we struck
up a friendship. Akiba is a most unusual Japanese politician, for he
spent nearly 20 years in the U.S. before returning to his homeland.
A mathematician, he earned a Ph.D. at the Massachusetts Institute of
Technology and taught at Tufts University. He came into world prominence when he founded Mayors for Peace, which, as of 2008, had as
members 2,226 mayors in 129 countries. He has made Mayors for
Peace into a leading force in the drive to build world opinion against
nuclear weapons. He launched the Vision 2020 Campaign, which he
calls an emergency campaign to eliminate all nuclear weapons by
2020, the 75th anniversary of the atomic bombings of Hiroshima and
Nagasaki. Akiba's steadfastness and courage continually inspire me.

Rotblat, Epstein, Akiba—these men are heroes to me. They have
been unflagging in their grit and determination to stand up to the
proponents of nuclear weapons and tell them they are wrong. They
devoted their lives to the eradication of this evil so that future generations would not have to live with the threat of Armageddon hanging
over them.

A Greater Illegality

In 2004, as I was researching *Beyond Hiroshima*, I travelled to the
federal penitentiary in Danbury, Connecticut, to visit Sister Ardeth
Platte, who was sentenced to three and a half years for her protest
against nuclear weapons. With two other Dominican sisters, Carol
Gilbert and Jackie Hudson, Platte had broken into a nuclear weapons
base in Colorado. The three women tapped on the rails leading to
a missile silo cover with baby bottles containing their own blood to
symbolize turning swords into ploughshares. With a crucifix, rosaries
and prayer books, they prayed, sang songs and sat down to await arrest.

The U.S. government pressed sabotage charges and the women were convicted.

Wearing a drab olive-green prison uniform, Sister Ardeth greeted me with a smile. I asked her for a message for the people I reach in my work. "We are all one creation," she said. "If we do not stop violence and care for one another, we are all diminished. Nuclear weapons are the ultimate evil. We must hold the U.S. accountable for dismantling nuclear weapons. They are instruments of murder."

I have never gone to jail for my beliefs. And as a public official for so many years, I have trouble with the concept of civil disobedience. But what are we to do when governments themselves are breaking the limitation and proportionality laws of humanitarian warfare? Nuclear warfare is a crime against humanity. The actions taken by Sister Ardeth and her colleagues, illegal as they may be, are designed to address an infinitely greater illegality: the threat to kill massively.

If nuclear weapons could be done away with by the commitment of the most passionate abolitionists, the advice of military leaders or sheer logic itself, we would long ago have achieved the goal. At least four independent international commissions over the past quarter-century pointed to the extreme dangers the world is facing by maintaining nuclear weapons. In 1982, a commission headed by Prime Minister Olof Palme of Sweden published a report, *Common Security*, that argued that nuclear weapons could destroy human civilization and that security could be attained only through co-operation and disarmament. In 1996, the Canberra Commission warned that as long as one state retains nuclear weapons, others will want them, and when others get them the risk of use expands exponentially. In 1998, the Tokyo Forum presented an action plan for nuclear disarmament. In 2006, the Weapons of Mass Destruction Commission, headed by Hans Blix, warned that the number of nuclear weapons in the world, 27,000, is "alarmingly high," and called for a World summit. When he was UN Secretary-General, Kofi Annan repeatedly called for a global summit on nuclear dangers. Just before he left office, he warned that the world risks "sleepwalking" towards nuclear catastrophe. The High-Level Panel on Threats, Challenges and Change, which Annan set up to mark the 60th anniversary of the UN, said, "We are approaching a point at which the erosion of the non-proliferation regime could become irreversible and result in a cascade of proliferation …."

The evidence of the danger is irrefutable. Nuclear weapons are not only immoral, not only is their use illegal in any circumstances whatsoever, not only are they militarily useless, they are now devoid of any intellectual credibility. Non-governmental organizations and academics do not hold panels called "Why Nuclear Weapons Are Good for the World." Yet countries maintain nuclear arsenals because their political and bureaucratic systems are locked inside their internal dynamics, in denial one moment, in apathy the next. The media virtually ignores the volcano of the existing nuclear weapons, which could erupt at any time, and concentrates its attention on the flash points of Iran and North Korea. Of course, those two countries—and every other country—should be prevented from acquiring nuclear weapons. But that task is impossible as long as the five permanent members of the Security Council, charged with maintaining peace and security in the world, retain their nuclear weapons. If the major powers had heeded the legal responsibilities flowing from their signatures on the NPT, India, Pakistan and Israel would never have acquired nuclear weapons.

In October 2006, Pax Christi, an international Catholic peace movement established in 1945 to promote reconciliation at the end of World War II, invited me to London and Edinburgh to lecture on the nuclear dilemma, to add my voice to the chorus of protest against the duplicitous policies of the U.K. government. While proclaiming its fealty to the NPT, it has put in motion plans to modernize its Trident nuclear weapon, thereby assuring that the U.K. will carry nuclear weapons well into the second half of the 21st century. In Edinburgh, Cardinal Keith O'Brien, a doughty fighter, is not afraid to criticize forthrightly the political establishment on its nuclear policies.

The Cardinal has asked that the Trident be replaced not with more weapons but "with projects that bring life to the poor." This wise approach would underscore the relationship between disarmament and development and lead to true human security. The amount of money governments around the world spend on arms, now more than $1 trillion annually, dwarfs the amount they spend on sustainable development. The gross disproportion is a scandal that mocks the poor and vulnerable of the world. Since nuclear weapons were invented, governments have so far spent a total of at least $12 trillion on these instruments of mass murder, which is a theft from the poorest people of the world. This madness must stop.

Would that all bishops and religious leaders of every faith spoke out as strongly as Cardinal O'Brien. But they seem preoccupied, in most cases, with internal concerns. For their part, the political leaders will sit on their hands on this issue until a chorus of public opinion deafens them.

The Net Is Closing

Despite the setbacks on the road to abolition, the net is gradually closing on the countries that possess nuclear weapons. The gains may seem slight, but they are occurring. Governments around the world have voted overwhelmingly at the UN to take steps to a nuclear weapons–free world. Even in the U.S. and Russia, large majorities (73 per cent of Americans and 63 per cent of Russians) favour completely eliminating nuclear weapons once advanced methods of international verification are established. Four senior U.S. political figures, Henry Kissinger, George Shultz, Sam Nunn and William Perry, all of whom previously defended U.S. nuclear arsenals, have come out for active steps to abolition. They have been joined by leading figures of the Washington establishment. The Holy See has stipulated that its limited acceptance of nuclear deterrence during the Cold War no longer applies now that continued modernization of nuclear arms is preventing genuine nuclear disarmament.

With the indefinite extension of the NPT, the ruling of the International Court of Justice and the "unequivocal undertaking" pledged at the 2000 NPT review conference all serving as a backdrop, I feel that current events are beginning to provide historical momentum towards the end of nuclear weapons. The tensions and dislocations of the moment often cloud our judgment about long-range gains. By stepping back, we can see better the evolution of societal thinking against war and the means of destruction. The world is still afflicted by the forces of greed, power and corruption. But change is coming.

Perhaps the change won't occur in my lifetime. After all, the great theologian Reinhold Niebuhr said that nothing worth accomplishing can be achieved in one's lifetime. I take heart whenever I walk in the mountains and see a flower blooming in the rocks. That flower is resilient. It defies the odds. Its beauty lies in its staying power.

20

Never Quit!

And now I am in my 80th year. I sigh not for the past but cry for the future. It is not my lost youth that I pine for but a lost future for my grandchildren.

Much of my public career has been marked by dissent, and I'm not stopping my protest now. I dissent from the anti-humanitarian policies of war for peace. I dissent from the perpetuation of poverty through the greed of the rich. I dissent from the despoliation of the planet by short-sighted industrialism. Most of all, I dissent from the fabric of lies spun by the proponents of nuclear weapons who would have us believe that these heinous instruments of mass murder make us safer.

I am outraged at what has happened to the Canada I love. This country, which used to be rated by the UN as number one in the world for human development, has become a pale imitation of the United States, itself torn by the belligerent policies of the Bush administration. Canada, blessed beyond belief with natural resources of land, minerals, forests and water, and with space, a stable population base, industry and technology, has become stingy in the amount of aid it sends to the developing countries. Too many politicians cater to a me-first attitude to the diminishment of the common good. Peace-keeping has been virtually abandoned as military spending has risen to its highest level since World War II. The top military commanders brag about the Canadian military's ability to kill in Afghanistan: those who think that the soul of our country can be found in combat are now militarizing our culture.

All this I dissent from.

The perpetrators of militarism are succeeding, for the moment, because they are trading on fear. Our political leaders are failing—disastrously—because they are afraid to speak out against fear. Political leadership today is bereft of vision not just for Canada but for the world. Never in the history of Canada have we been so lacking in political courage.

It's the Future, Stupid!

The eminent historian Barbara Tuchman adroitly observed that governments are afflicted with "wooden-headedness," the source of self-deception. "It consists in assessing a situation in terms of preconceived fixed notions while ignoring or rejecting any contrary signs." she said. "It is acting according to wish while not allowing oneself to be deflected by the facts."

Governments go on pretending that military might and bombing innocent civilians will bring security. They continue to ignore the technological reality that the world has become one place, interlocked in all its dimensions, and that national borders mean nothing in terms of protection.

It isn't that globalization is just too much for us to figure out, that we lack the brainpower or the international instruments to bring stability to a world in the midst of change. Far from it. We have immense stores of knowledge and, in the United Nations, we have the essential machinery to address the problems of armaments, poverty, pollution and human rights violations. But the captains of our society—the politicians, the diplomats, the media and the corporate structures—cannot, do not, will not, all to varying degrees, lift up their vision and work together to make the world a fitting habitat for all of humanity.

I want a world that is human-centred and genuinely democratic, a world that builds and protects peace, equality, justice and development. I want a world in which human security, as envisioned in the principles of the UN Charter, replaces armaments, violent conflict and wars. I want a world in which everyone lives in a clean environment with a fair distribution of the earth's resources and international law protects human rights.

To my critics, who say that this is just Doug Roche dreaming again, I say, have you got better policies for the future? The policies of the past have brought us untold wars and suffering, massive poverty, environmental destruction and repression of human beings, and have taken us, with the invention of weapons of mass destruction, to the edge of human annihilation. Isn't it time to try something better? Isn't it time to bring our heads and hearts together to produce true human security? Isn't it time to raise the standards of civilization for the sake of survival? Spare me the charge that this is mere idealism. The agenda for survival is no longer a dream but a demand of the human race.

Let my critics write a book and state why 25,000 nuclear weapons are good for the people of the world, why it is good for the global economy that a quarter of humanity lives in destitution while the profits of arms merchants soar, why it is good for the planet that the glaciers are melting and the seas rising. I want my critics to explain to me why it is coherent for governments to pledge to help the children of the world but then fail to provide the necessary money because they have diverted it to war. I need to hear from my critics a rational argument why the United States and Russia keeping nuclear weapons on high-alert status—meaning they can be fired on fifteen minutes' notice—makes the world a safer place. I want to hear why it is not possible to put a plan into motion to rid the world of nuclear weapons by 2020.

To the policymakers of the present, I say, to paraphrase Bill Clinton's famous election slogan, "It's the future, stupid!" Get over your wooden-headedness. We are hurtling into a future of more discord, more terrorism, more danger. As Kofi Annan said, "We are asleep at the controls of a fast-moving aircraft."

As the human security issues play out, particularly in the intertwined relationship of development and disarmament, I have found myself in many political battles, and I have the scars to prove it. In my career as a parliamentarian and diplomat, the greatest lesson I learned was how difficult it is to get governments to focus on problems "upstream"—that is, before they have happened, while they react with alarm, and often panic, when the problem occurs "downstream." Governments will devote political energy and money to dealing with the effects of a problem, but it is virtually impossible to get them to pay attention to and put money towards problems over the horizon.

It is not hard to predict that nuclear weapons will one day be used if they continue to proliferate among countries, to foresee rising terrorism that exploits discrimination and inhuman living conditions, to anticipate that rising temperatures and waters will force the dislocation of millions of people who will swamp already overcrowded systems.

Patience and Creativity

If I have experienced frustration in my career, I have also learned patience. Cardinal Léger's assessment that it would take a hundred years for the full effects of the Second Vatican Council to take will likely prove accurate; his wise comment helps me to understand better the slowness of human beings to adapt to change. The world, including the Church, is passing through a great transformative moment in which local exigencies are now caught up in global interdependencies. Adjusting our thinking, conditioned by centuries to deal with that which we can touch, to the broader realities of planetary existence is painful, threatening and just plain hard to do. It seems that we have to drag our minds into the future that we are at the same time creating. We have opened up that future by delineating human rights and inventing weapons of mass destruction. The two are incompatible. Two sides of our human nature are struggling for control. Denial, apathy, delay, obfuscation—these and a host of other reactions delay the human journey.

Governments have shown that they cannot muster the will to lead the public to a peace that is now necessary in the age of weapons of mass destruction. So it is the leading edge of civil society that is today trying to prompt governments to develop public policies that emphasize the core values of respect for life, freedom, justice and equity. The real creativity of today is found in civil society movements.

I have found that for me, personal creativity is the best way to overcome political intransigence. Parliamentarians for Global Action and the Middle Powers Initiative provided outlets for me to inject energy into the political systems. Both of these instruments have spurred progress. Rather than taking satisfaction from this, however, I regard the achievements of both organizations as beacons of hope. Dissent can become creative when we care enough about failed public policies to do something to move forward. Out of our griefs and anxieties, we build a new basis of hope.

What I feel most is that the human journey cannot be stopped. We are, often in spite of ourselves, raising up our civilization. An alliance of civilizations lies ahead—if we can avoid blowing up the earth. The photograph of Earth taken from space by the astronauts reveals our wholeness and, street fighting notwithstanding, our unity as a human family. Our vulnerability is apparent, but so is our strength—in knowledge, technology and creativity.

It takes time for both the Church to move out of its internal preoccupations and the world's political systems to move to a culture of peace. Time is running out for me, but I am not unhappy about that. I have had a marvellous life and I know how blessed I am. To have had the opportunities I have had as a journalist, educator, Member of Parliament, ambassador and senator is a rare privilege. To have participated in the struggles of our time to advance human security has developed me as a person. To have been sustained by the love and support of my family has enriched me in countless ways.

Though often in turmoil at the news of the day, I am at peace with the world, and I think I have found peace within myself. This is perhaps another paradox, like the world going in two directions at the same time. Because I want peace in the world so much, I feel it, and this in turn makes me want to keep working for it. I could not stand up and lecture about peace or write books about it if I did not feel peace within me. The words of Isaiah guide me: "Peace, peace to the far and near, says the Lord, and I will heal them."

Though relinquishing positions of responsibility, I'll go on working for peace until God decides otherwise. The grandstand has no appeal for me. "Never quit!" Bill Epstein used to say to me. He was right. There's too much to do.

Epilogue

India: A Double Faith

The Indian legislator challenged me directly.

"How can you say the people of the world are moving towards peace when the U.S., the big daddy, won't let them have it?"

I was in the Lok Sabha, the lower house of the Indian Parliament, speaking to 125 legislators and assistants at a breakfast meeting. I was attempting to tackle the delicate subject of why India should pursue the global elimination of nuclear weapons even though it, too, has joined the nuclear club.

"India cannot escape the global spotlight that will fall on it during the post-Bush U.S. administration," I replied. "The right-wing extremism of the Bush policies on war is already being challenged from within the U.S. A new day for peace is coming, and India, to be true to its values, should help lead the way."

When Michael Christ, executive director of International Physicians for the Prevention of Nuclear War, asked me to give the keynote address at the organization's world congress in New Delhi in March 2008 (the writing of my memoirs finished), I jumped at the chance to return to India, the country that was instrumental in forming my views on the human condition. It had been a decade since I had visited, and I was keen to see it again. Nor could I decline the invitation from Professor M.S. Swaminathan, the former president of International Pugwash and one of India's great scientists (he has been called "the father of economic ecology"), to give lectures to several important audiences there.

Patricia and I flew from Edmonton straight through to Delhi, a door-to-door journey of 30 hours. The India that I first saw 45 years ago has developed into two societies: the elite, who are well off, and the masses of the poor, who struggle every day just to survive. An emerging middle class is concentrated in the high-tech industries, fashion and Bollywood, but for those who cannot make the leap, despair is a daily companion.

On our first morning, Pat and I were out walking near the YMCA Hotel in Jai Singh Road. Scenes of people sleeping in the streets, mothers begging with infants at the breast and hustlers determined to "guide" us to great shopping were common and disturbing. An auto-rickshaw driver told us to jump into his three-wheeler. I liked the look of him—clean shaven and with a freshly pressed shirt—so we got in. Bobby became our escort to the museums and bazaars. When we needed him, we called him on his cellphone to navigate us through the traffic-choked streets.

Bobby is but one of thousands of rickshaw drivers careering around Delhi, trying to get a leg up on constant poverty. Some 70 per cent of Indians live below the poverty line. It's hard to maintain your humanity if you ignore the ravages of poverty but that, it seems to me, is what the new middle class in India is doing.

Pat and I took an early-morning train to Agra to see—*experience* is a better word—the Taj Mahal, the white marble tribute of an emperor to his wife, and one of the seven wonders of the world. As people travel to and from this majestic monument to love, beggars and hustlers prey on visitors. The contrast between beauty and squalor in India is astounding.

There is intense pressure to succeed in the new India. Aggressive-ness is in the air, at least in the cities. The rural areas are now known for the suicides of thousands of farmers who fall into debt as a result of shifting world commodity prices. The problem is so serious that the government recently moved to write off farmers' debts to ease their burden. There has also been a wave of suicides among students who, caught up in the succeed-or-perish attitude of the new India, fear failure in exams. When I called on Delhi's Archbishop Vincent Concessao, he was grieving the death of a student who had recently celebrated his first Holy Communion but had later hanged himself after receiving a failing grade in class. "We must do more to give our young people an appreciation of the fullness of life so that they can put their classroom work in perspective," the archbishop said. School authorities are starting to offer courses to help teachers identify signs of stress in students.

There is indeed a shadow over India. The country is said to be on its way to being the most populous in the world (its 1.1 billion people are exceeded only by China's 1.3 billion), and its economy will soon rival that of the U.S. But what of India's soul? Is the human heart uplifted or hardened in modern India? Why do people tolerate severe water shortages and mass homelessness while the government pumps money into nuclear weapons? Is the quest for the high life replacing the peace of the heart?

Already, India considers itself a big power in the world, and there is no doubt that its possessing nuclear weapons is a major factor in this pride. International Physicians for the Prevention of Nuclear War secured an appointment with Indian Prime Minister Manmohan Singh. I was invited to join the small group for the meeting in his heavily fortified residence. About eight of us sat in a sitting room sipping tea as the prime minister listened attentively to the organization's brief to have India play a role in nuclear disarmament. When my turn came to speak, I suggested that the principles for nuclear disarmament expressed so well in Rajiv Gandhi's 1988 proposal to eliminate all nuclear weapons by 2010 be rejuvenated, noting that India, precisely because it had since become a nuclear power, was well placed to take a leading role in a new world effort. The prime minister heard me out, then replied that India's desire for a nuclear weapons–free world had never waned, and that the current government of India would not be found wanting in supporting global efforts. But I sensed that this was as far as Singh could go: support but not leadership. In this and other meetings, it became clear that India would respond only to U.S. leadership.

In fact, India got the bomb in order to keep up with the U.S. and the other nuclear weapons states. The government is watching closely to see how and where the U.S. moves under the next administration. Even my old friend K. Subrahmanyam, with whom I had breakfast one morning, is watching to see what the new trend will be. Subrahmanyam, a defence expert who has always held that India needed to acquire nuclear weapons precisely because they had become the currency of power, now says it would be "logical" for India to support a new worldwide plan, going beyond the Nuclear Non-Proliferation Treaty, to get rid of nuclear weapons.

Al Gore was in India at the same time I was. He pushed hard for India to lead the global movement on climate change. That's exactly how I feel about the nuclear weapons issue. On the overarching problems of our time—global warming and nuclear weapons—it is in India's interests to show new leadership; it is also India's gift to give to the world. India's culture of non-violence must infuse sustainable development writ large.

I brought ideas for these new approaches into my lectures on the culture of peace, the alliance of civilizations and the need to incorporate thinking about nuclear annihilation into holistic development. I spoke at the Indira Gandhi Open University, which has 1.85 million students, and my lecture was telecast. Knowing I was reaching even a fraction of that number by television was daunting. I built on Professor Swaminathan's teaching on sustainability to make my case that nuclear weapons and human rights are incompatible in the 21st century: "Harmony with nature should become a non-negotiable ethic." When I lectured at the Rajiv Gandhi Foundation, I urged active follow-through on the words of Indian President Pratibha Patil a few days earlier, that India "remains committed to universal, non-discriminatory and comprehensive nuclear disarmament as reflected in the Action Plan … presented by Rajiv Gandhi."

Even the President's words must be filtered through the diversity and complexity of India. The government seems overwhelmed by the pressures to provide food and housing to the people and to get through the next election. I took heart in leaders such as Swaminathan, who is striving to integrate sustainability science into the natural and social sciences, and Muchkund Dubey, a fellow ambassador from the 1980s with whom I worked on the International Conference on the Relationship Between Disarmament and Development. Dubey, over a cup of tea one afternoon, told me that he is now concentrating his attention on education. "If India is to survive as one nation and claim its rightful place in the community of nations, it will have to come to terms with mobilizing resources on the required scale for school education," he said.

The M. S. Swaminathan Research Foundation is focusing on developing a new generation of sustainability scientists "who would combine modern science with Gandhian values." To my regret, one doesn't hear much in the modern India of Mahatma Gandhi. I went to Gandhi's shrine to feel once again his passion for leading people upwards through non-violence. There weren't many people around. Thankfully, he is not entirely forgotten, though. The new Parliament Museum—the best attraction for the tourist in India, in my view—features an animated display in which one can walk with Gandhi on his Satyagraha march. Over a lifelike depiction of Gandhi are his prophetic words: "Non-violence requires a double faith: faith in God and also faith in man."

India—one sixth of the world—seems to contain the enchantments and frustrations of the entire planet. At times, the problems seem overwhelming. As Gandhi did, I believe that only faith in God and humanity will see us through.

Index

Books by Douglas Roche

The Catholic Revolution (McKay, 1968)

Man to Man (with Bishop Remi De Roo) (Bruce, 1969)

It's a New World (Western Catholic Reporter, 1970)

Justice Not Charity: A New Global Ethic for Canada (McClelland and Stewart, 1976)

The Human Side of Politics (Clarke, Irwin, 1976)

What Development Is All About: China, Indonesia, Bangladesh (NC Press, 1979)

Politicians for Peace (NC Press, 1983)

United Nations: Divided World (NC Press, 1984)

Building Global Security: Agenda for the 1990's (NC Press, 1989)

In the Eye of the Catholic Storm (with Bishop Remi De Roo and Mary Jo Leddy) (HarperCollins 1992)

A Bargain for Humanity: Global Security by 2000 (University of Alberta Press, 1993)

Safe Passage into the Twenty-First Century: The United Nations' Quest for Peace, Equality, Justice and Development (with Robert Muller) (Continuum, 1995)

An Unacceptable Risk: Nuclear Weapons in a Volatile World (Project Ploughshares, 1995)

The Ultimate Evil: The Fight to Ban Nuclear Weapons (Lorimer, 1997)

Bread Not Bombs: A Political Agenda for Social Justice (University of Alberta Press, 1999)

The Human Right to Peace (Novalis, 2003)

Beyond Hiroshima (Novalis, 2005)

Global Conscience (Novalis, 2007)

Using 2 306 lb. of Rolland Enviro100 Print instead
of virgin fibres paper reduces your ecological footprint of :

Tree(s): 20
Solid waste : 565 kg
Water : 53 444 L
Suspended particles in the water : 3.6 kg
Air emissions : 1 241 kg
Natural gas : 81 m3